All of the electronic resources you need—in one place!

The third edition of *Bookmarks* contains marginal icons that refer you to its Companion Website, located at http://www.ablongman.com/bookmarks.

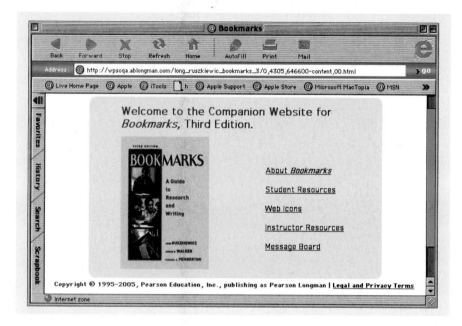

Welcome to the Companion Website for *Bookmarks*, Third Edition.

About *Bookmarks*

Student Resources

Web Icons

Instructor Resources

Message Board

Resources on this Companion Website include:

 Tutorials that will assist you in planning and preparing your research project. Learn how to find a topic and develop a research question; conduct searches of electronic databases and use the Internet; evaluate print and Internet sources for credibility; paraphrase source material; and integrate and balance outside material with your own voice.

 Additional aids, including **sample research documents** at various stages of the research process and a time line to keep you in check with your due dates.

Additional **writing and research activities** that will help you strengthen your skills and improve your projects. These interactive activities will help you focus your ideas, brainstorm about your topic and about related research issues, discover different ways to approach research projects, organize your ideas and your draft, and revise your draft.

 Annotated links for the **Web Sites Worth Knowing** that appear at the end of each chapter in Parts I–V. These sites will help you get the information you need for your research project.

THIRD EDITION

Bookmarks

A Guide to Research and Writing

John Ruszkiewicz
University of Texas at Austin

Janice R. Walker
Georgia Southern University

Michael A. Pemberton
Georgia Southern University

PEARSON
Longman

New York Boston San Francisco
London Toronto Sydney Tokyo Singapore Madrid
Mexico City Munich Paris Cape Town Hong Kong Montreal

Senior Acquisitions Editor: Lynn M. Huddon
Development Editor: Anne Brunell Ehrenworth
Senior Marketing Manager: Alexandra Rivas-Smith
Production Manager: Bob Ginsberg
Project Coordination, Text Design, and Electronic Page Makeup: Nesbitt Graphics, Inc.
Cover Design Manager: Wendy Ann Fredericks
Cover Designer: Kay Petronio
Cover Photos: Top to bottom: David Hanover/Stone/Getty Images, Inc.; Arthur
    Tilley/Taxi/Getty Images, Inc.; and Photodisc Red/Getty Images, Inc.
Manufacturing Buyer: Mary Fischer
Printer and Binder: Courier/Westford
Cover Printer: Coral Graphic Services, Inc.

For permission to use copyrighted material, grateful acknowledgment is made to the
copyright holders on pp. 403–405, which are hereby made part of this copyright page.

Library of Congress Control Number: 2005922644

Please visit our Web site at http://www.ablongman.com/bookmarks

ISBN 0-321-27134-3

6 7 8 9 10—CRW—08

Contents

4   Planning Your Research Strategy   31

PART **II**
GATHERING IDEAS AND INFORMATION   44

5   Using Library Resources   46

PART III
WORKING WITH SOURCES   98

9   Understanding Academic Responsibility and Avoiding Plagiarism   100

10   Evaluating Sources   108

PART IV
DEVELOPING THE PROJECT   152

PART **VI**
DOCUMENTATION   258

Preface

What's a *bookmark*? A decade ago the answer would have been simple: a strip of metal, fabric, or paper inserted between the pages of a book to hold a reader's place. Today a bookmark can also be understood as a feature in a Web browser, a way to store Web addresses one expects to consult often, or even a digital tag in an e-book to mark where a reader paused in an electronic manuscript. Someone familiar with the World Wide Web might even use the term as a verb: *to bookmark*.

What has happened to this simple word provides a rationale for *Bookmarks: A Guide to Research and Writing*. Just as electronic technology has complicated the meaning of *bookmark*, it has similarly transformed every aspect of *research* for college writers and instructors. So we offer *Bookmarks* as a new-generation research handbook, one built on the assumption that students need to know how electronic sources, materials, and methods are altering their relationship to knowledge.

An intriguing—but sometimes frustrating—feature of digital technology is that it is constantly changing. Older software is upgraded to include new features, almost on a monthly basis; cutting-edge computing systems are fit for the scrap heap after only a couple of years; dynamic new Web tools appear, sweeping the Internet in a fraction of the time required by older ones; and useful, familiar Web pages disappear, with virtually no sign of why or how. This third edition of *Bookmarks*, then, continues its quest to stay current with the dynamic information resource we know as the World Wide Web, to point you to the newest tools, sites, technologies, and programs that will enable your research.

Yet we insist that not everything has changed. Bookmarks still hold readers' places, and research still involves familiar activities such as finding topics, browsing indexes, summarizing and paraphrasing sources, and organizing ten-page papers. For this reason we have carefully designed *Bookmarks* as a bridge between old and new traditions—a guide for researchers who expect to work regularly in both print and electronic environments.

Bookmarks assumes that students are using technology to do research and to present their research. Throughout the volume we refer to research *projects*, not papers, and we treat Web pages, brochures, oral presentations, and multimedia displays as plausible options for reporting research findings in many situations. We take technology seriously because it creates new opportunities for undergraduates to do serious research in both their local and their professional communities. At the University of Texas at Austin, the University of South Florida, the University of Illinois, and Georgia Southern University, we have watched students who use the Web and other technologies grow as writers and researchers, and we have been excited by their achievements.

We've also been chastened occasionally by Web projects that were more glitter than substance—offered by writers who failed to read, organize, document, or edit carefully. While much of *Bookmarks* is genuinely new, the framework for describing research processes and the detailed chapters on documentation draw on materials refined over more than a decade. The result, we are confident, is a research guide that offers writers state-of-the-art advice about college research: the best of an older tradition merged with a thoughtful assessment of the new. In keeping with this philosophy, the third edition of *Bookmarks* extends its focus on audience and rhetorical issues, considering the many ways in which digital technologies affect process, research, and presentation in diverse rhetorical settings.

Our focus in this book is on offering **comprehensive, practical advice for student researchers,** including the following:

- **More than twenty engaging, accessible chapters** that explain the process of research.

- An opening section **encouraging students to think of themselves as researchers** (Section 1a).

- Specific advice for **sizing up research projects and assignments** (Section 1b). In particular, writers learn how to read and interpret assignments.

- A chapter on **field research** (Chapter 7). Not all research occurs in the library or online, so *Bookmarks* includes suggestions for conducting interviews, using questionnaires, and making systematic observations.

- A chapter on **handling quotations** (Chapter 14), offering guidelines for selecting and using quotations.

- New coverage of **outlining as an organizational tool**, with illustrative examples (Chapter 17).

Bookmarks pays extra **attention to rhetorical matters**, offering these features:

- A chapter on **finding a topic** (Chapter 2) as well as a chapter that helps writers **focus and narrow** their theses (Chapter 4).

- A chapter on **establishing the purpose of a research project** (Chapter 3). **Research hypotheses and claims** steer the development of thesis sentences and other aspects of the research process.

- A chapter asking writers to **reflect on what they have** (Chapter 15) and review the results of their research at a critical point, before they begin committing themselves to a draft.

- A new chapter on **document design** for both print-based and Web-based projects (Chapter 20).

- A new chapter on **oral and visual presentations** (Chapter 21) that shows students how to draft, design, and deliver oral and visual presentations.

- A new chapter on **presenting research in different genres** (Chapter 22) that shows how a student can communicate research results in a presentation, a report, a brochure, or a Web site.

Bookmarks emphasizes the process of **evaluating and working with sources,** research skills critical for success today. We include these valuable resources:

- A chapter on **evaluating sources** (Chapter 10) with a chart that explains the differences between research materials.

- Expanded coverage of **library databases and indexes** (Chapter 5), with database sources cited in the documentation chapters (Chapters 23–27).

- An updated discussion of **intellectual property issues** (Chapter 9), with guidelines for using academic sources responsibly and avoiding plagiarism.

- A chapter on **annotating research materials** (Chapter 11). The chapter shows writers how to engage in an active dialogue with their reference sources.

- A revised and updated chapter on **drafting the project** (Chapter 18) that includes new information about synthesizing sources.

- A chapter on **using search engines** (Chapter 6). The chapter helps writers manage electronic indexes and search engines efficiently.

- A chapter on **positioning sources** (Chapter 12). Writers learn how to detect and assess the biases in the materials they are using.

- A chapter on **summarizing and paraphrasing** (Chapter 13).

To illustrate how the techniques and guidelines discussed in these chapters apply to a real writing situation, this edition of *Bookmarks* traces a single research topic—the legal and social consequences of MP3 downloading—from the beginning stages of the process (finding a topic) to the production of a final draft (completing the project). Throughout the text, this topic is used in examples and illustrations of the research process, and at the end of each part, writers can see how this project develops by following the advice in the preceding chapters.

A key feature of *Bookmarks* is its **comprehensive coverage of documentation formats,** including **Columbia Online Style (COS).** This system of documentation for electronic sources is presented authoritatively by its creator (Chapter 23). In addition, *Bookmarks* includes detailed treatment of **MLA, APA, CMS,** and **CSE** documentation styles (Chapters 24–27), with comprehensive indexes to documentation items and clear examples of citations as they should appear both in the body of a paper and in the list of Works Cited or References. *Bookmarks* includes complete **sample papers** in MLA, APA, and CMS styles, as well as excerpts from papers illustrating COS style. Handy checklists help writers set up important items in research papers, including title pages, Works Cited and References pages, and abstracts.

Bookmarks itself exemplifies the way technology is reshaping the writing process. The book features a **strong visual component,** with graphical elements highlighting important parts of the research process.

Each part begins with a new profile of **Everyday Research,** which describes how professionals in diverse fields use research in their everyday lives and work.

Focus On . . . boxes appears throughout the book, featuring issues that students are likely to encounter in the research and writing process, and teaching them how to overcome these issues successfully.

Each chapter in Parts I through V concludes with **Web Sites Worth Knowing,** a useful feature that guides researchers to reliable and intriguing online sources.

Managing Your Project exercises follow Chapters 1 through 22, leading student writers step by step through their own academic work.

A **Glossary of Computer Terms** facing the inside back cover provides easy reference for new or unfamiliar terminology.

Supplements

Accompanying *Bookmarks* is a large array of supplements for both instructors and students. Most notable are the following:

- The Companion Website, *Bookmarks Online* at http://www.ablongman .com/bookmarks, includes numerous writing activities, links to other helpful Web sites, sample projects, and other useful tools.

- *MyCompLab* provides the best multimedia resources for writing, grammar, and research in one easy-to-use site. Students will find guided assistance through each step of the writing process; *Exchange,* Longman's new online peer-review program; newly revised "Avoiding Plagiarism" tutorials; "Exercise Zone" with diagnostic grammar tests and more than 3600 practice exercises; "ESL Exercise Zone" with more than 600 practice exercises; and *Research Navigator*™, a database with thousands of magazines and academic journals, the subject-search archive of the *New York Times,* "Link Library," library guides, and more. Tour the site at http://www.mycomplab.com.

- An updated *Instructor's Manual,* available to adopters of the third edition of *Bookmarks.*

Acknowledgments

Many people contributed to the development of *Bookmarks.* In particular we would like to thank the following reviewers, who have given us the benefit of their expertise: James Allen, College of DuPage; Arnold J. Branford, Northern Virginia Community College; Betty L. Hart, University of Southern Indiana;

Sharon James McGee, Southern Illinois University–Edwardsville; Warren Moore, Newberry College; Robert Schwegler, University of Rhode Island; Meryl Soto-Schwartz, Lakeland Community College; and Bill M. Stiffler, Harford Community College. We would also like to thank Betty Hart for her work on the updated Instructor's Manual and Sharon James McGee for her work on the revised and expanded Companion Website

We would like to thank our colleagues working in libraries and online environments for their professional guidance on this project as well. Much of what we present in *Bookmarks* is based on information gathered over decades of teaching and research, both in dusty stacks and in front of terminals. The faculty and especially the graduate students at the University of Texas at Austin's Computer Writing and Research Labs deserve a special round of thanks. This facility of the Division of Rhetoric and Composition has pioneered many of the electronic research and pedagogical strategies described in *Bookmarks*. A special thanks as well is due to the Information Literacy Committees at the University of South Florida and Georgia Southern University libraries for keeping us informed of student and faculty concerns about research and writing from sources in the information age. Our appreciation also extends to the Technology and Writing Committee in Georgia Southern University's Writing and Linguistics Department for continuing suggestions and advice about how to integrate computing technologies comfortably into a writing curriculum.

We are grateful, too, to the editorial team at Longman, especially to Lynn Huddon and Anne Brunell Ehrenworth, who provided us with superb editorial advice and assistance (and also managed to keep us on track with deadlines). Esther Hollander, too, has been helpful as we assembled the final manuscript. The contributions of Adam Beroud, Anne E. Smith, Sharon Balbos, Bob Ginsberg, Kelly Mountain, David Munger, Heidi Beirle, Jennifer Bracco, and Dan Seward to the first two editions of *Bookmarks* were substantial, and the strength of their work is continually evident throughout this text. We would certainly be remiss if we didn't express our indebtedness and gratitude to all those involved in the online conversations we have participated in throughout the years, whose questions, commentary, suggestions, and support have all contributed to this book.

Last, but certainly not least, we would like to thank our students in dozens of research-based writing courses for helping us understand how college research projects typically begin, develop, advance, collapse, and recover. We hope that the practical knowledge we gained from them is evident throughout this project.

JOHN RUSZKIEWICZ
JANICE R. WALKER
MICHAEL A. PEMBERTON

To the Writer

Welcome to *Bookmarks: A Guide to Research and Writing*. This textbook provides a fresh perspective on undergraduate research because the work you'll do in college has changed. Papers are not just papers anymore. Today, instructors expect you to delve deeply into new research materials and use a wide variety of innovative resources, both textual and graphic. They aren't surprised to see illustrations, charts, and photographs in your papers—in fact, they anticipate them. Some instructors may even encourage you to put your work online. Yet these same teachers will likely assume that you have command of all the traditional research skills, from reading an assignment sheet carefully to formatting a Works Cited page properly.

Bookmarks provides comprehensive information to guide you through contemporary college research projects. It will help you choose a topic, find and evaluate sources, and prepare your project efficiently, using up-to-date research and writing tools. Whether your path leads you to printed or electronic sources or to conduct your own field research, *Bookmarks* can do more than help you avoid the pitfalls of a research project. It can make the project an exciting introduction to genuine research.

Bookmarks provides ready access to the materials you will need. The chapters are arranged in a step-by-step sequence that helps you work systematically. The opening sections introduce preliminary skills such as reading an assignment sheet, discovering what is in your library, and choosing a topic. There's also an essential chapter on starting a research project (Chapter 1)—don't miss it. Then the research process advances, chapter by chapter, from finding a topic right through the completion and editing of a final project. The concluding section offers a comprehensive guide to the major systems of documentation, with a full chapter given to each type: COS, MLA, APA, CMS, and CSE.

You may treat *Bookmarks* as a reference tool as well. Use the comprehensive table of contents and the index to locate any information you need from *Bookmarks*. The "Don't Miss" lists at the beginning of each part give you a glimpse at the material contained in each section, and the convenient glossary of terms inside the back cover will explain unfamiliar computer terminology. Throughout the book you will find comprehensive treatment of electronic research forms, including illustrations of suggested Web sites, detailed instructions on using search engines, and important information on intellectual property for the modern researcher.

Be sure to visit the Companion Website for this text, at http://www.ablongman.com/bookmarks. This site offers tutorials, sample papers, activities, a valuable annotated listing of links to essential Web resources to help you find information online, and other useful tools.

As we hope you'll discover, undergraduate research is becoming more exciting because it is, more and more, real research with consequences for readers beyond individual classrooms. We sincerely hope that you enjoy using *Bookmarks* as much as we have enjoyed working with students like you to develop it.

JOHN RUSZKIEWICZ
JANICE R. WALKER
MICHAEL A. PEMBERTON

Bookmarks

A Guide to Research and Writing

I

BEGINNING RESEARCH

DON'T MISS . . .

- **The guide to project scheduling in Section 1f.** Time management is important to the success of any research project.
- **The list of Internet resources in Section 2d.** There's more to the Internet than just the World Wide Web.
- **The annotated research proposal on page 40.** A well-written prospectus can give you a clear focus and a strong start on your project.

EVERYDAY RESEARCH

STEPHEN SHERMAN, Chef de Cuisine
Union Bar and Grille, Boston, Massachusetts

Stephen Sherman began his career as a chef the same way so many others do—he was a dishwasher at a restaurant in Rhode Island the summer before he entered college. Throughout college, he worked in a variety of restaurants; after college, he attended the Culinary Institute of America. He has worked in a variety of high-end restaurants in both New York City and Boston, where he is currently Chef de Cuisine at an upscale eatery in Boston's South End.

Photo courtesy of Thiago "Elvis" DaCunha.

"Most of the research I do consists of keeping up with the trends and newest developments in restaurants and food service. I read many industry publications, including *Food Arts, Chef, Saveur,* and other magazines." Steve also conducts research on the Internet, accessing Web sites about food and competing restaurants to stay abreast of trends in the industry. "In doing this, I also get ideas for the development of my own menu," he says. In some cases, his research involves scouring the many cookbooks he owns or using local libraries to hunt down specific books or recipes. He even refers back to the notes he kept from college.

Steve is a strong proponent of research: "Even in the restaurant industry, it is necessary to use research every day; searching for old recipes or favorite recipes, using periodicals to stay abreast of current industry trends or developments, or even researching a new purveyor or supplier for a particular or new product."

CHAPTER 1

Starting Your Research Project

Students often do not look forward to the dreaded "research project" required in many courses. But all of us do research every day: we check the weather to decide what to wear; we check the TV listings or call the local theater to see what's playing; we look up an address or phone number in the telephone book or online.

In college, your research will ordinarily have two dimensions: you will discover information, and you will discuss what you have discovered—with friends and family, classmates and teachers, and perhaps with others through the medium of the Internet. Yet scholarly research isn't only about reporting on what others have already said; it's about joining the conversation. Research doesn't become real knowledge until your discoveries are shared, digested, tested, and reformulated by a community of people, a process that in turn will spur more ideas and more discoveries. College projects can open conversations that last a lifetime; many students even find themselves changing majors or redirecting their careers as a result of the topics they selected for college projects.

If you think of research as an active process of creating knowledge rather than a passive one of reporting information, you'll be more comfortable with another notion: that almost every college paper and project should be supported by research. The information explosion of recent years makes this prospect exciting. Today, in the library or online, you can locate more useful (as well as not so useful) material on almost every subject. Just as important, you'll have real opportunities to explore your subject with other writers locally and across the world. You may even be able to select the medium by which you'll share what you discover in a research assignment, exploring the rhetoric of document design, hypertext, or multimedia.

Of course, along with these new opportunities come new responsibilities: as a researcher, you'll find it important that you choose your sources wisely and that you credit the sources you include in your project accurately. Perhaps even more important, you will learn that, as a researcher, you have ethical responsibilities—to your subjects, to your readers, and to your ideas. From the time of Plato and Aristotle, philosophers and rhetoricians have held that a writer's goal must always be the pursuit of truth, and it will be your responsibility as a writer and researcher to remain faithful to that pursuit.

1a Think of yourself as a researcher and writer

All of us are capable of doing research, and we often do it without realizing that's what we're doing. Research develops from curiosity, the simple need to learn things and to share discoveries with others. While research may take patience, skill, method, and some training, it's not beyond the talents of anyone intrigued enough by a subject or a problem to do something about it. People learn to do research just as they learn to write, and they get better at both skills the more they practice them. Just as important, people in the professional world usually do research as part of a team. They work toward common goals, argue about how to get there, collaborate on their reports, and (usually) share the credit.

So don't begin a research project—especially one that will involve writing—by underrating your talent and potential. Expect to be challenged and to work hard. Expect to involve others in your work. And expect to succeed.

1b Size up your assignment carefully

Writing is a response to a particular set of requirements and demands, what is often referred to as the *rhetorical situation*. In many cases, a college research project assignment will be spelled out on an assignment sheet. In others, you may be expected to determine the shape of the assignment for yourself. Your instructor may specify the number of words or pages and a due date but leave other considerations for you to decide. Make sure you understand the assignment sheet, ask questions, and pay attention to the key words in the assignment that will help you define the scope of your project; each of these terms has its own significance. Think of the assignment sheet as a contract, and annotate and highlight its key features. As in any contract, rules, regulations, and requirements will be spelled out—and there may even be some fine print. Read your assignment sheet carefully and consider the following points.

Scope. An instructor may give you options for presenting a project—as a conventional paper, an oral report, an electronic presentation, a Web project. Understand those options in terms of what you must do and at what length. Find out whether the project has word or page limits or time limits at *both* ends (no less than, no more than).

Due dates. There may be due dates for separate parts of the project: topic proposal, annotated bibliography, outline, first draft, final draft. Take each due date seriously, and assume that an assignment is due at the *beginning* of class on the date appointed, not by the end of class or later in the school day.

1.1

Rhetorical approach. Sometimes an instructor will specify the rhetorical approach you should take in your paper, indicated by the presence of certain *key research terms* in the assignment sheet. (See the chart "Key Research Terms.") Make sure you understand what you are expected to *show* through your research and how you are expected to present it.

Audience. Think carefully about the audience that will be reading your research. Why would someone be interested in the information you plan to present? What is your purpose in presenting this information? What can you assume that your audience already knows about your topic? What kinds of evidence will you need to convince your audience? Remember, too, that while

---

CHART

Key Research Terms

Analyze. Examine. Break your subject into its parts or components. Discuss their relationship or function.

Classify. Define. Place your subject into a more general category. Distinguish it from other objects in that category. What are its significant features? What makes it unique?

Compare and contrast. Show how your subject resembles or differs from other things or ideas.

Discuss. Talk about the problems or issues your subject raises. Which issues are the most significant? What actions might be taken? Look at the subject from several points of view.

Evaluate. Think about the subject critically. What criteria would you use to judge it? How well does it meet those standards? How does it compare to similar subjects?

Explain. Show what your subject does or how it operates. Provide background information about it. Put your subject in its historical or political context so readers understand it better.

Persuade. Come to a conclusion about your subject and explain why you believe what you do. Use evidence to convince others to agree, or provide good reasons for someone to think or act in a particular way.

Prove or disprove. Provide evidence in support of or contrary to an idea or assertion.

Review of the literature. Examine a field or subject to see what the key issues are and what positions have been staked out by various researchers.

Survey. Measure opinion on a question by using appropriate methods to guarantee an adequate, random, and representative sample of the population.

your instructor is an important audience, he or she will not always be your *only* audience.

Presentation. Note and highlight exactly what your final paper or project must include: a cover sheet, an abstract, appendixes, bibliographies, illustrations, charts, and links? Check, too, whether your instructor expects you to turn in all your materials at the end of a project, including notes, drafts, photocopied sources, and peer editing sheets. If so, keep this material in a folder or an envelope or keep an electronic copy on disk from the start of the project.

Format. Will your project be typed or printed, or will it be submitted or published electronically? Notice specific requirements the instructor may have for margins, placement of page numbers, line spacing, titles, headings, illustrations, graphics, and so on, or specific formats required for electronic projects. If an instructor doesn't give specific directions for such items, you may want to follow the guidelines for your discipline of study.

Documentation. Be sure you understand your instructor's preferences for documenting a project. Some instructors may specify MLA, APA, or COS documentation; others may give you the option of choosing any system, providing that you handle it consistently. Make the decision about your documentation system early because you'll want to use it for your bibliography and notes or in your electronic files.

Collaboration. Instructors may encourage or require collaboration on research projects. If that's the case with your project, learn the ground rules to see how the work can be divided and what reports and self-assessments may be required from project participants. Pay attention, too, to how the project itself will be evaluated. See the Focus On . . . Collaboration box on page 8 for more information.

1c Establish the hard points of your project

Hard points are those features of a project you can't change—they are usually described in the assignment. When an instructor asks for a ten-page paper on genetic engineering using CSE style and due in two weeks, you have four hard points.

1. Format: ten-page paper
2. Topic: genetic engineering
3. Documentation: CSE
4. Due date: two weeks from today

All four points will shape your planning, but perhaps none more so than the due date. Researching and writing ten pages in two weeks is a lot of work. But instructors rarely show tolerance for late projects, particularly when there has been plenty of time to complete them. So do take due dates seriously.

FOCUS ON . . . Collaboration

You may need to work as part of a team for some college projects. Careful management is an important part of any collaborative effort.

Decide how to make decisions. Choose a project leader or meet regularly (even by email) to reach a consensus through discussions or voting. Team members must agree on how to make decisions and then respect that process.

Make sure someone has an overview of the process. Even small groups can lose sight of project goals, resources, or timelines. Choose one team member to allocate resources and adjust schedules to bring a project in on time.

Talk with each other. Team members must communicate throughout a project. Practice "simultaneous engineering"—that is, a team should be aware of the impact that choices might have on each component of a project, especially in the early stages.

Assess the strengths of team members. While every member of the team should be exposed to almost every part of the project, people should work chiefly on those parts of a project for which they have skill, talent, and experience. The team must be sure people don't undertake responsibilities they can't handle. A little diplomacy and honesty early in a project can save a lot of heartache later. Team members must understand their assignments and those of their colleagues—and expect to be held responsible for them. If you can't complete part of your assignment for some reason, let your colleagues know immediately so they can make adjustments. Don't string your team members along and lead them to expect work you can't or won't produce.

Some instructors may give you a series of due dates for a major project, asking that you submit items such as the following at specific times:

- Project proposal, prospectus, or thesis
- Annotated working bibliography
- Storyboards (for projects with graphics)
- First draft
- Web site design specifications
- Responses to peer editing

When you are given multiple due dates, they can be arranged to form a timeline into which you can fit the remaining hard points of your project. (See Section 1f for more on creating a schedule for your project.)

1d Define the stages of your project

Your hard points will provide a starting point for your project, but different kinds of projects may follow vastly different paths. If you are gathering information in a library, you might have to allow time for creating a bibliography and for locating documents and then taking notes from them. If you are planning a field project that involves interviews, you have to determine *whom* to interview about *what*, prepare the questions, conduct the interviews, and then review and report your findings. If you are searching the Web for articles and resource documents, you will need time to search, determine which resources are the most useful, print out hard copies of Web pages or save them to disk, and keep track of your research.

At the outset, however, there is no sure way of knowing all the elements a project might involve. The best you can do is estimate your work. In planning a project, it will certainly help to talk to more experienced researchers, to librarians, to instructors, and to colleagues. You might also review sample research projects, asking yourself, What did the authors have to do to create this work or get these results?

Finally, you might review the activities that research projects typically require. No project would include all the items listed in the checklist [below], and many projects might include tasks and activities not mentioned here. Use the checklist to stimulate your own thinking and to help you arrange your activities in a rough sequence.

CHECKLIST 1.1

Research Activities

Stage 1: Beginning Research

○ Size up the assignment.
○ Determine your purpose and audience.
○ Establish the hard points of your project.
○ Choose a topic that fits the assignment and matches your interests.
○ Define the stages of your project.
○ Prepare a proposal or prospectus for your research project.
○ Check campus research policies if people will be used as subjects.

Stage 2: Gathering Ideas and Information

○ Determine what information you need.
○ Decide where to look for information.
○ Consult bibliographies.

(Continued)

Research Activities–(*Continued*)

○ Locate sources (in libraries, online databases, on the Web, etc.).
○ Request materials through interlibrary loan, if necessary.
○ Prepare questionnaires and/or surveys, if appropriate.
○ Create a plan for systematic observation of subjects or objects of study.
○ Keep track of information systematically.
○ Establish a database or method of compiling results.
○ Determine the best format to present your findings.

Stage 3: Working with Sources

○ Generate a working bibliography.
○ Evaluate your sources.
○ Annotate research materials.
○ Prepare an annotated bibliography.
○ Read and position sources.
○ Summarize and paraphrase sources.
○ Conduct interviews.
○ Distribute questionnaires or surveys.
○ Conduct studies or observations.

Stage 4: Developing the Project

○ Refine your claim.
○ Organize your materials.
○ Decide on a design for your project.
○ Begin drafting your project.
○ Submit a draft or prototype.
○ Get feedback on your project.
○ Respond to feedback and make any necessary changes or revisions.
○ Meticulously document all sources used in your project.
○ Fine-tune your project, making any last-minute revisions or edits.
○ Test and carefully proofread your final project.
○ Submit your final project.

1e   Assess your strengths and weaknesses

Once you have a comprehensive idea of what your research project will require from you (or your team), plot those responsibilities against your time-line and decide how much effort to devote to each stage. If you know you are a competent researcher but a slow writer, or if you are prone to procrastination, you might allot extra time to draft a research paper. Similarly, if you are a novice at interviewing, you may want to schedule more interviews than absolutely necessary, figuring that the earlier ones might not be entirely successful. (See also Chapter 8, "Keeping Track of Information.")

This is the point at which to acknowledge any personal limitations. For example, if you have no experience with document design or managing graphics, you should rethink the wisdom of creating a project heavy on illustrations. Or perhaps you'd like to prepare a paper comparing great American novels, but you realize that you aren't a particularly fast reader. A paper about great American short stories might be more successful.

You also have to measure your resources. What kinds of materials can you find in your local community? Do you have the tools and the money to produce exactly what you want? Do the members of your team have the experience to do the kind of project you envision? Adjust your plan accordingly and expect to make similar adjustments throughout the project.

Sometimes circumstances outside your project will change the timeline. Try to anticipate minor calamities: interlibrary loan operating more slowly than expected, fewer respondents replying to your survey than predicted, campus computer access growing more difficult at the end of the term.

Factor in a little extra time for problems such as writer's block or a tendency to procrastinate. To overcome a tendency to procrastinate, you might make a commitment to write *something* every day, no matter what. Or try breaking a large task down into smaller, more manageable components. For example, instead of attempting to produce an entire draft, why not write just a one- or two-paragraph introduction? You could even "talk" your draft into a tape recorder, then transcribe it. One way to overcome procrastination is by setting a schedule and sticking to it. (For more tips, see "Web Sites Worth Knowing" at the end of this chapter.)

1.2

1f Create a schedule for your project

When you have established your hard points, listed the steps and stages of your project, and assessed your capabilities, you are ready to sketch out your project in a calendar or timeline. You can create a calendar simply by listing the due dates of a project and leaving sufficient space between them to insert the activities necessary to meet those deadlines. Then estimate the time necessary and/or available for each step in the project. Your initial calendar should not be too detailed; you'll waste time if you try to account for every movement in what is largely an unpredictable process.

You can also mark off your research project on an actual calendar, listing each day's activities along with due dates. With such a calendar you can get a clear sense of the time available to do your work, perhaps coordinating it with your other commitments. Then look at the time available to complete the entire job, counting the actual days if it helps. If you are given only a completion date, estimate the halfway point of your project and decide what you must accomplish by that point—perhaps a complete first draft or a working Web site design. Whatever type of calendar you create, allow some slack toward the end to make up for time you will almost certainly lose earlier in the project.

A third type of planning tool for projects is a Gantt chart. Imagine a line moving steadily forward while various activities proceed through stages that may be overlapping or even circular. You can design a timeline that illustrates this process by mapping ongoing responsibilities below the due dates you identified in your hard points.

Whatever form of calendar you create for your paper or project, build in some flexibility. Sometimes a carefully considered plan will have to be reshaped when things don't go quite as you expect. Always remember that the point of having a schedule is to produce a product; all is not lost if you have to change a schedule to fit altered circumstances. Few projects meet all their initial goals.

More than anything else, we want to impress on you the value of forethought as you plan your research project, even before you decide exactly what your topic is going to be. An understanding of your assignment, its requirements, and the time frame you're working in will definitely pay off in the long run. Armed with a clear sense of what you have to accomplish, you're ready to move onto the next step: choosing a topic.

WWW Web Sites Worth Knowing

WWW 1.3

- "Procrastination and Writer's Block,"
  http://owl.english.purdue.edu/workshops/hypertext/ResearchW/procrast.html
- *Group Work and Collaborative Writing,* http://www-honors.ucdavis.edu/vohs
- "Time and the Writer," http://www.writing-world.com/basics/time.shtml

MANAGING YOUR PROJECT

1. Photocopy your assignment sheet for a project, and then annotate it thoroughly. Highlight the actual assignment and the due dates. Note the special features the project must have. What parts of the assignment emphasize information? What parts encourage dialogue, conversation, or collaboration?

2. Identify the two or three parts of the assignment that you expect will cause you the most difficulty, and then explain exactly why you are nervous about those requirements or expectations. Consider what steps you might take to make the difficulty more manageable. Will more reading

help? Could the instructor or a librarian help? Might the project be easier if you found someone to collaborate with?

3. Examine your entire project carefully and break it down into four or five major stages. You might imagine steps such as the following:

For a Paper	For a Web Project
Finding/focusing on a topic	Determining purpose
Locating information	Determining basic site design
Reading and assessing sources	Assigning and developing pages
Producing a first draft	Establishing links
Getting feedback	Getting feedback and testing
Revising and editing	Fine-tuning the design

Look at your stages in terms of the time available for completion, and establish a firm timeline for completing the paper. Be sure that the calendar leaves ample time for feedback from colleagues. The more time you allow for revision and fine tuning, the better your final project will be.

CHAPTER 2

Finding a Topic

How often have you complained—even if only to yourself—about the "boring" topics you are assigned to write about by your instructors? Most instructors do try to choose topics they hope will interest students, or from which students can learn something of importance, of course, but even when students choose their own topics to research and write about, they often find the experience less than thrilling. The problem isn't that the topic—whatever it may be—is inherently boring; the problem is that writers sometimes don't put enough thought into finding ways to make their topic interesting.

When asked to find their own topics, writers may select issues that are both controversial and familiar. Most people have opinions about topics such as capital punishment or abortion and can rehash arguments they've been hearing all their lives, but such topics are the intellectual equivalent of the Dairy Queen—filling, familiar, and always just around the corner. Little is ventured to produce such a project and little gained. Unless you can discover a unique and interesting focus within such a topic, you would do well to avoid it. Have more confidence in your ability to make fresh discoveries about issues and problems close to you and your community.

Finding a topic to write about begins with your own questions and ideas, often prompted by class discussions and readings. Listen to what others have to say and ask yourself the following questions about your readers:

- What are their concerns?
- What are their questions?
- What do they already understand about a topic, and what do they need or want to know?
- Why are they interested in a subject, and what sort of approach are they most likely to listen to?

Knowing something about your audience is vitally important as you begin working on your research project. Not only will it help you decide on a research plan, but it will also guide you in organizing and presenting your information as you write.

Discussions with classmates, instructors, friends, and others you know well can help you clarify your own thinking as well. Consider the following:

- What aspects of the subject do you already know a lot about, and which do you feel less certain of?
- Do other people raise points you hadn't thought of?
- Do they introduce related issues or make connections that you find intriguing?
- Do they agree with your views completely, or are there areas where they disagree with you dramatically?

The cues you get from these discussions can be a valuable part of your initial discovery and research process.

But you must also extend these discussions beyond the classroom by participating in further conversations and discussions, face-to-face or online, through outside reading, watching television, browsing electronic newsgroups or the Web, and thinking about your topic.

2a Find a topic in your world

Many college research projects are open-ended—that is, your topic will be connected in some way to the general subject of the course, but its specific focus will be determined by you. In a history class you might write about an era, a movement, or a conflict (the Gilded Age, the Civil War); in a philosophy course, a movement (Thomism, Existentialism); in government, a theme or concept (balance of power); in the natural sciences, an experiment; in the social sciences, a field project. Within these broad areas, you will have much room to choose specific topics. The following considerations can help.

Connect assignments to your own experiences and interests and to issues of consequence in local, regional, or national communities. You're more likely to do original research when your project explores real turf, not abstract ideas. For example, you may be uneasy after watching a *Crossfire* debate on standardized testing in schools. Do the participants' views reflect your experience in taking such tests? Are the facts and assumptions you have heard accurate, the claims justified? A serious project might grow from such a query. Similarly, a history assignment on the civil rights movement could lead you to inquire about local concerns: Was your school or community ever segregated? How did your city or town react to civil rights initiatives or legislation? Do contemporary concerns for women or gay rights have roots in this earlier political movement?

2.1

Try freewriting about your topic for ten minutes. Write as quickly as you can without pausing to reread or correct mistakes. That way you'll have some words on paper to get you started or to keep you going. Freewriting can often lead you to discover the questions your research project may need to answer, as well as helping you to discover where your interests may lie.

Keep a journal to record ideas you may have while watching a television show or eating lunch. You may be surprised to find that issues of personal interest to you also have wider implications.

Read critically. Don't expect a cogent topic to drop from the sky, and don't rely on sudden inspiration to strike you. Open yourself up to the world by reading everything you can get your hands on: local newspapers, university journals, trade magazines, minutes of influential committees, fliers distributed by offbeat groups, and online discussion forums. Note questions you have as you read.

Watch TV, especially the news channels (CNN, MSNBC, Fox News) and that most valuable and unfiltered political source, C-SPAN. What is going on in your school, your community, or your world that you want to know more about?

Surf the Net, checking out political, cultural, and social sites of interest to you—or even those that offend you. (You're more likely to be moved to action by encountering something you don't like.)

Talk with other people, face-to-face or via electronic forums. Remember that you need to find out what others think, what's important to them, and how they will respond to what you want to say.

2b   Connect your topic to a wider community

2.2

Look for campus events, clubs, or forums that might be related to your topic. Browse the special collections in your local or university library; check museums or exhibitions; and consult the local papers for information about lectures, film groups, or community meetings where you might meet people interested in your work. When you find such people, network with them to find more people and organizations invested in your subject. To begin research on a paper about MP3 downloading and its impact on the local community, for example, you could talk with the employees of a nearby music store or attend a meeting of your campus's computing services committee. The people you encounter at these meetings might be able to point you to resources and reference materials far more quickly and efficiently than you could manage on your own.

2.3

If you are in a course with access to an electronic discussion list or chat room (see Figure 2.1 on page 21), invite classmates to join you in a session to discuss research ideas. As you explain your topic to others, you'll grasp it better yourself: its features will stand in sharper relief when viewed side by side with the projects your colleagues are planning. You may be able to set up your own electronic discussion list through such sites as *Yahoo! Groups* or *Tile.net* (see "Web Sites Worth Knowing" at the end of this chapter).

2c   Browse the library in your topic area

Look for a subject about which you can honestly say, "I want to learn much more about it." The enthusiasm you bring to a project will be evident in the work you produce. Stay clear of stale controversies that have been on the national or local news without resolution for a long time—you'll find plenty of material on such subjects, but it is unlikely you'll add much to the debate. Your paper should be different; it should spark interest and stand out from the others in the stack. The best way to do that is to go beyond "obvious" content and learn as much as you can about your subject.

Get closer to your subject by spending a few hours browsing in the library or on the Web. (See Section 2d and Chapter 6 for a full discussion of online resources.) A little preliminary research, reading, and talking about ideas can help you discover what to say about a topic that hasn't already been said over and over. Exploring your topic in this way can also help you determine what the actual controversies are by helping you focus your ideas.

Efficient sources for the preliminary exploration of academic topics are specialized encyclopedias that provide broad overviews of many subjects, outline important issues within a particular field, and focus more on general concepts than on details. Library reference rooms have dozens of specialized encyclopedias covering many fields, and many libraries also offer electronic access to them. The checklist on page 18 points you to some of the most commonly available specialized encyclopedias.

FOCUS ON . . . **Finding a Topic**

According to Webster, "heuristics" are devices that serve as an aid to discovery. In writing, heuristic devices are basically questions to help you discover a topic to research and write about, a focus for your topic, or evidentiary requirements for your project. Try asking yourself the following:

- What am I interested in?
- What kinds of activities do I enjoy?
- What do I like to read about?
- What kinds of Web sites do I enjoy visiting?
- What kinds of TV shows or movies do I enjoy?

Once you have a general subject area, browse through the subject indexes in your library's catalog (see Chapter 5) and general or specialized encyclopedias (see page 18), and surf the Web (see Chapter 6).

As you consider possible topics, consider what you would like to accomplish. Perhaps you want to express your feelings about something, to learn more about it, to inform other people about it, or to persuade other people of something. But don't stop there: your *purpose* is the reason *why* you want to do these things, what you hope to accomplish. Without a clear purpose, your research and writing will be drudge work, and your audience will likely come away from reading your work wondering why you have written about your topic at all. (For more information on establishing a purpose, see Chapter 3.)

When no specialized encyclopedia is available, or if the volume you select proves too technical, use one of the general encyclopedias available in print or electronic format.

Print	Electronic
The Encyclopaedia Britannica	*Britannica Online*
Encyclopedia Americana	*Encarta*
Collier's Encyclopedia	*Grolier Multimedia Encyclopedia*
Columbia Encyclopedia	*Academic American Encyclopedia*

To get a feel for your topic area, examine books and journals in the field as well. What are the major issues? Who is affected by them? Who is writing on the topic? You can learn more than you might expect from quick but purposeful browsing. You will learn fairly quickly whether or not sufficient reliable resources exist to support your project in the time available. If you have a difficult time finding information about your research topic, you might consider changing it. On the other hand, if a wealth of information is available, you should survey your subject so you can identify key issues and narrow the scope of your project as appropriate. Even more important, you should use the time you spend browsing to confirm whether you are in fact interested in your topic and want to read about it more deeply.

CHECKLIST 2.1

> ### Specialized Encyclopedias

Doing a paper on . . . ?	Begin by checking . . .
American history	○ *Encyclopedia of American History*
Anthropology	○ *International Encyclopedia of the Social Sciences*
Art	○ *Encyclopedia of World Art*
Astronomy	○ *Encyclopedia of Astronomy*
Communication	○ *International Encyclopedia of Communication*
Computers	○ *Encyclopedia of Computer Science*
Crime	○ *Encyclopedia of Crime and Justice*
Economics	○ *Encyclopedia of American Economic History*
Environment	○ *Encyclopedia of the Environment*
Ethics in life sciences	○ *Encyclopedia of Bioethics*
Film	○ *International Encyclopedia of Film*
Health, medicine	○ *Health and Medical Horizons*
History	○ *Dictionary of American History*

Law	○ *The Guide to American Law*
Literature	○ *Cassell's Encyclopedia of World Literature*
Multiculturalism	○ *Encyclopedia of Multiculturalism*
Music	○ *The New Grove Dictionary of American Music*
Philosophy	○ *Encyclopedia of Philosophy*
Political science	○ *Encyclopedia of American Political History*
Politics	○ *Oxford Companion to Politics of the World*
Psychology, psychiatry	○ *International Encyclopedia of Psychiatry, Psychology, Psychoanalysis and Neurology; Encyclopedia of Psychology*
Religion	○ *The Encyclopedia of Religion; Encyclopedia Judaica; New Catholic Encyclopedia*
Science	○ *McGraw-Hill Encyclopedia of Science and Technology*
Social sciences	○ *Encyclopedia of the Social Sciences*

2d Browse the Internet

The quality of materials on the Web varies enormously (see Chapter 10). Still, a well-constructed Web site should provide a helpful overview of a subject as well as links to other sources. Use search engines (see Chapter 6) to find the best locations. Many libraries also offer access to databases and other reference sources through the Web (see Section 5b).

Like Web sites, Internet discussion groups can help you understand the dimensions of a subject—what it involves and what the issues are. Internet discussion groups include both *asynchronous* communications and real-time *synchronous* communications, such as IRC (Internet Relay Chat), MUDs (multiuser domains) and MOOs (MUDs, object oriented), and chat rooms. In an asynchronous discussion, participants read messages that have been posted earlier and leave messages of their own for others to read at their convenience. In a real-time discussion, the participants are online at the same time, reading and responding immediately to each other, as they might in an actual conversation.

Asynchronous Online Forums	Synchronous Online Forums
Email	MOOs and MUDs
Listservs	Instant Relay Chat (IRC)
Newsgroups	Instant messaging
Blogs	Text messaging
Wikis	
Web boards	

Email and discussion lists. Many people use the Internet to communicate about a wide variety of topics. Email and electronic discussion lists, such as listservs, newsgroups, blogs, and wikis, enable people with common interests to share information with others online. Sifting through messages in these forums can help you focus a general topic into a workable research project. The forums can also be good places to ask questions and to learn about other potential sources. However, before using information obtained from these sources, make sure you get permission, and always give proper credit (see Chapter 14).

Some email lists are informal discussion lists; others may be more formal or moderated discussions. You can find listservs with search engines such as *Tile.net*, or you can search through newsgroups using a specialized search engine such as *Google Groups* at http://groups.google.com/. Some listservs and newsgroups such as *HyperNews* can be read on the World Wide Web using a browser, or you may be able to read them in your Internet email editor. It is usually best to "lurk" for a while, read the FAQs (frequently asked questions) and other information about the list, and get a sense of the conversation before asking questions.

Newsgroups come in all shapes and sizes, from raunchy or eccentric *alt.whatever* groups to moderated groups offering expert information on a wide variety of topics. A very small sampling will illustrate something of the range these groups cover.

alt.algebra.help	*rec.animals.wildlife*
alt.dorks	*red.folk-dancing*
humanities.classics	*soc.history.ancient*
info.academic-freedom	*talk.environment*

You can usually do a quick text search in the list of available groups to find those that might be related to your subject area.

Blogs, or Web logs, are actually Web pages with links and commentary; they are updated whenever new information is added. Many blogs are more or less personal journals, but some may allow for anyone to subscribe and add to the conversation. Wikis are also Web pages created by users, but unlike blogs or most Web pages, most wikis allow any user not only to add to the page but to change what others have added.

MOOs and MUDs, Internet Relay Chat (IRC). MOOs and MUDs (real-time synchronous communication sites on the Internet) and Internet Relay Chat (IRC) or other chat rooms can be spaces to meet other people from around the world, discuss topics of mutual interest, and get ideas for your own research project. You can conduct online interviews in these spaces with a wide variety of people, conduct surveys or ethnographic studies, or meet with group members to discuss your findings. Different "channels" or "rooms" represent distinct communities or topics. Figure 2.1, for example, shows the list of public

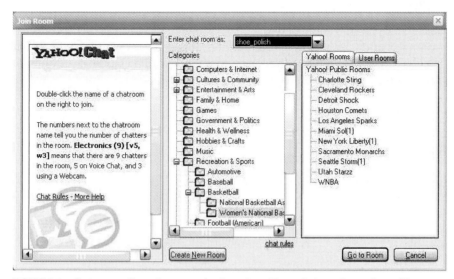

FIGURE 2.1 Chat rooms offer online spaces for discussion with people from all over the world, centered on various topics of interest.
(Source: Yahoo! Chat, http://chat.yahoo.com)

rooms available in *Yahoo! Chat's* "Recreation and Sports" category. Before logging a conversation or using information in your research, however, make sure you ask permission, and make sure that you cite your sources accurately.

Instant messaging and text messaging. Many people are now familiar with some of the hundreds of instant messaging programs (IMs), such as Apple's *iChat*, AOL's *Instant Messenger*, or *Yahoo! Messenger*. Many of these programs now allow for real-time audio and video as well as text conferencing, easy file sharing, and more. Many cell phones include text messaging services as well. Using IMs to chat with a variety of people from all over the world can sometimes help you discover topics where there is reasonable disagreement. These topics, then, can often be turned into full-fledged research projects.

Web boards. Some professional Web sites have discussion areas or "electronic bulletin boards" where others can share opinions, ask questions, pool resources, and help newcomers. Cable Network News (CNN), *Time* magazine, and *U.S. News and World Report* have Web sites that invite people to share their views of current events on a Web board. Professional organizations like the National Council of Teachers of English (NCTE) offer similar services—and members at the NCTE site, for example, might be very responsive to an inquiry on a topic such as standardized testing. Before posting a question as a new user, however, be sure to look through the archived discussions (which are usually available online) to make sure that the topic has not already been raised—and discussed thoroughly—within recent weeks.

Finding a topic for your research project is not always an easy task. Although it's possible you will find a topic relatively quickly, one rich in resource material that interests both you and others, it is equally possible that you will have to give some time to rethinking and refining your subject (see Chapter 4). Take the time to find a topic with a high potential for success; then you will be ready to consider how to give that topic—and your research project—a well-defined purpose.

WWW Web Sites Worth Knowing

- Writing Center at Colorado State University's Guide to Writing Processes, "Audience,"http://writing.colostate.edu/references/processes/audmod

- Purdue's Online Writing Lab, "Writing a Research Paper: Introduction to Topic," http://owl.english.purdue.edu/workshops/hypertext/ResearchW/topic.html

- Tile.Net Discussion List and Newsgroup Search Engine, http://tile.net

- Blogs and Wikis, http://ferret.bemidjistate.edu/~morgan/cgi-bin/blogsandwiki.pl?WikiAndBlog

WWW

2.4

MANAGING YOUR PROJECT

1. What issues or problems most concern your campus at the present time? Do any of these issues have a history you might explore in a class project or research paper? Explain how your library work or fieldwork might illuminate the issue or add an important voice to an ongoing conversation.

2. What connections might you make between the project you are considering for a course and your local community? Could your project draw on the resources of people around you or involve local people or institutions? How might a group or institution benefit from your research into archives, local or regional history, or current issues or controversies?

3. Investigate any special resources, collections, museums, institutions, or groups in your community that might help you in shaping a project.

4. Use the Web to look at newsgroups, listservs, or telnet sites that focus on your topic. (For information on searching and evaluating such resources, see Chapters 6 and 10.)

CHAPTER 3

Establishing a Purpose

Have you ever gone into a major chain bookstore like Borders or Barnes and Noble and scanned the magazine racks? If so, you've probably been taken aback by the sheer number of magazines available in virtually every area of recreational or professional interest. How do they all manage to create and sustain a demand for their publications, and how do they manage to avoid repeating themselves (and each other) month after month after month?

The answer is that these magazines all have different purposes, different audiences, and different takes on the subjects they cover. Sometimes their purpose is to provide factual information; sometimes it's to persuade people to accept a particular point of view; sometimes it's purely to provide entertainment. As you might suspect, there's an analogy here to your own research. Just as these publications have had to make important decisions about how to focus their articles and how to appeal to a specific group of readers, you too must make decisions about the purposes your paper or project might serve.

Imagine that you want to use a writing course assignment to investigate the controversy over MP3 file sharing, something that you've seen a lot of among your classmates. You know that piracy is wrong, but you also know lots of people who make copies of CDs for friends or who listen to music they've downloaded illegally from the Internet. Sharing media files with other people doesn't seem like such a serious crime, but your university has recently warned students against downloading music illegally on the campus network, and there have been threats of disciplinary action against those who are caught. You decide to explore the details of this issue and, based on your research, offer suggestions to resolve the problem.

Given this scenario, exactly what issues might you address, and how might you best approach them? You'll certainly need to consider your potential audience. The issues that interest politicians and record executives on the subject of MP3 file sharing are likely to be quite different from those that interest computer specialists or musicians or college students. In the same way, the arguments and evidence that are persuasive to members of one group might be far less effective with another. Hard numbers, numerical data, and detailed sales figures could appeal to an industry executive, but a group of college students might find these

www
3.1

23

FOCUS ON . . . **Audience**

Whenever you write, you're writing for an audience. Some people imagine that they're writing to one reader in particular; others try to imagine a specific, well-defined audience—readers of *Seventeen* magazine or a group of *Star Trek* fans, for example. Whichever approach works best for you, ask these questions about your audience and use your answers to guide you as you research and write:

- What will my readers already know about my topic?
- What will they likely want to know about my topic?
- What beliefs will they already have about my topic, and how can I address those beliefs?
- What parts of my topic will concern them most?
- How can I persuade them to value the results of my research?

You might decide, for example, that an audience of college students would be predisposed to favor MP3 downloading, but they might not know how it actually affects local businesses. Emphasizing the harm it does to people they know personally might be an effective persuasive strategy.

numbers far removed from their own concerns. Always keep your audience in mind as you reflect on how to approach and present your subject to your readers.

Deciding on a rhetorical approach for your project at this stage will help focus your thinking and give you direction as you think about how to develop and research your project. Though there are many possible approaches you could take, to make your choice manageable we'll focus on just five, considering your topic as:

- a question of fact
- a question of definition
- a question of value
- a question of causality, or
- a question of consequence

These five approaches have their roots in classical rhetoric and reflect rhetorical approaches found in all disciplines. We'll illustrate these strategies, examining the approaches one at a time, through an imaginary research project on MP3 file sharing. You should understand, however, that these questions will almost always overlap in your work, one question leading naturally to another.

3a Consider the topic as a question of fact

You can approach almost any subject by exploring factual questions, reporting what is known about a subject or what remains to be discovered. Queries of fact include the familiar journalist's questions: *who, what, where, when,* and *how.* By answering these questions you could develop the topic and purpose for a project.

Ask questions that make sense for your topic. For example, in researching the issue of MP3 file sharing, you might explore its impact on CD sales: Have CD sales declined over the years? If so, how much of this decline can be attributed to illegal downloading? Are there instances where music downloading has actually *increased* album sales? To answer these questions you may have to visit archives and record stores. A search of government documents might turn up congressional testimony by record executives about the impact of music piracy on sales. A local record store might be able to provide detailed information about how much its business has been hurt by illegal CD copying. Gathering and correlating these facts would be genuine research.

Factual questions such as the following provide a great way to begin your exploration of a topic.

- What is known about this subject?
- What remains to be discovered?
- What might readers find new or surprising about this subject?
- Are important factual matters relating to this subject in dispute?

As a result of considering these queries, you may decide to frame your project as a report, a brochure, or an informational Web site. Or, should your research show that the facts are in dispute, you may write an argument favoring one set of facts over another.

SUMMARY

Questions of Fact

You are dealing with factual matters when your research leads you to verify what is already known about a subject. You'll likely begin your research with specific questions—and other questions will arise as you learn more about your topic.

Projects based on questions of fact . . .

- Tell readers something they don't know.
- Prove that something known *is* so.
- Discredit false information.
- Explain how something came to be.
- Enumerate the parts or elements of a situation.
- Explain how something occurred.

3b Consider the topic as a question of definition

You can examine almost any subject by studying the meaning of its key concepts. You might find the standard meanings of these crucial terms in dictionaries and encyclopedias, or you might have to come up with definitions on your own—for example, by creating questionnaires to discover how the public understands the terms, concepts, or ideas. (See Chapter 7 for information on developing surveys and questionnaires.)

An issue such as MP3 downloading may not raise obvious questions of definition. But certain terms might quickly become controversial if your research places them in the public sphere. Should technicians or computer specialists use the terms *peer-to-peer networks* or *digital fingerprints,* you might examine the question by looking more closely at the meaning of those terms. Lawyers and copyright experts, on the other hand, might refer to *intellectual property* or *the doctrine of fair use,* and these terms too may lead to matters of definition.

Questions of definition may lead either to reports or to arguments. Your research effort might, for example, provide an extended definition of a concept in which you both define an idea and furnish examples and illustrations to help readers understand it. Or a research project based on issues of definition may become an argument when the terms of the definition are in dispute.

S U M M A R Y

Questions of Definition

You are dealing with matters of definition when you examine questions about the nature of things. You'll be trying to understand definitions, create them, or refute them. Or you may be trying to decide whether something fits the criteria of an established definition. Your exploration may begin with general sources (dictionaries) but will likely branch out to include more specialized information.

Projects based on questions of definition . . .

- Explore the classes to which things belong.
- Enumerate distinguishing features.
- Examine basic similarities.
- Point out fundamental differences.
- Move to include someone or something in a group.
- Move to exclude someone or something from a group.

3c Consider the topic as a question of value

You can examine almost any subject by framing it as a question of value. In fact, almost every day you make snap judgments about the value of dozens of things—movies, food, music, athletes, politicians, automobiles. These informal evaluations are not all that different from the more studied judgments you might make in a full research project, where you might evaluate the work of a contemporary poet or judge the merit of a new social program. In these more formal situations, you will need to support your evaluations with convincing evidence because you become more accountable when you go public with an opinion, whether in print or online.

How might issues of value shape your research on MP3 downloading? You'll have to explore many aspects: the value of an "open" Internet where information can be freely exchanged versus a "regulated" Internet where information sharing is restricted, the actual value of a group's music compared to the price of its CD, or even the value of a college education at an institution that places (possibly unreasonable) restrictions on technology. The purpose of research here is to go well beyond mere opinion. You would have to find strong evidence to support any claims of value you might offer, getting testimony from the opinions of experts, from public surveys and questionnaires, from systematic observation, and from articles and reports on the subject.

Think carefully about how to present your findings. To show all sides of an issue, you might write a feature article for the campus newspaper or create a Web site that offers a variety of opinions—using tables, charts, or graphics to display information. However, most evaluations will end up as persuasive pieces, with researchers taking definite stands supported by evidence they have gathered to support their judgment. (To learn more about choosing a format for your project, see Chapter 20.)

SUMMARY

Questions of Value

You are exploring a question of value when you judge the merit of an idea, concept, policy, institution, public figure, or activity. You'll have to decide on the valid criteria for judgment and then determine whether what you are evaluating meets those standards. In a few cases, particularly in the sciences, standards of performance or quality may be defined precisely. In other arenas, criteria for evaluation may be controversial. You'll need to understand the controversies in order to make convincing judgments of your own.

Projects based on questions of evaluation . . .

- Assess strengths and weaknesses.
- Explain why something has or has not worked well.
- Advise others in a course of action.
- Assess the competition.
- Praise or blame someone or something.

3d **Consider the topic as a question of cause and effect**

Examining why things happen the way they do is one of the most important jobs of researchers. Cause-and-effect analyses are among our culture's most powerful (and habitual) operations. Consider how regularly our leaders and the news media trace effects back to causes in order to dole out praise and blame: in describing the success or failure of policy decisions, in tracing the reasons for disasters, in tracking the consequences of various actions, in attributing behavior to societal influences.

You can find specific topics easily by thinking about cause-and-effect relationships. For example, you might design a project to investigate the effects of MP3 downloading on CD prices or Internet service. How would decreased CD revenues affect business in the recording industry? Would fewer musicians get recording contracts? Would royalties be smaller, particularly for "unknown" groups? Does MP3 downloading slow down network service for everyone else? Why and how much?

Questions of cause and effect can lead to reports when the causal analysis is more factual than speculative. The more speculative your analysis, the more likely it will move in the direction of argument. But even such arguments can be informative when, for example, research suggests many possible causes for a particular phenomenon.

SUMMARY

Questions of Cause and Effect

You are exploring a cause-and-effect question when you seek to know why something happened. You can explore such questions from two directions: by looking at an existing event or phenomenon and researching its causes or by examining a potential force and speculating what its consequences might be.

Projects based on cause-and-effect questions . . .

- Explain why something happened.
- Consider what might happen as a result of certain trends or movements.
- Question complex explanations for simple phenomena.
- Challenge simple explanations for complex phenomena.
- Explore the relationships between causes and effects.
- Probe the complexity of political and social relationships.

3e Consider the topic as a question of consequence

You might approach any subject by making a proposal for action. Proposals often begin with a problem, a gap, or an uncertainty. You might begin with evidence that a given situation—in school, at home, in the country—must change. First you have to define the problem, appreciating its complexities; then you have to think creatively about its implications. For example, were you to support university restrictions on illegal MP3 downloading, you might have to offer other proposals that would make the restrictions easier for students to accept, such as open access to "public domain" music archives or special discounts on downloads from commercial sites. One approach to the problem might be to learn what other colleges or universities have done to confront this issue. Another approach might be to look at the recommendations made by professional organizations such as the Recording Industry Association of America or the Electronic Freedom Foundation and then survey students, school administrators, and recording artists for their opinions. Finally, you'd have to consider the best way to convey your information: a detailed report both in print and online might be an impressive strategy.

Questions of consequence often lead to papers or projects that are exploratory. Such work asks people to consider alternatives to existing situations along with offering a particular solution. If your research leads you to recommend strongly a specific course of action, then you might write a formal proposal.

In thinking through the consequences of a proposal, remember that it's important to analyze public or professional attitudes toward your subject. You'll often need to explain what's wrong with current thinking on a subject before you can persuade readers to consider new proposals. And of course you'll have to defend your own proposal thoroughly—its consequences, its feasibility, its advantages.

S U M M A R Y

Questions of Consequence

You are addressing a question of consequence when you study a problem (local or national) to determine why current solutions aren't working and to suggest alternatives. First, you will have to establish the facts of the present situation and examine different perspectives on the problem. Then you'll offer a solution of your own, backed by information on its costs, feasibility, and likelihood of acceptance.

Projects based on questions of consequence . . .

- Present solutions to problems.
- Offer alternatives to the status quo.
- Consider the advantages of change.
- Consider the consequences of change.
- Consider the costs of change.

Selecting a rhetorical purpose for your project allows you to make important decisions about how to proceed as you do your research and prepare to present your information. The goals you decide on, as we have shown here, will

WWW
3.2

determine the sorts of questions you ask, what you look for, what counts as useful information, and how you might present your results to an audience. Decisions about purpose may also have a direct impact on your research topic; you will probably need to consider narrowing or focusing it to fit the purpose you have chosen. Chapter 4 will help you consider ways to fine-tune your focus.

WWW Web Sites Worth Knowing

3.3

- *Silva Rhetoricae: The Forest of Rhetoric*, http://humanities.byu.edu/rhetoric
- Writing Center at Colorado State University's Guide to Writing Processes: "Purpose," http://writing.colostate.edu/references/processes/purpose
- "Writing with a Sense of Purpose," http://webster.commnet.edu/grammar/composition/purpose.htm

MANAGING YOUR PROJECT

1. Identify two general subjects that might be appropriate topics for a research paper, and explore each one using the five approaches described in this chapter. You'll likely find that some perspectives work better for your subject than others.

2. List the most interesting questions or perspectives your topic generates (see Exercise 1). Then look for connections between the questions to see whether different questions might be pursued in the same paper.

3. When you have connected your potential topic to a specific purpose, locate an example of research that resembles the project you have in mind. If you decide to create a factual Web site, look for a Web site that presents documentary evidence. If you expect to prepare a proposal document, look for a proposal argument. When you locate an appealing model, note its features and decide which ones you might emulate and which ones may not fit your project.

CHAPTER 4

Planning Your Research Strategy

Early in the movie *The Matrix*, Neo (played by Keanu Reeves) experiences a shocking moment of discovery. Rising from the fluid-filled pod in which he has lived, unknowingly, his whole life, he looks out over a huge vista of billions upon billions of similar pods, each holding another person just like him. The sight is staggering, an overwhelming vision of just how expansive the Matrix has become.

Sometimes, after choosing a general topic or subject for a research paper, writers begin to feel much the same way as Neo. There are so many possibilities, so many directions to go, it can seem overwhelming. The only way to take control of your project, to manage the possibilities, is to limit the scope and establish a clear, well-defined focus. Some writers narrow and focus their topics by posing a *research question* or *query* for which they do not yet have a satisfactory answer.

Research question
Why is criminal violence increasing among juveniles at a time when the overall crime rate is decreasing?

Other writers prefer to guide even their early research by constructing a *hypothesis*, a statement that makes a *claim* that will be tested in the project.

Hypothesis
Despite a drop in the overall crime rate, violence among juveniles is increasing because of the pernicious influence of rap music.

As a general rule, a research question might be better when you want to consider a variety of explanations to an interesting or puzzling phenomenon. A hypothesis might be more useful if you have a pretty clear understanding (or a strong opinion) about your subject and you want to focus on proving or disproving it. Until the evidence comes in, you should strive to be open-minded and always ready to revise your claim. However, your question or hypothesis

4.1

will be important if your instructor asks you to prepare a proposal or prospectus as part of your research plan (see Section 4g). How you frame your research subject—as an open-ended query or a narrowly focused claim—will also guide the decisions you make about what sources to consult and what kinds of evidence to gather.

4a Pose questions

To gain more perspective on a topic, learn what the issues are. In your reading or field research, be curious about the following matters:

- The focal points of chapter titles and section headings
- The names of important people or experts
- The names of events or institutions related to the subject
- Issues or questions that come up repeatedly
- Issues about which there is controversy

Consider, too, what the implications of an issue might be. Ask questions and write down your observations. Above all, while reading and discussing your topic, be curious and adventurous in the questions you pose as you consider a subject.

TOPIC: MARINE PARKS

Does the confinement of whales and dolphins at marine parks constitute cruelty to animals?

Do marine mammals live longer in the wild than in protected environments? If so, why?

Who profits from keeping marine mammals in captivity—scientists or businesspeople?

TOPIC: DOWNLOADING MP3S

Do all music companies object to MP3 file sharing, or just some of them? Why?

What copyright protection schemes can companies use to safeguard their recordings? What technologies are required to make them work?

Are legal threats against individual downloaders an effective way to stop music piracy? How do we know?

You can turn some questions into tentative hypotheses by making them claims.

Selectively prosecuting individual downloaders of illegal MP3 music files is not an effective means of protecting copyrighted audio material.

But you couldn't turn some other questions into hypotheses without gathering additional information. (For example, you might not know for sure whether marine mammals in the wild live longer than those in captivity.)

In most cases, narrowing subjects early in the writing process can make subsequent searches of print and electronic resources more efficient. If you've narrowed a subject too much, you'll know it soon enough.

4b Focus your topic choice carefully

When you think about the research question or claim you want to address in your project, consider the *level of generality* at which you will be expected to write.

> CLAIM
> Cars are better than trucks.

> CLAIM
> The Mercedes S500 is superior to the Lexus LS430.

The second of these two claims is clearly more specific than the first. Because the first claim is made at a more general level, the comparisons you make in supporting it will likely be more general too (gas mileage, size, comfort, price). Because the second claim is more specific, the comparisons you offer can be more specific as well (relative size of the wheel base, ergonomic design, airbag deployment, emission controls).

Topics that are either too general or too specific can both lead to research problems down the road. When your topic is too general, you may have a hard time distinguishing between relevant and irrelevant information. When it's too specific, you may not find much information published about it. Ideally, you should aim for a topic general enough to provide lots of information but narrow enough that you can sift through the information easily and determine what's important.

If you are working on a class project, read the assignment sheet carefully. Sometimes there are clues or even suggested topics that will indicate the level of generality that the instructor will accept. If you are uncertain about your topic choice, you can always run it by your instructor for advice and suggestions.

4c Identify the information your project requires

As we demonstrated in Chapter 3, different projects serve different purposes and require different kinds of research. Your research techniques and sources will often depend on whether your preliminary question or hypothesis involves a question of fact, of definition, of value, of cause, or of consequence.

Questions or claims of fact have as their primary goal the demonstration of what is true, with "true" being defined as something that can be proved or disproved by clear, unambiguous evidence and data. The information you discover, as long as it comes from reputable, reliable sources (see Chapter 10), will probably be sufficient to establish your position as either true or false.

EXAMPLES OF FACT-BASED QUERIES AND CLAIMS

QUERY

How do children raised in day-care environments compare emotionally and intellectually with children raised at home by parents?

RESEARCH STRATEGY

Look at published studies comparing children from each environment and then write about the most striking results.

CLAIM

Violence among teenagers is higher now than in any decade in modern American history.

RESEARCH STRATEGY

Search for crime statistics that made comparisons—decade by decade—of young people aged 13 to 19 and then determine whether or not there has been an increase.

Questions or claims of definition, on the other hand, try to clarify an ambiguous term or concept. Our world is filled with abstract ideas—freedom, justice, obscenity, good manners, discrimination—which many people understand or define quite differently. Even relatively concrete concepts such as bilingual education and affirmative action can be subject to disagreements about how they should be defined. As you research and write about a definition-based project, you will be trying to help readers understand a concept more fully.

EXAMPLES OF DEFINITION-BASED QUERIES AND CLAIMS

QUERY

How do copyright laws define "fair use," and how do courts apply it?

RESEARCH STRATEGY

Locate court documents that define fair use in different cases. Perhaps you could contact a local courthouse and ask for assistance in finding this information.

CLAIM

Solitary confinement in prisons constitutes a form of cruel and unusual punishment forbidden by the Constitution. (What is "cruel and unusual punishment"?)

RESEARCH STRATEGY

Explore what authoritative sources have had to say about the subject. Court documents, legal records, and editorials in magazines and newspapers should provide rich resources for discussions of "cruel and unusual punishment" and the experience of solitary confinement.

A query or claim about value makes a judgment about something on the basis of reasonable criteria. We make judgments every day—I like that teacher; I want to buy the Sony receiver, not the Aiwa; the Beatles were much better musicians than Elvis—and we always have reasons for making those judgments, reasons that are based on personal criteria, or standards, for evaluation. Sometimes you make your standards explicit when you talk about them, and sometimes you don't. In an evaluative project your goal is to spell out your criteria, justify them, and show how the focus of your project measures up.

EXAMPLES OF VALUE-BASED QUERIES AND CLAIMS

QUERY

Is the quality of American filmmaking in decline?

RESEARCH STRATEGY

You'll have to make sure the criteria you choose are ones that your readers will value as well. Some people might consider screenwriting or cinematography or special effects the most important element; other people might talk about production values, merchandising, or box-office revenues.

CLAIM

Diomedes, not Achilles, is the real hero of *The Iliad*.

RESEARCH STRATEGY

A project attempting to justify this claim will need to define what a hero is—how a hero acts, how a hero differs from a "brave warrior," what features distinguish a hero from other people. To substantiate this claim, you could read what scholars have to say about heroes and heroism in literature and research the criteria that others have used to describe heroes.

A query or claim about cause, as you learned in Chapter 3, explores cause-and-effect relationships that are linked in time. We want to know *why* something happened in the past, and we want to be able to predict what *will* happen in the future if we follow a particular course of action. For this reason, projects that focus on cause will often begin either with an effect (something of special interest in the present) and consider what causes brought it about or with a cause (again, something of special interest in the present) and speculate what its eventual effects might be.

EXAMPLES OF QUERIES AND CLAIMS BASED ON CAUSE

QUERY

Why is the quality of American filmmaking in decline?

RESEARCH STRATEGY

Research the claims or reasons that have been advanced by film scholars or industry professionals to explain the decline (assuming, of course, that such a "decline" exists). Investigate the history of a single studio or significant event such as the proliferation of VCRs or DVDs that could have had a significant impact on the movie industry.

CLAIM

Enforcing new EPA pollution standards will endanger the economy of regions that rely on mining.

RESEARCH STRATEGY

This claim predicts what *will* happen as a result of strictly enforced pollution standards. You can use evidence from the past to make predictions about the future. Perhaps there are towns that have been seriously affected by existing standards; their history would make your argument about future effects all the more powerful. Web sites maintained by the mining industry and the EPA could provide useful information about predicted effects as well.

A query or claim about consequence is also forward-looking in that it argues in favor of (or against) a course of action. To some extent, projects based on this type of research question or hypothesis will incorporate elements of cause and effect. If you want to argue why we should do something in a certain way, you need to argue that the outcomes or effects will be beneficial. But the purpose of a proposal or consequence-based project goes one step further: it doesn't just predict what the effects will be—it demands that we pursue them.

EXAMPLES OF CONSEQUENCE-BASED QUERIES AND CLAIMS

QUERY

What can be done to improve math education in American secondary schools?

RESEARCH STRATEGY

Consider a variety of alternatives and gauge which among them are best. Read math journals for possibilities, or survey teachers for their opinions about weaknesses in math education.
Professional Web sites by groups such as the National Council of Teachers of Mathematics, or even by universities that train future math teachers, might provide a wealth of material.

CLAIM

Science literacy in local high schools might be improved by creating adjunct teaching positions for practicing scientists.

RESEARCH STRATEGY

Conduct research into whether this approach has been tried and studied in the past and whether concrete benefits have been documented. Is there evidence to support the belief that enough "practicing scientists" would want to teach high school for the proposal to be a reasonable solution to the problem? If you can provide evidence like this and present it carefully, you will go a long way toward convincing your audience to support your recommendation.

FOCUS ON . . . **Ethics**

When you begin your research, you may have strong feelings about your subject and you may want to focus on a hypothesis right away. It's fine to do so, but be careful! One student recently set out to argue that downloading MP3s should be legal. However, after researching copyright laws, he realized that such downloading constituted theft of intellectual property. As a result, he changed his thesis to argue that music companies should consider offering free MP3 downloads as a way to increase sales of CDs.

You have an ethical responsibility to present evidence fairly, not to ignore or conceal information when it doesn't agree with what you want to believe, and to choose sources that do the same (see Chapter 9). More than a few students (and professionals) have discovered that the positions with which they began were contradicted by the scientific evidence and expert opinions they uncovered in their research. You may need to modify, refine, or completely change your hypothesis on the basis of what you learn as your project progresses.

4d Determine where to locate the information your project requires

Given the glut of information on every subject imaginable now available in books, articles, newspapers, and databases and on the Internet, you're likely to find something about your topic no matter which resource you turn to first or which rhetorical approach you decide to use. If you had all the time in the world to research your subject, one starting place would be as good as any other and it wouldn't matter where you began. Unfortunately, deadlines and due dates make it important that you be selective in doing your research and focus on resources that are likely to have the best and most pertinent information for your project's goals.

The chart on page 38 can help point you to the most profitable research sources, depending on the type of research question or hypothesis you form. This is not to say that other sources in the chart should be overlooked or ignored, just that you are likely to find more immediately useful information for your project in the sources identified here.

4e Review library catalogs, databases, and Web directories

Library catalogs, databases, and Web directories can be powerful tools for generating topic ideas because they break complex subjects into manageable parts. To find topic suggestions, learn to browse these resources strategically. For ex-

CHART

Useful Sources for Research Material

Research Source Materials	Fact	Definition	Value	Cause
Encyclopedias	✓	✓		
Dictionaries		✓		
Other reference works, almanacs	✓			
Books, both scholarly and popular	✓	✓	✓	✓
Journal articles and magazines	✓	✓	✓	✓
Popular and special-interest magazines			✓	✓
Newspapers and online news services	✓			
Newspaper editorials and columns			✓	✓
Book reviews, film reviews, product reviews				✓
Scientific experiments and observations				✓
Interviews with experts	✓		✓	
Fieldwork	✓			
Surveys of opinion		✓	✓	✓
Institutional and government Web sites	✓		✓	
Issue-oriented Web sites	✓	✓	✓	
Listservs and Usenet groups		✓	✓	
Individual Web sites, blogs			✓	

ample, under a very broad category such as "English literature" you may find library catalog divisions such as "postcolonial authors," "Oriental influences," and "Renaissance." Similarly, the *Yahoo!* Index for "Arts and Humanities" offers the subcategories "Countries and Cultures," "Electronic Literature," "History of Books and Printing," and "Storytelling." These subheads and those that follow may lead you to topics that pique your interest. (For more information on using the library catalog and online databases, see Sections 5b and 5e.)

4f Talk to other people

Let the questions and comments of colleagues guide you to key issues. You'll be surprised how often a classmate will raise an issue you hadn't considered. Other people may even be able to broaden your appreciation for a subject. For a research project about the long-term effects of childhood abuse, you could join a newsgroup or chat room discussion to find firsthand accounts of the experience. You should approach such accounts carefully and sensitively, using the information you find mainly to stimulate your own thinking. After all, people may not want their lives to become part of your research project. A conference with your teacher during the early stages of your project can also help ensure you're on the right track and provide the opportunity to get advice when you're unsure what to do next.

4g Prepare a research proposal or prospectus

For many research assignments you may be asked to prepare a research proposal or prospectus that outlines your topic, plans, and resources. By outlining your ideas early, you enable an instructor or supervisor to give you the advice or suggestions you need to keep a project on track.

We can't offer a single form to cover all types of projects you might explore. However, any prospectus will likely include many of the following elements:

- **Identification of topic or topic area.** If required, also provide a rationale for selecting this subject.

- **Statement of hypothesis or research question.** This will form the basis for the rest of the prospectus, particularly the kind of research you will do and the ultimate goal(s) of the project itself. If required, discuss the hypothesis in detail and establish its significance, relevance, or appropriateness.

- **Identification of background information or a review of literature.** For major projects, provide a full review of the professional work already done in your area of research.

- **Review of necessary sources and archival materials.** Identify the kinds of materials you expect to review for this project: books, articles, newspapers, recordings, videos, artwork, databases, Web sites, email lists, and so on. You might also be asked to identify where and how you expect to gain access to these materials.

- **Description of your research methodology.** Outline the procedures you will follow in your research and justify your choice of methodology. For many types of research, this section will be the most demanding part of the prospectus. For example, if you intend to do a survey, you need to explain how you will generate and test your survey questions, how you will tally and validate responses to them, and how you will select your respondents to assure a valid and adequate sample.

- **Assessment of resources and/or costs.** Identify any special equipment, library resources, and other materials you expect to need for the project. Outline any travel that the work may entail. Provide a detailed estimate of costs for equipment, salaries, and printing. In major research projects, the budget may be a separate part of the prospectus; for simpler projects, this step may not be necessary.

- **Schedule or timeline.** Estimate the stages of your project and provide firm dates for each item that must be submitted.

A prospectus builds the research query or hypothesis into a complete research plan. It incorporates nearly all parts of the research process you have completed up to this point: choosing a topic, reviewing resources, thinking about an audience, finding a focus, and managing your time. For example, see the sample proposal on pages 40–42 on the topic of MP3 downloading.

With a research query/hypothesis or prospectus in hand, you will be well prepared to leap into the most exciting and rewarding part of your project: doing the research itself. But be warned! Investigators are only as good as the tools they use and their skill in using them. You will have to learn about the full range of research tools available to you, and you must pick your tools well and wisely. In Part II of this book we will look at all the strategies, techniques, and options you have in your research toolbox.

Annotated Research Proposal

Nelson Murdock

English 1102

Dr. R. Richards

Prospectus for Research Project

1

Overview

For my research project, I plan to study the current policy of the

Recording Industry Association of America (RIAA), which is selectively

prosecuting individual downloaders as a way to stop the illegal sharing

of copyrighted MP3 music files. I believe that the current furor over

MP3 file sharing is misguided and that MP3 downloading benefits,

rather than harms, the music industry. The hardline stance currently

taken by music companies toward file sharing and copying is

unwarranted, and it will only cause more resentment about artificially

2   inflated CD prices and, perhaps, an eventual boycott of all CD albums.

The arguments made by record executives that MP3 downloading is

dramatically affecting CD sales are contradicted by scholars such as

Felix Oberholzer-Gee and Koleman Strumpf, who claim that "sharing

digital music files has no effect on CD sales" (Potier). In fact, they say,

"for the most popular albums . . . file sharing actually boosts sales"

3 (Potier). If this is truly the case, then the RIAA's aggressive response to MP3 file sharing may be called into question. Clearly, there are serious disagreements between the two sides of this controversy, and my goal in this project will be to investigate the facts used to support both sides and argue–if the evidence supports it–that the RIAA should actively pursue alternative approaches that will protect copyrights without

4 alienating consumers.

Research Plan

I intend to research a wide variety of resources for this project, beginning with books and articles that discuss the effects of MP3 file sharing. Two books I have found already seem especially helpful in addressing this issue: *How to Survive the Scams and Shams of the Music Business* (Moses Avalon, 2002) and *Digital Copyright: Protecting*

5 *Intellectual Property on the Internet* (Litman, 2000). I will also look into recent congressional testimony by the RIAA about the economic impact of MP3 downloading on the music business and will check professional and trade journals for musicians, such as *Spin Magazine, Billboard*, and *Digital Audio*, that would likely include articles expressing a musician's point of view.

There are several online sources I plan to research as well. The organization MP3 Is Not a Crime.org at http://www.mp3isnotacrime.org maintains an archive of articles and research that addresses the MP3 debate, and the Electronic Frontier Foundation keeps a list of many links to sites that deal with the issue of MP3 downloading at

6 http://www.eff.org/share. In addition, at least one Usenet newsgroup, alt.music.mp3, hosts occasional discussions of MP3 copyright issues and current events, and I will use this board to see what MP3 aficionados around the world have to say about the issue. If I find some of the comments on the chat board to be useful for my paper, I will make

7 sure to get the authors' permission before quoting them directly.

I believe that this approach will allow me to see both what industry professionals are saying about MP3 downloading as a national issue and what consumers are saying about it as an issue that affects their

8   personal interests and their pocketbooks. I anticipate no special difficulties in being able to conduct this research, as the materials are either available in the library or easily accessible online.

Project Timeline

I anticipate that the preliminary research and note taking for my project will take two weeks to complete and that I will have my annotated bibliography done by November 2. The first draft of the project will be finished by class time on the due date, November 16, when I will share it with class members for their review and comments. I would like to schedule a conference with you by November 21 to discuss my project's progress and set an agenda for my work on the next draft. I plan to have the second draft finished by December 1 and will make an appointment in the Writing Center to go over the paper once more. The final draft will

9   be turned in on the due date, December 7.

Works Cited

Potier, Beth. "File Sharing May Boost CD Sales." *Harvard University Gazette*. 15 April 2004. 20 Aug. 2004 <http://www.news.harvard. edu/gazette/2004/04.15/09-filesharing.html>.

Annotations

1. This prospectus begins with an overview that incorporates several of the elements detailed in the earlier list: the statement of the topic and hypothesis and a brief description of the positions held by opposing sides in the controversy.
2. The writer clearly states the position that he intends to defend in his research project.
3. The writer points out two opposing points of views on this issue, and he also identifies some of the sources he's consulted in his preliminary research.
4. The writer reaffirms his goal for the paper and indicates a willingness to modify his hypothesis if the evidence proves him wrong.
5. The writer mentions specific book and journal titles he intends to review, including those that will give him a variety of perspectives on the issue.

6. The type of Web site and the nature of the information that can be found there are included.

7. The writer shows an awareness of the ethical issues involved in quoting people on an open forum like a chat board.

8. This paragraph justifies the scope of the research plan and its likelihood of success.

9. All deadlines and due dates are specified, including those set by the author himself.

WWW Web Sites Worth Knowing

- Online Newspapers, http://www.onlinenewspapers.com

- Cornell Institute for Social and Economic Research, Links to Public Opinion Surveys, http://www.ciser.cornell.edu/info/polls.shtml

- University of Pittsburgh, "Selected Proposal Writing Websites," http://www.pitt.edu/~offres/proposal/propwriting/websites.html

- Brigham Young University, Preparing a Prospectus for a Project, http://www.byu.edu/ipt/program/ms_prospectus_guide.html

WWW

4.3

MANAGING YOUR PROJECT

1. Put your preliminary topic in the form of a research question. This is the question that your paper might answer or that guides a brochure or Web site you are designing. ("Is it likely that explorers will find water under the surface of Mars?" "What volunteer opportunities do students have for improving literacy in our community?")

2. Put your preliminary topic in the form of a hypothesis. This is the statement that your paper may support or that provides a rationale for your brochure, Web site, or other project. ("Explorers are likely to find water under the surface of Mars." "The community provides many opportunities for students to volunteer for literacy projects.")

3. Draft a proposal for your project. Include a clear statement of your research question or hypothesis, a description of why this is an interesting and/or critical area to study, and your plan for finding resources. Share this proposal with your classmates and the instructor—in class, during office hours, or by email—and get feedback to use as you continue your research.

II

GATHERING IDEAS AND INFORMATION

DON'T MISS . . .

- **The library tour in Section 5a.** Explore your library and learn how to use its diverse collections and facilities.

- **The strategies for advanced keyword searching in Chapter 6.** Learn how to focus your Web searches with a few simple techniques and commands. Get useful results quickly, without having to wade through thousands of useless "hits."

- **The guidelines for conducting surveys in Section 7b.** Useful survey information depends upon questions that are bias-free.

- **The annotated bibliography on page 93.** Brief summaries of your resources' main points are an excellent way to keep track of critical information.

EVERYDAY RESEARCH

ANNE NATHAN, Broadway actress and singer
Currently starring in the musical *Chicago*

Anne Nathan has come a long way since her debut on the stage at age four. She is an actress and singer by trade and is presently a member of the Broadway company of *Chicago,* where she plays the role of Matron "Mama" Morton.

"I majored in musical theater, with a minor in directing," says Anne. "The training I received in college was rather helpful in teaching me how to take a script and make sense of it: how to read it, research it, and honestly play the scene. I think that it's important to be well-read and informed as an actor. I find that the more informed you are about the play and the characters, the easier it is to do the work."

Anne has portrayed several historical figures in her almost twenty years as an actress: "Recently, I was in the Broadway production of Stephen Sondheim and John Weidman's *Assassins,* where I played the role of Emma Goldman, a 1920s anarchist who was linked to the attempted assassination of President William McKinley. It was rather daunting at first because this was a woman whom people knew and had a certain expectation of. Because she is a historical character, there was a ton of information for me to research. I read her autobiography; I went online and found a wonderful Web site, *The Emma Goldman Papers,* which was filled with photos, documents, speeches, and even a brief interview with her. I also was able to find a film about her life, 'The Anarchist Guest'."

CHAPTER 5

Using Library Resources

Tennis legend Arthur Ashe once said, "I spent many, many hours in public and school libraries. Libraries became courts of last resort, as it were. The current definitive answer to almost any question can be found within the four walls of most libraries." Ashe's observation may be especially relevant to you and your project at this point, because once you have a research question or hypothesis, your next goal will be to prepare a *working bibliography*—that is, a preliminary list of materials relevant to your topic—and libraries are a great place to begin. (See Chapter 8 for more on preparing a working bibliography.) The type of information you will need depends on your audience, purpose, and topic. A paper on MP3 file sharing for an academic audience, for instance, might require you to scour scholarly journals in the fields of communications and copyright law.

Obviously, you don't want to rely on luck to support serious research in a library. Although it might be possible to go to your university library and browse the shelves until you find sources useful to a research project, the books you find would likely represent only a small portion of the information available in the library, and many of those books would be out of date. You need to work systematically with bibliographies, indexes, library catalogs, and librarians to find the information you need. Systematic research is even more important today when you have to deal with an explosion of electronic sources, many of which were not designed with researchers and scholars in mind. The very strength of the World Wide Web—its robust connection of millions of computers, files, and databases—is also its weakness: it presents a jumble of information, leaving users to screen nuggets of gold from mountains of slag. So it's essential that your searches be efficient.

In this chapter we explain the basic tools and resources you will use when sorting through information. You want to learn how to find relevant and reliable sources that fulfill the requirements of your specific situation as quickly and efficiently as possible—without sacrificing thoroughness.

5a Learn about your library

A first priority for any college student is to become familiar with the arrangement of campus libraries and research facilities. Most university libraries offer tours or workshops to help you learn how to use their resources. Many libraries even offer these services online. Don't be intimidated. Take a tour of the buildings and take advantage of all available help.

5b Use library catalogs efficiently

Library catalogs can usually be searched by author, by title, by subject, by Library of Congress classification (see Section 5g), and by keywords. If you know the title or author of a work, a catalog can tell you whether the library owns the item and, if so, where to locate it in the stacks. A subject search will help you locate sources in which a given topic is the main focus; a keyword search can help you locate sources in which your topic is mentioned, even though it may not be the focus of the piece. Thus a keyword search provides a potentially richer range of source material. Keyword searches can be very powerful; to learn how to use them effectively, see Chapter 6. When the catalog is electronic (as most now are), you can also determine immediately whether a document is checked out, lost, or otherwise unavailable, thereby saving you much time.

Figure 5.1 shows the search menu screen for the online library catalog at the University of Texas at Austin at **http://dpweb1.dp.utexas.edu/lib/utnetcat/keyword.html.** Notice that the screen supports a variety of keyword combinations and permits a user to specify the location, format, and language of the research material.

Thanks to the Internet, you can also search the catalogs of other libraries. This capability can be especially useful if your library is small or your topic unusual. For a list of online library catalogs, examine LIBCAT at **http://www.metronet.lib.mn.us/lc/lc1.cfm.** You may be able to borrow the items your library doesn't own through the Interlibrary Loan (ILL) program; find out if your library participates and how to request items.

Online library catalogs will usually give a short entry first—typically, the author or editor, title, publishing information, date, and call number—with an option to select a fuller listing. The fuller listing will describe additional features of the book—whether the book is illustrated and whether it has an index or a bibliography, for example. Be sure to follow up any new subject headings provided: they can be keywords for additional searches. Additional subject headings in online catalogs may also link to more sources of information that you might not have found with your original keyword search, such as the subject link "Intellectual Property—United States" shown in Figure 5.2. The book also includes a bibliography that can point you to further sources. The screen tells you the location of the book, the call number, and whether or not it is checked out.

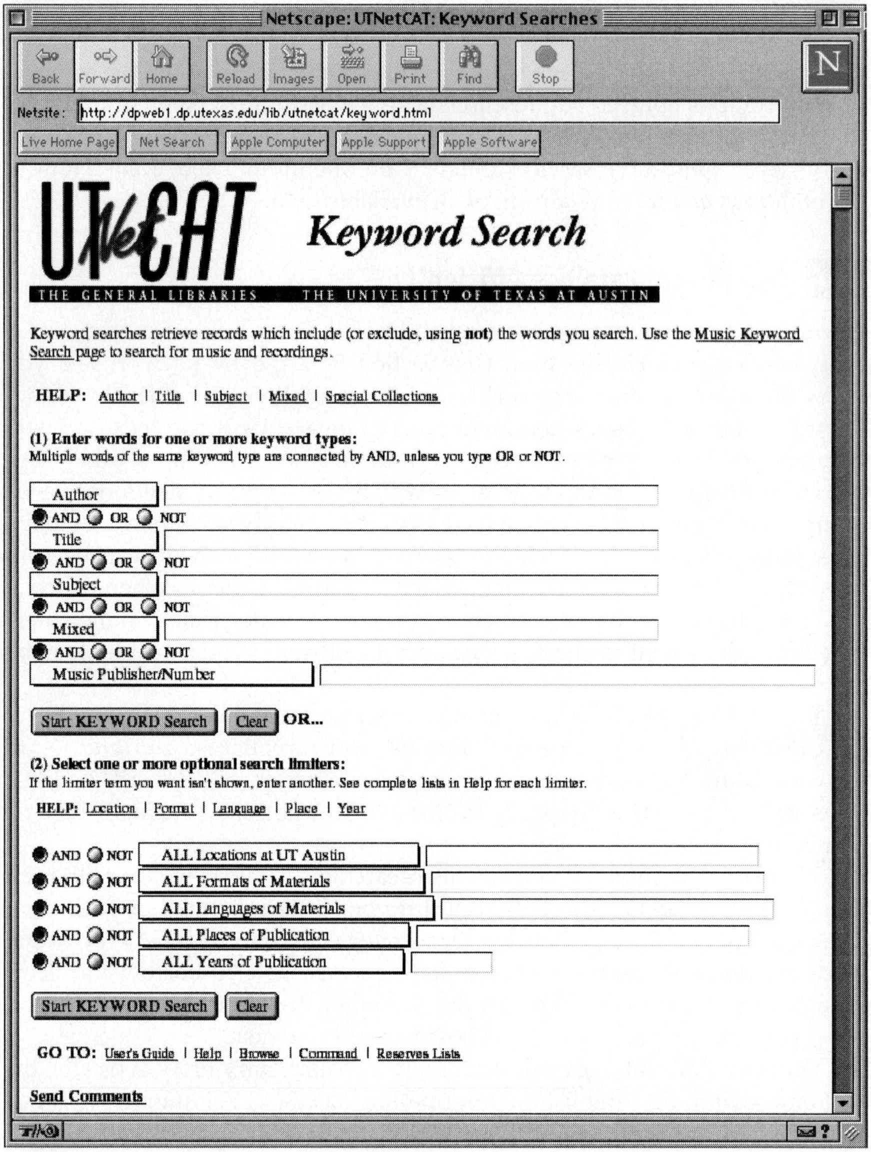

FIGURE 5.1 Search menu screen for an online library catalog.

5c Locate the reference room

Most libraries have a special section or room that houses reference materials, including dictionaries, encyclopedias, indexes, bibliographies, and many other types of sources. Usually these materials cannot be checked out. You will want to learn what materials are available to you here and how to access

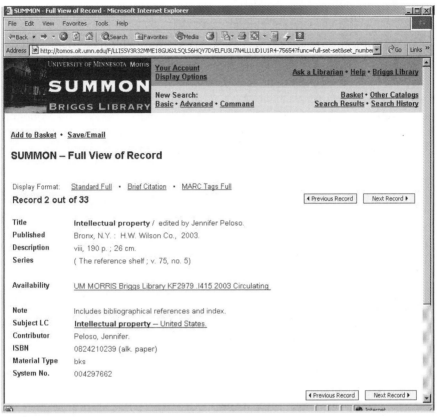

FIGURE 5.2 Sample online library catalog.

them. Reference librarians are there to help you; don't hesitate to ask. You may need to sign up for time on computer terminals to search online or CD-ROM resources; find out your library's policy.

5d Locate suitable bibliographies

Bibliographies are lists of books, articles, and other documentary materials that deal with particular subject areas. You can save considerable time if you can locate an existing bibliography—preferably an annotated one—on your subject, rather than attempting to search through all the literature on your own.

There are four major types of bibliographies. Depending on your topic, you may need to consult one or more of the following:

- *Complete bibliographies* attempt to list all the major works in a given field or subject.
- *Selective bibliographies* usually list the best-known or most respected books in a subject area.

5.1

- *Annotated bibliographies* briefly describe the works they list and may evaluate them.

- *Annual bibliographies* catalog the works produced within a field or discipline in a given year.

To determine whether a bibliography has been compiled on your subject, check your library's reference room or catalog. If you can't find a bibliography on your precise subject area, you may have to use one of the general bibliographies available for almost every field. Your instructor or a reference librarian should be able to suggest an appropriate bibliography or a computerized index for your subject area. A brief list of specialized bibliographies in selected disciplines is provided in Checklist 5.1.

Although printed bibliographies are quickly losing ground to electronic indexes and databases, they are still available on many subjects. In addition, the bibliographies you'll find at the back of scholarly books, articles, and dissertations may prove invaluable. They represent a selective look at a field and are usually compiled by an expert, not by a search engine. Pay special atten-

---

CHECKLIST 5.1

Bibliographies of Selected Disciplines

Doing a project on . . . ?	Check this bibliography . . .
American history	○ *Bibliographies in American History*
Anthropology	○ *Anthropological Bibliographies: A Selected Guide*
Art	○ *Guide to the Literature of Art History*
Astronomy	○ *A Guide to the Literature of Astronomy; Astronomy and Astrophysics: A Bibliographic Guide*
Classics	○ *Greek and Roman Authors: A Checklist of Criticism*
Communications	○ *Communication: A Guide to Information Sources*
Engineering	○ *Science and Engineering Literature*
Literature	○ *MLA International Bibliography*
Mathematics	○ *Using the Mathematical Literature*
Music	○ *Music Reference and Research Materials*
Philosophy	○ *A Bibliography of Philosophical Bibliographies*
Physics	○ *Use of Physics Literature*
Psychology	○ *Harvard List of Books in Psychology*
Social work	○ *Social Work Education: A Bibliography*

tion to works that are cited repeatedly; they may be important references that you should not overlook

5e Locate suitable periodical databases or indexes

Library catalogs list the titles of journals and periodicals that are included in the library collection and tell which issues your library owns and where they are located (see Figure 5.3), but in order to search for specific articles in these journals and periodicals, you will need to use an index.

Databases may be organized by subject (you can use these to look up a particular subject to find resources about it located in a variety of periodical publications). Many subject databases cover a wide range of topics. Bibliographic databases, on the other hand, may present comprehensive bibliographical information within a specific subject area. Nowadays, researchers also have access to a variety of full-text databases, that is, searchable databases that contain the entire article online rather than merely providing the bibliographic information to locate the article in print.

Indexes generally offer the tables of content for specific periodical publications, allowing you to search through years of a journal's issues to locate specific articles. In the past, all periodical indexes were printed works, and you may still need to rely on those volumes to find older sources. For more current materials, however, you'll likely use electronic indexes. Many indexes

GALILEO
An Initiative of the University System of Georgia

GEORGIA'S VIRTUAL LIBRARY

Home | About GALILEO | Policies | Contact Us | Help
Kids | Database List | Georgia Southern Zach S. Henderson Library | Ask-a-Librarian

Title:	College English.
Publisher:	[Urbana, Ill.] National Council of Teachers of English, 1930-
Description:	v. ill. 25 cm. Monthly (Sept.-Apr.) v. 1- Oct. 1939-
Subject(s):	English philology--Periodicals. English philology--Study and teaching--Periodicals. English language--Periodicals.
Continues:	English journal College edition
Linked Resource:	Click Linked Resource below for online access.
Location:	Periodicals (First Floor)
Call Number:	PER PE1 .E521
Number of Items:	14
Status:	Not Charged
Notes:	Recent issues shelved alphabetically by title in Current Periodicals. For pre-1971 holdings, ask at Circulation / Reserve Desk.
Recent Issues:	v. 66, no. 6 (2004 July) v. 66, no. 5 (2004 May) v. 66, no. 4 (2004 Mar.) v. 66, no. 3 (2004 Jan.) v. 66, no. 2 (2003 Nov.) v. 66, no. 1 (2003 Sept.)
Volumes Owned:	v. 1- 1939-

FIGURE 5.3 The library catalog shows which issues of a journal your library owns.

provide abstracts (short summaries) of the pieces in addition to bibliographic facts—who published an article, as well as where and when it was published. Some electronic indexes even furnish the full texts of news stories, magazine articles, literary works, and historical documents that you can print out or download to your computer (depending on copyright rules).

Ordinarily you can access indexes in your library's reference room, through the library catalog, or from your library's Web site, and a few indexes are available on the World Wide Web for free. Electronic indexes usually support title, author, and keyword searches (see Chapter 6), and they may permit searching by other "fields"—that is, the categories by which data are entered. For example, a database may be searchable not only by author and title but also by publisher, place of publication, subject heading, government document number, and so on.

You may want to begin periodical searches with general and multidisciplinary indexes such as the following:

Academic Search Premier. Abstracts and indexing for over 3,800 scholarly journals and general magazines.

ArticleFirst. Bibliographic citations for articles in journals of science, technology, medicine, social science, business, the humanities, and popular culture.

EBSCOhost (electronic). A collection of online databases in business, education, the sciences, and more.

Ingenta. Citations for over 26,000 multidisciplinary journals.

JSTOR. Full-text, full-image collection of core journals in the humanities, sciences, and social sciences.

LexisNexis Academic. Indexes for approximately 5,000 publications, mostly full text, including newspapers, legal news, general-interest magazines, medical journals, company financial information, wire service reports, government publications, and more.

Periodical Abstracts. Multidisciplinary index of over 1,600 publications in the humanities, social sciences, and general sciences, including scholarly journals, popular magazines, and business publications.

Readers' Guide to Periodical Literature (print). Index to popular magazines and periodicals.

All major academic fields have specialized indexes for their periodical literature, most of them now computerized. Because new indexes may be added to a library's collection at any time, check with your reference librarian about the best sources for a given subject and how to access them. Checklist 5.2 gives just a sampling of the many specialized indexes to specific academic areas that may be available.

Learning to use these powerful research tools is essential. Figure 5.4 shows some of the results of a simple keyword search in the *Academic Search Premier* online database. The list provides important information about each

CHECKLIST 5.2

Specialized Academic Indexes and Databases

Doing a project on . . . ?	Check this index . . .
Anthropology	○ *Anthropological Literature*
Architecture	○ *Avery Index*
Art	○ *Art Abstracts*
Biography	○ *Biography Index*
Biology	○ *Biological and Agricultural Abstracts; BIOSIS Previews*
Business	○ *Business Periodicals Index; ABI/Inform*
Chemistry	○ *CAS*
Computer science	○ *Computer Literature Index*
Current affairs	○ *LexisNexis*
Economics	○ *PAIS (Public Affairs Information Service); EconLit*
Education	○ *Education Index; ERIC (Educational Resources Information Center)*
Engineering	○ *INSPEC*
Film	○ *Film Index International; Art Index*
History	○ *Historical Abstracts; America: History and Life*
Humanities	○ *Francis; Humanities Abstracts; Humanities Index*
Law	○ *LegalTrac*
Literature	○ *Essay and General Literature Index; MLA Bibliography; Contemporary Authors*
Mathematics	○ *MathSciNet*
Medicine	○ *MEDLINE*
Music	○ *Music Index; RILM Abstracts of Music*
Philosophy	○ *Philosopher's Index*
Physics	○ *INSPEC*
Psychology	○ *Psychological Abstracts; PsycLit; PsycINFO*
Public affairs	○ *PAIS*
Religion	○ *ATLA Religion Database*
Science	○ *General Science Index; General Science Abstracts*
Social sciences	○ *Social Science and Humanities Index; Social Sciences Index; Social Sciences Abstracts*
Technology	○ *Applied Science and Technology Abstracts*
Women	○ *Contemporary Women's Issues*

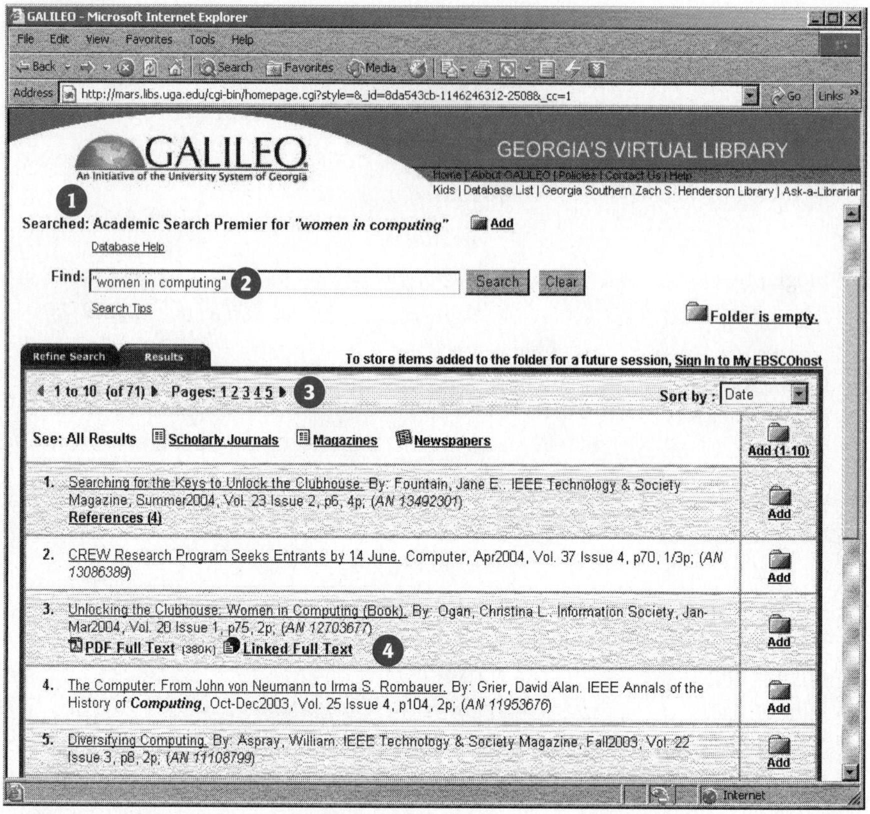

FIGURE 5.4 Results of a keyword search using the *Academic Search Premier* online database.

Annotations to Figure 5.4

1. *Academic Search Premier* database accessed through GALILEO library index
2. Search term is in quotation marks to indicate whole phrase.
3. Don't forget to look at more than one page of results.
4. Some articles are available in full-text and/or PDF format.

entry, including the title, the name of the author, and the year of publication. The title can give you some idea of whether the content of an article will be useful before you look for it. Similarly, if you want only more recent information, the dates of publication will help you eliminate sources.

Some databases, such as *ERIC*, may provide abstracts of articles along with full bibliographic records for each entry (see Figure 5.5). The screen may also enable you to access other information, such as a listing of libraries that own a particular source, options for obtaining the source via fax or email, or links to view the document in full-text or full-image (including pictures) versions.

When searching by keyword, see whether a list of subject headings is available. To save time, match your search terms to those on the list before you

Title:	How Forcefully Should Universities Enforce Copyright Law on Audio Files?
Author(s):	McCollum, Kelly ①
Source:	Chronicle of Higher Education v46 n13 pA59-A60 Nov 19 1999
Publication Year:	1999
ISSN:	00095982
Descriptors:	*Audiotape Recordings; *Compliance (Legal); *Copyrights; *Music; *Privacy; Access to Information; Administrative Policy; College Students; Computer Mediated Communication; Ethics; Higher Education; Information Technology; School Policy; Technological Advancement ②
Identifiers:	*Recording Industry; Carnegie Mellon University PA
③ Abstract:	The Recording Industry Association of America is aggressively pursuing copyright violations on campuses concerning *MP3* music recordings being exchanged on computer networks. Carnegie Mellon University (Pennsylvania), to avoid litigation, has been searching public folders of students' computers to find illegally copied *MP3*s. Controversy over privacy has ensued.(MSE)
Language:	English
Clearinghouse:	Higher Education (HE540175)
Publication Type:	Journal Article (080) Reports - Descriptive (141)
Journal Code:	CIJMAY2000
Entry Month:	200005
ERIC Number:	EJ595369
Persistent link to this record:	http://search.epnet.com/direct.asp?an=EJ595369&db=eric
Database:	ERIC

FIGURE 5.5 Sample abstract of an article from a database.

Annotations to Figure 5.5

1. Find other articles by this same author by clicking here.
2. Descriptors can be used as new search terms or subject areas.
3. An abstract can help you decide quickly whether an article will be relevant to your project.

begin. If your search doesn't return the number of items you had hoped for, or if you need to ensure that your search has been thorough, try your search again using synonyms of your initial keyword(s). (For more on keyword searching, see Chapter 6.)

You may be able to search electronic databases from home or from terminals in open-use computer labs as well as in the library; other databases may be available only on certain library terminals or on CD-ROM. Some electronic indexes and databases may require that you enter your library or student ID number for access. Check with your reference librarian for details.

5f Consult biographical resources

Often in preparing a research project you'll need information about famous people, living and dead. Good places to start are the *Biography Index: A Cumulative Index to Biographic Material in Books and Magazines; Bio-Base; LexisNexis; Current Biography;* and *The McGraw-Hill Encyclopedia of World Biography.*

FOCUS ON . . . **Electronic Databases**

Students often begin—and end—their search of the library with the library's catalog. They then turn to the Web to locate online articles and Web sites. While the books listed in the library catalog and the articles published on the Web may be valuable sources, you will be missing a tremendously valuable resource if you don't take advantage of the powerful electronic databases available to you, many of which offer a wealth of full-text scholarly articles, newspaper and magazine articles, government documents, and more. When the subject you are researching is something as current as MP3 file sharing, databases can be especially valuable as they often index the most up-to-date sources. These electronic databases are perhaps the single greatest boon to researchers in our time, making searches of these sources, which once could have taken years, available in only seconds.

Various *Who's Who* volumes cover living British, American, and world notables, including African Americans and women. Deceased figures may appear in *Who Was Who*. Probably the two most famous dictionaries of biography are the *Dictionary of National Biography* (British) and the *Dictionary of American Biography*.

On the World Wide Web you might check out the database maintained by the A&E program *Biography* at http://www.biography.com. For the wisdom of famous people, see the Web version of the 1910 edition of *Bartlett's Familiar Quotations* at http://www.bartleby.com/100 or, for more recent remarks, *The Quotation Page* at http://www.quotationspage.com. To search for private individuals, you can use features such as *Yahoo!*'s "People Search" on the Web; it provides addresses and phone numbers with almost frightening ease. And for information about writers and authors, consult the Internet Public Library's "Literary Criticism" page at http://www.ipl.org/div/litcrit, where you can find links to sites that provide bibliographies, abstracts, and even full-text biographies of famous authors.

Examples of the specialized biographical resources available to you are included in Checklist 5.3. Check with your instructor or reference librarian for additional resources.

5g Consult guides to reference works

The reference room in most libraries is filled with helpful materials. How do you know what the best books are for your needs? Ask a reference librarian whether guides to the literature for your topic are available, or check the reference section using the call number that you used to locate circulating books. Most libraries arrange books according to the Library of Congress Classifica-

CHECKLIST 5.3

Specialized Biographical Resources

Your subject is in . . . ?	Check this source . . .
Art	○ *Index to Artistic Biography*
Education	○ *Biographical Dictionary of American Educators*
Music	○ *The New Grove Dictionary of Music and Musicians*
Politics	○ *Politics in America; Almanac of American Politics*
Psychology	○ *Biographical Dictionary of Psychology*
Religion	○ *Dictionary of American Religious Biography*
Science	○ *Dictionary of Scientific Biography*

Your subject is . . . ?	Check this source . . .
African	○ *Dictionary of African Biography*
African American	○ *Dictionary of American Negro Biography*
Asian	○ *Encyclopedia of Asian History*
Australian	○ *Australian Dictionary of Biography*
Canadian	○ *Dictionary of Canadian Biography*
Female	○ *Index to Women; Notable American Women*
Mexican American	○ *Mexican American Biographies; Chicano Scholars and Writers: A Bibliographic Directory*

tion System (see below). Reference books are usually shelved in a noncirculating section or room but are usually arranged following the same classification system.

Library of Congress Classification System

A	General Works	N	Fine Arts
B	Philosophy, Psychology, Religion	P	Language and Literature
		Q	Mathematics, Science
C–F	History	R	Medicine
G	Geography, Anthropology	S	Agriculture
H	Social Sciences, Business	T	Technology, Engineering
J	Political Science	U	Military Science
K	U.S. Law	V	Naval Science
L	Education	Z	Bibliography, Library Science
M	Music		

Also useful in some situations are printed or electronic indexes that list all books currently published, their publishers, and their prices. Updated frequently, such indexes include *Books in Print* (print or electronic) and *Paperbound Books in Print*. Dictionaries, encyclopedias, atlases, and other reference works can also be good starting points for many research projects. Of course, you should not rely on dictionaries and encyclopedias alone for your research, but you should not ignore them either.

The following chart lists popular online reference works that will help you locate suitable information for your project.

CHART

Online Reference Works

American School Directory	http://www.asd.com
Bartlett's Familiar Quotations	http://www.bartleby.com/100
CIA World Fact Book	http://www.odci.gov/cia/publications/factbook/index.html
Electronic Statistics Textbook	http://www.statsoft.com/textbook/stathome.html
Encyclopaedia Britannica Online	http://www.eb.com
Merriam-Webster's Dictionary	http://www.m-w.com/dictionary
Occupational Outlook Handbook	http://www.bls.gov/oco
Perry Castaneda Map Collection	http://www.lib.utexas.edu/maps/index.html
U.S. Census Bureau American Fact Finder	http://factfinder.census.gov/servlet/BasicFactsServlet
U.S. Code	http://uscode.house.gov/usc.htm

WWW

5.3

5h Locate statistics

Statistics on every imaginable topic are available in library reference rooms and online. Be sure to find up-to-date and reliable figures, however. Consult resources such as *The New York Times on the Web* "CyberTimes Navigator" at **http://www.nytimes.com/library/tech/reference/cynavi.html** or the General Reference Collection of *The Internet Public Library* at **http://www.ipl.org/div/subject/browse/ref00.00.00**. Even *The Old Farmer's Almanac* is on the Web at **http://www.almanac.com**. Commercial online services such as *America Online* and *Prodigy* may offer access to additional reference sources. Other electronic sources may be available on CD-ROM, online through your library's home page or university network, or for free on the World Wide Web. For statistical

CHECKLIST 5.4

Resources for Statistical Information	
To find ...	**Check this source ...**
General statistics	*World Almanac; Current Index to Statistics* (electronic; check with your library for access)
Statistics about the United States	*Historical Statistics of the United States; Statistical Abstract of the United States* (online at http://www.census.gov/prod/www/statistical-abstract-us.html); *Stat USA* (electronic; check with your library for access); *GPO Access* (online at http://www.gpoaccess.gov/index.html)
World information	*The Statesman's Yearbook; National Intelligence Factbook; UN Demographic Yearbook; UNESCO Statistical Yearbook*
Business facts	*Handbook of Basic Economic Statistics; Survey of Current Business; Dow Jones–Irwin Business Almanac*
Public opinion polls	*Gallup Poll*
Census data	*Population Index* (electronic; check with your library for access)

information on specific topics, try the resources named in Checklist 5.4 or ask your reference librarian for additional sources.

5i Check news sources

Sometimes you'll need information from newspapers, particularly when your subject is current and your aim argumentative or persuasive. For information before about 1995, you'll have to rely on printed papers or microfilm copies since electronic newspapers and news services are a more recent phenomenon. When you know the date of an event, you can usually locate the information you want, or you can use a periodical index or search newspaper indexes to locate information. Only a few printed papers such as *The New York Times* and the *Wall Street Journal* are fully indexed. *The New York Times Index* provides chronological summaries of articles on a given subject.

Another useful reference tool for more recent events is *NewsBank,* an index available since 1982 in electronic format. It covers more than 400 newspapers from across the country, keyed to a microfiche collection. *Facts on File* summarizes national and international news weekly. For background information on major problems and controversies, check *CQ Researcher;* to report on what editors are thinking, examine *Editorials on File,* a sampling of world and national opinion.

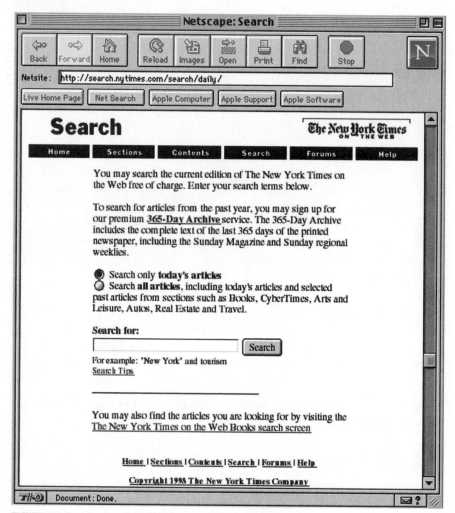

FIGURE 5.6 Search screen from *The New York Times on the Web.*

For very current events, you can search hundreds of newspapers and news services online. See, for example, the search page for *The New York Times on the Web* shown in Figure 5.6. A directory such as *Yahoo!* at http:// dir.yahoo. com/news_and_media/newspapers can point you to hundreds more online newspapers of every sort. Be careful, however; not all news sources are unbiased or even credible. (For more on evaluating sources, see Chapter 10.) Many schools also offer a Web version of *LexisNexis* that you may find helpful, especially with topics currently in the news. The following chart lists some online news resources worth consulting.

CHART

Online News Sources

CNN Interactive	http://www.cnn.com
C-SPAN Online	http://www.c-span.org
London Times	http://www.timesonline.co.uk
MSNBC	http://www.msnbc.com/news
National Public Radio	http://www.npr.org
The New York Times	http://www.nytimes.com
Reuters	http://www.reuters.com
USA Today News	http://www.usatoday.com
Wall Street Journal	http://www.wsj.com
Washington Times	http://www.washtimes.com

WWW

5.4

5j Check special collections

In addition to circulating materials and reference collections, your library may offer access to rare books, original manuscripts, special exhibits, or interesting artifacts. For example, the Zach S. Henderson Library at Georgia Southern University has on exhibit such items as a 1940 campaign banner for Franklin Delano Roosevelt's bid for reelection as president, an original fifteenth-century manuscript of a Dutch prayer book, and a handwritten slave deed dated February 17, 1845. These holdings are usually kept in a special room or area where they can be protected. Some items may be subject to copyright or other access restrictions, but most items in special collections are available for you to review. Your library catalog may allow you to search for items in special collections, or the library may index these items in a special catalog. Check with your reference librarian for information. Be sure to note any rules for using materials housed in special collections (such as limitations on photocopying) and be prepared to abide by them.

5k Consult government documents

Nowadays you can find many government documents online through the Web site for the Government Printing Office at http://www.gpoaccess.gov or on the World Wide Web sites for various government agencies. Many libraries are designated as official depositories for government documents, including documents or publications not available online. Your library may also house public records and official documents for local, state, or regional governments. Check with your reference librarian for more information.

51 Check book and film reviews

WWW

5.5

To locate reviews of books, see *Book Review Digest* (since 1905), *Book Review Index* (since 1965), and *Current Book Review Citations* (since 1976). *Book Review Digest* does not list as many reviews as the other two collections, but it summarizes those it does include—a useful feature. Many electronic periodical indexes also catalog book reviews, including *Academic Periodical Index* (since 1988) and *Readers' Guide to Periodical Literature* (since 1983). You can also find numerous book reviews online. Try searching with the *Yahoo!* directory at **http://dir.yahoo.com/Arts/Humanities/Literature/Reviews** or try searching for online book reviews on bookseller sites such as *Amazon.com.*

For film reviews and criticism, see the printed volumes *Film Review Index* (since 1986) or *Film Criticism: An Index to Critics' Anthologies* (since 1975) as well as the electronic *Film Index International*, or find reviews online at **http://dir.yahoo.com/Entertainment/Movies_and_Film/Reviews.**

Finding information is a time-consuming and sometimes frustrating process. However, with a little practice you can soon learn to locate the information you need more effectively. In Chapter 6 you will learn some techniques to make your electronic searches more efficient—whether you're searching the library catalog, a CD-ROM or an online database, or the World Wide Web.

WWW Web Sites Worth Knowing

WWW

5.6

- *iTools*, **http://iTools.com**

- *The Library of Congress*, **http://www.loc.gov**

- *Yale University Library*, "Research Guides by Subject," **http://www.library.yale.edu/guides**

- *Search Engine Watch*, "Web Searching Tips," **http://www.searchenginewatch.com/facts/index.php**

- "Internet Country Codes," **http://www.concentric.net/~Noshadow/countrycodes**

MANAGING YOUR PROJECT

1. Explore your subject in your library's catalog. Begin by looking specifically for books on your subject. If you're having trouble locating books using a simple keyword or subject search, try some of the tips in Chapter 6.

2. Locate a bibliography particularly suited to your subject. The more specific the bibliography, the better. But don't ignore the general bibliographies available in many fields.

3. Explore your topic on the Web using a search engine such as *Google*. But first come up with keywords that will help to both identify and narrow your subject. (For help, see Chapter 6.)

Locating Online Resources

"Shut down all garbage mashers on the detention level!" Luke screamed into the comlink. "Do you copy?" In an instant, R2D2 set to work and scanned the Death Star's online computer network, locating the master controls in a matter of moments. Sending a quick electronic command, the little droid stopped the deadly machinery, saving not only Luke's life but the lives of all his friends as well. Lives were saved, the Death Star was destroyed, and the Empire was eventually overthrown, all because R2D2 knew how to conduct an efficient online search.

Well, that might be overstating the case a bit, but it's not an overstatement to say that these days, print materials make up only one part of the research resources available to students and scholars. Online resources—digital databases, listservs, and the World Wide Web, for example—are now some of the most important tools that researchers can use to explore and learn about their topics.

Understand, however, that the Web has not been systematically designed to support research, so you cannot apply library research techniques or assume that what you find there is always reliable. You must approach the Web with caution and evaluate the information you find critically. (See Chapter 10 for further advice about evaluating sources.)

Because the resources of the World Wide Web are so vast, you'll appreciate the need for search engines and directories—tools that help you cull wanted information from the billions of Web pages now online.

6a Find the most useful search engines

The key to a successful search is to use a combination of "big" search engines and smaller specialized engines to look for information (see Section 6f). Among the biggest and most popular search engines and directories are *Yahoo!* at http://www.yahoo.com, *Google* at http://www.google.com, *AltaVista* at http://www.altavista.com, and *HotBot* at http://www.hotbot.com. More specialized search engines can be located at the *Big Search Engine Index* http://www.search-engine-index.co.uk, which currently indexes 910 search engines available on the Web. A few search portals, often called metasearch engines, such as *Dogpile* at http://www.dogpile.com, will run your searches through many search engines simultaneously.

6.1

6b Understand how a simple keyword search works

When you use the "find" feature of a word processor, you are performing a simple keyword search. Increase the power of this technique and apply it to much larger databases and you have a search engine, an instrument that can seek not only the word(s) you specify but related terms and phrases as well. When you visit a search engine's home page, you will be invited to enter one or more "keywords" or phrases into a text box. The search engine will then look for these keywords in the Web pages it has indexed and will return a list of all those that match. (Be sure to type keywords carefully. A misspelled search term can prevent you from finding available information.) A librarian or instructor may be helpful in guiding you to appropriate keywords for your searches, or you can use research tools creatively to find powerful keywords. For example, library catalogs usually offer cross listings for subjects—that is, other terms under which your subject is entered (see Chapter 5). If your project on Civil War ironclad ships leads you to search with the term "Monitor" (the name of a famous Union ship), a particular catalog entry might include cross listings such as "Civil War"; "Merrimac"; "U.S. Navy, history"; and "Ericsson, John." You could then probe the catalog using each of these terms.

Think about it like a detective following a trail of clues—each location you visit will contain new terms, new connections, and potential new directions for your investigation. For example, if you need to know why some organizations object to MP3 downloading, you could begin with the general keywords "MP3" and "downloading." But you'd be swamped by the number of responses, and you might never find the particular information you need. Here is where a little preliminary reading might pay off (see Section 2c). If you learn that one of the organizations leading the fight against MP3 file sharing is the Recording Industry Association of America, you could try searching with that term or, even better, its familiar acronym: RIAA. Once you locate the RIAA's official site on the Web, you could search it for "MP3" to find the information you were seeking (see Figure 6.1).

The keywords you choose—whether names, places, titles, concepts, or people—will shape your search. A comparatively small database, such as an online library catalog, may ask you to indicate whether a word you are searching for is a title (t), an author (a), a subject (s), or some other type of term the system recognizes. Imagine that you are preparing to write a report on *Master and Commander* by Patrick O'Brian, a novel that takes place in the time of the Napoleonic wars. Searching a library catalog for the title of the book (*Master*

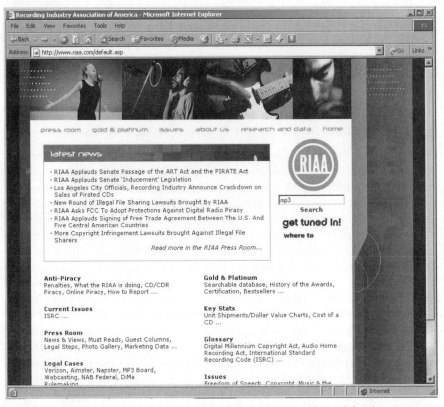

FIGURE 6.1 Home page for Recording Industry Association of America with search function.

and Commander), the name of its author (Patrick O'Brian), or a narrow subject keyword (Napoleonic wars) will often produce manageable numbers of items to examine.

t (title)	*Master and Commander*	8 items
a (author)	Patrick O'Brian	26 items
s (subject)	Napoleonic wars	25 items

However, a simple search of the same items on the World Wide Web, a huge database, might overwhelm you. Consider, for example, these results returned by three popular Web search engines.

	Google	AltaVista	HotBot
Master and Commander	2,390,000 items	806,812 items	798,875 items
Patrick O'Brian	230,000 items	36,115 items	36,438 items
Napoleonic wars	178,000 items	64,704 items	63,579 items

Similarly, typing even a narrowed subject listing into an online library catalog may provide too many items for you to read and research.

Naval history   1,800 items

In these situations you need more sophisticated search techniques. One such technique is called Boolean searching.

6c Refine your search with Boolean operators

There are more than four billion Web pages on the Internet, and chances are a great many of them will contain at least one of the words you're looking for. When *AltaVista* is told to search for the words *Master and Commander*, for example, it looks for every single Web page in its database that contains the words *master* and *commander* (it ignores the lowercase "and" altogether). The result? Thousands of links to pages or articles that will be of no use to you whatsoever.

One way to increase your chances of success in the search process is to use Boolean operators. When you do a Boolean search, you are actually doing two or more searches simultaneously and studying the point where those searches overlap. Most search engines in online catalogs, databases, and Web browsers allow some form of Boolean searching.

You control a Boolean search through a set of specific terms or symbols. For example, by linking keywords with the term AND, you can search for more than one term at a time, identifying only those items in which the separate terms intersect. One way to initiate a Boolean search is to insert AND (in capital letters) between terms you wish to search.

Patrick AND O'Brian

miniature AND schnauzer AND training

Washington AND Jefferson AND Constitution

Another way to search is to select an appropriate command from the search engine, such as *Google*'s "Exact Phrase" option, or try enclosing the phrase in quotation marks (see Section 6e). Asking the engine to search for a specific sequence of words usually reduces the information glut, but sometimes not enough to make the results manageable.

Master and Commander	from 2,390,000 to 861,000 items
Patrick O'Brian	from 230,000 to 129,000 items
Napoleonic wars	from 178,000 to 145,000 items

You can further refine a Boolean search by increasing the number of search terms—the more specific the better. Consider what happens when you add "Great Britain" to our earlier online library catalog search for "naval history."

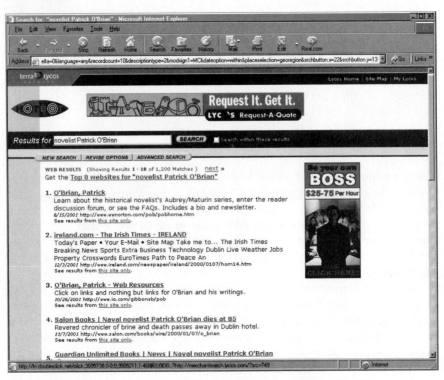

FIGURE 6.2 Search results for "novelist Patrick O'Brian" using the *HotBot* search engine.

> Great Britain naval history   from 1,800 to 450 items

Or look at what happens when we specify O'Brian's profession, using *HotBot*'s "All the Words" filter on the Web (see Figure 6.2).

> novelist Patrick O'Brian   1,200 items

At this point the logic of the *HotBot* search engine is trying to figure out which of the more than 1,200 items might be most helpful to us. As it turns out, the resulting search still produces little useful material, but that's not unusual in Web searches. You have to keep plugging away.

6d   Truncate terms to extend your search

Computers can search only for the exact string of letters you type in. They cannot always recognize different forms of a word. A search for the keywords "Napoleonic wars" would miss any articles or Web pages that contain variations of these words, such as "Napoleon" or "war." Truncating (literally, shortening) your terms allows you to search for words with a common root. For example, the word *vote* has the variants *votes, voting, voter,* and *voters.* List these words in a column and draw a line down the column following the last letter that is the same in all the words.

vot|e

vot|es

vot|ing

vot|er

vot|ers

The root common to all of the forms of the word is *vot*. Replacing the omitted (or variable) letters with an asterisk, the truncated term you would use in your search becomes *vot**.

Most databases use an asterisk (*) to indicate truncation, although some use other characters, such as a question mark (?) or an exclamation point (!). Be sure to read the instructions for the search engine or database you are using.

Of course, you need to consider carefully the effect of truncation on your search. Truncation can be quite effective in helping you to narrow your search; it can also help broaden your search when specific forms of a word are returning too few hits. But use the technique with caution; searching for *"vot*"* will help broaden your search for forms of the word *vote*, but it may also return irrelevant hits for words such as *votive* and the French *votre*. To eliminate these terms, use Boolean operators such as NOT (e.g., vot* NOT votive) and select English-only if your database allows you to limit your search.

6e Refine your search with exact phrases

To narrow a search even more, you can look for a specific and distinctive phrase either by placing it between quotation marks or selecting the "exact phrase" option on a search screen. Type "novels of Patrick O'Brian" into the search engine *AltaVista*, and it hunts its vast database for only those sites where that phrase occurs in its entirety (see Figure 6.3). The narrowing is dramatic.

WWW

6.4

  novels of Patrick O'Brian 287 items

These items include a Patrick O'Brian Web page, a newsletter, and, best of all, a list of other O'Brian links that leads to a newsletter index and a mailing list for online conversation about O'Brian's maritime novels.

You can use exact phrase searches creatively in many ways. When you can't recall who is responsible for a particular expression or quotation—for example, "defining deviancy down"—you can make it the subject of an exact phrase search. Using the *Yahoo!* search directory, you'll quickly find the expression attributed to Senator Daniel Patrick Moynihan, in the very first item located by a search of that directory.

CHART

Commonly Used Boolean Commands

OR Using OR between keywords directs the search engine to find examples of either keyword, widening your search by allowing you to locate all documents that cover related concepts.

> dog OR puppy
> Congress OR Senate

NOT Using NOT between terms permits you to specify sites with one term but not another, useful when you want to exclude certain meanings irrelevant to your search.

> Indians NOT Cleveland
> apple NOT computer

Some search engines use + and – signs for AND and NOT functions.

> +wetlands +definition
> +Nixon –Watergate –China

(Note that there is a space before each sign but not after it.)

( ) Putting items in parentheses allows for additional fine tuning of a search. As in mathematical equations, parentheses group terms together.

> Senator AND (Gramm OR Hutchison)
> church NOT (Mormon OR Catholic)
> pickup NOT (Ford OR Dodge)

" " Use " " (quotation marks) to search for exact phrases.

> "the quality of mercy is not strained"
> "The Sound of Music"

You can also combine exact word searches with various Boolean commands to find precisely what you need when you can identify appropriate keywords. For example, to find Web pages about the movie *The Ten Commandments* that specifically mention either Charlton Heston or Yul Brynner, your Boolean search would look like this:

"Ten Commandments" AND ("Charlton Heston" OR "Yul Brynner")

Or, to search for information on pickup trucks not manufactured by Ford or Dodge, try.

"pickup truck" NOT (Ford OR Dodge)

Some databases allow you to refine searches further by language or by publication type. The potential of such searches is limited only by your imagination and the speed of your modem or online connection.

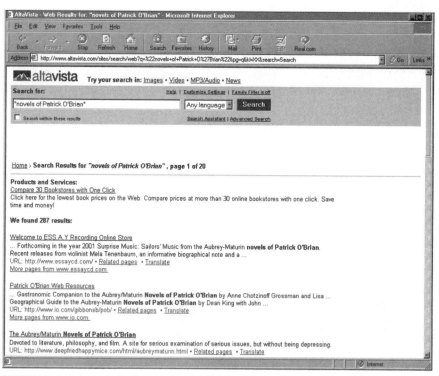

FIGURE 6.3 Search results for "novels of Patrick O'Brian" using the *AltaVista* search engine.

As with mathematical equations, there is a distinct order of operations in Boolean searching: Boolean operations are evaluated from left to right, with operations in parentheses evaluated first. Make sure you read the directions for the particular software or search engine you are using, and experiment with it until you feel confident.

6f   Use more than one search engine or database

No two search engines are alike—they perform their functions in different ways using different sets of criteria for finding and listing. Some engines are very selective about the pages they index and search; others are almost completely nonselective, including virtually every Web page they can find on the Internet. As a researcher, then, you need to take advantage of the strengths and weaknesses of several search engines to get the best and most useful results.

6.5

A good way to illustrate this is to take a close look at two of the more popular search engines on the Web, *AltaVista* and *Google*.

AltaVista, the first searchable full-text index of the Web (created in 1995), employs a Web "spider" or crawler to seek out and index new pages. Although this may give you the power to access nearly everything published on the Web about your topic, the sheer scope of "everything" means you have to focus your searches very carefully with Boolean operators. Here are the results of searches on *AltaVista* on the topic "MP3 downloading" before and after using Boolean terms.

MP3 downloading	822,544 items
"MP3 downloading"	8,151 items
"MP3 downloading" AND copyright	5,683 items
"MP3 downloading" AND copyright AND legislation	139 items

Though the prospect of wading through more than a hundred results may seem daunting, you will often find that the first few pages of results will provide the most useful resources. In this case, the first ten results in the last search include links to a *West Virginia Journal of Law and Technology* article by David Cheval on the case against Napster (a once popular resource for file sharing) as well as a paper by Paul Veravanich at the UCLA Online Institute for Cyberspace Law and Policy on the history of MP3 downloading and copyright issues.

Like *AltaVista*, *Google* automatically seeks out Web pages with a crawler (called *Googlebot*) and is one of the most widely used search engines on the Internet. As of June 26, 2004, it indexed 4,285,199,774 Web pages, a number that is estimated to be growing by 7 million pages every day. What makes *Google* distinctive is that it uses a sophisticated ranking system to list the pages most likely to be useful first. You should note that even though *Google* accepts the Boolean operators AND and OR in keyword searches, it doesn't accept NOT. Putting a minus sign (−) immediately before a search term performs the same function, however.

Here are the results of a *Google* search using Boolean operators (see Figure 6.4).

"MP3 downloading"	46,700 items
"MP3 downloading" AND copyright	7,660 items
"MP3 downloading" AND copyright AND legislation	91 items

The results for the last search on *Google*, somewhat smaller than the same search on *AltaVista*, include the Cheval and Veravanich articles, but they also list a number of significant articles that are either not mentioned or not easily found on *AltaVista*. Without conducting this second search, you might miss those articles.

For those who prefer a somewhat different approach to Web searching, *Google* offers a smaller directory of Web pages at **http://directory.google.com**, submitted by Web site owners and reviewed for content, that can be browsed independently. Current news articles about MP3 downloading, for example, can be found by looking under the category Computers>Multimedia>Music and Audio>Audio Formats>MP3>News and Media.

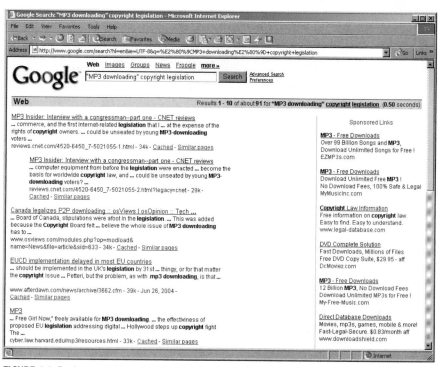

FIGURE 6.4 Boolean search results using the *Google* search engine.

If you're having trouble focusing your search and finding what you need, click on the "Help," "Advanced Search," or "Search Assistant" buttons available on most sites. They will guide you through the search process and give you extremely valuable tips on how to use the engine effectively.

You can also refine your online search by choosing search engines carefully. Instead of more general search engines, you can choose those that index academic sites.

6g Evaluate your electronic search

Don't be satisfied with your initial searches, even when they supply ample information. Another combination of keywords or a different search path might provide still better material.

6.6

Each time you search and get an unexpected response, ask yourself why. Ideas may be hidden under synonyms of the word you searched. When the first try doesn't work, look for clues in the results you receive (or don't receive). Check spellings and try synonyms. Use different combinations of Boolean operators. Don't give up.

CHART

Selected Internet Search Engines

About.com	http://home.about.com/index.htm
AltaVista	http://www.altavista.com
AOL Anywhere	http://search.aol.com
AskJeeves	http://www.ask.com
Excite	http://www.excite.com
Google	http://www.google.com
HotBot	http://www.hotbot.com
LookSmart	http://search.looksmart.com
Lycos	http://www.lycos.com
WebCrawler	http://webcrawler.com
Yahoo!	http://www.yahoo.com

6h Keep a record of your search

Whether you are conducting research on the Web, using an online information service or database, or searching an online library catalog, probably the most important research strategy of all is to keep track of your work. In addition to keeping a record of potential sources, you will want to remember the search terms you have used and keep a record of the indexes, databases, or catalogs you have searched. This way, you will be able to locate information again if necessary later in the research process by using the same search strings, and you can save yourself time by ensuring that you do not duplicate effort.

Compile an annotated bibliography—that is, a listing of all the potential sources you found, along with a brief summary or description of each one. (See the sample annotated bibliography on page 93.) This can be valuable if your project later develops in ways you had not anticipated.

You can also use the "Bookmarks" or "Favorites" feature in your Web browser or a separate computer file to keep track of Web sites and sources you have located, or you can keep photocopies and printouts in a folder. (See Chapter 8 for useful information and helpful tips on keeping track of and organizing your work.)

6i Join in electronic conversations

Search engines are not the only resources available to you for online research or feedback about your project. Usenet newsgroups, listserv discussion groups, MOOs, and other electronic forums can provide useful advice and in-

CHART

Academic Directories and Search Engines Online

Argus Clearinghouse	http://www.clearinghouse.net
Books on the Internet	http://www.lib.utexas.edu/ books/etext.html
eserver.org	http://eserver.org
Infomine	http://infomine.ucr.edu
InfoSurf	http://www.library.ucsb.edu/subj/ subject.html
Internet Public Library	http://www.ipl.org
Librarian's Index to the Internet	http://lii.org
Library of Congress Research Centers	http://www.loc.gov/rr/ research-centers.html
The Universal Library	http://www.ul.cs.cmu.edu/html
Voice of the Shuttle	http://vos.ucsb.edu

WWW

6.8

sights into the most current work. Many online course packages such as *WebCT* and *Blackboard* offer discussion boards or chat rooms, and many online chat rooms such as *Yahoo! Chat*, or online service providers such as *America Online*, offer real-time chats with public figures, including authors, actors, and musicians.

Usenet groups, listservs, and similar tools can furnish you with interactive and up-to-the-second information on a topic from many points of view. They offer you the chance to question people who are doing the research or living the experiences you are writing about. But you must be careful when you take factual information from these environments: make it a habit to confirm any statistic, fact, or claim with information from a second and different type of authority—a book, an article, a reference work, or another credible source.

Some Web search engines now cover Usenet groups so that you can find and even join online conversations on your topic when such a discussion group exists (try searching *Google Groups* at **http://groups.google.com**).

Usenet groups and other electronic conversations can help you place your own work within an existing community of thought. But keep the bigger picture in mind too; rely on traditional resources—journals, books, encyclopedias—to keep the full subject in perspective and to balance individual and idiosyncratic points of view you may find online.

The following summary describes major characteristics of and uses for listservs and Usenet newsgroups and offers tips for searching these resources for information.

SUMMARY

Listservs and Usenet Newsgroups

A **listserv** is a type of mail program that maintains lists of subscribers interested in discussing a specific topic. Users must subscribe in order to read or post messages.

Major characteristics: Subscribers may be experts working in fields related to the list topic or simply interested participants. Some lists may be moderated. Old messages may sometimes be archived.

Use for: Listening in on the practitioners' conversations, discovering opinions, noting solutions to common problems, and learning about other available print or online resources.

Searching: When you subscribe, check the welcome message for instructions for searching the archives and for rules governing participation.

A **Usenet group** works like a listserv except that you need not subscribe to the list either to read its messages or to participate in the discussion.

Major characteristics: Thousands of groups on nearly every conceivable topic. There is wide variation in the expertise of contributors. Anyone may read or post messages.

Use for: Conversations about popular topics and about little known, obscure subjects. Almost every political group, social interest, religion, activity, hobby, and fantasy has a Usenet group.

Searching: Check the welcome messages and frequently asked questions (FAQ) file for information on how to search. Some lists have archives of older discussions.

6j Write or email professional organizations

Almost every subject, cause, concept, and idea is represented by a professional organization, society, bureau, office, or lobby. It makes good sense to write or email an appropriate organization for information on your topic; ask for pamphlets, leaflets, and reports. Many organizations offer detailed information on their Web sites as well. For mailing addresses of organizations, consult *The Encyclopedia of Associations,* published by Gale Research, or use a search engine to find Web sites.

FOCUS ON . . . **Listserv Etiquette**

Most listservs welcome new members, but before subscribing to a list, check out its frequently asked questions (FAQ) posting if there is one—or "lurk" for awhile, reading the messages and getting a sense of the conversation. Although some groups may discourage students or researchers from asking questions, many listserv members are happy to share information with students whose questions show thought, knowledge, and advance preparation. Make sure that you acquire permission from the author(s) to use any information you obtain through listserv or Usenet discussions.

The following guidelines—called "netiquette," or Internet etiquette— help make electronic discussions courteous and productive:

- Keep postings relevant to the topic of the list; for most lists, keep postings as brief as possible.
- Avoid using all-capital letters, usually considered the electronic equivalent of shouting.
- Do not send advertisements, chain letters, or personal messages to the entire list.
- When replying to previous messages, quote only those portions of the message to which you are referring.
- Avoid flaming (posting messages that attack other members of the list or their beliefs and ideas). Keep discussions and arguments on topic and courteous.
- Avoid "me too" messages. Do not reply to the list simply to express agreement; your posting should have something to contribute to the conversation.

Remember that the U.S. government publishes huge amounts of information on just about every subject of public interest. Check the *U.S. Government Periodicals Index* or the *Monthly Catalog of U.S. Government Publications* for listings. Or use a Web site such as *Fedworld Information Network* at http:// www.fedworld.gov to look for the material you need.

Not all of your research will or should rely solely on print materials or online resources. Some projects will require that you conduct your own experiments or field research. Chapter 7 provides important information about conducting interviews, administering surveys and questionnaires, and using careful observation as additional sources of support for your project.

WWW Web Sites Worth Knowing

6.9

- *AltaVista* "Advanced Web Search Help Page,"
  http://www.altavista.com/help/search/help_adv
- Purdue's OWL, "Searching the World Wide Web,"
  http://owl.english.purdue.edu/handouts/research/r_websearch2.html
- Boolean Logic and Boolean Operators, http://www.josts.net/tec3012/5a5.htm
- *Search Engine Watch*, "Web Searching Tips,"
  http://searchenginewatch.com/facts/index.php
- Search Engine Showdown: The Users' Guide to Web Searching,
  http://notess.com/search/

MANAGING YOUR PROJECT

1. Explore your subject in the library catalog. Check for other subject listings under which your topic may be cataloged, and ask the reference librarian for useful search terms. Use these new terms as keywords for additional searches.

2. Consider various combinations of keywords that might help you narrow your search, or vary the forms of words by which you are searching.

   alcohol → alcoholism → alcoholic OR alcoh*
   "House of Representatives" → "U.S. House" → Congress

3. Explore your subject with at least two Web search engines or directories. Keep track of the tools you use and the search terms you try.

4. Begin to assemble your preliminary bibliography. Create note cards for sources you consider valuable, or print out or download useful material. Keep track of all bibliographical data, including the dates you accessed electronic items.

5. Create a special "Bookmarks" or "Favorites" file for pages and sites from the Web you expect to visit again.

7

Conducting Field Research

What is research but a blind date with knowledge?
—William Henry

Although much college research occurs in the library or online, some projects may lead you to seek information through your own interviews, surveys, and close observation. This *fieldwork* is common in disciplines such as psychology, anthropology, and education; if you are pursuing a degree in these areas, you'll learn formal techniques for field research. But informal fieldwork can be useful in other, less rigid research situations provided that you describe your procedures accurately and qualify your conclusions properly.

Why do fieldwork at all? For one thing, fieldwork (sometimes referred to as *primary research*) gives you an opportunity to collect and interpret data yourself, without having to rely on someone else's interpretations and conclusions. It is also possible that some questions in your research project can't be answered any other way. If you wanted to include information about the effects MP3 downloading has had on local retailers, for example, it is unlikely you would find much relevant information on the Web or in the library. Your best bet would be to pay a visit to nearby music stores and interview the owners about the effect on their business. Not only will that give you insights about MP3 downloading you probably couldn't find anywhere else, but current, poignant observations from local retailers might be very persuasive to an audience of residents in the same community.

Of course, you must be careful about trying to generalize from such small samples; reviewing published reports of research (secondary research) can aid you in both planning and interpreting your results.

The sort(s) of fieldwork that will work best for you will depend on your project, your research question and/or hypothesis, and the time and resources you have available. Field research requires careful planning and perseverance to be successful, and the process of gathering and interpreting data can be complex and time consuming. Budget your time wisely as you think about the kind of fieldwork that will contribute the most to your project's rhetorical goals. In this chapter we'll look only briefly at basic information for conducting interviews, using surveys and questionnaires, and making observations.

7a Conduct interviews

Sometimes people are the best sources of information. When you can discuss your subject with an expert, you'll add credibility, authenticity, and immediacy to a research report. If possible, you will want to meet in person to conduct your interview. However, you may need to interview people by telephone or by mail, and of course it is possible to consult with knowledgeable people via email, newsgroups, or listservs (see Section 6i). Although online chats tend to be less formal than face-to-face conversations, your queries will still require appropriate preparation and courtesy. For a directory of experts willing to consult via email, browse the "Ask an Expert" links at *CIESE* at **http://k12science.ati.stevens-tech.edu/askanexpert.html**.

FOCUS ON . . . **Ethics in Field Research**

In his well-known book *How to Lie with Statistics*, Darrell Huff shows how survey results can be skewed by deceptive or careless wording in questions. As an investigator, your role should be to gather information in honest and ethical ways. That means asking questions fairly and interpreting the responses without prejudice.

You are also obligated to present your results fully and without an intent to deceive your readers. If you discover, for example, that a majority of the people you survey disagree with your position on MP3 downloading, you must report the results regardless. If you obscure relevant information or falsify your results, you violate the whole purpose of doing research.

You also have an obligation to your research subjects. You must present their opinions and statements fairly and accurately, protect them from repercussions by protecting personal information, assure anonymity (when appropriate), and obtain their informed consent to participate in your research project. You may also need parental consent if your subjects are under eighteen. Most colleges and universities have an institutional review board (IRB) that you may need to check with before conducting research that involves human subjects; ask your instructor to see if that is the case at your school.

Conducting a formal interview is not the same thing as chatting with a friend over the phone. You're there with a specific purpose, and you're often talking with someone you've never met before. You should make every effort to conduct the interview as professionally as possible. Checklist 7.1 will assist you in achieving that goal.

7b Conduct surveys

Research projects that focus on your local community may require surveys of public opinion and attitudes not available from other sources. So you may have to supply the information yourself by creating questionnaires and conducting studies. Yet polling is demanding, and even creating a useful questionnaire requires ingenuity; you'll have to work hard to produce research results that readers will respect.

To begin with, you should have a clear idea about the information you are seeking. In other words, you distribute questionnaires as a way of answering research questions you have already formulated.

Asking the right question isn't easy, whether you are gathering factual information or sampling public opinion. You don't want to skew the answers by posing vague, leading, or biased questions.

CHECKLIST 7.1

Conducting a One-on-One Interview

○ Write, telephone, or email your subject for an appointment, making clear why you want the interview.

○ Confirm your appointment the day before, and be on time.

○ Be prepared. Learn all you can about your subject's professional background, education, work history, and publications.

○ Dress appropriately; show that you take the interview seriously.

○ Have a list of questions and possible follow-ups ready. When appropriate, pose questions that require more than one-word answers.

○ Be alert and interested: make frequent eye contact.

○ Take careful notes, especially if you intend to quote your source.

○ Double-check direct quotations, and be sure your source is willing to be cited "on the record."

○ If you plan to tape or log an interview, get your subject's approval first.

○ Thank your subjects for their time.

○ Send a written thank-you note to everyone you interviewed, and offer to send them a copy of your completed project.

VAGUE	What do you think about MP3 downloading?
REVISED	Do you feel it's acceptable to share MP3 files of copyrighted music with others?
LEADING	Do you believe citizens should be able to protect their children by censoring violent, sexually explicit music videos?
REVISED	Should music videos be censored or regulated?
BIASED	Do you support the homosexual assault on the holy sacrament of marriage?
REVISED	Should gay couples be allowed to marry?

To make responses easy to tabulate, you will often want to provide readers with a range of options for answering your questions. This kind of survey instrument is called a Likert scale.

How do you feel about the following statements?

Respond using the appropriate number.

1. I disagree totally.

2. I disagree somewhat.

3. I agree somewhat.

4. I agree totally.

Our bus system serves the whole community.

Our bus system operates efficiently.

Our bus system runs on time.

Bus fares are too high.

A sales tax increase for buses makes sense.

I am unfamiliar with our bus system.

Experts recommend that you provide an even number of choices for responses; otherwise, answers often tend to hover in the middle.

In addition to exploring specific issues, you may want to gather demographic data on the people you are surveying; this information may be useful later in interpreting your findings. You must be able to protect the privacy of the people you survey and offer reasonable assurances that any information they volunteer will not be used against them in any way. But personal data can reveal surprising patterns, particularly when you ask questions about political and social topics.

About you. Knowing a little about respondents to this survey will make interpretation of the data more significant. Please answer the following questions as best you can. Leave off any information you would rather not offer.

1. What is your gender?

   M   F

2. What is your marital status?

   Married

   Single, divorced/separated/widowed

   Single, never married

3. What is your age?

4. What is your race or ethnicity?

   Asian

   Black/African American

   Hispanic

   White

   Other

5. What is the highest level of your education?

   Elementary school or less

   Some high school

   High school graduate

   Some college

   College graduate

   Postgraduate or professional school

   Other

Try to anticipate the questions your queries might raise in a respondent's mind, and work for a reasonable mix of "quick response" and "open-ended" questions. People are not often willing to spend a lot of time completing surveys. Whenever possible, ask questions in ways that your respondents can answer with minimal effort. Save open-ended questions for those issues that can't be satisfactorily answered any other way.

Be sure you survey enough people from your target group so that readers will find your sample adequate. Ordinarily those polled should represent a cross section of the whole population. Surveying only your friends, only people who agree with you, or only people like yourself will almost certainly produce inadequate research.

You may have to provide an incentive to get people to cooperate, particularly when your survey is lengthy. In most cases this means suggesting that their responses may help solve a problem or serve others in some way. J. D. Powers, the company famous for surveying new-car owners, sends a crisp dollar bill with its survey to thank potential respondents. You may not be able to go that far, but you do need to consider whether you can offer some incentive for a response.

SUMMARY

Conducting a Survey

- Understand the purpose of your survey or questionnaire before you create it. What information do you need to gather?
- Prepare clear, fair, and unbiased questions. Test your questions to be sure participants in your actual survey will understand them.
- Consider the types of responses you need. Should people respond on a scale? Choose from a list of options you provide? Fill in blanks?
- Create questionnaires that are easy to read, fill out, and tabulate.
- Create questionnaires that are convenient to return. If necessary, provide properly addressed envelopes and return postage.
- Give respondents appropriate assurances about the confidentiality of their responses and then abide by your commitment.
- Keep track of your sampling procedures so you can report them accurately.

Finally, you'll have to tabulate your findings accurately, present the results in a fashion that makes sense to readers, let readers know the techniques you used to gather your information, and, most important, report the limits of your study. Those limits provide the qualifications for any conclusions you draw. Don't overstate the results.

Like interviews, surveys and polls can be conducted face to face, by telephone, by mail, or online. Figure 7.1 shows a simple online poll created using the free *Yahoo! Groups,* which automatically tabulates results for you.

7c Make systematic observations

Some of the best field research you can do may come simply from the close study of a phenomenon. On their own, people are notoriously unreliable in recounting what they have seen; their observations are often colored by their expectations, experiences, and assumptions. (Not surprisingly, the sworn testimonies of eyewitnesses to events are often conflicting.) So in making research observations, you want to employ techniques that counteract your biases as much as possible and ensure the reliability of your claims.

You might begin with a double-column spiral notebook to separate your actual observations from your immediate reactions to them. Your written notes should be quite detailed about time, place, duration of the study, conditions of the observation, and so on. You may have to summarize this information later.

You need not rely on notebooks alone for your records. To assure an accurate account of what you are studying, use any appropriate technology:

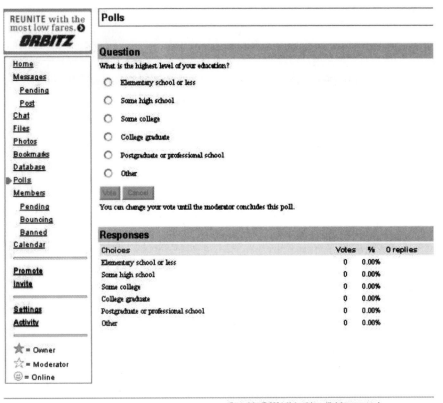

FIGURE 7.1 Create an online poll with *Yahoo! Groups.*
(*Source:* http://groups.yahoo.com)

photography, tape recording, video recording, transcription of online conversations, and so on. Remember to get permission to gather this type of information. If you make multiple observations over a period of time, follow the same procedures each time and note any changes that might affect your results. For example, students conducting a traffic count of persons entering a major campus facility would want to perform the counts on typical campus days—not during spring break or on days when the weather is unusually bad.

Between going to the library, conducting searches on the Web, and collecting data from field research, you may soon begin to feel yourself awash in information. With so many new sources of information available to us these days, it's all the more important to find ways to keep track of it all. In Chapter 8 we'll look at handy ways to make keeping track a bit easier.

S U M M A R Y

Making Observations

- Understand the purpose of your observations. What information do you hope to gather? In what forms can that data be gathered and reported?

- Look at the literature on your subject and become familiar with the subjects you are studying. What background information do you require to make informed and perceptive observations?

- Plan your method of observation. How can you gather the information you need? How can you minimize your own impact on the situation you are observing? Will you need to obtain permission from an institutional review board or another regulatory authority?

- Work with others to confirm the reliability of your observations. Cross-check your field notes with those of fellow researchers.

WWW Web Sites Worth Knowing

WWW
7.1

- *Ask the Experts*, http://www.refdesk.com/expert.html
- *Suite 101.com*, "Field Research: Planning an Efficient Out-and-About," http://www.suite101.com/article.cfm/academic_writing/26071
- "Survey Design, Questionnaire Design Tips," http://www.surveysystem.com/sdesign.htm
- U.S. Department of Health and Human Services, Office for Human Research Protections, http://www.hhs.gov/ohrp

MANAGING YOUR PROJECT

1. Decide whether your subject would benefit from interviews with experts or others involved in your topic. What might you learn from these interviews that you might not discover in printed or electronic sources?

2. Does your topic need information from a survey or questionnaire? Even if it seems that a formal survey is unnecessary, might your project benefit from the results of an informal survey of opinion? For example, a survey might reveal apprehension or general ignorance about your subject, so you could introduce your subject by reporting the results of that survey.

3. Does your subject require systematic observation of any kind? If so, sketch out your methodology for the observation and share the report with your

instructor or colleagues. Get feedback on the techniques you will use to be sure they are valid and reliable.

4. Will you need approval from an institutional review board to conduct your research? Check policies at your institution, or check with your instructor.

CHAPTER 8

Keeping Track of Information

In the late 1990s, a man named Edmund Trebus gained a small amount of notoriety in Great Britain for being a compulsive hoarder. His home and his garden were so full of accumulated papers, toys, and trash that he needed ladders to get in and out of his house. Eventually, responding to neighbors' complaints, the local health services stepped in and hauled away 515 cubic yards of rubbish. His behavior (and the British love of quirky eccentrics) made him the focus of a BBC documentary, *Mr. Trebus: A Life of Grime.*

Perhaps, at times, you've felt a bit like Mr. Trebus, awash in stacks of photocopies and printouts of Web sites, notes from interviews, data from surveys or experiments, lists of electronic addresses, image files in various formats, MOO transcripts, audio and video files, and software copies of your own work, perhaps in several versions. It's probably at that point you realized that organizing your research materials is at least as important as collecting them. Somehow you have to find a way to bring all this information together and make sense of it.

8a Organize and safeguard your materials

Plan from the beginning where you will keep all the materials you accumulate while working on a project. A good organizational strategy will help you keep track of everything as you assemble your list of Works Cited and, more important, allow you to locate the sources again if necessary.

- Invest in a rugged, closable folder with ample pockets and safe storage for papers and disks. Write your name and phone number inside.
- Put your name, email address, and phone number on all computer disks.
- Make a backup copy of your work and keep in a safe place.
- Buy a hard case for your working disk to protect it from dust and dirt that can damage it and cause you to lose data.

- If you're working with images or audio or video files in a project, use a Zip disk, jump drive, or CD-R (compact disc–recordable) to store your files.
- If you must learn how to construct a database to study your findings (perhaps using commercial software such as Microsoft *Access*) do so at the start of your project. Don't leave this hurdle until the end.

It also helps to organize your computer information intelligently: keep your data in one location on your hard disk, name your files in a logical way (such as "Testing Project-Kohn Article Notes.doc"), and use version numbers or dates to ensure you are always working with the latest version of a document. You can also create directories (or folders) on your hard drive and disks to help you organize information, and you can use your "Bookmarks" or "Favorites" file to help you keep track of Web sites.

8b Prepare a working bibliography

It doesn't matter whether you are using print or electronic sources or whether your project will culminate in a paper, a Web site, or a brochure. You need to know where your information came from, and the best way to keep track is to record bibliographical data as you move through your sources, developing a working bibliography.

CHECKLIST 8.1

Bibliography Checklist

○ Name(s) of author(s), editor(s), translator(s), Webmaster(s), or others responsible for the publication, along with a notation of their contribution (e.g., "ed.")
○ Date of publication
○ Title information
○ City of publication and name of publisher (for books)
○ Journal, magazine, or newspaper title, along with volume and issue numbers (for journals) or section or edition name(s) for newspapers
○ URL (uniform resource locator, or the Internet address) for World Wide Web sites
○ Database name and identifying file or accession numbers (for full-text or full-image articles accessed through an online database)
○ Date of access for electronic materials
○ Page number(s) for articles or book chapters

Regardless of what format you must follow (MLA, APA, Chicago, etc.), you will have to record the same information about each source you use.

Recording this information will ensure that you can locate the source again if need be and that you will have the information necessary to compile your list of References or Works Cited. You may also want to record notes about the source, such as a brief summary or description of the information it contains. If you are using a database or bibliography software, you might want to include keywords to help you search your entries quickly. And you might want to record particularly succinct or well-stated sentences or phrases if you think you will want to use a quotation from this source. Make certain that you copy direct quotations accurately and that you carefully denote them as quotations! Include page numbers for any information you quote or summarize as well.

There still may be no simpler way to create the bibliography and track your sources than to keep an accurate set of bibliography cards, either in electronic format or on 3-by-5-inch note cards. Each bibliography card should contain all the information you need to find a source again or to record when you accessed an electronic source such as a Web site. For printed sources, be sure to include a library call number or a location (current periodicals, for example, may not have call numbers). Typical bibliography cards might look like those in Figure 8.1.

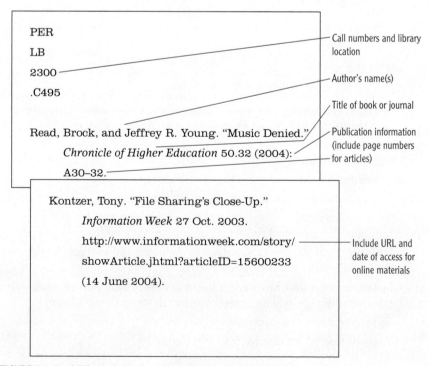

FIGURE 8.1 Use bibliography cards or files to keep track of information.

FOCUS ON . . . Citing Databases Correctly

While it may seem like the easiest thing in the world to cite the URL of a Web site—copying and pasting it from the address bar of your Web browser—you have to be careful about just what sort of URL you're citing, especially when the information comes from an online database or newsbank. Sometimes the database you use will be *password protected* or *site limited*; you have access because your school has subscribed to the database, but others don't. Other times the URL information may be created "on the fly" and will change depending on the particular user and date of access.

A search through the State of Georgia's GALILEO portal (a site that provides access to online databases) for full-text articles on "MP3 copyright," for instance, turns up the article "MP3.com founder fights to save the music," by Mike Freeman. The URL for this article, http://web.lexis-nexis.com/universe/document?_m=764af00cda85d5efb6bba90b20a8f763&docnum=21&wchp=dGLbVtz-zSkVA&_md5, shows that it comes from a licensed database, *LexisNexis*, and includes coded details on all the Boolean and other search terms used to find it. If nonregistered users try to find the same article with this URL, they will get only an error message. Cite the article using all the information from the original publication (in this case, the November 27, 2003, issue of the *San Diego Union-Tribune*) and then indicate that it was located via the *LexisNexis* database.

Nowadays most writers prefer to print out a list of potential sources from online library catalogs, electronic databases, and Web search engines (see Chapter 5). But this strategy can be risky because the information on a Web search page printout is usually insufficient for preparing a Works Cited page or References list. Printouts can also be misplaced among the many papers a research project typically generates. So if you rely on printouts for bibliographical information, keep the lists in one place and know what's on them. Use a highlighter to indicate important sources and annotate them when possible. If you download or print out Web pages, make sure you record carefully the URL and the date of access in a separate file or handwrite the information on your printed copies (see Section 8d).

An even better alternative to note cards might be an electronic program such as *EndNote* or *ProCite* that keeps track of your notes and sources. Database software of this kind is often easy to use and quite powerful, though you may need a laptop computer to take it into the library. Figure 8.2, for example, shows screens in a bibliography program that can automatically format in-text entries following whatever style you use. Built-in templates for various types of sources help you list the necessary information. Some software packages

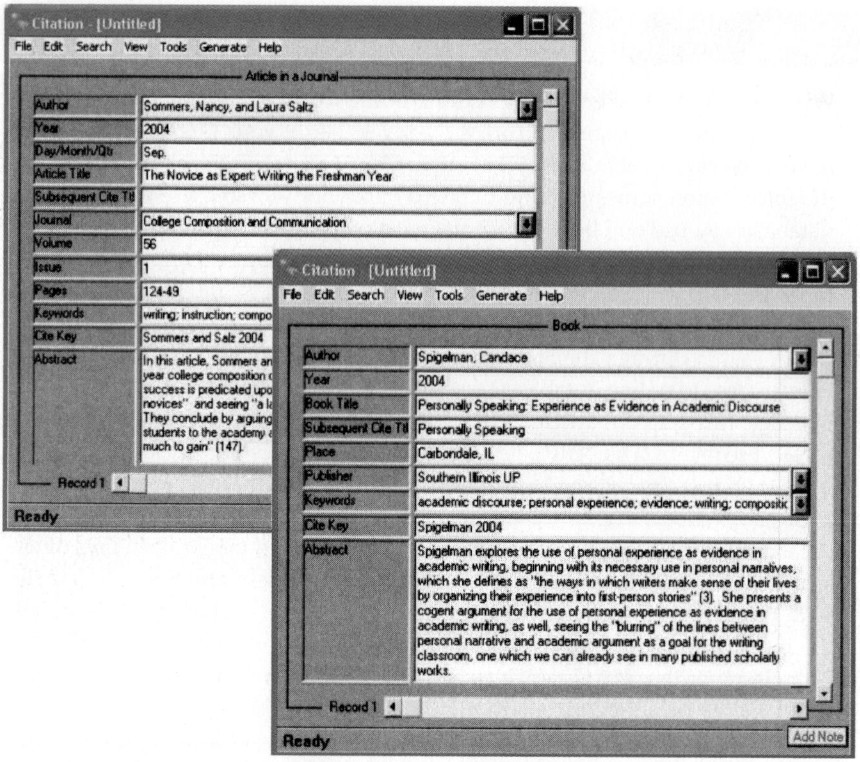

FIGURE 8.2 Bibliography programs such as this are excellent means of keeping track of sources and notes.
(*Source: Citation 8* for Windows.)

can be configured to work from inside your word processor to help you ensure that your citations are accurate.

8c Prepare an annotated bibliography

Your instructor may require you to prepare and submit an annotated bibliography, that is, a listing of sources that includes a summary or description of the main points covered in an article. Even if your instructor doesn't require it, you may want to compile one. An annotated bibliography can be useful for keeping track of the information contained in the many sources you review. If at a later stage you realize that you need information from a source you reviewed early on and discarded, you can check the annotated bibliography to help you recognize the source and retrieve it. For each entry in your bibliography, include a brief annotation, or summary, of the information it contains. (See Chapter 13 for more information on writing effective summaries). An example of an annotated bibliography appears on pages 93–95.

Some software packages such as *EndNote* and *ProCite* will help you compile an annotated bibliography quickly (see Figure 8.3). Of course, you may

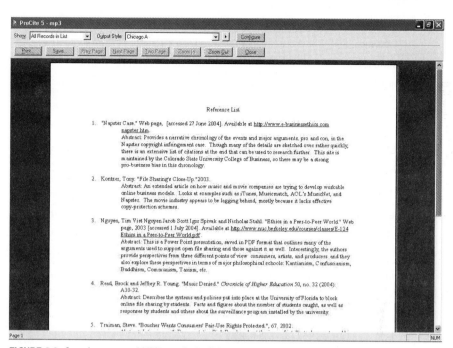

FIGURE 8.3 Sample annotated bibliography in Chicago style created with ProCite5.

need to modify or correct the files generated by such software to adhere to your instructor's guidelines (see Figure 8.3 above). You don't need to invest in special software tools, however; you can easily create an annotated bibliography in your word processor or Web page editor.

Annotated Bibliography

Kontzer, Tony. "File Sharing's Close-Up." *Information Week* 27 Oct. 2003. **1**

    http://www.informationweek.com/story/showArticle.jhtml?articleID=

    15600233 (14 June 2004).

An extended article on how music and movie companies are trying to develop workable online business models. Looks at examples such as Apple's iTunes, **2** Musicmatch, AOL's MusicNet, and Napster. The movie industry appears to be lagging behind, mostly because it lacks effective copy protection schemes.

"Napster Case." *E-center for Business Ethics*.

    http://www.e-businessethics.com/napster.htm (27 June 2004). **3**

Provides a narrative chronology of the events and major arguments, pro and con, in the Napster copyright infringement case. Though many of the details are sketched over rather quickly, there is an extensive list of citations at the end that can be used to research further. This site is maintained by the Colorado State University College of Business, so there may be a strong pro-business bias in this chronology.

Nguyen, Tim, Viet Nguyen, Jacob Scott, Igor Spivak, and Nicholas Stahl. "Ethics in a Peer-to-Peer World." 2003. http://www.nuc.berkeley.edu/courses/classes/E-124/Ethics in a Peer-to-Peer World.pdf (1 July 2004).

4

This is a *Power Point* presentation, saved in PDF format, that outlines many of the arguments used to support open file sharing and those against it as well. Interestingly, the authors provide perspectives from three different points of view—consumers, artists, and producers—and they also explore these perspectives in terms of major philosophical schools: Kantianism, Confucianism, Buddhism, Communism, Taoism, etc.

Read, Brock, and Jeffrey R. Young. "Music Denied." *Chronicle of Higher Education* 50.32 (2004): A30-32.

Describes the systems and policies put into place at the University of Florida to block online file sharing by students. Facts and figures about the number of students caught, as well as responses by students and others about the surveillance program installed by the university.

Traiman, Steve. "Boucher Wants Consumers' Fair-Use Rights Protected." *Billboard* 114.28 (2002): 67.

Interview with Representative Rick Boucher about the issue of intellectual property and his work to guarantee Internet users fair use rights. He's concerned about the actions of a number of CD producers who want to introduce copy-protection schemes that will deny consumers this right.

Annotations

1. Bibliographic entry for each source follows the same format as Works Cited or References page.
2. Annotations (brief summaries) describe each source, including the information it contains and any special features.
3. Entries are listed alphabetically by author's last name or by the first major word of the title if no author is listed.
4. Include page numbers for print articles, URLs and date of access for online sources.

8d Make copies of important sources

This may sound like a fairly obvious point, but you'd be surprised how frequently researchers forget this simple step.

- Photocopy or print out passages from sources you know you will quote from directly and extensively.
- Make sure your copies are complete and legible, including the page numbers.
- When you are copying from a book or a magazine, record the bibliographical information right on the copy. You'll be glad you did later on.
- Use highlighter pens to mark printed passages you expect to refer to later. Some word-processing programs allow you to highlight passages in different colors or insert comments. *Never highlight or write in library books.*
- Store the URLs of important Web sites in your "Bookmarks" or "Favorites" file for easy retrieval.

It is possible to copy many electronic sources directly to disk, and copyright regulations usually allow you to make copies for personal use. Be especially careful that you know where all downloaded images come from and who owns their copyrights. As with printed sources, you must document and credit all copyrighted pictures, photographs, and images borrowed from the Web, whether you use them in a paper or in an electronic project. If your project is to be published on the Web or distributed outside the classroom, you may need to acquire permission from the copyright owner to use the material (see Chapter 9).

8e Back up your work frequently

It's happened to all of us: a notebook or disk left behind in the library or a public lab. And if there's one thing that computers can always be relied on to do, it's to crash at inopportune times. Sometimes you're lucky and you can recover the lost notebook, disk, or file intact. But better than relying on luck is taking the time to back up your work frequently. If you've made substantial changes to a paper, click "save." When you finish a work session, copy all your files—word-processed documents, bibliographic files, "Bookmarks" or "Favorites" files, graphics files, and so on—to another disk or to your hard drive. Make two sets of photocopies and keep one in your desk drawer. And remember to update your backup files and copies regularly; otherwise, you may have to retrace all the work you did for however long it has been since your last backup.

An old adage summarizes much of what we've covered in this chapter: An ounce of prevention is worth a pound of cure. Paying attention to detail at the beginning can save you a lot of frustration at the end. If you are a thorough researcher and organize your information carefully, you'll find yourself well

8.1

prepared to *use* that information in your own research project. As you think about ways to do so, you will have to be certain you incorporate outside sources fairly and ethically.

WWW Web Sites Worth Knowing

8.2

- "How to Write Annotated Bibliographies," http://www.library.mun.ca/guides/howto/annotated_bibl.pdf
- Arizona State University, "Writing Annotated Bibliographies" (*PowerPoint* presentation), http://www.asu.edu/duas/wac/annbib.html
- Note Taking, http://student.bvsd.k12.co.us/~blackl/school/nvhsresearch/ notetaking/notetaking.html
- "Bibliographical Management and Note Taking," http://www.kcl.ac.uk/ humanities/cch/pg/course/bib_management/bib_management.html
- "Bibliography Software," http://www.educational-software-directory.net/ reference/bibliography.html

MANAGING YOUR PROJECT

1. Plan your research strategy. Begin by considering how you will keep track of the data you will list for each source on a Works Cited or References page. Set up a routine for listing all sources you examine, even those you might not use at all.

2. Set up a procedure for taking notes from your sources. Make sure the link between your notes or photocopies and your bibliography is always clear.

3. Always consider the possibility that some part of your project might be lost or erased. Plan a strategy to avoid such problems (such as a regular schedule of backups).

4. Compile an annotated bibliography of potential sources. You can use a word processor, Web page editor, or database program to keep track of the entries. If you are working on a group project, share your resources with other members of the group. Photocopy important sources, especially any material you anticipate quoting, and take notes directly on the photocopied text. Be sure to photocopy the title page of a source because it will have bibliographic information you'll need later.

III

WORKING WITH SOURCES

DON'T MISS . . .

- **The discussion of plagiarism in Chapter 9.** Documents, charts, and other graphics are not free for the taking, even if they're published on the Web. Learn how and why you must cite borrowings from all your sources.
- **The explorations of purpose and bias in sources raised in Section 10b.** As a researcher, you must weigh the special interests served by even the most "objective" sources.
- **The annotated editorial in Chapter 11.** Learn how to read your sources critically and respond in writing to the points they raise.
- **The sample bibliography with positioning information and quotes in Chapter 12.** As you compile your resources, you need to choose effective quotes and think about how they will "fit" in your paper.

EVERYDAY RESEARCH

TIM COCKEY, Author

With his first published poem at the tender age of ten, Tim Cockey knew he wanted to become a writer. "I was one of those kids who loved to read and whose imagination took me not only to the places in the books, but to the writers who had written the books," he says.

Tim attended college, where he majored in English and creative writing. After landing a series of public relations and advertising jobs, he moved to New York City, where he read for television and movie productions and wrote screenplays. At the age of 42, he hit on the idea of writing a mystery novel: "The moment I began the first book, I knew I had located the kind of writing where my skills could really flourish."

Although the majority of his material comes from imagination and invention, Tim does a good deal of outside research for each book. He reads other mystery novels and pores over synopses of new books, both in print and on the Internet, just to ensure that his "big ideas" aren't already in place in someone else's book. He interviews others (for his last series, he spoke with a number of undertakers about particular aspects of their trade) and travels to places where he wants to set certain scenes. He also takes notes on what other writers have written, particularly when they discuss legal matters and the workings of a district attorney's office: "It's always nice to have a storehouse of investigating tactics, just in case."

CHAPTER 9

Understanding Academic Responsibility and Avoiding Plagiarism

WWW

9.1

On May 2, 2003, *New York Times* reporter Jayson Blair was forced to resign after it was discovered he had plagiarized portions of one of his stories from an article in a San Antonio, Texas, newspaper. The uproar that resulted ultimately led two *Times* editors to resign as well. Clearly, *plagiarism* (stealing another writer's words) can have serious consequences, so it's no wonder that college writers often bridle when they hear the word, knowing that being accused of this offense can undermine one's integrity and ruin a career. No one wants to commit plagiarism, but sometimes writers are uncertain just how to avoid it. Many writers have been surprised to discover that they have plagiarized material, even when they have tried to be careful not to. That's unfortunate, because research ought to be regarded as an exciting journey, not as an obstacle course full of traps. But simply crediting the sources you use in a research project is not always enough. It is important, therefore, to follow guidelines for the use of resource materials based on common sense, ethics, and a desire to give credit where credit is due. More important, citing sources accurately shows your readers that you are responsible and reliable and contributes to the credibility of your own work.

9a Understand the ethics of research

You should summarize, paraphrase, quote, and document research materials carefully, not merely to avoid charges of plagiarism but because you have an ethical responsibility to represent the ideas of other writers accurately, and to assist readers in verifying your research or gathering additional information.

Readers and writers alike depend on the integrity of their sources. Thus you need to ensure not only that you are using sources ethically but that the sources on which you rely are honest as well (see Chapter 10). Most students do understand that it is wrong to buy a paper, to let someone heavily edit a paper, or to submit someone else's work as their own, but many students do not realize that taking notes carelessly or documenting sources inadequately may also raise doubts about a paper's integrity.

Representing the words, ideas, or creations you found in a source as your own, intentionally or not, constitutes plagiarism, and instructors take this seriously. Luckily, plagiarism is easily avoided when you take good notes (see Chapter 8) and follow the guidelines discussed in the following sections.

9b Avoid intentional and unintentional plagiarism

The ease with which entire papers can be found on Web sites or in databases can be a powerful temptation to cheat: a quick search, a quick cut, a quick paste, a quick printout, and presto, the paper is done! Who's to know, right?

Wrong. The Web has also made it much easier for instructors to catch plagiarism. Often all they have to do is take a short phrase from a paper and type it into a search engine; every Web document that includes that phrase appears in the results. The process can take less than a minute. Some companies, such as Turnitin.com at http://www.turnitin.com and Glatt Plagiarism Services at http://www.plagiarism.com, specialize in plagiarism checking, comparing student papers to the thousands upon thousands they have in their databases; other companies, like Canexus at http://www.canexus.com, perform detailed Web searches for instructors on request.

More than a few students have discovered to their surprise that the time they "saved" on research and writing resulted in an F on their transcripts and, in some cases, expulsion from school. Students who plagiarize ultimately cheat only themselves. College writing courses offer the opportunity to learn how to communicate your own ideas in writing, a skill that you will need throughout your life. You may squeak through your first-year composition courses by relying heavily on someone else's work, but getting through the rest of your life that way will be much more difficult.

Most students recognize that intentional plagiarism is cheating, whether one buys a paper from a term paper mill or copies it from a friend or a fraternity cache. However, you need to understand that copying *any* portion of a source word for word or presenting ideas, facts, and figures from other sources without giving proper credit—even if you present them in your own words—constitutes plagiarism.

WWW
9.2

The following example shows how easily you can be guilty of unintentional plagiarism when you are not careful in copying and pasting information from an online source into your notes.

ORIGINAL SOURCE

Quality of sleep habits was found to be a factor in self-perceived academic competence. If college students experience REM sleep deprivation more than the average population, then the findings of this study need to be passed on to college students. The findings in this study suggest that college students with poor sleep habits may perceive themselves as having lower academic competency. The study also showed that self-perceived academic competency was positively correlated to academic performance. Thus, according to Hobson (1989), Webb & Bonnet (1979), and this study, those college students who do have poor sleep habits will negatively affect their academic performance.

It was also found that test anxiety and grade point average are negatively correlated, and that quality of sleep and grade point average are positively correlated. This, and the fact that quality of sleep and test anxiety are negatively related, suggest interrelationships among the variables test anxiety, sleep habits, self-perceived academic competency and academic performance. This highlights the fact that professors need to instruct their students on how to manage test anxiety. Students also need to be aware of the effects that poor sleep and low self-perceived academic competency have on academic performance. Thus, the phrase "I think I can, I think I can . . ." may be beneficial only if students reduce their test anxiety and develop better sleep habits. More research needs to be done to find other variables that affect self-perceived academic competence.

The following paragraphs are based much too closely on material from the original essay, now archived on the Web. This reformulation of the material amounts to plagiarism, even though the author of the plagiarized paragraphs credits the source. The boldfaced material looks like it was copied and pasted directly from the online original.

PLAGIARIZED PARAGRAPHS

Getting a good night's sleep before an examination makes sense psychologically. According to Briggs (1999), **quality of sleep habits was found to be a factor in self-perceived academic competence.** That is to say that college students with poor sleep habits may perceive themselves as having lower academic competency. **Those college students who do have poor sleep habits will negatively affect their academic performance.**

There also seems to be a connection between self-perceived academic competency and academic performance. **This highlights the fact that professors need to instruct their students on how to manage test anxiety.**

FOCUS ON . . . **Avoiding Plagiarism**

Sometimes it is easy to forget which ideas are your own and which were culled from the many sources you have reviewed in the course of your research. After reading many articles, Web pages, and books about MP3 file sharing, for example, it might be difficult to remember whether a particular opinion about fair use was yours or someone else's. The following tips can help you avoid unintentionally plagiarizing the work of others:

- **Take careful notes.** Make sure you enclose any direct quotations—even a single cogent word or phrase—in quotation marks, carefully noting the page number and source.
- **Paraphrase carefully.** Paraphrasing means more than changing a few words. Although a paraphrase should follow the order of the original, it should be written entirely in your *own* words.
- **Summarize ideas in your own words** whenever possible. Think about the meaning of what you have read, and try to explain the ideas to your reader in your own words.
- **Carefully acknowledge *all* borrowings**: quotations, ideas (including paraphrases and summaries written in your own words), factual information, statistics, and so on.
- **Cite the source of any graphics or figures** you use as well as the source of information contained in tables and graphs. Usually, you will need to include a "source" line to give credit to the creator or publisher.

Students also need to be aware of the effects that poor sleep and low self-perceived academic competency have on academic performance. Thus, the phrase, "I think I can, I think I can . . ." may be beneficial only if students reduce their test anxiety and develop better sleep habits. So a student really can improve performance in college courses by making more time for sleep.

Chapter 13 shows how to summarize and paraphrase sources responsibly and how to correctly acknowledge your borrowings. Chapter 14 explains how to handle quotations in your paper accurately and honestly. For more help, try the tutorial on recognizing and avoiding plagiarism at http://www.indiana .edu/~wts/pamphlets/plagiarism.html.

9c Understand the special nature of collaborative projects

Collaborative work is an important part of many writing projects in the classroom as well as in the workplace. Sometimes the group takes credit for the entire project; at other times, individual authors are credited for separate sections or components of a project. Check with your instructor before you decide to work with someone else on a project.

Many colleges and universities offer professional consultations for students free of charge in writing centers or academic tutoring centers (see Chapter 18). These consultants are trained to offer guidance and feedback to students without taking over a project. Sometimes, however, a well-intentioned friend or family member (or even an overzealous tutor) will offer too much "help," essentially writing the paper for you. Remember, *you* are the author; while you do want to take advantage of proffered feedback and assistance, you want to ensure that your project reflects your own voice and ideas, not someone else's.

9d Understand intellectual property rights

Patents, trademarks, and copyrights are all ways of protecting original creations and ideas. When we create an original machine or process, we patent it, which means we own the rights to produce the invention: we can sell (or rent) those rights to others, and we can receive compensation for such use. When we create an original work of words or art, online or in print, the same principles apply, only the concept is called *copyright* instead of patent. We still own the rights to reproduce our work; we can sell (or rent) those rights to others, and we have the right to receive compensation or recognition for such use.

Copyrighted material may be included in other works, such as research projects, without prior permission or payment of royalties, under the doctrine known as *fair use.*

> The fair use of a copyrighted work, including such use by reproduction in copies or phonorecords or by any other means specified . . . , for purposes such as criticism, comment, news reporting, teaching (including multiple copies for classroom use), scholarship, or research, is not an infringement of copyright. (17 U.S.C. Sec. 107)

A good rule of thumb for fair use would be to take no more than 10 percent of a work (a poem, paper, or other document) and give proper credit to the author or creator (see Chapter 19). Violations of fair use can bring legal penalties as well as charges of plagiarism. In terms of your own project, then, place reasonable limits on the amount of material you borrow from your sources.

9e Understand the special nature of online resources

Governments around the world (including our own) have yet to decide what the laws will be regarding copyrights, fair use, and electronic sources. However, some guidelines for handling electronic materials have been developed, based on current laws. For example, the controversy surrounding the original Napster site (which allowed users to share copyrighted music files without paying royalties) hinged on legal definitions of fair use. You will need to un-

CHECKLIST 9.1

CHECKLIST 9.1

Guidelines for Fair Use

○ **Always give credit where credit is due.** Citing sources serves several purposes beyond avoiding academic penalties and/or lawsuits. It gives credit to the originator of the idea, it shows that you have done your research, and it tells readers where to find your sources if they want further information.

○ **If it's on the Web, it's published.** Information published on Web pages must be cited like any other source. In addition to citing text and Web sources, you should properly cite all graphics and audio and video files included in your work (see Chapter 19).

○ **When in doubt, ask.** If it is unclear whether or not a given use of material (electronic or otherwise) is permitted, ask the owner or author, if possible, explaining the nature of the intended use and noting the portion or portions of the work to be included in your work. If asked by a copyright owner to remove material or links from your project, do so promptly.

derstand the guidelines and principles of fair use and consider carefully how you use information, ideas, graphics, and other elements created by others in your own projects. Use Checklist 9.1 as a guide.

The Web is an international publishing space. As such, many images, texts, and other files may fall under the copyright laws of other nations, whose attitude toward ownership of intellectual property may be different from our own. Thus a key word in our consideration of intellectual property should be *respect*—respect for the moral and ethical as well as the economic and legal rights of authors, creators, and publishers.

9f Using graphics, audio, or video files

Graphics and audio and video files may not fall under the shelter of fair use guidelines. Although it is easy to download files from the Internet or scan images from books, usually it is illegal to do so unless you have permission from the copyright owner. Luckily, there are many sites online that offer free graphics for Web page authors. Make sure, however, you read the fine print carefully and follow any rules or stipulations (see Figure 9.1 for an example).

Whether your images and files are free or are being used with permission, you still need to cite the source. Images may have a "source" or "credit" line underneath them as in Figure 9.1, or you may include a "credits" page or a list of figures with source information. For example, a Web page or a research pa-

---

TERMS OF USAGE

THE RULES
You can do whatever the heck you want with these pieces of clip art. You can place 'em on Web pages, snort 'em, do whatever—as long as you follow these rules:

1. ONLY USE CLIP ART FOR THE SOLE PURPOSE OF ENHANCING YOUR PERSONAL/ COMMERCIAL PROJECTS
I have come across a site that actually took an entire collection of clip art and posted it for his users. **Under no circumstances can you do this.** Do not take clip art for the sole purpose of creating your own clip art or offering a collection to your visitors to download or buy. There are only two circumstances in which you may take the clip art:

1. **Personal use**—as imagery for your Web site, for desktop publishing projects, greeting cards, school projects, home, etc.
2. **Commercial use**—Web sites you are building for clients, t-shirt business, mugs, graphic design projects, etc.

In other words, the clip art must be used specifically to enhance (decorate) projects, whether personal or commercial. You may not under any circumstances simply pick clip art to create your *own* clip art site or clip art collection to redistribute commercially. Really, now—I shouldn't have to say this, but I have to be very clear on this. This site was created to help people find clip art for their projects, not to help people build their own clip art sites.

2. DO NOT—I REPEAT—DO NOT REMOTE LINK TO IMAGES!
In case there is any confusion, here's what remote linking is: linking to the images in **any** way or form for **whatever** reason. This includes linking to an image here for use as an avatar on message boards. Download images to your hard drive and upload to your own server! If you need a place to store your graphics and remote load them, then check out Village Photos com, which will allow you to host and remote link images for free. But do not remote load from here, as you would be engaging in bandwidth theft.

3. Please place a link to **The Hassle Free Clip Art Guide** as a courtesy on your pages somewhere if you use these pieces. You don't have to, but it would be nice! :-)

FIGURE 9.1 "Terms of Usage" for clip art on the Hassle Free Clip Art Page, http://www.hasslefreeclipart.com/pages_terms.html.

---

per with multiple images from a free online graphics site may include a note like this: "All images on this page courtesy of FreeGraphics.org, **http://www .freegraphics.org.**"

It is not necessary to include a citation for graphics or audio or video files used in your project in your list of Works Cited or References unless you are actually citing or referencing the images or files. See Part VI for information on how to cite graphics and audio or video files in your Works Cited or References pages when necessary. (See Chapter 21 for more information on formatting graphics for use in print-based projects.)

If you are feeling intimidated at this point, don't worry. In the next few chapters we'll show you how writers commonly bring research material into their texts and how you can do so without falling into the plagiarism trap.

WWW Web Sites Worth Knowing

- University of Kansas Writing Guide, "Academic Integrity," http://www.writing.ku.edu/students/docs/integrity.shtml
- Center for Academic Integrity, http://www.academicintegrity.org
- Purdue University Online Writing Lab, "Avoiding Plagiarism," http://owl.english.purdue.edu/handouts/print/research/r_plagiar.html

WWW

9.3

MANAGING YOUR PROJECT

1. If you expect to rely heavily on materials borrowed from online sources, be sure to acquire permission early in your project. If you wait until the last minute, you may be in trouble if you are denied permission to use material central to your thesis or project. In making such a request, be sure to mention the following:
   - Who you are
   - Your academic institution
   - The character of your work
   - The nature and scope of the material you are borrowing
   - The context in which you intend to use the material

2. If you are involved in a collaborative project, discuss with your colleagues how the work will be distributed and credited before you get too deeply into the project. Decide not only who will do what but how performance within the group will be monitored during the project and then reported when the project is done.

CHAPTER 10

Evaluating Sources

According to an article by Nick Jeffreys in the August 12, 2004, edition of the popular newsstand tabloid *Weekly World News,* Michael Jackson's real parents may be an alien couple from the planet Zertonia named Mr. and Mrs. Zortron. A man claiming to be their attorney has recently filed a lawsuit that seeks to return Jackson to his distraught Zertonian parents.

Do you find this information or the source it came from credible? Not many people would, so you might think twice before including it as "evidence" in a research project you wanted people to take seriously. Before you can expect your readers to rely on the information you give them, you must be certain that the sources from which you gathered your information are reliable and relevant. Experience teaches us to trust some people more than we do others.

For many subjects, traditional research resources—books, articles, and newspapers—now form just the tip of an iceberg. You may also have to consider pamphlets, microfilm, maps, field data, transcripts of interviews, CD-ROMs, databases, Web sites, videos, listservs, email, and more. Because electronic sources often come to you almost directly from their authors, many judgments about the credibility of research materials that used to fall on publishers and librarians now fall squarely on your shoulders.

Before you use any source, you have to consider its relevance, purpose, authority, and timeliness (see Checklist 10.1 on evaluating sources). In this chapter we present information that will help you answer these questions and ensure that your use of information gleaned from outside sources is successful.

10a Consider the relevance of your sources

Search tools such as electronic catalogs and indexes may point you to thousands of potential resources. When you find yourself with an embarrassment of riches, first try narrowing the scope of your project even more than you did initially (see Chapter 4), or scan the titles in your working bibliography (see Section 8b); you'll usually be able to cut irrelevant items.

www
10.1

Some library catalogs, indexes, and search engines provide summaries or abstracts of the works they contain. Such summaries may also suggest whether a full article or site deserves your attention. Recognize the limits of these brief descriptions—you may still have to examine the source itself to appreciate its value.

There is no magic formula for determining how relevant a source is to your topic—other than exercising critical judgment. You are conducting research to find answers to questions or to support your arguments. Each source you include should provide such answers or add something that will help you build your case. You must decide what the material in question adds to your project: Crucial information? Supportive commentary? An alternative perspective? For example, if you are arguing that downloading music files from the Internet has had no effect on music sales, you might include statements from musicians, mu-

---

CHECKLIST 10.1

Evaluating Sources: Questions to Consider

Relevance

○ Does the information answer important questions that you have raised?

○ Does it support your propositions or present counterarguments that you need to address?

○ Does it present examples or illustrate important points in your project?

Author's Purpose and Audience

○ Is the author's purpose apparent or explicit?

○ Can you detect any biases that may affect the author's choice to present or omit facts or ideas?

○ Does the author's choice of audience affect the presentation?

Authority

○ Does the author have firsthand knowledge or experience?

○ Are arguments and supports presented logically and in an easy-to-follow format?

○ Are facts and figures from reliable sources used to support the author's position when necessary?

Timeliness

○ How current is the information?

○ Has more recent work substantiated claims or provided more information that is pertinent?

○ Are the statistics or other information still relevant?

sic industry moguls, or legal experts to support your arguments—or to help you (and your readers) understand any opposing viewpoints. On the other hand, merely including information about how much (or little) money musicians earn is *not* relevant unless you compare that information with what they would have earned if the music were purchased instead of downloaded.

Never include sources in your project simply to pad your bibliography. Choose sources carefully; push yourself to learn more, and be prepared when necessary to reconsider your approach. Often you will need to reconsider your entire hypothesis.

10b Consider the purpose and bias of a source

10.2

The value of a source will depend both on its trustworthiness and on the uses you intend to make of it. If you were writing a report on the official positions taken by the two major political parties in a past presidential election, you'd probably depend on scholarly books and articles published by reputable writers and on newspaper accounts archived in the library. But if you were developing a project about a current political campaign, you might examine less scholarly materials, such as the candidates' Web sites. You could also conduct interviews or cite polls. Such sources, of course, need to be approached with caution: the Web site for a candidate running for office intends to convince readers to vote for the candidate. It is likely such a site would omit information that would make the candidate appear in a less than stellar light.

10.3

Of course, not all biases are as easy to detect. Almost all sources have points of view that shape the information they include (and determine what they exclude). Even cold facts and hard figures can be interpreted in various ways. We've summarized some of the features you will want to consider in the chart on pages 112–113, but our guidelines should be taken with the understanding that any single source can differ from these characterizations.

10c Consider the authority and reputation of a source

10.4

You'll soon recognize the names of important scholars and key works on your topic because you will find them cited repeatedly in other works. If you haven't included these sources in your own collection of data, then your research is incomplete. Don't rely only on someone else's summary of the ideas or arguments they contain—track them down and determine their usefulness for yourself.

Consider, too, the types of sources you have gathered. The chart on pages 112–113 lists some of the key features of sources you might consider. Make sure the types of sources you use match the needs of your readers, your topic, and, of course, your own purpose. Which types of sources are your readers most likely to find convincing?

Sometimes you can find clues to the authority of a source outside the work itself. For printed sources, the title page or book jacket gives important information: a university press such as Columbia University Press or Oxford University Press will probably wield more authority than a trade press that targets a popular market (see Section 10b). Yet no single press or place of publication is ideal for all subjects. Authorities on extreme sports or fashion are more likely to write for monthly magazines than for Harvard University Press. Even a comic book or a video game might be an authoritative source for a project on popular culture.

Establishing the authority of online sources can be more of a challenge. Virtually anyone can become a "published" author on the Web without the benefit of comments from editors, corrections from fact checkers, or advice from reviewers. However, the Web does offer a kind of book jacket: the *domain name*. The domain name is usually the first part of an Internet address (called the *uniform resource locator*, or URL), and it can provide important clues to the location of the author (and hence perhaps to her or his authority). The URL itself breaks down into specific parts: the type of protocol used to access the resource, the domain name where the file resides, any directories and/or subdirectories, and the file name and type.

The following table illustrates how three URLs break down into their component parts.

http://www.cas.usf.edu/english/walker/mla.html

http://www.m-w.com

http://www.ibm.com/ibm/ibmgives/grant/grantapp.shtml

Protocol	Domain	Directory	Subdirectories	File	File Type
http://	www.cas.usf.edu	english	walker	mla	.html
http://	www.m-w.com			(index)	(.html)
http://	www.ibm.com	ibm	ibmgives/grant	grantapp	.shtml

Generally, the domain name identifies where the information resides. A document at **http://www.cas.usf.edu** resides on the Web server (*www*) for the College of Arts and Sciences (*cas*) at the University of South Florida (*usf*), an educational institution (*edu*). The last part of the domain name gives important information about the type of site. The most common designations are these:

.com   Commercial site

.edu   Educational site

.gov   Government site

.mil   Military site

.net   Network site

.org   Organization (usually a nonprofit) site

Of course, no source is automatically credible, or even useful, merely because the domain at which it is published is an educational site, nor is a commercial site necessarily biased or useless.

There are also some tools to help you evaluate the quality of online materials. *The Argus Clearinghouse* at **http://www.clearinghouse.net** offers a collection of guides to Web sites on a wide variety of topics, along with ratings of the information contained there. You can use similar criteria to evaluate sites

CHART

Assessing Sources

Source	Purpose	Authors	Audience/ Language
Scholarly books	Advance or report new knowledge	Experts	Academic/Technical
Scholarly articles	Advance or report new knowledge	Experts	Academic/Technical
Serious books and articles	Report or summarize information	Experts or professional writers	Educated public/ Formal
Popular magazines	Report or summarize information	Professional writers or journalists	General public/ Informal
Newspapers	Report current information	Journalists	Popular/Informal
Sponsored Web sites	Varies from report information to advertise	Varies	Varies/Usually informal
Individual Web sites	Varies	Anyone	Varies/Depends
Interviews	Consult with experts	Experts	Varies/Technical to colloquial
Listservs	Discuss specific subjects	Experts to interested amateurs	Varies/Technical to colloquial
Usenet newsgroups	Discuss specific subjects	Open to everyone	Varies/Technical to colloquial
Databases	Provides searchable access to indexes, articles, or information	Varies	Varies

you find on your own. The *Librarian's Index to the Internet* at http://lii.org and *ICYouSee* at http://www.ithaca.edu/library/training/think.html are additional sites that could be useful in locating and evaluating online sources.

10d Consider the credentials of experts, authors, and sponsoring agencies

As you read about any subject, you'll pick up the names of people mentioned frequently as experts or authorities. You may even hear your instructors speak of writers who deal with your topic. When scanning a printout of potential sources, look for those familiar authors. But don't be drawn in by celebrity

Publisher or Medium	Reviewed/ Documented?	Current/ Stable?	Dialogic/ Interactive?
University or scholarly press	Yes/Yes	No/Yes	No/No
Scholarly or professional journal	Yes/Yes	Usually no/Yes	No/No (unless online)
Commercial publishers	Yes/Not usually	Depends on subject/ Yes	No/No (unless online)
Commercial publishers	Yes/No	Yes/Yes	No/No (unless online)
Commercial press or online	Yes/No	Yes/Yes	No/No (unless online)
Online WWW/ Commercial sponsor	Sometimes/ Links to other sites	Yes, if regularly updated/Sometimes	Sometimes/Often
Online WWW	Usually no/ Links to other sites	Varies/Varies	Sometimes/ Sometimes
Notes, recordings, email	No/No	Yes/No	Yes/Yes
Online email	Not usually/No	Yes/Sometimes	Yes/Yes
Online email	Not usually/No	Yes/Sometimes	Yes/Yes
Commercial publishers; electronic	Yes/Usually	Usually/Usually	No/Usually

alone, particularly when the names of famous people are linked to subjects about which they may have no special expertise.

With Web sites, listservs, and other online materials, you may find yourself in a quandary about the credentials of your "authors." When you report factual information from such sources, you will usually want to confirm those facts with additional sources. (Reporting opinion is a different matter.) On personal Web sites, check the credentials that writers claim for themselves. When Web authors offer email addresses, you can follow up their claims with a one-on-one exchange, asking for the sources they used to support claims on their pages.

Some electronic information is sponsored by agencies you already trust in print environments. Acquiring information online from Reuters News Service or *USA Today* is *almost* equivalent to seeing the same information in print. On

10.5

FOCUS ON . . . **Evaluating Web Sites**

One advantage of conducting research online is that you may find sources not available in library collections, and thereby you give your work a fresh perspective. You will need to apply careful critical reading skills to determine the logic, validity, and bias of the information before including it in your own work. You might decide, for example, that the *Boycott-RIAA* Web site at **http://www.boycott-riaa.com** is too strongly biased in favor of MP3 file sharing and against the RIAA. A more objective source might work better with your readers.

Links in Web documents should be easy to follow. Navigational aids and transitional statements should guide readers through arguments, and sources should be documented so that users can verify the claims presented or find additional information. Authors or author affiliations (for example, a sponsoring organization such as a news service, an educational institution, or a corporation) should be clearly designated, along with the date of publication or last revision of the site.

When considering information from online sources, ask yourself these questions:

- Is the site sponsored by a reputable group you can identify?
- Do the authors of the site give evidence of their credentials?
- Is the site conveniently searchable?
- Is the site easy to navigate?
- Does the site provide an email address where you might send questions?
- Is the site updated regularly or properly maintained?
- Does the site archive older information?
- Is the content of the site affected by commercial sponsorship?

the other hand, books, magazines, or Web sites published by commercial organizations may need to be approached with caution. That means you should remain sensitive to issues that apply to any source: questions of purpose, timeliness, and completeness, as well as the credentials of the author.

10e Consider the timeliness and stability of a source

10.6

Timeliness is relative. You will want your projects to be supported by the most current and reputable information in a field, but your instructors and librarians may also point you to classic pieces that have shaped thinking in your topic area. For many college papers you should have a mix of sources—some from the past, some quite recent.

Not every site you visit will provide dates of publication. You'll want to check, though, since the Web is full of outdated sites, posted and largely forgotten by their authors; approach such sites with caution. Currency is less a factor in listservs, Usenet groups, and other email postings because the turnover of material is rapid, changing from day to day. That also means that something you read today may be gone tomorrow—or sooner. Many researchers prefer to use material from sites that archive their postings so that the information will continue to be available.

Web sites pose similar problems. Some sponsored sites enable you to search their archives for past stories or postings, but those archives may not be complete or may not go back many years. We are a long way from having electronic sources that are as stable, comprehensive, and dependable over the long run as printed books and articles. At the same time, you cannot ignore important information online merely because it may not be permanently available.

One more note about timeliness: if you are researching a topic that is currently in the news or that has been the focus of a lot of attention over the past several years—genetic engineering, online file sharing, or terrorism, for example—make certain that you draw as much of your information as possible from up-to-date sources. If you want to sound well-informed, you'll need to be aware of—and ready to discuss—the most recent developments and innovations in the field.

10f Consider how well a source presents key information

A well-designed Web site identifies its purpose clearly, arranges information logically, uses graphics wisely, furnishes relevant and selective links to other responsible resources, and provides basic bibliographical information: the identity and email address of the author or sponsor, the date of the posting, the date of the most recent update, and so on. Yet standards for Web documentation are still developing. You cannot automatically discount a site that does not include this information, for an author's authority is not solely dependent on his or her knowledge of technology and the constraints of electronic publishing, but you will need to consider what a lack of documentation may mean to your research.

10.7

The design of a source is probably of greater concern with Web sites than with printed books and articles, for which the conventions were established years ago. But print sources are "designed" as well, as you'll learn about in more detail in Part V.

10g Consider commercial intrusions into a source

Books today rarely contain advertising, and we are accustomed to dealing with ads in print magazines. But commercial intrusion into Web sites is growing enough to warrant our concern when assessing resources. Sponsored Web sites—especially search engines—are often so thick with commercial appeals that they can be difficult to use. Moreover, your search itself may bring up specific advertising messages in an effort to direct you to a sponsor's material. No library catalog ever exerted this kind of pressure.

Sponsored sites may also reflect the commercial connections of their owners, especially when news organizations are owned by larger companies with commercial interests. What appears—or doesn't appear—on a site may be determined by who is paying for the message. You shouldn't automatically discount commercially sponsored sites, but you should consider how advertising may affect the information you find and what effect using information from these sources will have on your reader's evaluation of your own credibility.

10h Consult librarians and instructors

Librarians and instructors can help you assess the quality or appropriateness of a source. They have the expertise to cut right through a long list of references to suggest the three or four you should not miss. Those leads will often enable you to make subsequent judgments on your own.

Librarians and instructors may even correct biases in your own research strategies, directing you to sources you might have avoided or considered suspect. And they may suggest solutions to problems you are having with experiments, interviews, or statistical sampling.

10i Conduct interviews

Interviews with authorities are important sources of information, both the questions you ask and the answers you receive. Interviews can be especially useful in obtaining personal opinions and insights. The opinion of a musician about the harm caused by MP3 downloading, for instance, would carry more weight than the opinion of a student; however, the student's opinion might provide an important point of view that needs to be considered as well. The information you gather from interviews will be useful to the extent that you have carefully selected interviewees to suit your purpose, carefully chosen your questions, and carefully recorded the responses. See Chapter 7 for more on conducting effective interviews.

10j Consult listservs and Usenet groups

A *listserv* is a program that allows a group of people who subscribe to the list to have extended email conversations about their ideas and their research. If you join a group germane to your subject, you can quickly learn a great deal about the nature of current interests and debate. However, listservs have all the advantages and disadvantages of any extended conversation: participants may vary widely in what they know; facts and figures may be reported unreliably; the credentials of participants may not be well known.

A Usenet group works like a listserv except that you need not subscribe to the list either to read its messages or to participate in the discussion. Anyone with access to the Internet can participate in any of the thousands of Usenet groups. As you might guess, these groups are often more valuable for what they reveal about the range and depth of feeling on a subject than for any information you may find there. You'll have reasons to cite Usenet discussions in some projects, but you'll need to use these materials with caution because you cannot confirm their credibility.

As you locate information, you will want to take careful notes and record summaries of the information contained in them, along with your responses or questions that the material raises that you will want to find answers to. Chapter 11 presents useful strategies for annotating sources to help make your research efforts more productive.

WWW Web Sites Worth Knowing

- "Critically Analyzing Information Sources,"
  http://www.library.cornell.edu/okuref/research/skill26.htm
- "Critically Analyzing Information Sources,"
  http://www.library.cornell.edu/olinuris/ref/research/skill26.htm
- *The Good, the Bad, and the Ugly: OR Why It's a Good Idea to Evaluate Web Sources,*
  http://lib.nmsu.edu/instruction/eval.html
- "Thinking Critically About World Wide Web Resources,"
  http://www.library.ucla.edu/libraries/college/help/critical/index.htm

10.8

MANAGING YOUR PROJECT

1. As you recall your preliminary reading and scan your preliminary bibliography, do certain names stand out—people of authority on your subject whose names are cited often? Find out all you can about these authors. Be sure they are cited for the right reasons, and check what they have to say about your topic.

2. For each source, answer any of the following questions that apply.

   - Is the source appropriately timely? Would a more recent source be more up-to-date or less reflective?
   - Is this a source a reader will be able to locate reliably? If not, can you still afford to use it?
   - What are the biases of this source? How should you adjust your reading of the source to account for the bias? How will you describe the bias to readers?
   - How does the source present its information? Does the author cite sources and provide evidence for all assertions? Is the presentation clear and well organized?

CHAPTER 11

Reading and Annotating Sources

Imagine you have a distant great-granduncle who dies and wills you a map to the legendary Lost Dutchman's gold mine. You know the mine contains millions and millions of dollars' worth of gold ore. Yahoo! You're rich! Well, no, you're not, because no matter how much gold the mine might contain, it's only a hole in the ground until you get in there and start digging for nuggets. Research is like that too. Once you have collected print and online sources and evaluated them for timeliness, reliability, authority, and usefulness, you can take full advantage of the riches they offer only by mining them for nuggets of information. One way to do that is to *annotate* the material you've gathered— that is, to attach comments, questions, and reactions to it. Some instructors refer to this process as *critical reading*—not just accepting information at face value but always questioning it, looking for biases, and thinking about how credible the evidence is. Most important, annotation focuses you on this question: How does this information relate to my research question or affect my hypothesis?

Annotation is not an option when you are reading library books and materials; it is irresponsible to mark up books and magazines that do not belong to you—that would be a form of vandalism for which you could be prosecuted. When responding to library texts, you will want to record your reactions in notes, summaries, and paraphrases (see Chapter 13). Much research material today is also photocopied, downloaded, or read online—and these media support different forms of annotation.

The annotations you make while reading critically have a distinctly different rhetorical purpose from those you made in your annotated bibliography (see Section 8c). In an annotated bibliography your notes *capture* the substance of an entire text briefly yet as accurately as possible. Critical reading annotations, on the other hand, *expand* the text you are reading by adding your own responses and making connections to other texts.

11a Highlight key information

Many researchers use highlighting pens to tag important passages, but sometimes their highlighting is both too frequent and too random to be useful. If you underscore every passage that strikes you as interesting, you will end up with pages glowing pointlessly with color. Use color chiefly to help you locate material you intend to use later. Consider these strategies:

- Highlight sentences you expect to quote directly. Potential quotations should be *very* limited in number. Give attention to other interesting information in your notes or with marginal comments.
- Highlight important dates, facts, and figures that you might have difficulty locating later. Such highlighting can be smart when you're dealing with especially dense passages of prose.
- Highlight sentences that might contain a thesis or an important summary of the piece. Such sentences should be relatively rare. Don't merely highlight the topic sentences of paragraphs.
- Highlight key names or sources you might wish to consult later.
- Never mark a text that is not your own property.

11b Use marginal comments to start a dialogue with your sources

A marginal comment is a more powerful tool for critical reading than a highlight. A comment responds actively to texts; it doesn't just point out what someone has said.

Record your reactions to the materials you are reading, either on paper, note cards, or directly into a word processor, carefully noting the source you're responding to (see Chapter 19). You can also use the annotation features of word-processing programs to record your reactions to files you download to your computer. Even pages from the World Wide Web can be marked with comments and, in some cases, annotated as part of an ongoing online discussion.

The following guidelines can help you as you think about when and how to add marginal comments.

WRITE A MARGINAL COMMENT WHEN YOU WANT TO . . .

Critique the author's arguments.

Point out any facts, evidence, or positions that the author is *not* including.

Reflect on the author's rhetorical strategy.

Point out the author's use of significant facts or details to build credibility.

Indicate important shifts in the author's position or arguments.

Identify when the author is using humor or irony or some other stylistic device to affect readers.

Record your personal reactions to what the author is saying.

The following sample shows how a source (an unsigned editorial from *Broadcast Engineering* magazine) might be annotated in its margins.

As you read and make your annotations, you are assessing the author's position on your subject as well as her or his credibility and authority. Does the author agree with your views, disagree with them, or fall somewhere in the middle? Is the author an expert in the field or someone expressing a personal opinion? The answers to these questions will be central when you decide how to *use* sources in your research project, and that is the topic of our next chapter.

File Sharing Is Not Threat to Music Sales

April 12, 2004

http://broadcastengineering.com/new/
  broadcasting_file_sharing_not

Internet music piracy has no negative, according to a study released last week by two university researchers.[1] This contradicts the music industry's assertion that the illegal downloading of music online is taking a big bite out of its bottom line.

[1] No negative? That doesn't seem to fit with what is said later about "niche" music.

Songs that were heavily downloaded showed no measurable drop in sales, the researchers found after tracking sales of 680 albums over the course of 17 weeks in the second half of 2002. Matching that data with activity on the OpenNap file-sharing network, they concluded that file sharing actually increases CD sales for hot albums that sell more than 600,000 copies.[2] For every 150 downloads of a song from those albums, sales increase by a copy, the researchers found.

[2] Interesting statistic that seems to run counter to "common sense." If true, that could be a striking way to begin my paper.

"Consumption of music increases dramatically with the introduction of file sharing, but not everybody who likes to listen to music was a music customer before, so it's very important to separate the two," said Felix Oberholzer-Gee, an associate professor at Harvard Business School and one of the authors of the study.[3] The results were reported by *The Washington Post*.

[3] His position as a Harvard business professor makes him a pretty reliable source.

Oberholzer-Gee and his colleague, University of North Carolina's Koleman Strumpf, also said that their "most pessimistic" statistical model showed that illegal file sharing would have accounted for only 2 million fewer CD sales in 2002, whereas CD sales declined by 139 million units between 2000 and 2002.[4]

"From a statistical point of view, what this means is that there is no effect between downloading and sales," said Oberholzer-Gee.

For albums that fail to sell well, the Internet may contribute to declining sales. Oberholzer-Gee and Strumpf found that albums that sell to niche audiences suffer a "small negative effect" from Internet piracy.[5]

The study stands in opposition to the recording industry's long-held assertion that the rise of illegal file sharing is a major cause of declining music sales over the past few years. In making its case, the Recording Industry Association of America (RIAA) points to data showing that CD sales fell from a high of more than $13.2 billion in 2000 to $11.2 billion in 2003—a period that matches the growth of various online music piracy services.[6]

Wayne Rosso, president of the Madrid-based file-sharing company Optisoft, said he hoped the study would spur the RIAA to abandon litigation and look for ways to commercialize file sharing. "There's no question that there is a market there that could easily be commercialized, and we have been trying for years to talk sense to these people and make them see that," he said. Rosso formerly ran the Grokster file-sharing service.[7]

Eric Garland, chief executive of Big Champagne, an Atlanta company that tracks file-sharing activity, said the findings match what his company has observed about the effect of file sharing on music sales. Although the practice cannibalizes some sales, it may promote others by serving as a marketing tool, Garland said.

[4] This is a great contrast; what could account for the remaining drop of 137 million CDs?

[5] Small-market bands would still be hurt by downloading. Aren't there other sources that say file sharing helps them? What's the real story here?

[6] The decline in sales matches an increase in file sharing piracy? Could this be a coincidence?

[7] This person's connection to Grokster may make him a biased source, so his statement may be suspect.

FIGURE 11.1 Sample article on file sharing with annotations.

WWW Web Sites Worth Knowing

- "7 Critical Reading Strategies," http://www.salisbury.edu/students/counseling/New/7_critical_reading_strategies.htm
- "Critical Thinking—Critical Reading" (*Power Point* slide show), http://www.kcmetro.cc.mo.us/longview/ctac/powerpoint/ct.ppt
- "Annotation and Critical Reading" (*Acrobat* document), http://www3.uark.edu/qwct/resources/handouts/37%20Annotation%20and%20Critical%20Reading.pdf

11.2

MANAGING YOUR PROJECT

1. If you prefer highlighter pens for marking sources, highlight only those passages or bits of information you need to find quickly or cannot afford to lose when you come to assemble your project or write your paper.

2. Annotate in the margins of photocopied material carefully. Record your responses, whether you agree with your sources or find yourself doubting what you read. You may well want to read both ways, what the scholar Peter Elbow describes as "believing and doubting."

3. Review your note-taking process carefully at this stage. Are the methods you are employing working? Are you keeping track of your sources and your comments on them? Modify any procedures that are not working now, before you get deeper into your project.

CHAPTER 12

Reviewing and Positioning Sources

Every election season, politicians everywhere accuse their opponents of "waffling" on issues, changing opinions so often it's hard to figure out where they stand. For the most part, these accusations are untrue and just another ploy to sway voter opinion. But the tactic is sometimes successful and underlies the importance of having a clear position supported by the best evidence. As you gather or create materials for a project, therefore, you will need to review them critically in terms of your research question or hypothesis (see Chapter 4). To incorporate any material into your research effort, you must understand its impact on your work. Does source material or the data you generate advance your argument or undermine it? Does it fill a hole in your background information or raise new questions? Does it change or validate your opinion? Read and respond to research materials carefully, thinking deeply about their implications and ideas.

When you review and position sources, you're thinking about three things in particular: *what* your sources have to say, how *credible* the information is, and how well it *fits* with your research query or hypothesis. Reviewing and positioning are activities that are chiefly concerned with how source materials extend, clarify, or otherwise affect *your* arguments and ideas.

12a Review data and resources critically

Skimming materials may make sense when you are browsing a subject early in the research process, but (as you learned in Chapters 10 and 11) your subsequent research requires careful, *critical* reading. You can learn a lot about a source by asking the questions in Checklist 12.1. (For more on determining the authority of print and online sources, see Chapter 10.)

CHECKLIST 12.1

> **Critical Review of Data and Resources**

Ask yourself about your own research methods.

○ Are my findings valid and repeatable?

○ Was I careful not to skew my methods to generate data favorable to my thesis or hypothesis?

○ Was I careful to incorporate a variety of perspectives into my research or reading?

Question all facts and figures you encounter in your sources.

○ Do the authors have firsthand knowledge or experience of their subject matter?

○ Are all critical claims adequately documented?

○ Do my sources appeal to logic, or do they make unwarranted appeals to emotions?

○ If facts and figures are presented, where did they come from?

○ Are the figures presented in a biased way? Could the figures be used to support different arguments?

○ Can controversial facts and figures be verified by other sources?

Consider carefully the sources included in bibliographies.

○ Are the references used authoritative?

○ Does the author include references to works that might disagree with his or her point of view?

○ Are the facts and figures presented in the work from reliable and diverse sources?

WWW
12.1

12b Position your research materials

After you've decided that source materials or data are appropriate and reliable, you'll want to "position" them within your project to identify their perspectives and biases. Where do they fit in your project? Do the sources support your arguments, provide examples or definitions, or represent opposing viewpoints you need to consider?

Sources often reflect generational, political, social, and economic biases and attitudes (see Chapter 10). Differences of gender, religion, or worldview may shape the materials you gather in ways that bear on your research. Even the methods used in creating the source material will influence how you present them: Was a survey scientific? Was a study sponsored by a group with a

---

FOCUS ON . . . **Balanced Arguments**

Readers are a lot more likely to accept your position on an issue if you can show them that you've considered alternative points of view fairly. An argument in favor of MP3 file sharing, for example, will be much more persuasive if you consider the arguments of those who hold a different point of view. If you include comments from the Electronic Frontier Foundation on the pro-MP3 side, include anti-MP3 comments from the Recording Industry Association of America as well. But make sure the sources you include on both sides are equally valid, reliable, and credible. A comment posted on the *alt.i-hate.the-riaa* newsgroup (which really exists) will not stand up well against an official document posted on the Web site of a large organization.

---

stake in its outcome? Does a document you cite represent a person's carefully considered judgment, or is it a paid endorsement, a political creed, or a parody?

The answers to such questions will help you define how to use sources responsibly. You owe it to readers to be honest with information and to share what you learn about your sources when that information affects your conclusions. When an expert who provides statistics in support of nationalized health care is a scholar at a liberal think tank, you and your readers should know; if a columnist you quote as supporting a flat tax proposal is wealthy enough to benefit significantly from the policy change, that's relevant information. The Web sites in Figure 12.1 are positioned in ways that reflect their origins as well as their political biases.

Keep an eye on the positional balance of the articles and Web sites you collect. If you realize that many of them lean overwhelmingly in one direction, you might want to refocus your research strategy to find information that presents alternative points of view. One of the most effective strategies for persuading an audience to see things your way is to show you have made an effort to be fair, to be open to a range of possibilities. If your readers sense that you're overlooking important points or not giving other perspectives a fair shake, your arguments will lose much of their persuasive force.

Figure 12.2 shows how a short article might be positioned. Your own efforts to position a source might be much less formal than this, but the example should help you formulate the questions you need to ask in order to appreciate what a source is and does.

Mother Jones at http://www.motherjones.com appeals to a predominantly left-of-center readership concerned with issues of social justice. You might discover its point of view quickly by clicking the "About Us" link.

The titles of articles in *National Review Online* at http://www.nationalreview.com might suggest its right-of-center politics. Or you might recognize the names of some of its authors.

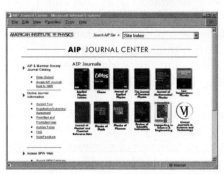

The American Institute of Physics publishes a dozen specialized journals, described at http://www.aip.org/ojs/service.html. The titles of journals such as *Chaos* or *Physics of Fluids* will quickly reveal the journals' academic orientation. (Reprinted with permission. Copyright 2002, American Institute of Physics (AIP).)

FIGURE 12.1 Positioning Web sites.

Music Industry Hits Wrong Note Against Piracy

Peter K. Yu

This past week, the Record Industry Association of America filed 261 law-suits against individuals who downloaded music illegally via peer-to-peer file-sharing networks, such as KaZaA, Grokster, iMesh and Gnutella. Unlike what the industry did a few months ago, it offered carrots in addition to sticks this time. Along with the lawsuits came a new amnesty program that allows individuals to avoid lawsuits from the RIAA if they remove all illegal music files from their computers and promise not to [download illegally] again.

On its surface, the new program is quite attractive and creative. In reality, it represents another ineffective, costly and disturbing attempt to fight the copyright wars.

The most egregious offenders would [be] unlikely [to] participate in the program. Many of them don't think what they are doing is illegal. Nor do they feel guilty about what they have done. The RIAA will end up with a list of only mild, and perhaps occasional, offenders. The list is far from what the industry wants.

There are other problems as well. First, the music industry is not the only copyright holder out there that can go after illegal file swappers. There are other equally powerful industries, like the movie and software industries. The amnesty program also would not protect individuals from federal prose-cutors, music publishers and independent labels not represented by the RIAA. A "clean slate" with the recording industry group is not very clean if many others can sue you the next day.

. . .

So what's wrong with going after shoplifters? First, copyright law is not as clear as laws against theft and shoplifting. There are a lot of "muddy" rules, like the fair use privilege, the first sale doctrine and various statutory exemp-tions that allow people to have limited sharing of copyrighted works.

In addition, there are better alternatives. In Europe, many countries im-pose taxes on blank recording media and equipment to compensate com-posers and authors whose works have been copied without authorization. And proposals are on the table that call for a compulsory licensing scheme and campus-wide licenses in universities.

Lawsuits are not necessarily the best and most effective way to deal with online piracy. In the meantime, file swappers might want to consult their lawyers and "plead the fifth."

FIGURE 12.2 Sample of a short article.
Source: From the Detroit News, *September 14, 2003.*

POSITIONING

"Music Industry Hits Wrong Note Against Piracy" is an editorial that appeared in the Entertainment section of the Detroit News on September 14, 2003. It was written by Peter K. Yu, the founding director of the Intellectual Property and Communications Law Program at Michigan State University-DCL College of Law. The author's position as a law professor specializing in intellectual property issues makes him a credible authority on music file sharing, and the tone he takes in the editorial is logical and reasonable. The editorial page of the Detroit News seems evenly balanced between liberal and conservative views, though it's possible that the music industry's strong presence in Detroit (Motown) might predispose readers against file sharing. This article was accessed on July 8, 2004, at http://www.detnews.com/2003/editorial/0309/14/a13-269781.htm.

CHECKLIST 12.2

Positioning Your Sources

- ○ What are the background and interests of the author(s)?
- ○ What are the interests and biases of the publisher?
- ○ Does the source purport to be objective and/or scientific?
- ○ Does the source present itself as subjective and/or personal?
- ○ Whose interests does the source represent?
- ○ Whose interests does the source seem to ignore?
- ○ What do readers need to know about the source?

As you can see, positioning is more than deciding which side of an argument a piece of writing falls on. You have to assess an author's background and expertise as well as a publication's potential editorial bias. Good research means not always believing everything you read or taking information at face value, even when you agree with it.

12.2

As you annotate, review, and position your sources, you will always be on the lookout for ways to bring information *from* those sources into your own project. One easy way of doing this is by summarizing important points or paraphrasing what other writers have had to say. Using summary and paraphrase wisely can be complicated, however; Chapter 13 reviews guidelines to keep in mind as you proceed. A sample annotated bibliography with positioning information and sample quotations is included in Chapter 14.

WWW Web Sites Worth Knowing

- The Gale Group, *Bibliographic Instruction Support Program,* "Content Positioning," http://www.galegroup.com/customer_service/alise/content_position.htm
- Purdue University OWL, "Evaluating Content in the Source," http://owl.english.purdue.edu/handouts/research/r_evalsource3.html
- The Writing Center at Colorado State University, "Using Outside Sources in Your Writing," http://writing.colostate.edu/references/sources/working/index.cfm

12.3

MANAGING YOUR PROJECT

1. After you have assembled a working bibliography (see Section 8b), use Checklist 12.2 to position your major sources, describing, as best you can, the research context of the materials. Who is offering the material? What are their points of view and biases?

2. After positioning your sources, check that they are sufficiently diverse. If all your sources reflect the same perspectives, come from the same publishers, and show similar biases, you may need to expand your preliminary bibliography.

3. Position yourself within your project. What assumptions and biases do you bring to the material? Is your work influenced by a particular social, ethnic, religious, sexual, or political orientation? What experiences or training directed you toward this inquiry? To help you position yourself, think about how someone outside the project might view you.

4. Assess what you have learned from positioning your sources and methods. You may discover that the mainstream research in a field reflects selected interests or points of view. Or certain ideas or voices may be ignored while others receive unexpected emphasis. Consider why this may be so. Are the possible reasons institutional, political, cultural, economic? Ponder this information and use it as you see fit in your own treatment of the research materials.

CHAPTER 13

Summarizing and Paraphrasing Sources

Why bother taking detailed notes today when you can mark up copies of actual sources or download the texts and images you want? Because you're far more likely to understand sources when you have read them carefully enough to put their claims into your own words. In moving from reading to writing, you also demonstrate how well you understand key concepts in research materials. Even more important, you help your readers better understand how sources connect with your own ideas when you include summaries or paraphrases of your sources.

13a Choose whether to summarize or paraphrase a source

Summarizing and paraphrasing are far more active processes than scribbling comments in margins or sweeping photocopied texts with highlighter pens—although both techniques may help you (see Chapter 11). Your choice of summary or paraphrase will be determined by both the source and the use you intend to make of it.

A *summary* captures the gist of a source or some portion of it, boiling it down to a few words or sentences. Summaries tend to be short, extracting only what is immediately relevant from a source and highlighting key concepts. The summary should make sense on its own—as a complete statement you might use later in your project itself. Don't be surprised if you try out several versions of that statement before you come up with one that satisfies you.

You might also want to summarize the main idea of articles from which you plan to use important facts and figures, information, or direct quotations in order to position these materials (see Chapter 12) and connect them to your own ideas.

FOCUS ON . . . Summaries and Paraphrases

The most dangerous and academically dishonest sort of summary or paraphrase is one in which a researcher borrows the ideas, structure, and details of a source wholesale, changing a few words here and there in order to claim originality. This sort of borrowing is considered plagiarism even if the material is documented in the research project. Writers can't just change a few words in their sources and claim the resulting material as their own work. Make sure that the words you use are truly your own.

When an article is quite long, you might look for topic ideas in each major section. If you have a photocopy of the source, highlight sentences that state or emphasize key themes. Then assemble these ideas into a short, coherent statement—in your own words—about the whole piece. You may also need to summarize the key idea or concept depicted in visuals (tables, charts, graphics) to ensure that your reader understands the information depicted in the way that you intend. (For more on including visual components in your project, see Part V.)

A *paraphrase* reviews a complete source in much greater detail than a summary, recording both important ideas and supporting details. When paraphrasing a work, you report its key information or restate its core arguments point by point *in your own words.* You will typically want to paraphrase any materials that provide specific facts or ideas your readers will need. Predictably, paraphrases run much longer than summaries, often as long as or even longer than the original.

WWW
13.1

Paraphrases generally follow the same structure as the original source, and often they include details or supporting evidence in addition to arguments. As in summaries, material that is paraphrased must be cited and connected to your own ideas (see Section 13c).

13b Summarize sources effectively

In Chapter 12 we read Peter Yu's editorial "Music Industry Hits Wrong Note Against Piracy" with an eye to positioning it rhetorically. In this section we will refer to the same article (page 127) to frame our discussion of summary and paraphrase.

You might begin by highlighting and annotating the information most relevant to your project (in this case, focused on the research question, "Should MP3 downloading be regulated?").

Next you would assemble the key claim and supporting elements into a concise restatement of the overall argument.

EFFECTIVE SUMMARY

Peter Yu, the director of the Intellectual Property Communications Law Program at the Michigan State University--DCL College of Law, argues that even though the new amnesty program offered by the RIAA looks attractive on the surface, it is likely to be ineffective. The worst copyright violators probably won't participate, and there's no guarantee that downloaders who take advantage of the offer won't be sued by parties other than the RIAA. A better solution might be taxes on recording media.

How can something as simple as a summary go wrong? In a number of ways. You might make the summary too succinct and leave out crucial details; a summary scribbled on a note card might be useless when you try to make sense of it days later.

INEFFECTIVE SUMMARY

RIAA proposal won't work. 261 lawsuits. Worst ones will leave it alone. Get sued anyway. Don't think it's illegal. More taxes.

Or your summary might fail because it misses the central point of a piece by focusing on details that don't capture the substance of what the author wrote.

INACCURATE SUMMARY

Peter Yu, director of the Intellectual Property and Communications Law Program at the Michigan State University--DCL College of Law, writes in the Detroit News (14 Sept. 2003) that copyright law is too "muddy" for any regulation to work effectively.

Yet another danger is that you might use the actual words of the original author in your summary. If unacknowledged borrowings make their way into your project without both quotation marks and documentation, you would be guilty of plagiarism (see Chapter 9). In the following example, language taken directly and inappropriately from Roland's editorial is boldfaced.

PLAGIARIZED SUMMARY

Peter Yu, the director of the Intellectual Property Communications Law Program at the Michigan State University--DCL College of Law, writes in the Detroit News (14 Sept. 2003) that the RIAA's amnesty program **represents another ineffective, costly and disturbing attempt to fight the copyright wars.** The amnesty program **would not protect individuals from federal prosecutors, music publishers and independent labels not represented by the RIAA.**

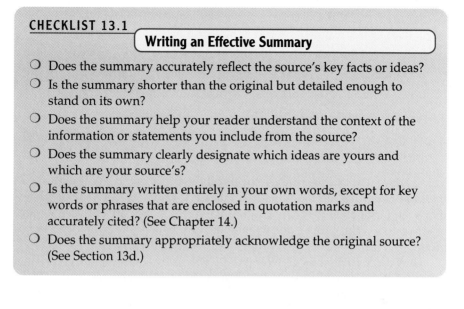

CHECKLIST 13.1

Writing an Effective Summary

○ Does the summary accurately reflect the source's key facts or ideas?

○ Is the summary shorter than the original but detailed enough to stand on its own?

○ Does the summary help your reader understand the context of the information or statements you include from the source?

○ Does the summary clearly designate which ideas are yours and which are your source's?

○ Is the summary written entirely in your own words, except for key words or phrases that are enclosed in quotation marks and accurately cited? (See Chapter 14.)

○ Does the summary appropriately acknowledge the original source? (See Section 13d.)

You can appreciate how tempting it might be to slip the plagiarized words from this summary into the body of a paper or project, forgetting that you didn't write them yourself. To avoid plagiarism, the safest practice is *always* to use your own words in summaries. Checklist 13.1 will help you write an effective summary.

13c Paraphrase sources effectively

A paraphrase of "Music Industry Hits Wrong Note Against Piracy" (page 127) would be appreciably longer than a summary because a researcher would expect to use the information differently, probably wanting to refer to the source in greater detail. Paraphrases are useful in your paper or project to help readers understand key sources or complicated ideas. Here's one possible paraphrase of the editorial.

EFFECTIVE PARAPHRASE

Peter Yu, director of the Intellectual Property Communications Law Program at the Michigan State University--DCL College of Law, writes in a Detroit News (14 Sept. 2003) editorial that the RIAA's recent "amnesty" proposal is seriously flawed. Even though it appears to provide an "out" to people who have downloaded music illegally, the worst offenders probably won't take the RIAA up on its offer, so it's not likely to make much of a dent in music piracy. An even worse aspect of the amnesty proposal is that it's not "true" amnesty. Downloaders could still be prosecuted at the federal level or sued by music producers who aren't RIAA members. Going after individual downloaders is inherently troublesome anyway, as copyright laws do permit people to use and share protected materials in some cases. In any event, Yu argues, there are better ways to address any monetary losses suffered by music producers, such as taxes on blank recording media and equipment. Lawsuits just don't seem to be the best solution to a complicated issue like this one.

You'll notice that this paraphrase covers all the major points in the editorial in the same order the ideas originally occurred. It also borrows none of the author's language other than a few incidental terms, which are enclosed in quotation marks. With proper documentation, any part of the paraphrase could become part of a final research project (see Sections 19e and 19d).

How can paraphrases go wrong? One way is by confusing the claims in a source with your own opinions. A paraphrase should accurately reflect the thinking of the original author, so reserve your comments and asides for annotations or other, separate notes. Consider how the following paraphrase might misreport the views of Peter Yu if the researcher later forgets that the bold-faced comments in the example are in fact personal notes and annotations.

INACCURATE PARAPHRASE

Peter Yu, director of the Intellectual Property Communications Law Program at the Michigan State University--DCL College of Law, writes in a Detroit News (14 Sept. 2003) editorial that the RIAA's recent "amnesty" proposal is seriously flawed. The RIAA is doing all it can to create a climate of fear among music downloaders. The RIAA hopes to persuade people that all music downloading is potentially illegal, and the only way to be safe is to download from RIAA-sanctioned commercial sites where you have to pay for the music. The RIAA's proposal also does not guarantee that downloaders couldn't be prosecuted by other parties like the movie or software industries, **which might lead some people to wonder whether these organizations are in collusion. What's to prevent the RIAA from making its list of amnesty applicants available to other copyright holders?**

The reactions to the editorial may be valid, but they don't represent an accurate paraphrase of the original article.

A paraphrase also should not reorganize or attempt to improve on the structure or argument of the original piece, since doing this does not accurately reflect the original and could skew the author's intended meaning. The following paraphrase doesn't add material to Yu's editorial, but it rearranges information radically.

INACCURATE PARAPHRASE

Copyright laws in this country are very complex, and it's sometimes difficult for people to know when sharing MP3 and music files is "fair use" or a violation of copyright. In an editorial for the Detroit News (14 Sept. 2003), Peter Yu argues that many people don't believe any sort of file sharing should be illegal, so they're likely to continue downloading copyrighted music on peer-to-peer networks like KaZaA and Gnutella, no matter what restrictions are imposed or what sorts of "amnesty" programs are offered. The RIAA, in fact, recently made a proposal to grant amnesty to people who had downloaded music illegally, but Yu feels that only infrequent or occasional downloaders are likely to take advantage of it. This has left the RIAA in the position of having to file individual lawsuits against the offenders it's been able to detect, 261 of them by early September 2003. Even with the amnesty program in place, movie companies, independent music producers, and others may be turning to individual lawsuits as well. This solution may not be as effective as taxes on blank recording media at reducing the financial hardships caused by file sharing, but it's the approach that the RIAA has chosen to pursue for the present, at least.

Checklist 13.2 will aid you in writing an effective paraphrase.

13d Acknowledge all borrowings

You *must* acknowledge ideas and information you take from your sources (unless you are dealing with common knowledge; see Section 19e) even though the exact words you use to express the ideas may be your own. Here are two acceptable summaries of the passage on the RIAA amnesty program that report its facts appropriately and originally. Notice that both versions include a parenthetical note acknowledging Yu as the source of information.

WWW
13.3

An editorial in the September 14, 2003, issue of the Detroit News recently argued that the RIAA's amnesty program is likely to be ineffective at reducing music piracy (Yu).

Though downloaders might hope the RIAA's program would give them a "clean slate," they will not be protected from prosecution by other media organizations or federal prosecutors (Yu).

CHECKLIST 13.2

Writing an Effective Paraphrase

○ Does the paraphrase reflect the structure of the original piece?

○ Does the paraphrase reflect the ideas of the original author, not your thoughts about them?

○ Is each important fact or direct quotation accompanied by a specific page number from the source (when possible)?

○ Is the material you record relevant to your point? (Don't waste time paraphrasing those parts that are of no use to your project.)

○ Is the paraphrase written entirely in your own words, except for clearly marked quotations?

Without documentation, both of these versions might be considered plagiarized even though only Yu's ideas—and not his actual words—are borrowed.

You are the author of your paper, and your paper should reflect *your* ideas and opinions. Don't make the mistake of patching together a paper that consists of nothing but the ideas and opinions of others, even if you summarize and paraphrase them entirely in your own words. At the same time, don't overlook the importance of including direct quotations when they are especially well phrased or when the reputation of the speaker will lend authority to your own arguments. In Chapter 14 you will learn more about handling quotations in your research project.

WWW Web Sites Worth Knowing

- University of Wisconsin–Madison Writing Center *Writer's Handbook*, "Quoting and Paraphrasing Sources," http://www.wisc.edu/writing/Handbook/QuotingSources.html

- Purdue University OWL, "Quoting, Paraphrasing, and Summarizing," http://owl.english.purdue.edu/handouts/research/r_quotprsum.html

- University of Northern British Columbia Learning Skills Centre, "Summarize, Paraphrase, or Quote?" http://www.unbc.ca/lsc/writing/Summarize,Paraphrase,orQuote.pdf

- Ohio University ESL, "Quotation, Paraphrase, Summary," http://www.ohiou.edu/esl/help/quotation.html

WWW
13.4

MANAGING YOUR PROJECT

1. Survey your working bibliography and decide which sources you expect will require full paraphrases, which ones will be handled adequately through summaries, and which ones may require a combination of approaches.

2. Using a word processor or note cards, write a summary for the sources in your working bibliography that you plan to use extensively in your project. For particularly important or complicated points, write a paraphrase of the original, including the main ideas and supporting information and following the structure of the original. Make sure you include page numbers and source information so you can accurately document the summaries and paraphrases if you use them in your project.

CHAPTER 14

Quoting Sources

Students often think of a "research paper" as one that includes multiple quotations, pasted together with a few lines of their own. And it is true that quotations can add texture and authority to your project, adding voices that confirm your positions, challenge them, or extend them.

However, including too many quotations can be distracting and ineffective—*your* voice should be the one that readers hear. This chapter will help you select and use quotations to fulfill your own rhetorical purposes.

14a Select direct quotations strategically

As much as possible, use your own words. Every quotation you include should contribute something your own words cannot. Use quotations for these purposes:

- To focus on a particularly well stated key idea in a source
- To show what others (experts, those involved with an issue, the general public) think about a subject
- To give credence to important facts or concepts
- To add color, power, or character to your argument or report
- To show a range of opinion
- To clarify a difficult or contested point
- To demonstrate the complexity of an issue
- To emphasize a point

In a project on MP3 file sharing, for example, a quotation from a scholar who has researched its economic impact on the music industry could be very powerful. It would provide useful, relevant information in a strongly authoritative voice. On the other hand, you should never use quotations to avoid putting ideas in your own words or to pad your work. A long narrative history of copyright legislation quoted directly from a source book might make your MP3 project longer, but readers would probably find it irrelevant and irritating.

You already know that you need to scrupulously acknowledge *all* borrowings from other sources: ideas, opinions, facts, and information, unless it is common knowledge (see Section 19e). Just as important, you need to make sure that your readers understand how you are using the quotations you select—what they mean in the context of your own project.

By the time you have reached this point in the research process, you should have found a substantial number of resources, kept track of their bibliographic information, positioned them carefully, and mined them for appropriate quotations and information. On individual sheets of paper or word-processed documents, you will have detailed summaries, annotations, and direct quotations such as these that you can later incorporate into a draft of your final project.

Fries, Bruce, and Marty Fries. "Digital Music and Copyright Law." *MP3*
 and Internet Audio Handbook 2000. http://teamcombooks.com/
 mp3handbook/5.htm (2 July 2004).

This site offers excerpts from a book by Bruce Fries and Marty Fries,
including a chapter on copyright law that quotes significant passages
from several recent pieces of copyright legislation verbatim (the Audio
Home Recording Act of 1992, the No Electronic Theft Act, and other parts
of U.S. Copyright Law that affect digital file sharing) and analyzes
several hypothetical cases of music "use" in terms of that legislation. This
chapter is just a prelude to the book's main focus: a step-by-step how-to
manual for creating, editing, and playing MP3 disks. Bruce Fries is an
associate of the Audio Engineering Society and founder of the media
publishing company TeamCom, so he seems to be a reliable authority to
speak about MP3s. He clearly favors MP3s as a medium and a technology,
but he also appears sensitive to the legalities of MP3 file sharing.

> "The Audio Home Recording Act protects consumers who use digital or
> analog audio recording devices to make copies of prerecorded music,
> as long as the copies are for noncommercial use. But, because
> computers are not considered recording devices, as defined by the
> Audio Home Recording Act, [rippers are] not protected by this law
> when [they rip] CDs."

> "Typically, songs are covered by two copyrights. The first is for the
> actual notes and lyrics, or what is referred to as the *musical work.*

(Continued)

Usually, copyrights on musical works are owned by the artist and his
or her publicist. The second copyright is for the artist's
interpretation of the musical work and the actual recording, referred
to as the *sound recording*."

Schultz, Jason. "File Sharing Must Be Made Legal." Electronic Frontier
Foundation. 12 Sep. 2003. http://www.eff.org/share/
20030912_jason_salon.php (1 July 2004).

This editorial, originally published on *Salon.com*, criticizes the RIAA's
move to file lawsuits against individual file sharers. The Electronic
Frontier Foundation has long been a leader in the fight against ill-
advised restrictions on the Internet, so it is unsurprising that this
editorial--with this particular position--is reproduced here. Jason
Schultz is also a staff attorney for the EFF, so he is certainly an expert
on the legal issues involved.

"A good solution will get artists paid, while protecting the privacy
and free-speech rights of fans."

"Congress could step in and force the record labels to accept file
sharing in exchange for reasonable compensation from file sharers.
This is what happened with webcasting. It is also how cable
companies and satellite companies pay for TV programming."

"Under the Digital Millennium Copyright Act (DMCA), any copyright
owner can issue a 'secret' subpoena to your ISP and force them to
reveal your name, address, e-mail, and personally identifying
information simply on the basis of a 'good-faith belief' that you are
infringing one of their copyrights."

FIGURE 14.1 Sample bibliography with positioning information and sample quotations.

14b Introduce all direct and indirect borrowings

Although quotation marks (see Section 14d) and indentions (see Section 14i)
will identify direct quotations, these typographical devices don't tell a reader
who wrote a passage, why it is important, or how it stands in relation to the rest
of an essay. And indirect borrowings (summaries, paraphrases, statistical information, graphics) have no quotation marks at all. So short introductions are

needed to orient readers to materials you've gathered from sources. To be sure readers pay attention, give all borrowed words and ideas a context or *frame*.

Frames can be relatively simple; they can precede, follow, or interrupt the borrowed words or ideas. The frame need not even be in the same sentence as the quotation—it may be part of the surrounding paragraph. Here are some ways that material can be introduced. Frames appear in boldface.

FRAME PRECEDES BORROWED MATERIAL

I wonder how often Einstein was infuriated by the phrase "Is *that* all there is to it!"

—Arthur C. Clarke

Profiles of the Future

FRAME FOLLOWS BORROWED MATERIAL

"One reason you may have more colds if you hold back tears is that, when you're under stress, your body puts out steroids which affect your immune system and reduce your resistance to disease," **Dr. Broomfield comments.**

—Barbara Lang Stern

FRAME INTERRUPTS BORROWED MATERIAL

"Your best action," **an Atomic Energy Commission booklet read,** "is not to be worried about fallout."

—Terry Tempest Williams

SURROUNDING SENTENCES FRAME BORROWED MATERIAL

Historian Charles Beard writes that most of the drafters of the Constitution viewed "democracy as something rather to be dreaded than encouraged." **Well into the nineteenth century, he insists,** "the word ["democracy"] was repeatedly used by conservatives to smear opponents of all kinds."

—Richard Shenkman

Legends, Life & Cherished Myths of American History

BORROWED MATERIAL INTEGRATED WITH PASSAGE

The study concludes that a faulty work ethic is not responsible for the decline in our productivity; quite the contrary, the study identifies "a widespread commitment among U.S. workers to improve productivity" **and suggests that** "there are large reservoirs of potential upon which management can draw to improve performance and increase productivity."

—Daniel Yankelovich

CHART

Some Verbs of Attribution

accept	argue	emphasize	reveal
add	believe	insist	say
admit	confirm	mention	state
affirm	deny	posit	think
allege	disagree	propose	verify

WWW

14.2
Borrowings in your research paper should be attributed in similar fashion. Either name (directly or indirectly) the author, the speaker, or the work the passage is from, or explain why the words you quote are significant. Many phrases of introduction or attribution are available, and they can shape significantly the way readers perceive a quotation. Verbs of attribution such as those in the above chart are more powerful than the repetition of the bland phrases "he said" and "she explained." (For more on using quotation marks correctly, see Sections 14d and 14e.)

Vary these terms sensibly; you needn't change the verb of attribution with every direct quotation.

FOCUS ON ... Quoting from Interviews

While it's relatively easy to ensure that you're quoting material accurately from print and Web sources—all you have to do is compare your quoted words with the original—it's a little more difficult to guarantee complete accuracy when you're quoting from an interview. You might not have been able to write fast enough to record someone's exact phrasing, or a tape recording you made of the interview might be noisy and garbled. Whenever you have any doubts about the accuracy of your quotation or its phrasing, you should verify it with the person you interviewed before including it in your project.

It's important to do this because sometimes even seemingly minor differences can have major consequences. In the 2004 presidential campaign, for example, candidate John Kerry said in an interview that the war in Iraq was "not a success," but two journalists subsequently wrote that Kerry had said the war was "a failure." While the two phrases may sound roughly the same, the conservative press seized on the misquotation and claimed Kerry had called American troops "failures." If you decide to quote from interview material in your own projects, you should always make sure to stay as close to the interviewee's original language and phrasing as possible.

The President of the United States **claimed** that ". . .

The members of the board **declared** that ". . .

Marva Collins **asserts**, ". . .

While you can avoid charges of plagiarism by simply naming the source of your quotation, you may need to note the author's credentials for his or her words to have the effect you desire. The sample bibliography with both positioning information and sample quotations on pages 139–140 will aid you in documenting information effectively.

In academic papers you will usually be expected to include in-text documentation (called *parenthetical citations*) when using direct and indirect quotation or other information from research materials. The format for such documentation is discussed in Section 14j.

14c Integrate graphical elements correctly

You will also need to frame your use of graphics, figures, tables, and other artwork. Usually that means referring to them in the text and summarizing the information they contain to ensure that your reader understands them in the way that you intend. Most style guides have explicit rules for labeling and citing tables, figures, and other graphical elements as well. For example, Table 14.1 is labeled above the item; the source of the information is identified under the table. In some circumstances, particularly when you want to give readers a

Table 14.1

Number of Automated Banking Machines per 1,000,000 Inhabitants

	1997	1998	1999	2000	2001
Belgium	492	564	606	657	669
Canada	652	775	873	1034	1142
France	452	490	538	580	606
Germany	505	556	563	580	603
Italy	444	487	524	549	593
Japan	924	934	944	922	918
Sweden	268	281	291	295	289

Source: Reprinted by permission of Secretariat of the Committee on Payment and Settlement Systems (CPSS), Bank for International Settlements, Basel, Switzerland, from Table 5, "Cards with a Cash Function and ATMS," in Statistics on Payments and Settlement Systems in Selected Countries, CPSS Publication No. 54 (April 2003), accessed from www.bis.org).

lot of numerical data encompassing many variables or an extended time period, it may be preferable to use a chart or graph rather than try to present all the information in a narrative or text form. Graphical elements can often demonstrate the relationships among many factors more easily and vividly than words can, but do not let graphical elements "speak for themselves." All pictures need to be introduced, and all graphics need to be explained or interpreted to make your point. Include a credit line citing the source of a graphic or include a separate listing of all graphical borrowings at the end of your paper or project. (For more information on using graphical elements, see Chapter 21.)

14d Handle quotation marks correctly

WWW

14.3

Quotation marks—which always occur in pairs—draw attention to the words, sentences, or passages they enclose. Use double quotation marks (" ") around most quoted material; use single quotation marks (' ') to mark quotations within quotations. Quotation marks are used around any material you borrow word for word from sources, even if you borrow only one particularly cogent term or a two- or three-word phrase.

Take care with the punctuation before and after quotations. A quotation introduced or followed by *said, remarked, observed*, or similar expressions takes a comma.

> Benjamin Disraeli observed, "It is much easier to be critical than to be correct."

> "Next to the originator of a good sentence is the first quoter of it," said Ralph Waldo Emerson.

Commas are used, too, when a one-sentence quotation is interrupted by a phrase.

> "If the world were a logical place," Rita Mae Brown notes, "men would ride side-saddle."

When a tag line comes between two successive sentences from a single source, a comma and period are required.

> "There is no such thing as a moral or an immoral book," says Oscar Wilde. "Books are well written, or badly written. That is all."

No punctuation is required when a quotation runs smoothly into a sentence you have written.

> Abraham Lincoln observed that "in giving freedom to the slave we assure freedom to the free."

Take care, too, to place quotation marks correctly with other marks of punctuation. Commas and periods go *inside* closing quotation marks except when a parenthetical note is given (see Part VI).

> "This must be what the sixties were like," I thought.

> Down a corridor lined with antiwar posters, I heard someone humming "Blowin' in the Wind."

When a sentence ends with in-text documentation, the period follows the parenthetical note.

> Mike Rose argues that we hurt education if we think of it "in limited or limiting ways" (3).

Colons and semicolons go *outside* closing quotation marks.

> Riley claimed to be "a human calculator": he did quadratic equations in his head.

> The young Cassius Clay bragged about being "the greatest"; his opponents in the ring soon learned he wasn't just boasting.

Question marks and exclamation points fall *inside* the closing quotation marks when they are the correct punctuation for the phrase in quotation but not for the sentence as a whole.

> When Mrs. Rattle saw her hotel room, she muttered, "Good grief!"

> She turned to her husband and said, "Do you really expect me to stay here?"

They fall *outside* the closing quotation marks when they are appropriate for the entire sentence.

> Who was it that said, "Truth is always the strongest argument"?

Quotation marks are also used to indicate dialogue. When writing a passage with several speakers, begin a new paragraph each time the speaker changes.

> Mrs. Bennet deigned not to make any reply; but unable to contain herself, began scolding one of her daughters.

> "Don't keep coughing so, Kitty, for heaven's sake! Have a little compassion on my nerves. You tear them to pieces."

> "Kitty has no discretion in her coughs," said her father; "she times them ill."

> "I do not cough for my own amusement," replied Kitty fretfully.

> —Jane Austen, *Pride and Prejudice*

14e Tailor your quotations to fit your sentences

To make quotations fit smoothly into your text, you may have to tinker with the introduction to the quotation or modify the quotation itself by careful selections, ellipses (see Section 14f), or bracketed additions (see Section 14g).

AWKWARD   The chemical capsaicin that makes chili hot: "it is so hot it is used to make antidog and antimugger sprays" (Bork 184).

REVISED   Capsaicin, the chemical that makes chili hot, is so strong "it is used to make antidog and antimugger sprays" (Bork 184).

AWKWARD   Computers have not succeeded as translators of languages because, argues Douglas Hofstadter, "nor is the difficulty caused by a lack of knowledge of idiomatic phrases. The fact is that translation involves having a mental model of the world being discussed, and manipulating symbols in the model" (603).

REVISED   "[A] lack of knowledge of idiomatic phrases" is not the reason computers have failed as translators of languages. "The fact is," says Douglas Hofstadter, "that translation involves having a mental model of the world being discussed, and manipulating symbols in the model" (603).

Take care that you do not change the context of the original or skew its meaning. There is obviously a significant difference in the meaning of these two statements:

MISLEADING   Thomas Paine argued that soldiers and patriots will "shrink from the service of their country."

REVISED   Thomas Paine argued that "[t]he summer soldier and the sunshine patriot will, in this crisis, shrink from the service of their country."

Remember, you have an obligation both to your sources and to your readers to ensure that the use you make of material from sources is ethical and accurate (see Chapter 9).

14f Use ellipses to indicate omissions

Three spaced periods (one space after each period) mark an ellipsis (. . .), omitted material in a sentence or passage. The missing material may be a word, a phrase, a complete sentence, or more.

COMPLETE	Abraham Lincoln closed his First Inaugural Address
PASSAGE	(March 4, 1861) with these words: "We are not enemies, but
	friends. We must not be enemies. Though passion may have
	strained, it must not break, our bonds of affection. The mystic
	chords of memory, stretching from every battlefield and patriot
	grave to every living heart and hearthstone all over this broad
	land, will yet swell the chorus of the Union when again touched,
	as surely they will be, by the better angels of our nature."
PASSAGE	Abraham Lincoln closed his First Inaugural Address
WITH	(March 4, 1861) with these words: "The mystic chords of memory
OMISSIONS	. . . will yet swell the chorus of the Union when again touched, as
	surely they will be, by the better angels of our nature."

Be sure to use the correct spacing and punctuation before and after ellipsis marks. When an ellipsis mark appears in the middle of a sentence, leave a space before the first and after the last period, and remember that the periods themselves are spaced.

chords of memory . . . will yet swell

If a punctuation mark occurs immediately before the ellipsis, include the mark when it makes your sentence easier to read. The punctuation mark is followed by a space, then the ellipsis mark.

We are not enemies, . . . must not be enemies

When an ellipsis occurs at the end of a complete sentence or when you delete a full sentence or more from a passage, include the period at the end of the sentence, followed by a space and then the ellipsis.

We must not be enemies. . . . The mystic chords

When an ellipsis appears at the end of a sentence or passage, the final period follows the ellipsis unless there is a parenthetical note.

"These are the times that try men's souls. The summer soldier and the sunshine patriot will, in this crisis, shrink from the service of their country. . . ." Thomas Paine is often quoted by students of U.S. history.

—Thomas Paine

When a parenthetical reference follows a sentence that ends with an ellipsis, leave a space between the last word in the sentence and the ellipsis. Then provide the parenthetical reference, followed by the closing punctuation mark.

passion may have strained it . . ." (102).

You needn't use an ellipsis, however, every time you break into a sentence. The quotation in the following passage, for example, reads more smoothly without the ellipsis.

> In fact, according to Lee Iacocca, ". . . Chrysler didn't really function like a company at all" when he arrived in 1978.

> In fact, according to Lee Iacocca, "Chrysler didn't really function like a company at all" when he arrived in 1978.

Whenever you use ellipses, be sure your shortened quotation accurately reflects the meaning of the uncut passage. It is irresponsible and dishonest to alter the meaning of a source by excising critical words or phrases.

14g Use square brackets to add necessary information to a quotation

Sometimes you may want to explain who or what a pronoun refers to, or you may have to provide a short explanation, furnish a date, or explain or translate a puzzling word. Enclose such material in square brackets: [ ].

> Some critics clearly prefer Wagner's *Tannhäuser* to *Lohengrin*: "the well-written choruses [of *Tannhäuser*] are combined with solo singing and orchestral background into long, unified musical scenes" (Grout 629).

Any change you make to material in a quotation—even changing an uppercase letter to a lowercase one or changing a mark of punctuation—must be designated by enclosing it in square brackets. But don't overdo it. Readers will resent the explanation of obvious details, and too many changes may lead the reader to question your use of the material.

14h Use *[sic]* to acknowledge errors in sources

Quotations must be copied accurately, word by word from your source— errors and all. To show that you have copied a passage faithfully, place the expression *sic* (the Latin word for "thus" or "so") in brackets one space after any mistake in the original.

> Mr. Vincent's letter went on: "I would have preferred a younger bride, but I decided to marry the old window [sic] anyway."

If *sic* can be placed outside the quotation itself, it appears between parentheses, not brackets.

> Molly's paper was titled "Understanding *King Leer*" (sic).

14i Present quotations correctly

Short quotations are arranged differently on a page than longer ones, but the exact format will depend on which documentation style you are using. MLA, APA, and Chicago styles vary slightly; be sure you follow the appropriate guidelines for the style you are using. (See Part VI for more information.)

Place prose quotations of four typed lines or fewer (MLA) or forty words or less (APA) between quotation marks.

> In "It's Only Rock 'n' Roll" (2004, May), Carrie Russell declares, "For strictly educational purposes, I would argue that the students who include copyright-protected images from the Internet in their assignments are exercising fair use" (p. 41).

Indent prose quotations longer than four typed lines (MLA) or forty words (APA). MLA form recommends an indention of ten spaces or one inch from the left-hand margin; APA form requires five spaces. (The right-hand margin is not indented.)

> Copyright law was, according to Thomas F. Cotter, a response to the new technology of the printing press:
>
> > Prior to the invention of the printing press, authors necessarily relied upon manual copyists to reproduce their works, and this technological limitation had two consequences. First, manual copying substantially limited the number of copies that could be made within a given time, which in turn made it virtually impossible for authors to earn a living from the commercial sales of their works. Second, unauthorized copying was unlikely to harm authors, since authors themselves made minimal profits from commercial sales, and unauthorized copies were just as laborious to produce as were authorized ones. (325–26)

Note that quotation marks are *not* used around indented material. If the long quotation extends beyond a single paragraph, the first lines of subsequent paragraphs are indented an additional three typed spaces (MLA) or five spaces (APA). In MLA papers, the indented material—like the rest of the essay—is always double spaced. Both APA and Chicago style permit quotations to be single spaced in student projects.

When you are quoting poetry, indent the lines if the passage runs more than three lines (MLA). Up to three lines of poetry may be handled just like a prose passage, with slashes marking the separate lines with a single space before and after each slash. Quotation marks are used when the lines are not indented.

As death approaches, Cleopatra grows in grandeur and dignity: "Husband, I
come! / Now to that name my courage prove my title! / I am fire and air"
(V.ii.287-89).

14.4

More than three lines of poetry are indented ten spaces and quotation marks
are not used. (If the lines of poetry are unusually long, you may indent fewer
than ten spaces.) Double-space the indented passage (MLA), and be sure to
copy the passage accurately, right down to the punctuation.

Among the most famous lines in English literature are those that open
William Blake's "The Tyger":

> Tyger tyger, burning bright,
>
> In the forests of the night;
>
> What immortal hand or eye,
>
> Could frame thy fearful symmetry? (1–4)

14j Document the source of all quotations

You must identify the author, work, publisher, date, and location of every direct quotation. In MLA documentation style (see Chapter 24), the parenthetical note and corresponding Works Cited entry would appear in this form.

By contrast, David Brown attributes the cause of the Titanic disaster directly
to the ship's captain: "Titanic's fatal chain of disaster always comes back to
Captain Smith's feeling of invincibility aboard his giant liner. Any danger
from the sea seemed so trivial when one stood 60 feet off the water,
surrounded by tons of steel" (11).

Works Cited

Brown, David G. The Last Log of the Titanic. Camden, ME: International
Marine/McGraw-Hill, 2001.

You must use *both* quotation marks and the parenthetical note when you
quote directly. Quotation marks alone would not tell your readers where
your source was. A note alone would acknowledge that you are using a
source, but it would not explain that some of the words in your paper are not
your own. For the same reason, providing complete references in Web documents is still necessary, even though you can (and often should) link a quotation to the original if it is available online. Online sources may move or disappear, making links inoperable (see Part V for more information). Part VI
presents more information on in-text notes and bibliographic formats for five
different styles. For other styles, you will need to consult the appropriate
guide for your discipline.

At this stage in your project, you should be well on your way through the research process. You've collected sources, found relevant information, and marshaled authoritative quotations, and you're no doubt beginning to get a sense of how all this research will fit into your developing project. Excellent! That means it's time to move on to the next phase and put your accumulated knowledge into writing. Part IV will guide you through developing your project, reflecting on what you already have, refining, organizing, drafting, documenting, and—finally—completing it.

WWW Web Sites Worth Knowing

- *Bartlett's Familiar Quotations,* http://www.bartleby.com/100
- "Big Dog's MLA Quick Guide," http://aliscot.com/bigdog/mla.htm
- "Incorporating Quotations into Sentences," http://www.wisc.edu/writing/Handbook/QuoLitIncorporating.html

14.5

MANAGING YOUR PROJECT

1. Review your notes and photocopied or downloaded material for passages, tables, charts, or images that you regard as essential to your project. Be sure you have a rationale for each direct borrowing (see Section 14a).

2. After you have drafted a version of your project, check to see that you have framed every direct quotation in some way (see Section 14b) and provided an appropriate label or title for any table, chart, or figure. Remember that no borrowed element should simply be dropped into the paper without an explanation or context.

3. Review every point of entry into a quotation for readability. Be sure that reading is not disrupted by a shift in verb tense, person, or sentence structure (see Section 14e). Revise your frame or modify the quotation appropriately to make any difficult passage more readable.

IV

DEVELOPING THE PROJECT

DON'T MISS . . .

- **The questions for reflecting on what you have in Chapter 15.** Don't rush into the final stages of your project before you're ready. Take a few moments to reassess what you've done and what you still need to do.

- **The strategies for organizing your material in Section 17b.** Tailor the organization of your project to fit your rhetorical goals.

- **The sample introduction and conclusion on pages 182–183.** A strong beginning and memorable ending will impress and persuade your readers.

EVERYDAY RESEARCH

FREDERICK L. WHITMER, Partner

Brown Raysman Millstein Felder & Steiner LLP

Frederick's affinity for the dramatic and an early interest in courtroom actions led him to a career in law. He is currently a litigation trial lawyer who specializes in intellectual property.

For Fred, research is important in several ways. "There is no substitute for preparation in trying a case. Understanding the law and researching into the factual content of a controversy is vital to representing a client effectively." In addition, "a fully prepared lawyer is informed about the court in which a case is to be tried and the adversary he faces." Fred always researches the judge who will be trying the case, as well as the opposing lawyers.

In important or substantial cases, employing jury consultants such as sociologists and psychologists "is key to getting advice on what kind of juror is most likely to be sympathetic to the position I'm advocating. Research on this level entails a deep understanding of the ethnic, cultural, and philosophical backgrounds of jurors. This understanding also helps shape the kinds of arguments I make to persuade them."

CHAPTER 15

Reflecting On What You Have

When you look around you at the wealth of materials you have collected—your notes and files, CDs and diskettes, and so on—it's tempting to think, "I'm done!" But before you move into the next phase of your project, step back, take a critical look at what you've got, and consider what you may still need. You probably have a good feeling for what the major issues are and how well the information you've found is likely to fit into your research project. Now you should assess the scope and balance of your materials.

Think of your project as a lively conversation and see that no single voice dominates that conversation or goes unchallenged. This means that you shouldn't compose a major part of your work without drawing on a variety of sources. And every part of the project should reflect the depth of your research and reading.

In some projects you'll want to cite sources that reinforce each other, especially when you're trying to build a persuasive case. In other situations, you may find authoritative sources that differ significantly; then you have to decide which to endorse, or perhaps you'll leave that choice to readers. When sources have pronounced biases (political or otherwise), be sure to read them "against" pieces with alternative views to keep your own perspectives broad (see Chapter 12). And when you borrow materials from questionable sources, make sure you confirm the information before you ask your readers to rely on it.

15a Consider whether you need to do more research

Look at the material and resources that relate directly to your research hypothesis. How comprehensive are they? Do your resources provide you with both a broad overview of the subject area and a detailed look at the specific topic you're researching? In a project about MP3 file sharing, for example, you

FOCUS ON . . . **Logic**

Logical fallacies, syllogistic reasoning, Toulmin logic—these are all ways of helping to ensure that your arguments are presented, well, logically! That is, in order for a reader to accept your evidence and be persuaded, the reader must first agree with the *premise* on which your evidence relies.

For example, in papers on MP3 downloading, many students begin with the often unstated assumption that recording artists "make enough money." But unless this assumption is always, or even almost always, true, *and* accepted as such by your reader, any argument that relies on it will fall apart.

What you, as the writer, are left with, then, is an important question: do you know that what you believe to be true *is* true? If not, then it is your job to provide evidence for your reader.

15.1

would probably want to have information about the growth of file-sharing networks like Napster and Kazaa, general commentaries on benefits and drawbacks of peer-to-peer file sharing technologies, and articles and research studies that focus on the specific effects that MP3 downloading has on CD sales and the music industry. In order to write convincingly about the little picture, you need to know what the big picture looks like (and vice versa). Examine your materials and ask yourself these questions:

- Do my materials give me a sense of the larger subject area in which my project is based, including a sense of any controversies?
- Do I have a sufficient number of studies and articles on my topic to support my hypothesis?
- Does the information I've gathered come from reputable authorities my readers will accept?
- Have I gathered my information from an appropriate range of print, online, and other resources?
- Are there other avenues of research or published resources my readers would expect me to include?

Consider, too, whether your argument relies on assumptions that may need to be supported with additional evidence. If you are left with lingering doubts about the completeness of your research, you will probably want to continue your investigations until you can answer the questions more confidently.

15b Consider whether you have a fair balance of sources and opinions

Look again at the reviewing and positioning you did in Chapter 12 and think about the results in terms of rhetorical balance. Do virtually all the articles, Web sites, and book chapters you've uncovered take basically the same position or talk about the subject in the same way? If so, then you should probably return to your research to look specifically for alternative points of view. Remember, to be fair and ethical in your research and to be persuasive to your audience, you will need to show respect for other voices and other opinions. If you find that you've been favoring one position unjustly, you'll want to do a bit more research to balance your approach.

Sometimes a little creativity with the key terms you use in search engines (see Chapter 6) can turn up different perspectives; sometimes Web sites will provide links to pages that express positions you might not expect. You might even ask friends or instructors to look over your hypothesis, evidence, and arguments and come up with every possible objection they can to your position. Your reference librarian should be able to point you to resources you can use to identify and locate diverse points of view, particularly on controversial subjects. Several publications specialize in oppositional views: *Current Controversies*, *Ideas in Conflict*, and the aptly named *Opposing Viewpoints* series.

15c Consider whether you need to revise your purpose

One of the most rewarding—and occasionally frustrating—aspects of research is that you learn a lot about your topic. It's rewarding because you expand your knowledge; it's frustrating because sometimes the things you learn will contradict the beliefs you started out with.

Reflect on what you've learned in researching and reading about your topic, and gauge whether your beliefs or opinions have changed since you began. If you find yourself answering *yes* to any of these questions, then you may want to consider revising your purpose:

- Do I see the topic in a different light now?
- Have the things I've learned altered my views in any way?
- Am I beginning to feel that my original purpose for the research project is changing, that maybe a different focus, a different approach, or a different research question might work better?

Imagine that you began a research project on MP3 file sharing, intending to see it as a question of fact (see Section 3a) and setting out to show how downloading or sharing MP3 files is a violation of copyright and, therefore, a crime. As you conduct your research, however, you notice that the issue is not as clear-cut as you first thought. There are a lot of disputes over exactly what fair use of copyrighted material is and to what extent it should be allowed. Some people argue that fair use entitles them to download and listen to a song, as long as they delete it from their computers afterward; others claim that the downloading itself is a violation of fair use. Some people say they have a right to make backup copies of CDs and store the files on open networks if they wish; others say that the concept of fair use does not extend that far. The more you read, the more you might realize that what's really needed is a clearer definition of "fair use." If that's the case, you may find that you want to revise your purpose from a question of fact to a question of definition (see Section 3b).

15d Consider whether you need to narrow your focus

Sometimes when you conduct research, you find that your original topic turns out to be larger and more complex than you thought. A research project on the Bay of Pigs incident in 1961, for instance, might seem to be a narrow, well-focused topic for investigation. Once you get into the research, however, you find yourself immersed in articles about the Cold War; U.S. policy toward Cuba, Cuban exiles, and refugees; and President John F. Kennedy's relationship with Fidel Castro. Even those articles that center on the day of the invasion itself could point in many directions, with widely varying opinions about what happened and who was responsible. Suddenly your narrow topic has broadened considerably, and you will probably need to refine your topic further, perhaps by looking only at the kinds of pressure Cuban exiles put on Eisenhower and Kennedy to support the invasion.

In the next chapter you'll learn strategies you can employ to make your topic manageable again. While it's certainly easy to be sidetracked by new discoveries and research topics only slightly related to your subject, you have to know when to stop doing research and move on to the next phase of your project.

WWW Web Sites Worth Knowing

- University of Arizona Library, "Revising," http://www.library.arizona.edu/rio/write8.html
- New England Institute of Technology, "Everything's an Argument: EN 102 Sources," http://library.neit.edu/argument.htm
- Colorado State University Writing Center, "The Toulmin Method," http://writing.colostate.edu/references/reading/toulmin/index.cfm

15.3

MANAGING YOUR PROJECT

1. Divide a sheet of paper into two columns. In one column, list all the evidence, arguments, and resources in support of your research question or hypothesis. In the other column, list all the information and resources that argue against your position or that hold an alternative view. Do the two columns seem unbalanced? If they seem clearly uneven, you might want to do additional research. Do you have sufficient evidence to refute or at least make a good case against opposing viewpoints? Can you make your case without ignoring the opposition?

2. What is the relationship between the "big picture" (overall context) and the "little picture" (specific topic) in your research project? Has your research provided you with enough background information to show readers why your project is important to a larger community? Conversely, do you have enough specific information to answer the particular research question you've posed for yourself? If you feel something is lacking in one or the other of these areas, you should do further research to fill in the gaps.

CHAPTER 16

Refining Your Claim

Sometimes your project presents you with so many different directions to explore, it can make you feel like you've walked into a Chinese restaurant with a huge buffet. There are forty or fifty delicious main dishes to choose from, and it's hard to resist piling your plate high and sampling absolutely everything. If you do, though, you run the risk of a generally unsatisfying meal and a huge stomachache at the end. Overall, it's usually better to limit yourself to a few dishes that you really like and consume them in moderation.

For the same reason, you should resist the impulse to tackle too broad a topic in your project or to explore too many points in detail. In most cases you'll want to narrow the scope of your project early in the writing process and give it a design that reinforces clear, though not necessarily simple, points. Some projects will support specific thesis statements or arguments; others may explore alternatives to the status quo or offer proposals to solve problems. Your role is to create whatever framework will work to make your project an effective response to the original assignment. This shaping must be deliberate and strategic. In a research project, you can't rely on chance to bring the parts together.

16a Be sure you have a point to make

It doesn't matter whether your research supports a report, a Web site, or a series of online conversations; you need to have a point and a purpose. All the while you're reading, responding, taking notes, and conducting surveys or interviews, you should be testing your preliminary assumptions and objectives. As we've indicated in previous chapters, you may want to revise your original purpose or rethink your initial focus based on what you learn from your research. Use Checklists 16.1 and 16.2 on pages 160 and 163 to test your ideas against the material you are reading or gathering.

CHECKLIST 16.1

> **Evaluating Your Purpose**

If the purpose of your research project is primarily *argumentative*—that is, if its thesis makes a strong claim about where you stand on an issue and supports that position with evidence from your research—then you should ask the following questions:

○ Does the project focus on a debatable issue that deserves readers' attention?

○ Will the issue affect or interest your audience?

○ Will readers understand how the issue affects them?

○ Does the information you are finding support your hypothesis or research claim?

○ Are you using information from your sources to support your own claim, or are you merely repeating a claim made by others?

○ Do you need to *qualify* your hypothesis and claim? In other words, would it make more sense to say your position or approach is true under *some* rather than *all* circumstances?

If the purpose of your research project is primarily *informational*—that is, if it intends to educate your readers and deepen their understanding of an issue by presenting the results of your research—then you should ask the following questions:

○ Does the project focus on a substantial issue that deserves readers' attention?

○ Does the project focus on an issue or a topic that your readers are presently unfamiliar with?

○ Will the issue affect or interest your audience?

○ Will readers understand how the issue affects them?

○ Are you using sources to *supplement* your own presentation, or are you relying on them too heavily?

○ Do you need to narrow the scope of your project to keep from being too general or too lengthy and detailed?

WWW

16.1

16b Grab your reader's attention

For many writers, developing a significant point or thesis is the real challenge of a research project. Your thesis is the claim you make as the result of your research, the answer to your research question, or the confirmation of your original hypothesis (see Chapter 15). It is tempting to rely on thesis statements that only break huge research ideas into smaller parts because the material then seems easy to organize. For example:

Child abuse is a serious problem with three major aspects: causes, detection, and prevention.

Common types of white-collar crime are embezzlement, mail fraud, and insurance fraud.

Simple classifications like these can work well when you need to divide issues or ideas into their components, but for research projects that make arguments, theses that just break an idea into parts can seem more like shopping lists than engagements with compelling ideas. More interesting and useful theses might explore how child abuse might be prevented if we could understand what causes it, or why white-collar crime poses a threat to the work ethic.

When issues are laid out piece by piece, readers can lose a sense of what connects them. One way to avoid such loose structures is to focus on problems and conflicts connected to your life or community. Look for claims that demand the attention of readers and that place a burden on you to provide convincing supporting evidence.

TENTATIVE THESIS	The practice of downloading and sharing copyrighted music files has had a dramatic impact on CD sales.

You may quickly learn that the point you're developing can't be supported by reliable studies. If that's so, share this discovery with readers.

FINAL THESIS	Though some people in the music industry claim that file sharing has hurt them significantly, the evidence does not support their position.

Ask basic questions about your topic, particularly *how* and *why*. Get to the heart of a matter in defining a topic. Examine issues that affect people.

LIFELESS	Child abuse is a serious problem with three major aspects: causes, detection, and prevention.
CHALLENGING	Prosecutors in some communities have based charges of child abuse on types of hearsay evidence that now receive tougher scrutiny from judges.
LIFELESS	Common types of white-collar crime are embezzlement, bank fraud, and insurance fraud.
CHALLENGING	White-collar crime is rarely punished severely because many people think that misdeeds aimed at institutions are less serious than crimes against people.

16c Limit your claim

The more you learn about a subject, the more careful you're likely to be in making claims. The thesis that eventually guides your project will almost certainly be more specific, restrictive, and informative than your initial research

---

FOCUS ON . . . **Refining Your Topic Using Indexes and Tables of Contents**

If you're having a hard time narrowing your focus or refining your topic, an index or a table of contents that appears in a reference book can be a source of inspiration. Pull out some of the books that you've uncovered in your research and spend some time browsing through the indexes at the end. What you'll find are lists of terms, topics, and people that are referred to in the texts, along with page numbers that give an indication of how important they are. (The more often they're mentioned, the more important they're likely to be.) Consider using a frequently mentioned topic as the central focus of your own project. A table of contents can also give you a good idea of what other authors consider to be significant subtopics within a broad area of study. The focus of a single book chapter might work as the central idea for your whole project.

---

question or hypothesis. The thesis itself or the paragraph surrounding it should address questions such as: Under what conditions? With what limits? With what scope?

The shape you give a project will depend on what your thesis promises. One way to understand that commitment is to recall the point of your research inquiry (see Chapter 3). Does it ultimately involve a claim of *fact*, a claim of *definition*, a claim of *value*, a claim of *cause*, or a claim of *consequence*?

ORIGINAL CLAIM OF *FACT*

AIDS is the greatest killer of the young.

> CLAIM SPECIFIED AND LIMITED BY RESEARCH
> In the United States, AIDS has recently replaced automobile accidents as the leading cause of death among teenagers.
>
> COMMITMENTS
> * Present figures on mortality rates among young people.
> * Find figures on deaths from auto accidents.
> * Find figures on deaths from AIDS.
> * Draw out the implications of the studies for AIDS prevention.

ORIGINAL CLAIM OF *DEFINITION*

Zoos constitute cruelty to animals.

> CLAIM SPECIFIED AND LIMITED BY RESEARCH
> Confining large marine mammals in sea parks for public amusement is, arguably, a form of cruelty to animals.

CHECKLIST 16.2

> ### Refining Your Claim

If you suspect at this point that your topic is a bit too broad, you may want to consider narrowing or refining your original claim. This does not mean you have to abandon all the research and thinking you have invested so far. Not at all! It just means you need to find a focus that will help you organize and present your research effectively. Here's a short checklist you can use to help you refine your claim:

○ Identify any issues or questions that keep coming up over and over again in your research. If other writers seem to be focusing on a few specific issues, you might choose one or two to be the central point of a revised thesis.

○ Pinpoint where most disagreements are coming from. Find a critical point in the debate and take your stand on that point alone.

○ Look for broad terms in your original thesis (MP3 file sharing, cruelty to animals, cloning) and break them into smaller parts (*cloning*: human cloning, animal cloning, therapeutic cloning, etc.). Use one of these subcategories as the central topic of your revised thesis.

COMMITMENTS
- Define specific criteria for "cruelty."
- Examine what experts say about the condition of animals in marine parks or do fieldwork in such a park.
- Find statistics on animal health in and out of marine parks.
- Show that conditions in marine parks meet or do not meet criteria for "cruelty to animals."

ORIGINAL CLAIM OF *VALUE*

Frankenstein is one of the most influential books of all time.

CLAIM SPECIFIED AND LIMITED BY RESEARCH

Because of its strong technological elements and its focus on the moral questions that accompany any new scientific achievement or discovery, Mary Shelley's *Frankenstein* is considered to be the first great work of science fiction, one that had a lasting impact on that literary genre.

COMMITMENTS
- Examine the work of scholars who study and define science fiction.
- Demonstrate that the features that define science fiction as a genre appear in *Frankenstein*.

- Present statements from literary scholars and current science fiction writers attesting to the book's influence.

ORIGINAL CLAIM OF CAUSE

Higher speed limits are not the cause of increased traffic deaths.

CLAIM SPECIFIED AND LIMITED BY RESEARCH

The general, gradual rise in traffic deaths is not due to recent higher speed limits on interstate and limited-access highways.

COMMITMENTS
- Provide accurate facts on increase in traffic deaths.
- Explain where, when, and by how much speed limits have increased.
- Refute the inference that the rate of traffic deaths has risen uniformly on four-lane, limited-access highways.
- Present other potential causes for any observed increase—including increases in travel, number of vehicles and drivers, road rage.

ORIGINAL CLAIM OF CONSEQUENCE

MP3 downloaders should not be prosecuted.

CLAIM SPECIFIED AND LIMITED BY RESEARCH

The RIAA and other media organizations should discontinue their policy of selectively prosecuting individual MP3 downloaders because it has had virtually no impact on the amount of file sharing that takes place, and it may, in fact, cost the entertainment industry more money than it saves.

COMMITMENTS
- Describe the RIAA's policy of selectively prosecuting individual down-loaders.
- Demonstrate that file sharing has not been significantly affected by this policy.
- Show how consumer resentment over this policy may lead to a decline in CD sales and other revenues.
- Offer an alternative proposal to show how media companies could take advantage of file sharing to increase profits.
- Defend the advantages and feasibility of the proposal.

One result of thinking about your project in terms of its thesis, claims, and commitments at this stage is that you will begin to get a sense of the structure you need to develop as you organize your project. Considering how to introduce the topic, what background information to provide, and what order your points should be presented in will be key to the success of your project and the effect it will have on your audience. In the next chapter we examine useful rhetorical strategies for organizing research materials.

WWW Web Sites Worth Knowing

- "University of Illinois Writers' Workshop, "Developing a Thesis Statement," http://www.english.uiuc.edu/cws/wworkshop/advice/developing_a_thesis.htm
- TeachWeb at the University of Pennsylvania, "Thesis Construction," http://www.english.upenn.edu/Grad/Teachweb/thesis.html

16.2

MANAGING YOUR PROJECT

1. Can you connect your project in some way to your world or local community? Why should readers care about what you have discovered? How will they benefit, directly or indirectly?

2. What limits on your thesis can help make your project both more true to the facts you are uncovering and more manageable? Write out your thesis fully, stating both your claim and supporting reasons. Then either add the necessary qualifications or note the qualifications already in the statement.

3. How would you characterize your project and thesis: Are you making a claim of *fact, definition, value, cause,* or *consequence*? Or does your project fall between categories, combine them, or fit in another realm entirely? (Review Chapter 3 on these categories.) If you are unable to categorize the nature of your claim, it may be because your claim is either changing or still unfocused. This might be a time to ask an instructor or your colleagues for suggestions.

17

Organizing and Outlining

Have you ever had the experience of watching an avant-garde movie such as Luis Buñuel's *The Andalusian Dog* or a TV show such as David Lynch's *Twin Peaks* and feeling totally confused by the way scenes and images jump from place to place? Have you ever visited a Web site and been frustrated by your inability to find a simple piece of information, no matter how hard you try to figure out how the site is organized? If so, then you've learned an important lesson: from the humblest two-page research report to the most complex Web site, structure matters. Structure helps readers move purposefully from point to point in a project—whether they are heading in straight lines as they usually do in most papers or blazing paths of their own through the nodes of a Web site.

Organizing a project might seem easy. We even have the classic academic design for papers, the five-paragraph essay, that looks like a model of clarity. Make a statement in an introductory paragraph, prove it with at least three paragraphs of supporting evidence, tack on a conclusion, and you've got a paper.

Unfortunately, a statement isn't proven just because you can line up three ideas in a row to support it. Three or more reasons can be marshaled in favor of most propositions, and using such a pattern of organization can produce sheer nonsense.

Thesis: Large Doses of Radiation Must Be Beneficial to Human Health.

- Atomic power produces useful energy.
- People are exposed to radiation all the time.
- Radiation is used to cure cancer.

These "supporting arguments" aren't related to the main point or to each other, and they certainly don't prove that radiation in large doses is good for people. Yet some writers will believe that they have done their jobs just because they have corralled ideas into a similar five-paragraph structure.

When organizing research materials, you want a plan that reflects the complexity of your ideas while serving your readers' need for clarity; no single formula will work for all your projects.

17a Create a blueprint for your project

The design of your paper, brochure, Web site, or other project may be rough at first, but you do need to sketch out a shape of some kind. For a paper, that shape may be a scratch outline that does no more than list what you know you must cover.

I. Thesis
II. Background information
III. Claim
IV. Evidence
V. Conclusion

The equivalent of a scratch outline for a Web project or brochure might be a *storyboard,* a drawing that positions the major features or elements of a design. Scratch outlines and storyboards help you set large-scale priorities in arranging and positioning information.

Organizing your research effort means deciding what parts or features a project must have and in what order they'll appear. At least five priorities will typically compete for your attention.

Logical order. You will want material to follow a pattern that seems coherent to readers, with claims and reasons backed by evidence. Readers should have the impression that ideas are being presented thoroughly, fairly, and systematically.

Chronological order. In some cases the structure of a project will follow a sequence: *first, second, third; beginning, middle, end; step 1, step 2, step 3.* Portions of a project may follow chronological order even when the rest of the work doesn't.

Order defined by genre. In some cases the structure of a project will be determined for you by precedent or professional guidelines. This will be the case with laboratory or research reports in many fields.

Order of importance or significance. Sometimes you may need to present the most compelling evidence near the end of the presentation where readers will remember it. Other times, you'll have to decide whether information belongs in the body of a paper, in notes, or in an appendix. With a Web site, order of significance may play a major role in determining what goes on the home page and how "deep" the site goes.

Order of interest. Depending on your purpose, interest may be a consideration in arranging material. You may decide that it is necessary to present important information early just to keep readers involved. In a Web site or a brochure, you may decide to forgo the most logical arrangement in order to present an appealing face.

It's up to you to manage these competing interests as you create a design for your work.

17b Consider general patterns of organization

Projects that prove a thesis can be organized in various ways, and your choice of organizational pattern will depend on your topic, your hypothesis, your evidence, and the effect you want to have on your audience. Some research hypotheses will lend themselves to common organizational patterns. The following patterns may be useful when your project builds a connected sequence of arguments, makes an evaluation, establishes a cause-and-effect chain, or proposes a solution to a problem.

Connected sequence of arguments. In a connected sequence of arguments, each claim is based on the one that precedes it: "If X is so, then Y is true, and if Y is true, then so is Z." A structure of this kind presents arguments that build on each other. You cannot remove any portion of such a structure without demolishing the whole.

Introduction: Thesis
Recent legislation that increases the fines that the FCC can impose on broadcasters for "indecency" undermines freedom of speech.

Argument 1 + examples/illustrations
Members of Congress passed this legislation quickly in response to the public furor over a single accident at the Superbowl. In an election year, they were afraid of appearing soft on immorality.

Argument 2 + examples/illustrations
As a result, the FCC and conservative watchdog groups are now threatening broadcasters with prosecution and massive fines for shows whose "indecent" content is only vaguely defined.

Argument 3 + examples/illustrations
Consequently, rather than risk huge fines, broadcasters may choose to prohibit any content that could offend listeners, thereby undermining constitutionally guaranteed rights to freedom of speech.

↓

> Conclusion
> *Although the FCC is certainly within its rights to fine broadcasters who air obscene material, its attempts to impose a vague and politically conservative definition of "indecency" on broadcasters by threatening huge fines are an unconstitutional infringement on freedom of speech.*

This pattern of organization is potentially more complex than the basic five-paragraph essay because each part of the project depends on its connection to a previous part, not to the thesis statement alone. However, you must be sure that readers can follow the chain of evidence from link to link, so strong transitions are essential.

Evaluations. Similar organizational patterns may seem simple in outline but will grow in complexity as you fill in the blanks. When your project involves evaluating something, you know the project has to fulfill certain commitments:

- To provide a rationale for the evaluation
- To establish criteria for making evaluative judgments
- To measure the subject against the standards

When you know what the big pieces of a project are, you can begin arranging them. You might test a structure in which you present all the criteria of evaluation first and then apply them to the particular subject of the paper.

WWW
17.1

> Introduction: What's being evaluated
> *This evaluation judges whether the selective prosecution of MP3 downloaders by the RIAA has the effects its advocates claim.*

↓

> Criteria for evaluation presented

> Criterion 1
> *Selective prosecution should reduce the amount of MP3 downloading.*

> Criterion 2
> *Selective prosecution should result in increased CD sales.*

> Criterion 3
> *Selective prosecution should teach people to respect copyright and intellectual property.*

↓

Evaluation/judgment of subject

By criterion 1 *Selective prosecution does not appear to have reduced the amount of MP3 downloading or file sharing overall; it has only reduced the number of flagrant violators.*

Evidence

By criterion 2 *Selective prosecution has not caused any significant increase in CD sales; in fact, this tactic has spurred numerous calls for a boycott of the music industry.*

Evidence

By criterion 3 *Selective prosecution has generated such anger and resentment against the RIAA that users may see MP3 downloading and file sharing as a form of legitimate protest.*

Evidence

↓

Conclusion *The RIAA's program to selectively prosecute individuals who download and share MP3 music files has had none of the effects its advocates claim and may even have made the problem worse. For these reasons, the music industry should find an alternative method to uphold its intellectual property rights.*

If, however, you believe that readers would understand your argument better if you explained and supported each criterion in the same part of the paper, you would craft a different outline.

Introduction: What's being evaluated *This evaluation judges whether the selective prosecution of MP3 downloaders by the RIAA has the effects its advocates claim.*

↓

Evaluation of the subject

By criterion 1 *Selective prosecution should reduce the amount of MP3 downloading, but it appears to have reduced only the number of flagrant violators.*

Evidence/counterevidence

> By criterion 2
> *Selective prosecution should result in increased CD sales, but just the opposite may be occurring; the tactic has spurred numerous calls for a boycott of the music industry.*

> Evidence/counterevidence

> By criterion 3
> *Selective prosecution should teach people to respect copyright and intellectual property, but it has actually generated such anger and resentment against the RIAA that users may see MP3 downloading and file sharing as a form of legitimate protest.*

> Evidence/counterevidence

↓

> Conclusion
> *The RIAA's program to selectively prosecute individuals who download and share MP3 music files has had none of the effects its advocates claim and may even have made the problem worse. For these reasons, the music industry should find an alternative method to uphold its intellectual property rights.*

Which pattern will work best? That's a question you alone can answer, knowing the purpose of your work, your audience, your evidence, your medium, and your own preferences.

Cause and effect. A project that examines a cause-and-effect question offers similar structural options. Once again, you'd begin by determining the project's major components. The typical cause-and-effect paper will probably make at least two major commitments:

- To examine a phenomenon or event
- To explore causes and/or effects of the event

The first part of such a project might introduce the phenomenon or situation the project will explore, explaining it in some detail. The bulk of the project will then be concerned with interpreting the phenomenon.

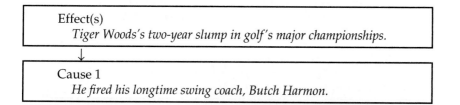

> Effect(s)
> *Tiger Woods's two-year slump in golf's major championships.*

↓

> Cause 1
> *He fired his longtime swing coach, Butch Harmon.*

> Cause 2
> *The emotional pressure and unrealistic expectations of being ranked #1 for so long are having an effect.*

> Cause 3
> *The rest of the golfing field has gotten better, and Tiger's no longer quite so intimidating.*

> Cause 4
> *Knee surgery affected his stance and his swing.*

This arrangement is solid and simple, yet it still might require rearranging the causes from the most obvious, specific, or uncontroversial to the more subtle, abstract, and challenging ones. Your readers might have no trouble accepting Tiger Woods's knee surgery or the loss of his swing coach as reasons for a slump, for instance, but they might need a bit more convincing before they would agree that emotional pressure and stronger competition were equally important.

Proposals. Sometimes the components of a proposal don't fall to hand as easily as they do for evaluative or cause-and-effect projects. A proposal will likely have several parts, each organized by a different principle. You might have to explain the history of a problem, evaluate the seriousness of the situation, explain the causes of the current situation, enumerate alternatives, and argue for your own solution. Each of these considerations might require its own section of the project. Again, you'd want to set down the essential components of the paper and arrange them in a coherent order based on the principles described in Section 17a.

> The problem
> *A continuing occurrence of typos and layout mistakes in the local newspaper*

> History of the problem
> *For nearly as long as anyone can remember, the* Herald *has had typos and other mistakes in every issue. The newspaper's problems have become a standing joke among members of the local community, particularly those who teach journalism at the local college.*

> Causes of the problem
> *Small-town newspaper is underfunded, with a poorly trained staff, deadline pressures, and low standards.*

Crisis: Need for solution
The newspaper is an embarrassment to the community.

Alternatives to the current situation (rejected)

Alternative 1: Advantages/disadvantages
Hire more and better proofreaders: Would solve the problem, but the newspaper's budget won't permit it.

Alternative 2: Advantages/disadvantages
Rely more frequently on pretyped wire stories from the Associated Press: They'd still need to be proofread, and they wouldn't cover the local news.

Alternative 3: Advantages/disadvantages
Publish less frequently: More time for proofreading, but news would be less current and subscribers might cancel.

The proposed solution
Increase subscription fees by a small percentage.

Explanation of solution
The increased revenue would pay for additional and/or better-qualified proofreading staff.

Feasibility of solution
An increase in subscription rates is easy to implement and announce; the increased revenue would easily pay for a staff person; qualified people can be hired from the local college community.

Disadvantages
Some people might cancel their subscriptions because of increased rates.

Advantages
Increased professional appearance of newspaper; increased respect inside and outside the community; more people might subscribe; new job(s) created.

Implementation of solution
Make recommendation to newspaper's board of directors, editors, and accounting department.

FOCUS ON . . . **Low-Tech Cutting and Pasting**

The computer is a superb tool for many purposes, but it has one limitation that can be a serious drawback when you're trying to organize your thoughts and ideas: it can display only one screen of text at a time. When you're working on a complicated project with lots of arguments and evidence, cutting and scrolling and pasting and scrolling over and over again can be a time-consuming (and confusing) way to test different arrangement strategies.

Try this instead: Print out each of your main points and supporting pieces of evidence and cut them into strips or paste them onto note cards. Arrange these notes on a table or floor space in an order you think will work well. Move the cards around and experiment with other arrangements, keeping an eye on how all the parts fit together in terms of the whole presentation. You'll find that this process can be much easier than moving text piece by piece on a small screen, and it also allows you to see the project's entire structure all at once.

In research this complex, the key points in the scratch outline may eventually become headings within the project itself.

Remember that patterns such as these are not simply "writing containers" into which your content can be poured; even when one of them looks like it will work for you, you will probably have to modify the pattern to fit your particular evidence, audience, and rhetorical goals.

17c Accommodate dissenting voices

In many projects you must deal with opposing arguments by presenting them fairly and strategically. If you don't acknowledge them, your project may seem unbalanced, uninformed, or narrow. But this is not just a matter of dividing positions into "those in favor" and "those against." Most debatable issues offer a range of positions, and most problems have a variety of solutions; you will need to recognize these positions and demonstrate why your position is the more reasonable or preferable one. You do this by using *counterargument*. Here are two sample scratch outlines that take counterarguments into account; the first deals with all objections to a thesis at once, and the second deals with objections one by one.

Introduction: Thesis

Counterarguments: Possible objections to the thesis

Responses to the counterarguments

Main arguments to support the thesis

Argument 1 + examples/illustrations

Argument 2 + examples/illustrations

Argument 3 + examples/illustrations

Conclusion

Introduction: Thesis

Main Point 1

Argument 1 + examples/illustrations

Counterargument 1 and your response

Main Point 2

Argument 2 + examples/illustrations

Counterargument 2 and your response

Main Point 3

Argument 3 + examples/illustrations

Counterargument 3 and your response

Conclusion

While these models may suggest that all components of an essay would receive comparable treatment, in practice, you would give your best points more attention, using all the examples and illustrations you need to make your case. Minor points would receive less coverage than major ones.

17d Follow professional templates

For some projects you will have to learn and apply the conventions of organization already established within a profession or field. If you're asked to prepare a formal business report, your project may require elements such as a table of contents, an executive summary, a statement of the problem with background information, and conclusions and recommendations, as well as appendixes and a bibliography of references. These parts make up your organization. As you flesh out each section, you create your report.

Some software such as Adobe *PageMaker*, Broderbund *Print Shop*, or Microsoft *Publisher* will walk you through the task of creating newsletters, brochures, and other kinds of presentations. Many newer word-processing packages include templates for typical MLA- and APA-style reports, as well as electronic presentations for various purposes and samples of spreadsheets and databases for common uses. Before using the templates, however, make sure they conform to the requirements of your project (see Chapter 1), and learn how you can customize them to best suit your purpose. If your project is a Web site, you will find yourself constricted by the "interfaces" of online communication—the places where you and your readers meet the computer. What you present will be defined by the tools available to you and the expectations readers have for Web sites and Web designs. (See Part V for more information on designing documents following professional guidelines.)

17e Create a formal outline

You might also try a formal outline to help you organize your thoughts and build a structure for your project. Outlines can keep you focused on the main point in each part of your developing project, and they can also help you visualize how all parts of the project work together.

A formal outline is organized hierarchically, meaning that the central or most important points of the project are placed at a "higher level" than the supporting points or examples. The levels in a formal outline are generally indicated by letter and number *tags* and by *indentation*, and they typically take this form:

> I. **Main point 1**
>   A. **Subpoint 1**
>   1. **Example 1**
>   2. **Example 2**
>   B. **Subpoint 2**
> II. **Main point 2**

By convention, the highest-level topics in a formal outline use Roman numerals, but unless your instructor specifies a particular format, there is no reason you can't use a different system if it works better for you. Whatever system you decide on, though, make sure it allows you to distinguish between your project's most important major points and less important minor ones. Part of an outline for a project on "Women in the Comics" might look something like this.

Sample Outline

> I. Introduction: There are a lot of strong female comic book characters today—Storm, She-Hulk, Dawn, Huntress. Are these positive role models?
> II. Background: Roles of women in the comics have changed.
>   A. Women were often clueless, helpless victims.
>   1. Superhero comics were written for young boys.

    2. Lois Lane was always rescued by Superman.

    3. Rare exceptions were Wonder Woman, Sheena.

  B. Women were often sex objects.

    1. Provocative "headlight" covers

      a. Fiction House comics

      b. Phantom Lady, Torchy, Venus

    2. Recurring bondage motif

    3. "Evil seductress" character type

  C. Women's liberation in 1960s led to stronger female characters.

III. Current female comic book types: has anything changed?

With an organizational plan in place, one that reflects the purpose of the project, your audience's needs and expectations, and your personal goals, you should be ready to begin your first full draft. The research and groundwork you have done thus far should have prepared you to take this next step with confidence.

WWW Web Sites Worth Knowing

- *Web Style Guide,* http://www.webstyleguide.com
- University of Chicago Library—Style Guides for Science Writing
  http://www.lib.uchicago.edu/e/su/chem/science_writting.html

WWW
17.2

MANAGING YOUR PROJECT

1. Create scratch outlines or storyboards for your overall project, and identify the major divisions of your work. Don't settle too quickly on a single design; try alternatives. Be sure to examine these tentative outlines (or storyboards) from the point of view of readers coming to your project with no idea of what you may be doing.

2. Once you have settled on the major divisions of your project, prepare a more formal outline or sketch that subdivides each of the major headings into component parts. You may discover places where a traditional paper might repeat itself or where a Web site might run into navigational problems.

3. If you have kept your notes on cards, you might now lay out the entire project. Create note cards for all your major headings and subheadings, then arrange your other cards under those headings in the order you expect to follow in the project. Many writers find that laying out their projects on cards in this way helps them spot weaknesses in their organization.

CHAPTER 18

Drafting Your Project

Professional writers have agonized over it, researchers have written about it, and all of us have experienced it: that cold moment of truth when you sit down at your desk, look at that blank screen or piece of paper, and *know* you have to start writing. It can be tempting to retreat into more research or reading, to promise yourself to "think about it tomorrow," or to go to a movie. That's precisely when you have to gather up your confidence, your determination, and your co-authors—and push ahead. It's time to write.

18a Prepare a version of your project early

Think of the first draft as the prototype for your project. Will it stand up to calls for facts, evidence, logical argumentation? Will it survive potential counterarguments? Will it keep readers interested and engaged? Will readers understand references to events or people?

Finish a first draft of your project well in advance of the final due date. You'll need time to revise and redesign based on the feedback you receive from colleagues. You may find yourself returning to the library or the Web or visiting your university writing center for help, but the more polishing you do, the better your project is likely to be.

Remember, too, that the final stages of producing a research project can involve additional steps such as preparing a Works Cited or References page, checking Web page links and graphics, or tinkering with a color printer. You have to allocate time for all these activities, appreciating that something can always go wrong.

18b Draft your project for an audience

Reflecting on the needs and interests of your audience, as we've said, is important throughout your research project, but it's vital at the drafting stage. Here you will make critical choices about how to present your material, what to include, and what can be safely left out. You should be able to make reason-

CHECKLIST 18.1

Writing for an Audience

○ **Tailor your examples, illustrations, and allusions to the group you are addressing.** With a professional audience, you can select technical sources and explain them, knowing that many concepts and terms will be familiar. With a less knowledgeable audience, you'll have to surround technical materials with more detailed explanations or choose simpler evidence and examples.

○ **Write in language suited to your audience.** Language changes from audience to audience, and you'll find differences in tone, style, organization, and vocabulary in the work of writers who want to be "heard" by their various readers. To address an academic setting, you must master something vaguely described as *college writing*. College writing is semiformal in tone, careful about grammar and mechanics, and scrupulous about evidence and documentation.

○ **Convince readers that your project deserves attention.** You may be certain that your subject is important, but readers presented with a paper, brochure, Web site, or other project need some reason to take notice. This isn't a matter of grabbing readers with sensational claims or pulsing graphics; it *is* about supplying a rationale for your work based on your own thoughtful study of an issue or a problem.

able guesses about your readership and adjust your presentation accordingly. Checklist 18.1 offers some ways in which you can accomplish this.

18c Present your material thoroughly

The organization of your research project (see Chapter 17) will guide many decisions you make about content and coverage, but always remain aware that your readers will probably not know as much about your topic as you do. Whether your audience is composed of novices or experts, it's your job to make sure they understand what you're saying and can follow you from point to point.

State ideas clearly. Explain your ideas in language as direct as the facts will allow (see also Section 18f), answering as many basic questions as readers are likely to have. Here, for example, is a topic sentence that would leave most readers puzzling over *who* is doing *what* to *whom*. It's from a paper examining the causes of an increasing pregnancy rate among teenagers.

> The most evident and changeable factor in the pregnancy increase in the
> past thirty years directly relates to the media.

In this sentence you won't find an explanation for the rising pregnancy rate,
only the suggestion that some evident and changeable factor *relates* to the media. *Relates* is an ambiguous verb; in what sense is this factor connected to the
media? Indeed, what is the factor? The topic sentence doesn't tell you. The
sentence needs to be revised to make the causal connection clear so that the
project (or paragraph) that follows from it will have direction.

> The clearest blame for the increase in teenage pregnancies in the past thirty
> years belongs to the national media--newspapers, magazines, films, and
> television filled daily with articles that make teens believe that early sexual
> activity is both normal and healthy.

That's quite an indictment. A reader might disagree with the claim, but at least
he or she has something to disagree with: an argument stated clearly and directly. Who would react to the original version of the topic sentence in the
same way?

Provide evidence for all key claims. You don't prove an assertion by
merely restating it or contradicting it, no matter how confident you are of your
views. Show readers how you came to your judgments. If possible, give them
an opportunity to arrive at similar conclusions. Consider this passage from a
paper about battered spouses.

> A common belief in society today is that spouses who put up with beatings
> over a long period of time are probably masochists who come to regard the
> assaults as signs of love. This belief is obviously not true.

The second sentence carries little weight as part of an argument or proof because it is presented as a mere assertion. In fact, the first sentence is not
obviously false; if it were, the belief would not be common. The writer needs to
provide evidence and alternative explanations for the willingness of spouses
to put up with long-term abuse.

Qualify generalizations. Sweeping statements attempt to generalize from
too small a sample. You may have seen advertisements that claimed or suggested that a product is "the physician's choice." The inference here is that *all*
physicians would choose it, when the more likely fact is that all (or most, or
some) of the physicians *they surveyed* chose it. Can you support all the evaluative statements and judgments you make? Qualifiers, such as the following,
help limit your liability.

Qualifiers

almost	many	often	some
in a few cases	most	possibly	sometimes
in many cases	occasionally	probably	with these exceptions

Cite authorities whenever you support assertions with figures or other data. Don't expect readers to take your word for any arguable claim, and don't assume that you know what the facts are because you've heard some generalizations. A statement as sweeping as the following would need authoritative evidence if it were to appear in a research project.

> It is a scientific fact that a marijuana cigarette kills more brain cells than a night of free drinks on Bourbon Street.

See how much more convincing this next statement (from the opposite point of view) sounds with its use of an authoritative source.

> In a study published in the July issue of the *Journal of the International Neuropsychological Society*, Dr. Igor Grant, a professor of psychiatry at the University of California, San Diego, noted that there was "very little evidence" of neurocognitive damage among habitual marijuana smokers.

Use multiple sources to support your thesis. Readers will probably not find your project or thesis convincing if you rely heavily on a small number of sources. Your readers might think you haven't done a very good job of researching your topic; worse, they might think you are purposefully showing bias by excluding relevant information. Your audience will be far more likely to accept your claims when you provide facts and opinions from several sources rather than just one or two. Again, it doesn't matter how authoritative you think your source is—be it the *Encyclopedia of American Biography* or the King James version of the Bible—you can't assume that all members of your audience will find that source so powerfully credible or valid that they'll consider other references unnecessary. Alternatively, mustering a long list of sources in support of your thesis won't be convincing if you have ignored important sources with opposing evidence (see Chapter 15).

18d Write a strong introduction and conclusion

Introductions and conclusions can sometimes be the hardest parts of a research project to write because they frame the contents of your research. Introductions draw readers into a project and persuade them to keep reading; conclusions ease readers out of a project report and convince them that what they read was meaningful and worthwhile. Perhaps the most useful advice we can give you here is that you don't have to write introductions first, and you don't have to write conclusions last! For extended research projects, it often makes sense to write a draft of your conclusion at the start. That way, you'll have a reasonably clear sense of what you want to "get to" as you draft the rest of your project. By the same reasoning, you may want to write your introduction last. After all, how can you introduce your research project effectively without knowing what appears in your final draft? On pages 182 and 183, you will find a sample introduction and conclusion to a paper about the RIAA's policy of "selectively prosecuting" individual users. Note that these are still preliminary drafts with many notes and questions that will affect the final versions that eventually emerge.

Sample Introduction

In 2003, Sarah Seabury Ward, a 65-year-old grandmother and retired teacher, was awakened late one night by a loud pounding on the door of her home. ~~On the other side of the door~~ It was not a burglar trying to break in, but someone almost as bad: a process server from the Recording Industry Association of America **[DO I NEED TO PUT THE ACRONYM "RIAA" HERE?]** informing her that she was being sued for illegally sharing thousands of MP3 music files, ~~many of them rap and hip-hop songs~~. Even though Ms. Ward's computer, an older Macintosh, was incapable of running file-sharing software, and even though she knew nothing about the practice of illegal music downloading, ~~and even though it seems ridiculous that a grandmother would listen to rap music~~, she nevertheless found herself accused of copyright infringement, threatened with jail time, and told she had to pay thousands of dollars in fines and penalties.

Ms. Ward is not alone. Hundreds of other computer users now stand accused of illegal file sharing using services such as Napster, Gnutella, and Kazaa, **[DO THESE NAMES NEED TO BE IN ITALICS?]** the latest targets in the RIAA's assault on copyright ~~violations~~ violators. Few people would disagree that musicians and the organizations that represent them have a right to protect their creative property. Copyright laws ensure that artists have the right to profit from their creations and "own" those creations for a limited period of time. **[IS THIS SENTENCE ABOUT COPYRIGHT LAWS NECESSARY?]** Still, many people are now arguing that the RIAA is going too far and being too ~~mean-spirited~~ heavy-handed in its enforcement of copyright laws, particularly in a digital age when questions about what constitutes "fair use" are still being debated in the courts. Some people, even those in the music industry, are beginning to wonder whether a policy that selectively prosecutes individual file sharers might stimulate a backlash among consumers and end up doing more damage to the industry than file sharing ever could. **[IS THIS A GOOD PLACE FOR A QUOTATION FROM A MUSIC INDUSTRY PERSON?]**

Sample Conclusion

So the critical question before the music industry is this: how are musicians and their professional organizations to protect intellectual property rights while also respecting the notion of "fair use" and not alienating their customer base? **[SENTENCE SOUNDS A LITTLE AWKWARD . . .]** ~~As can be seen~~ As I have shown in this paper, the question will not be an easy one to answer, and a successful solution will probably have to be extremely flexible. **[DO I NEED TO EXPLAIN WHAT I MEAN BY "FLEXIBLE" HERE?]** Unfortunately, however, the RIAA's hard-line policy of selective prosecution seems to be anything but flexible. Its unwillingness to pursue other avenues of enforcement or, even better, to offer alternatives to consumers that will be far more attractive than seeking out and downloading files illegally demonstrates a ~~rather~~ narrow-minded approach that could backfire in the long run. As we are now learning in Iraq, a policy of ~~unwavering~~ aggression and ~~strict~~ control will never win the "hearts and minds" of the people. In fact, it seems to do little more than stimulate resistance and encourage terrorism. **[IS THIS THE BEST METAPHOR TO USE? SOME PEOPLE MIGHT THINK THERE'S NOTHING WRONG WITH OUR POLICY IN IRAQ.]** The RIAA might be well advised to rethink its policy of "surgical strikes" against individual downloaders, as the result might not be capitulation and voluntary compliance but a growing underground network of file sharers that becomes larger, smarter, and more deeply entrenched than ever.

For those who are uncertain how to write an introduction or a conclusion, we summarize the tried-and-true techniques that authors have been using since the time of Aristotle. You may find that one of them works for you.

SUMMARY

Strategies for Introductions

Begin with a narrative. A brief attention-getting narrative or anecdote can catch readers' attention and make the topic more "real" for them.

Begin with a question or a series of questions that relates to your topic. Show readers that your subject is curious, provocative, interesting, or just plain puzzling. Direct questions invite readers to respond, and that will draw them into your presentation.

Begin by quoting a key source. Use a bold, striking statement from an expert, an interview subject, or another source to capture your readers' attention or introduce your topic. You may choose to set the quotation off by itself before the introductory paragraph, but more often it is integrated into the introduction.

Begin by showing that your subject has long been neglected, misunderstood, or misrepresented. This approach can be especially useful when you're writing about a subject that your audience thinks it knows relatively well. An introduction that begins "MP3 file sharing may be illegal, but it's the best thing to happen to the music industry in years" cannot help but increase a reader's interest.

Begin with your thesis. For some college papers or workplace reports, the best way to open your essay is simply to tell your readers exactly what you are going to write about.

SUMMARY

Strategies for Conclusions

Summarize the main points you have made. Reemphasize your main points without merely repeating what you have said in the same words or using "As I have shown in this paper . . . ." Link the project's main points together into a coherent argument or narrative.

Make a recommendation when one is appropriate. Any recommendation should grow out of the issue you have been discussing. This strategy brings a paper to a positive ending and closes the topic.

> **Link the end to the beginning.** Tie your conclusion back to your beginning to frame and unify your paper. If you began with an anecdote, your conclusion could refer back to those people or events.
>
> **Place your argument in a larger context.** Discuss how your findings are relevant to larger issues or have implications for your community. Concluding paragraphs of this sort are common in academic research projects.
>
> **Stop when you're finished.** Don't overdo your conclusion or bore your readers with unnecessary padding. When you have covered all your points satisfactorily, quit.

18e Make connections and use transitions

It is not enough to have pattern or structure within a project; you must also help readers follow it. In papers and other written work, we designate the components that hold a piece together as *transitions*.

For the sake of economy, writers often—and understandably—omit connectors when taking notes. Unfortunately, writers often fail to restore some of those connectors when they come to write about a subject themselves, mistakenly assuming that readers are just as familiar with the material as they are. The result can be sentences of information unsupported by connective tissue.

> The music industry does not like the idea of computer users downloading copyrighted songs for free. A lot of musicians think downloading costs them money. Some lesser-known musicians think file sharing makes them money, though.

This cluster of sentences frustrates readers more than it informs them. Readers will have to "rewrite" the paragraph to make sense of it. Worse, readers may infer meanings not intended by the author. The writer needs to make the connections implied in the sentences more explicit, spelling out the relationships.

> The music industry does not like the idea of computer users downloading copyrighted songs for free **because it believes that downloading negatively affects CD sales. For this reason,** a lot of musicians believe that downloading costs them money, **as fewer CD sales mean smaller royalty payments. On the other hand,** some lesser-known musicians feel file sharing makes them money **because it publicizes their music to a much wider audience**.

The concluding sentence of a paragraph can also function as a kind of connector. Not every paragraph requires a concluding statement that reinforces the thesis of the project. But when you've furnished considerable evidence in a paragraph, don't leave it up to readers to reckon how that evidence supports your thesis. Make the connection yourself in a competent concluding sentence like this one:

> The bulk of the evidence, then, shows conclusively that students who use word processors tend to write texts that are longer and freer from error than those who write by hand.

You can also make connections in an essay by using helpful transitional words and phrases such as the following:

Transitional Words

alternatively	finally	instead	similarly
although	first, second (etc.)	moreover	since
because	for example	next	then
consequently	however	not only, but	thus

18.1

Although transitional words may seem like small items, a timely *nevertheless* or a phrase such as *on the other hand* can help a reader enormously. As you will see in Part V, the strategic placement of headings and subheadings is highly effective and important. Even a well-chosen title—one that previews succinctly the content of a paper or project—can add to the coherence of a project.

18f Write stylishly

"One size fits all" does not apply to the writing style of a research project. You'll write one way when assembling a research report for a psychology course, another way entirely when posting a Web site designed to help elementary school children understand aspects of African American history. Many of your choices of language will seem fairly obvious: you know better than to joke around in a physics lab report or to insult people in a proposal. You've probably been drilled, too, in the virtues of stating ideas simply and directly. Here we explore general principles that apply to research reports and arguments. As always, the guidelines should be applied judiciously.

Find language that addresses readers intelligently. Be confident about the research you have done, but don't assume that positions other than your own aren't plausible. Remember that the readers most interested in your research may be suspicious of it. Make sure that the language you use welcomes skeptics and doesn't make them personally defensive. Put your own case in positive terms (when that's possible), and don't alienate readers by as-

FOCUS ON . . . **Writing Centers**

One of the most valuable resources available to you as a college student is the campus writing center, a place where skilled, interested writers and/or instructors will look over what you've written and give you valuable feedback. Writing centers are not just for "poor" writers, and they aren't just places where you can have your paper proofread for grammar mistakes. In fact, writing centers tend to be visited most by "good" writers who want to be even better, and writing center consultants will usually look first at the "higher-order" issues of discourse: organization, development, tone, argumentation, use of evidence, and focus on audience.

If you would like to get additional response to what you have written, you should locate your campus writing center and see one of the consultants.

suming a tone that suggests that only you have special insight or sensitivity on the issue.

Use specific details. Writing that uses a lot of abstract language is often harder to understand and less pleasurable to read than writing that states ideas more specifically. Abstract terms like *health-care provider system, positive learning environment,* and *two-wheeled vehicle* are usually harder to grasp than concrete terms like *hospital, classroom,* and *Harley.* Of course you have to use abstract words sometimes; it's impossible to discuss big ideas without them. But the more you use specific details, the clearer your sentences will be. For example, specialists might understand the following sentence if it appeared in a professional journal, but stating its ideas more concretely gives the statement broader appeal.

ABSTRACT   Some biologists used to believe that ontogeny recapitulated phylogeny.

REVISED   Some biologists used to believe that embryos went through all the stages of evolutionary development—fish, reptile, mammal—as they grew.

State ideas positively. Negative statements can be surprisingly hard to read. When you can, turn negative statements into positive ones. Your writing will seem more confident and may be more economical.

DIFFICULT   Do we have the right **not to be victims** of street crime?

CLEARER   Do we have the right **to be safe** from street crime?

DIFFICULT   It is **not unlikely** that I will attend the conference.

CLEARER   **I will probably** attend the conference.

"Chunk" your writing. Consider breaking lengthy sentences into more manageable pieces or creating a list to present unusually complex information. Chunking is the principle behind dividing telephone and social security numbers into smaller parts: the breaks make the long strings of numbers easier to recall. It's also a principle operating on many Web pages, where information is constricted to fit relatively small screens. (See Part V for more information on chunking as a design consideration as well.)

Condense sprawling phrases. Some long-winded expressions often just slow a reader's way into a sentence, especially at the beginning.

Why write . . .	**When you could write . . .**
at this point in time	now
in light of the fact that	since
in the event that	if
it is obvious that	obviously
on an everyday basis	routinely
on the grounds that	because
regardless of the fact that	although

We are so accustomed to these familiar but wordy expressions that we don't notice how little they convey.

WORDY   **At this point in time,** the committee hasn't convened.

REVISED   The committee hasn't convened **yet.**

Cut nominalizations. Nominalizations are nouns made by adding endings to verbs and adjectives. The resulting words tend to be long and vague, and they often sound awkward as well.

Word	**Nominalization**
customize	customi**zation**
historicize	historici**zation**
knowledge	knowledge**ableness**
prioritize	prioriti**zation**

Novice writers sometimes use nominalizations as a way of sounding scholarly or authoritative, but overusing them can have just the opposite effect, making a writer sound pompous or foolish. Avoid them whenever possible.

Condense long verb phrases to focus on the action. To show tense and mood, verb phrases need auxiliaries and helping verbs: I *could have* gone; she *will be* writing. But many verb phrases are strung out by unnecessary clutter.

Why write . . .	**When you could write . . .**
give consideration to	consider

make acknowledgment of	acknowledge
have doubts about	doubt
is reflective of	reflects
has an understanding of	understands
put the emphasis on	emphasize

Cut down on expletive constructions. Expletives are short expressions such as *it was, there are,* and *this is* that function like starting blocks for pushing into a sentence or clause. For example:

It was a dark and stormy night.
There are too many gopher holes on this golf course!

Some expletives are unavoidable. But using them habitually to open your sentences will make your prose tiresome. In many cases, sentences will be stronger without the expletives.

WITH EXPLETIVE	Even though **it is** the oldest manufacturer of automobiles, Mercedes-Benz remains innovative.
EXPLETIVE CUT	The oldest manufacturer of automobiles, Mercedes-Benz, still remains innovative.

Why write . . .	When you could write . . .
It is clear that	Clearly
It is to be hoped	We hope
There are reasons for	For several reasons
There is a desire for	We want
There was an expectation	They expected

18.2

Avoid vague evaluative terms. Writers often report information in evaluative terms too vague to make much of an impression. If you find yourself tempted to overuse the following terms, you may want to reconsider.

Vague Terms

bad	effective	good	little	nice
big	fine	great	neat	poor

Also avoid expressions that begin with vague qualifiers such as *pretty, sort of, kind of, such a,* and *so.*

The point of most research is to make ideas more robust, not to bury claims under vacuous adjectives. Every time you use a vague evaluative term in a draft, circle it and ask yourself, What do I mean by _____ ? What exactly makes my subject _____ ? Then incorporate those specifications into your prose, as shown in these examples:

Why write . . .	When you could provide details?
a bad estimate	an estimate 125 percent too high
good evidence	three refereed articles in JAMA
nice music	lush, romantic orchestration
sort of hot	a surface temperature of 104°F

At this point you should see the whole project—in all its component parts—coming together, and you should be prepared to move into the last phase of the task: revising your draft, verifying that all necessary documentation has been included, and preparing the project for presentation.

WWW Web Sites Worth Knowing

18.3

- "Writing a First Draft," http://daphne.palomar.edu/handbook/firstdraft.htm
- William Strunk's *Elements of Style*, http://www.bartleby.com/141
- Strategies for Overcoming Writer's Block, http://www.english.uiuc.edu/cws/wworkshop/advice/writersblock.htm
- International Writing Centers Association Home Page, http://www.writingcenters.org

MANAGING YOUR PROJECT

1. Find a place and a time to work on drafting your project. Don't underestimate the importance of this preparation. Gather all the materials you need in one location so that you don't have to interrupt your writing. Also claim the time you need from friends, other projects, and other concerns. Make yourself comfortable, too.

2. Review the timetable for completing your project, and adjust it to fit any changes in your project to date (see Chapter 1). Be sure the schedule remains specific and reasonable. You'll be more successful if you break the project into manageable parts and set goals that you can realistically meet.

3. Schedule a visit to your campus writing center and prepare for the visit in advance. What sorts of questions do you have about your draft? What things concern you most, and what would you like help with? Go in with a list of specific issues you would like to discuss.

CHAPTER 19

Revising Your Project and Reviewing Documentation

In "The Death of the Footnote (Report on an Exaggeration)," published in *The Wilson Quarterly* (Winter 1997), Anthony Grafton, professor of history at Princeton University, writes, "Footnotes give us reason to believe that their authors have done their best to find out the truth . . . they give us reason to trust what we read." Documentation is the evidence you provide to support the ideas you present in a research project. Effective documentation gives the material you offer readers credibility and authority.

But the unending conversation of ideas that makes academic work an adventure is always present too, as Grafton explains: "[Footnotes] democratize scholarly writing: they bring many voices, including those of the sources, together on a single page." Footnotes, in-text notes, and electronic hyperlinks encourage the conversation that has become essential to contemporary academic work.

Specific guidelines for formal documentation appear in Chapters 23 through 27. This chapter examines general strategies for revision as well as principles of acknowledging and using sources.

19a Review your project's content and focus

When you revise an early version of a paper or a project, you are not correcting it; you're making much bigger changes, the kind that might affect its subject, focus, structure, even its genre. Bring a fresh eye to your work and make major changes wherever they're needed—painful as such revisions may be. Ask yourself frankly whether you like the paper or the project and believe it has potential. If you really dislike what you've produced, consider starting over, perhaps by mining a vein in the original that shows more promise.

Review your purpose. Someone reading your draft should quickly understand what you are trying to accomplish. Ask yourself the following questions:

- What do I really want to achieve with my project?
- Will readers appreciate the point of the project?
- Have I chosen a project that is important and interesting to my readers or the community?

Check the focus of the project. Is your topic so broad that the work seems superficial or rambling? Ask these questions:

- Does the thesis sentence present a limited claim that I can support with specific evidence?
- Have I made broad generalizations I can't prove in the space available?

Recall your audience. Your first draft is very likely to be "writer-centered," which means that its ideas are stated mostly from your point of view. If so, it's time to become more "reader-centered"—to adapt your writing to the needs and expectations of your audience. Ask these questions:

- Have I decided whom I want to reach with this project? What would their interest in my work be?
- What do I know about this group (or these groups—you may have more than one type of reader in mind)? What kinds of examples and reasons will they respond to?
- How much do my readers already know about the subject? What questions might they have?
- What tone and style of writing is appropriate for these readers? Should my language or presentation be more or less formal?

When revising, your greatest asset is a clear sense of your audience.

Review the content of your project. You may need to add information and more detail to your project to make it important to readers. Ask yourself these questions:

- Have I answered the journalist's questions—*who, what, when, why, where,* and *how?*
- Do I need to quote authorities or offer more specific examples to give weight to my essay and add interest?
- Have I supported my claims with acceptable evidence?

Drafting your research project is likely to be a time-consuming process, but you will be well rewarded by the satisfaction you feel once you have a completed draft.

19b Evaluate the organization of your project

Organizing a sizable project involves seeing that all its parts fit together. Is the information in the body of your report clearly supported by the tables and charts you've placed in its appendixes? Will the separate panels in your brochure or the pages in your Web site work well together?

Sometimes you may be too close to your own project to review the material objectively yourself. Encourage others from outside your project group to review an early draft and give you feedback. You might then ask yourself and any reviewers these basic questions:

- Does the project need a more explanatory opening, one with more background information?
- Does the project need more signposts to keep readers on track? more logical divisions? better headings and subheadings? a site map or other graphics?
- Are links between claims and evidence solid?
- Are connections or transitions between parts of the project adequate?
- Do the verbal and visual elements of the project cohere?
- Does the closing require more summary?

Try the following method to check your structure:

- **Underline the topic idea, or thesis, in your draft.** It should be clearly stated in the first few sentences or paragraphs.
- **Underline just the first sentence in each subsequent paragraph.** If the first sentence is very short or closely tied to the second, underline the first two sentences.
- **Read the underlined sentences straight through as if they formed an essay in themselves.** Does each sentence advance or explain the main point or thesis statement? If the sentences—taken together—read coherently, chances are good that the paper is well organized.
- **If the underlined sentences don't make sense, reexamine those paragraphs or sections.** If the ideas really aren't related, delete the entire paragraph or section. If the ideas are related, consider how to revise your structure to make the connection clearer. A new lead sentence for a paragraph or a new section heading will often solve the problem.
- **Test your conclusion against your introduction.** Sometimes conclusions contradict their openings because of changes that occurred as the project developed. If you find this is true in your project, you may want to consider revising. (See Section 18d for more information on writing introductions and conclusions.)

19c Provide a source for every direct quotation

A direct quotation is any material repeated word for word from a source. (For integrating quotations in your project, see Chapter 14.) Direct quotations in college projects often require some form of parenthetical documentation—that is, a citation of author and page number (MLA) or author, date, and page number (APA).

> **MLA** It is possible to define literature as simply "that text which the community insists on having repeated from time to time intact" (Joos 51–52).

> **APA** Hashimoto (1986) questions the value of attention-getting essay openings that "presuppose passive, uninterested (probably uninteresting) readers" (p. 126).

Some systems signal notes with raised or highlighted numbers in the body of a text, keyed to either individual footnotes or endnotes (Chicago style) or to sources on a References page (CSE style).

> **CMS** Achilles can hardly be faulted for taking offense to this incident, as it "threatened to invalidate . . . the whole meaning of his life."[2]

> **CSE** Oncologists[1] are aware of trends in cancer mortality.[2]

Many electronically accessed sources—especially Web pages—do not have page numbers. For these types of sources, the parenthetical note or footnote usually includes only the author's last name. (For more on citing electronic sources, see Chapter 23.)

Famous sayings, proverbs, and biblical citations do not need formal documentation as they are considered forms of common knowledge (see Section 19e); however, if in doubt, it is better to give too much information than too little. Remember, too, that your own credibility rests on the accuracy and credibility of your sources and the uses you make of them.

19d Provide a source for all paraphrased material

Even when you express information from other sources completely in your own words, you still need to document it. Paraphrases and summaries of another person's ideas or information can be cited by placing a parenthetical note at the end of the paraphrase or summary, indicating the author's last name (see Chapter 13). You should also include page number(s) when you are summarizing or paraphrasing a specific section of the text. For example:

> Though so-called single-track trails might put mountain bikers in conflict with the hikers, such tracks are often empty and underutilized (van der Plas 106).

FOCUS ON . . . Citing Sources Responsibly

A student in a first-year composition classroom was surprised by the results when he submitted his paper to an online plagiarism detection service. Although he had carefully enclosed all direct quotations in quotation marks and scrupulously listed all of his sources in his Works Cited list, it wasn't enough. Much of his text was still identified as plagiarism.

In addition to citing direct quotations, you must cite your source for borrowed information.

- Statistics
- Paraphrased or summarized material
- Graphics, tables, and figures

Even material that you may consider common knowledge may need to be cited in order to lend your work greater credibility, and, of course, you want to make sure that summaries and paraphrases of information are truly in your own words as well as cited.

Every item in your list of Works Cited or References should be cited in the body of your paper, either in the text itself or in a parenthetical note, and every work cited in the body of your paper should have an entry in your list of Works Cited or References.

When you are summarizing or paraphrasing a complete work (book, article, movie), omit the page number. For example:

> Problems on the Russian space station *Mir* make it clear why a human mission to Mars may not be a good idea: people in space cause problems that robots don't (Roland).

When a work is important enough to summarize or paraphrase, you may want to cite the author in the text to lend your use of the information greater credibility. For example:

> Recent problems on the Russian space station *Mir*, Alex Roland argues in a *USA Today* editorial, make it clear why a human mission to Mars may not be a good idea: people in space cause problems that robots don't.

APA and other scientific styles also include the date of publication, either in the text after the author's name or in the parenthetical note if the author's name is not mentioned in the text (see Part VI).

19e Document all ideas not from common knowledge

Common knowledge includes facts, dates, events, information, and concepts that an educated person can be assumed to know. You may need to check an encyclopedia to find out that the Battle of Waterloo was fought on June 18, 1815, but that fact belongs to common knowledge, so you don't have to document it.

You may also make assumptions about *common knowledge within a field.* When you find that a given piece of information or an idea is shared among several of the sources you are using, you need not document it. (For example, if in writing a paper on anorexia nervosa you discover that most authorities define it in the same way, you probably don't have to document that definition.) What experts know collectively constitutes the common knowledge within a field; what they claim individually—their opinions, studies, theories, research projects, and hypotheses—is the material you *must* document in a paper.

COMMON KNOWLEDGE

The Internet is a vast network of computers that connects millions of people from many areas of the world.

NOT COMMON KNOWLEDGE

The Internet is a vast network of computers used by over 300 million people worldwide (USIC).

OR

The Internet is a vast network of computers which, according to the United States Internet Council, is used by over 300 million people worldwide.

When you're not sure whether the information you are using is common knowledge, document it. You should also consider documenting information if your readers are likely to question it or if your argument depends on your readers accepting the information as credible (see Section 19g).

19f Document information from field research

Some of the information you present may be the result of your own original research. While this information may not be included in your list of Works Cited or References, you will still need to acknowledge the source of your information in the body of your paper or project. Asserting that two out of three students in your class spent more than $50 on a pair of sneakers in the past year is not convincing, but you can make it convincing by providing the source of your information.

A survey of students in Dr. Smith's English 101 class at State University conducted during fall semester 2004 indicated that two out of three students spent more than $50 on a pair of sneakers during the 2003-04 school year.

For more formal research projects, you may need to provide information about your methodology. (How did you select students to survey? How many students were surveyed? How was the survey administered?) Sometimes the survey and complete results will be included as appendixes.

Similarly, citing the authority of interviewees can help corroborate the information you include.

> "Timed in-class writings are not usually the best way to assess students'
>
> writing abilities," cautioned Dr. Jones, professor of English at XYZ
>
> University, in an email interview with the author.

You may need to include the transcripts of interviews as appendixes as well; check with your instructor for specific requirements for your project.

19g Document all material that might be questioned

When your subject is controversial, you may want to document even those facts or ideas considered common knowledge. Suppose that, in writing about witchcraft in colonial America, you make an assertion that is well known by historians but likely to surprise nonspecialists, such as "Virtually no witch burnings took place in the American colonies." Writing to nonspecialists, you should certainly document the assertion. Writing to historians, you would probably skip the note.

Sometimes people's biases can be reflected in what they think of as common knowledge. Don't confuse personal opinion with fact. General statements such as "Men make better soldiers than women" and "Reagan was one of our country's best presidents" are common knowledge only to people who feel the same way. You should provide evidence to back up these claims.

Documentation should give readers confidence in your source. A traditional citation for a book usually tells them (at minimum) the name of the author, the title of the book, the place and date of publication, and the identity of the publisher—enough information to support a judgment about the authority of the work. However, you may want to provide additional information in the text, particularly if your argument hinges on the information. For instance, in the first paragraph of this chapter, we not only noted the author's name and the publication information for the quotation we used about footnotes, but we also included information about the writer's authority, identifying the author as a "professor of history at Princeton University."

19h Furnish source information for all graphics, audio files, and other borrowings

If you include graphics (either downloaded or scanned), audio, video, or other types of files in your project, you will need to provide source information. Make sure you have permission to use the files or graphics, and follow any instructions the permission specifies for citing your source (see Chapter 9). For online projects you may also need to include a link to the original Web site on which the graphic is published.

Often these kinds of sources will not appear in your list of Works Cited or References. Instead, you may include the source information as a credit line following the title of a figure or table (see Chapter 20). Alternatively, you may compile a separate Credits page (see Part V), especially if you make extensive use of copyrighted material.

19i Furnish dates and other useful information

Provide dates for important events, major figures, and works of literature and art. Also identify any people readers might not recognize.

> After the Great Fire of London (1666), the city was . . .

> Henry Highland Garnet (1815–82), an American abolitionist and radical, . . .

> Pearl (c. 1400), an elegy about . . .

In the latter example, *c.* stands for *circa,* which means "about" or "approximately."

When quoting from literary works, help readers locate the passages you cite. For novels, identify page numbers; for plays, give act, scene, and line numbers; for long poems, provide line numbers and, when appropriate, division numbers (book, canto, or other divisions). Some Internet sources provide paragraph numbers or links to specific sections of a page, usually indicated in the URL by a pound sign (#) followed by the name of the target (for example, *#AT2*).

> NCSA's "A Beginner's Guide to HTML" explains how to add alternative text
>
> for images (#AT2), which is often recommended to facilitate ADA
>
> compliance.

The reader may access the specific section cited by adding the information in parentheses to the end of the URL in the Works Cited entry.

> National Center for Supercomputing Applications (NCSA). "A Beginner's
>
> Guide to HTML." Rev. 23 Jan. 2001.
>
> http://archive.ncsa.uiuc.edu/General/Internet/WWW/HTMLPrimerAll.html
>
> (10 May 2004).

19j Use links to document electronic sources

Creating a link in a Web page to the original source (if it is online) can function as a type of documentation: such links take readers directly to supporting material or sources. However, it's important that readers understand where a highlighted passage is leading them; when they select a link, they should know where they are going.

But don't overwhelm a Web page with links that do not contribute significantly to the project. Note, too, that you may still be expected to provide a Works Cited or References page or traditional documentation in a scholarly paper that is posted online. The hypertext link may supplement, but won't necessarily replace, more traditional documentation.

19k Include all the parts your project requires

Before submitting a research project, reread the specifications of the instructor or the professional society to which you are submitting your paper. Must you, for instance, include an abstract or an outline? What leeway (if any) do you have in arranging the title page, notes, bibliography, and other features?

Don't forget to provide your reader with all the information necessary to cite your document and (when necessary) to contact you for permission to use your material. Essential bibliographical information for a Web site includes the following elements:

- Your name and email address or email link.
- Title of your work.
- Date of publication/creation and/or date of last modification or revision.
- URL for your document and/or your home page.

Finally, give credit to your sources. Don't just provide a link to an online source; include full bibliographical information, or at least the complete URL, in your Web text. Then people who print out your document from the Web won't lose track of the linked sources—which may print out only as underscored words or phrases. Include the source of any graphics or other files you used in your document as well.

Now is the time to review your project carefully. Make sure that you have met all the requirements of the assignment (the hard points), that your focus is clear and consistent, your arguments and supporting evidence are sound and logical, and your sources are correctly documented. Next comes the fun part: designing the project, testing it, and submitting the final version professionally. In Chapter 20 you will learn the basics of good design for both print and electronic projects.

WWW Web Sites Worth Knowing

- "Avoiding Plagiarism," http:// sja.ucdavis.edu/avoid.htm
- "Using Quotations Effectively," http://www.virtualsalt.com/quotehlp.htm
- University of Wisconsin–Madison Writing Center, "Using Literary Quotations," http://www.wisc.edu/writing/Handbook/QuoLitIncorporating.html

19.1

MANAGING YOUR PROJECT

An important decision you will make is to determine what system of documentation best suits your project. Consider these matters:

1. Did the assignment sheet ask you to use a specific form of documentation?

2. Do you expect to use electronic sources? You may want to use COS style (see Chapter 23).

3. Are you preparing a project in the arts or humanities? If so, you'll want to choose either MLA (Chapter 24) or CMS style (Chapter 26). Notes in these systems focus on individual authors and on particular passages within works.

4. Are you preparing a project in the social sciences? If so, you'll want to use APA style (Chapter 25). Notes in this system focus on complete research studies (rather than on individual passages) and the dates of their publication.

5. Are you preparing a project in the natural sciences? If so, you'll want to use CSE style (Chapter 27).

6. Do you prefer using in-text notes? If so, your options are MLA (Chapter 24) and APA style (Chapter 25).

7. Do you prefer traditional footnotes? If so, use CMS style (Chapter 26).

V

PRESENTING YOUR RESEARCH

DON'T MISS . . .

- **The guidelines for selecting a project format in Chapter 20a.** Choose the presentation method that works best for your material, your audience, and your goals.
- **The principles of document design in Section 20b.** Good document design will give your project impact and help readers understand how all the parts work together.
- **The advice for making oral and visual presentations in Chapter 21.** Careful preparation and well-designed materials will reduce any nervousness you might feel.
- **The annotated Web pages and technical reports in Chapter 22.** See how professional document designers make use of space, fonts, and graphics to present information clearly and stylishly.

EVERYDAY RESEARCH

DR. IRWIN HOLLANDER, Senior Research Biochemist (Oncology Discovery)
Wyeth Pharmaceuticals

As one of the research scientists involved in the recent discovery of a drug used to treat a form of leukemia, Irwin Hollander's job is truly a rewarding one, combining a love for chemistry and the added benefit of helping others.

Research obviously plays a key role in Dr. Hollander's daily work. In the laboratory, he measures the activity of key enzymes and proteins from cancer cells. Dr. Hollander then tests and retests certain compounds for their ability to block the activity of these enzymes, first in test tubes, and then inside the actual cancer cells. Compounds that seem effective are then tested for their ability to stop or slow the growth of cancer cells; compounds that are successful eventually lead to new drugs that treat cancers. When he is not in the laboratory, Dr. Hollander pores over the published work of other research scientists. The latter type of research is an essential part of his work in discovering and developing new drugs for the treatment of cancer.

"In high school, I had a great chemistry teacher, Mr. Zuckerman. Later, in college, I became specifically more interested in biochemistry through course work and lab research. I also reviewed literature and wrote reports." This work prepared him for the kind of responsibilities he now has in his current position.

CHAPTER 20

Designing Documents

Imagine yourself sitting in a dentist's office, looking for something to read while waiting for your appointment. Which would you be the more likely to pick up and browse through: a 50 page, all-text scientific research report on the effectiveness of a new treatment for gingivitis (complete with statistical analyses of clinical trials conducted over a five-year period) or a snappy little brochure with graphics and pictures that explained the same treatment in simple terms? Unless you happen to be a dentist yourself, chances are you'd pick up the brochure and use the research report as a footrest.

Document design is part of the process of creating *any* written work, even a conventional academic essay. The decisions you make as a writer about document design are rhetorical—that is, they will depend on your purpose and audience and on the requirements of your assignment and topic. This chapter will help you choose the best format for your project.

20a Consider the formats your project might take

WWW
20.1

A research project may take a variety of formats, depending on your purpose, audience, and topic. If your purpose is to present information from research to an academic audience, you will probably want to write a research paper. In the humanities, you will then need to follow the guidelines set forth by the Modern Language Association (MLA); in the social sciences, you may follow American Psychological Association (APA) guidelines; and in the hard sciences, you may need to follow Council of Science Editors (CSE) style.

Or your project may take other formats. A letter to the editor of your school or local newspaper would look very different from an academic essay, while a newsletter article or brochure might allow you to include different type fonts, colors, and graphics. Oral presentations may require electronic slide shows or other visuals (see Chapter 21). Even presenting a more-or-less traditional research paper as a Web site entails a considerable number of choices: whether to present your project on a single Web page or divide the material and present it on separate pages with links from one page to another; how to format headings, paragraphs, and your list of Works Cited or Refer-

Document Formats

Traditional Print Formats

Letters	Résumés	Papers/Reports	Booklets
Memoranda	Articles	Flyers	Spreadsheets
Pamphlets	Brochures	Books	Newsletters

Common Electronic Formats

Email	Web pages (.htm, .html)	Message forums
Word-processing files	Graphics files	Spreadsheets
Help files	Sound files	Animation files
Program scripts	Style sheets	Databases
Rich Text Format (.rtf)	Portable Document Format (.pdf)	

Other Presentation Formats

Speeches	Slide shows	Video clips
Dramatic performances	Colloquiums	Debates

FIGURE 20.1 Document formats.

ences; whether to include graphics, tables, lists, external links, multimedia, and other features allowed by electronic publishing.

Figure 20.1 lists some common document formats for print and electronic media. The basic principles of document design that follow apply to most of these formats, although different media may also require you to rethink some of them. For more information on oral and visual media, see Chapter 21; see Chapter 22 for examples of projects in a variety of genres and formats.

20b Understand the principles of document design

The most important consideration—for both print and electronic projects—is that your project meets the needs of your readers. Unlike writing style, which focuses on such things as word choice, sentence structure, and figurative language, document design is concerned with the ways in which you present your message through formatting and media. In Figure 20.2 you can see how a sample newsletter page makes use of colors, fonts, images, lines, and boxes to set off elements of the text, show relationships, and lead the reader's eye to important information. The following are some of the more common elements of document design you should be familiar with for both print and online projects (see Chapter 21 for more information on oral and visual presentations).

Suitability. Consider the requirements of the particular rhetorical situation for your project. The choices you make about document design will depend on your answers to the questions in Checklist 20.1 on page 207.

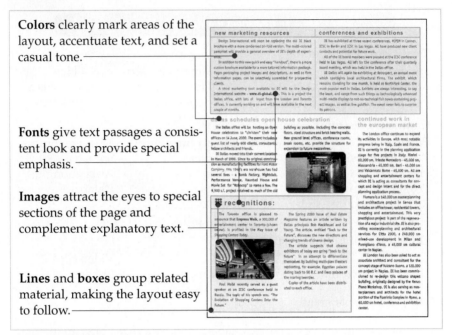

Colors clearly mark areas of the layout, accentuate text, and set a casual tone.

Fonts give text passages a consistent look and provide special emphasis.

Images attract the eyes to special sections of the page and complement explanatory text.

Lines and **boxes** group related material, making the layout easy to follow.

FIGURE 20.2 The basic elements of document style are at work in this newsletter page.

Accessibility. Considerations of access are twofold. First, of course, you must have access to the necessary equipment and skills to produce a document in the desired format. Second, and equally important (if not more so), your audience must have the necessary knowledge and means to access your work. That is, if your audience is unlikely to have a computer or Internet access, then a Web page is probably not the best format.

You may even need to combine or overlap formats to reach your whole audience. For instance, on the Web, you may want to provide a text-only version of your pages (many of which will likely feature images) to accommodate users such as the visually impaired who may need to access the Web through programs that read texts to them. Similarly, you may decide to provide your materials in downloadable formats such as portable document format (PDF) that retain your document formatting codes.

If you want your audience to be able to access *you*, then that goal will also dictate some of the format choices you will make. For example, if you want to encourage readers to respond to your work, you'll have to make it easy for them to do so—perhaps by furnishing an email address, a telephone number, or a mailing address. Or if you want readers to pressure their congressional representatives on an issue, your project might include a list of the representatives' names and addresses, as well as a sample letter identifying key points to make. For similar reasons, brochures and mailings might include tear-off response forms, or Web sites might include email addresses or automatic form submissions.

CHECKLIST 20.1

Document Design

Audience

○ Who is the primary audience for your project?

○ What are their needs and expectations, including their expectations about language and level of diction, structure, and format?

Purpose

○ What is/are your purpose(s) for writing?

○ How does this purpose affect your choices of language, structure, and medium?

○ How will your choice of format help you to achieve your purpose(s)?

○ What do you want your reader to know or do with the information you present?

Occasion

○ What occasions (or causes) you to write about this topic at this time?

○ What has prompted you to choose a particular audience and purpose for your project?

○ How is your choice of format at least partially—if not substantially—affected by the occasion, or context, within which you write?

Medium

○ For your particular audience(s), what are the usual choices of medium?

○ Why would a particular format (for instance, a text-only, double-spaced essay) be appropriate for certain types of media and not for others?

○ How will your choice of medium affect the presentation of your message?

○ What formatting choices are allowed—or prohibited—by your choice of medium?

Navigability. In traditional papers, navigational cues may be as basic as transitional words and phrases or headings and subheadings (see also Section 18e). Or they may be more complex—graphs, tables, appendixes, indexes, and so on. Traditional formatting cues such as paragraphing, page numbering, and even the use of upper- and lowercase fonts are all means of helping readers navigate through the structure of a document. On a Web page, in addition to or in place of more traditional navigational cues, you may need to supply hypertext links, instructions for downloading applications or plug-ins, buttons, site maps, drop-down menus, or other means to help your reader find their way through the information on your site. You'll also want to offer your information in formats that your audience can readily access.

As you consider possible designs for the presentation of your project, you will want to keep in mind any hard points or requirements of the assignment (see Chapter 1). In the next section, you will learn more about how the principles of suitability, accessibility, and navigability are applied in specific situations.

20c Apply design principles

As you apply these design principles to specific types of documents for different media, you will find many similarities. Since the invention of movable type in the fifteenth century, people have relied on printed texts for much of their information. Thanks to powerful software and high-speed printers, almost anyone today can produce documents that rival those from a print shop. But many writers have abused this design capability, sometimes forgetting that design should enhance a message, not become the message itself. A well-designed Web page is attractive and easy to read; it fulfills a purpose and provides the reader with something useful—information, links, entertainment value—that makes time visiting the site well spent. It does not distract readers with unnecessary clutter.

Fortunately, most professional and academic disciplines offer sensible guidelines for formatting documents. Consult the style guide for your field whenever you begin a major project—whether it's a paper or something less conventional. The following are important elements of document design that you should become familiar with, regardless of the type of document you will be producing.

Page size, margins, and line spacing. Most academic projects for print will use standard paper sizes (in the United States, $8\frac{1}{2}$ by 11 inches) with standard margins, usually one inch on all four sides. For paper projects that will be bound, however, the left-hand margin may need to be increased to 1.5 inches; if the bound project will have type on both sides of each page, the right-hand margin may be increased to 1.5 inches on even-numbered pages. Headers, required for many types of academic papers, are usually positioned one-half inch from the top margin. The draft should usually be double spaced throughout. For typical formats in different styles, see the sample papers in MLA style in Chapter 24, in APA style in Chapter 25, and in CMS style in Chapter 26.

Newsletters and brochures may use smaller margins than academic essays. Newsletters are often formatted in columns and may be printed on either standard or legal size ($8\frac{1}{2}$ by 14 inches) paper. A brochure may use either size paper, formatted in "panels" to allow it to be folded. Newsletters and brochures are often printed on both sides of a single sheet of paper (see Chapter 22).

For electronic documents, the "page" size often depends on the software used to view the document, the size of the screen, the browser window, and other factors. While a Web page may not have margins in the traditional sense, some Web page designers argue that information should be "chunked" to fit on one screen, and most agree that formatting that forces readers to scroll to the right or left should be avoided. Further, trying to force line breaks to emulate double spacing or the hanging indents used in print documents can result in a mess if your reader views your project with a different Web browser, screen size, or font than you intended. You will also need to ensure that your page design includes "white space" (areas of the page with no text or graphics) to enhance readability and avoid clutter.

A good site to visit for more information on Web page design is the Yale C/AIM "Web Style Guide" at **http://info.med.yale.edu/caim/manual**. While you could take a course in Web design (not a bad idea if you have the time and interest), you can learn much about good (and bad) Web page design simply by casting a critical eye at the pages you visit online. Think about the sites you like—those that are easy to navigate, attractive, and useful—and then consider how their design contributes to that ease of use.

Headings and subheadings. In academic papers, specific guidelines for headings and subheadings often apply. A short research paper (five or six pages) may need only a title. Longer papers may require subheadings that announce the content of major sections. Subheadings should be brief, parallel in phrasing, and consistent in format. MLA style provides fairly loose standards for headings and subheadings, with titles ordinarily centered on the first page and first-level headings flush with the left-hand margin. APA style (see Chapter 25) defines five levels of headings for professional articles, more than you are likely to need for most academic projects. While the rules vary, most styles agree that you must have at least two headings at each level and that you should be consistent in how you format headings and subheadings in your document.

Newsletters and brochures also use different levels of headers to indicate major and minor divisions. However, in addition to boldface, italics, and underlining, you may be able to choose different font sizes, faces, and colors, or you may use text boxes or background coloring to draw your reader's attention.

HyperText Markup Language (HTML) designates six levels of headers, as shown in Figure 20.3. You can also choose different font styles, sizes, or colors to designate various levels of headings. But be careful with your choices; professionals caution that mixing too many different font styles or colors makes a page difficult to read.

Headings and subheadings help the reader navigate your page and locate information quickly. They also help break the text into chunks, allowing addi-

<H1>Level One Header</H1>

<H2>Level Two Header</H2>

<H3>Level Three Header</H3>

<H4>Level Four Header</H4>

<H5>Level Five Header</H5>

<H6>Level Six Header</H6>

FIGURE 20.3 Six levels of HTML headers.

tional white space to make your page more attractive and less intimidating. Note the differences in the two pages in Figure 20.4: both pages use subheadings, but the right-hand page includes more white space, making that page more inviting.

Fonts and colors. For most academic projects, use a simple *serif* font (see Figure 20.5) such as Times New Roman 10- or 12-point type. Nonstandard, "fancy" fonts may actually detract from what you have to say, and fonts that are too large can be as difficult to read as those that are too small. Use a good-quality printer and white paper to increase contrast for easy readability.

With print projects such as brochures or newsletters, you have more freedom for artistic expression than with academic essays. For example, you can use colors and fonts for visual emphasis. But show restraint—using too many colors can be distracting and unattractive as well as expensive since commercial printers charge extra for each additional color.

Rules for Hiking in the Park

Don't go off the trail. The animal habitats in the park are extremely fragile. While we encourage people to enjoy the natural benefits provided inside, in order to maintain the survival of the fauna and flora, visitors must restrict themselves to clearly marked trails.

Don't take anything out of the park. Just as we don't want visitors leaving their marks, we don't want them removing what might be necessary parts of a fragile ecology.

Don't feed the animals. Wild animals can become dependent upon humans, if they expect to be fed. Once in the habit of receiving handouts they can become aggressive when refused—then they must be removed.

Report violations of these rules. It's your park. When other visitors violate these rules, they are destroying public property.

Rules for Hiking in the Park

Don't go off the trail.
The animal habitats in the park are extremely fragile. While we encourage people to enjoy the natural benefits provided inside, in order to maintain the survival of the fauna and flora, visitors must restrict themselves to clearly marked trails.

Don't take anything out of the park.
Just as we don't want visitors leaving their marks, we don't want them removing what might be necessary parts of a fragile ecology.

Don't feed the animals.
Wild animals can become dependent upon humans, if they expect to be fed. Once in the habit of receiving handouts they can become aggressive when refused—then they must be removed.

Report violations of these rules.
It's your park. When other visitors violate these rules, they are destroying public property.

FIGURE 20.4 Two examples of the use of headings and subheadings.

Font Styles

SERIF FONTS
Serif fonts are the most easily readable. The "feet" lead the reader's eye and help in recognition of letters and words. Use serif fonts for most body text. These are some of the more common serif fonts.

- Courier
- Times or Times New Roman
- Bookman Old Style

SANS SERIF FONTS
Sans serif fonts are generally not as easy to read as serif fonts, but they have a clean look that stands out. Use sans serif fonts for headings. These are examples of common sans serif fonts.

- Arial
- Futura
- Helvetica

FIGURE 20.5 Choose the font style to suit your project.

For electronic projects, the cost of reproduction is not a consideration as it is with print projects, but mixing too many colors on a page may result in a distracting mishmash. Use different type fonts, sizes, and colors only to enhance your project, to make elements stand out, or to designate related information. Don't fall into the "because I can" trap; use features to enhance your presentation, not simply because the technology allows them.

Tables and figures. Tables and figures can help readers understand your ideas better than words alone. You might want to use pie charts, graphs, and tables to make statistics easier to interpret or trends easier to spot. The use of tables, figures, and other visuals has been shown to aid in reader understanding and retention, especially when complicated or complex statistical information is being given.

Choose the right format to present information.

- Use *tables* to present complicated data in an easy-to-comprehend format and to allow comparisons among items.
- Use *bar charts* to allow ready comparison of quantities.
- Use *line charts* to show changes in quantities over time.
- Use *pie charts* to show the distribution of parts of a whole when exact quantities are not essential.
- Use *Gantt charts* to show progress over time toward a goal.

• Use *maps* to indicate geographic locations and relations.

• Use *flowcharts* to illustrate steps in a process or procedure.

Be careful, though, not to clutter your work with what design experts call "chartjunk." Develop an eye for clean and attractive presentations on paper or screen.

For academic papers, MLA format requires that you label tables (columns of data) and figures (pictures or illustrations), number them, and briefly identify what they illustrate. Spell out the word *table* and place the heading above the table, flush left, as in the following example. Short tables may appear on the same page as text material.

Table 1

Economic Dimensions of the Bond Market, 1980–90

	Year-End Amounts	Outstanding	(in billions)
Type of Issuer[a]	1980	1985	1990
U.S. Treasury	$159.8	$427.0	$1,023.6
U.S. agencies	17.6	276.1	447.3
States and municipalities	144.4	322.3	734.9
Corporations	181.0	421.7	752.3
Total	$502.8	$1,447.1	$2,958.1

Sources: Federal Reserve Bulletin, U.S. Treasury Bulletin, and Survey of Current Business.

[a]Excludes institutional issues; data are not available.

The word *Figure,* usually abbreviated in the caption as *Fig.,* appears below the illustration, flush left.

For an APA paper, check the complete coverage of figures and tables in the *Publication Manual of the American Psychological Association,* fifth edition. For APA-style student papers, figures (including graphs, illustrations, and photos) and tables may appear in the body of the text. Longer tables and figures are placed on separate pages, immediately following their mention in the text.

Chromosomes consist of four different nucleotides or bases which, working together, provide the code for different genes (see Figure 1).

Figures and tables are numbered consecutively. When an illustration or figured is borrowed from another source, you must get permission to reproduce it, and you need to acknowledge your source as in the following example:

Figure 1. The four bases of the genetic code: adenine (A), guanine (G), thymine (T), and cytosine (C). [Note: From *Your Genes, Your Choice,* by C. Baker, 1997. Copyright 1997 by the American Association for the Advancement of Science. Reprinted with permission.]

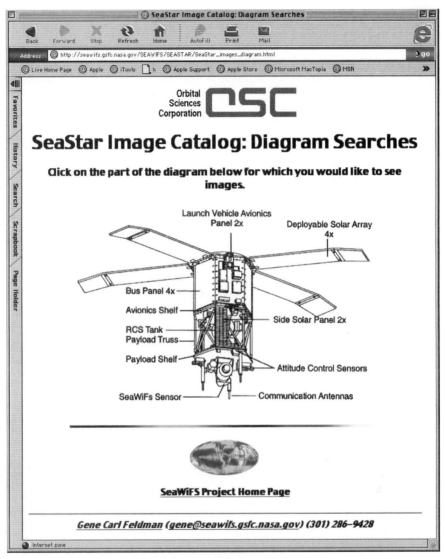

FIGURE 20.6 Appropriate labelling will help readers to understand all parts of a diagram.
(*Source: OrbView-2/SeaStar Satellite is reprinted by permission of Orbital Sciences.*)

A table title appears above the table; the source of information appears below the table.

In Web documents, you can use lists or tables to present information in rows and columns the same way you do with print documents, and you can place graphical or visual elements on your page in a variety of ways. Text and picture elements can be placed in a simple table, each element taking up one or more cells on a page as needed. While many professional Web designers argue that you should use cascading style sheets (CSS) to lay out elements on your page, you can also use tables without borders in your Web pages to make your layout more effective and aesthetically pleasing. You can use tables to achieve configurations that create the look you desire: changing the size or position of the table on the page and varying the height or width of rows, columns, or individual cells; nesting tables inside tables; or changing the width of the table's borders—or eliminating the borders altogether.

Figures of any kind should be introduced in the body of your project. You will then need to explain to your reader what the graphic shows. Don't rely on the reader to understand why you have chosen to include the figure and what it tells them (see Figure 20.6).

Photos, graphics, and multimedia. Photographs provide a realistic view of a person, place, or thing and can be useful when you want to "humanize" a project, while other types of visuals can depict what photographs cannot. For example, line drawings may show a rendering of a product that has not yet been developed; exploded views and cutaway drawings can allow readers an inside view of something (see Figure 20.7).

Figures and other graphical or multimedia elements are easy to include in Web projects, so easy that authors may often be tempted to fill all available space on a page with animated graphics, scanned photographs, and blinking text. Use graphics and figures to present data, clarify details, illustrate concepts, draw attention, or enliven your page, but use them with caution. A simple horizontal rule can be much more effective than a dozen blinking arrows. Avoid "busy" backgrounds that make information hard to read.

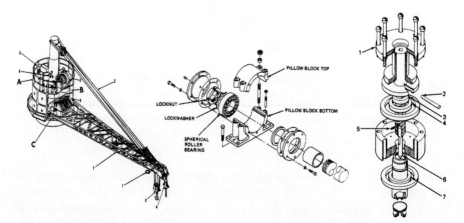

FIGURE 20.7 Line drawing, exploded view, and cutaway drawing used in technical reports.
(Source: Naval Systems Data Support Activity U.S. Navy, Technical Manual Management Program, Hull Mechanical and Electrical Equipment/System Technical Manual Production and Style Guide http://nsdsa.phdnswc.navy.mil/tmmp/axgyd010/toc.html*)*

FOCUS ON . . . **Creating Graphics and Visuals**

It makes sense to learn how to manipulate the graphics features in word-processing or data management programs. In the former you may be offered a wide range of drawing tools. In the latter you can typically choose how to present data (in tables, bar graphs, pie charts); the program itself produces the actual image, which you can modify to suit your needs.

Presentation programs like Microsoft *PowerPoint* and Corel *Presentations* make it easy to create professional-looking slides and overheads, and some even allow you to include sound or video elements. You can also learn to use desktop publishing programs such as Adobe *FrameMaker* or *PageMaker* to design sophisticated projects, including magazines and books.

If you have access to the Web, you can download pictures and other visual items for your projects, but you must both document the borrowings and get permission to use them from the authors or owners of the material. You also need to document images you scan in from published work, and you need to obtain permission to use them as well (see Chapter 9).

Lists and text boxes. Complicated information or instructions that must be followed in a specific order may be best presented as either an ordered list (if the instructions must be followed in sequence) or an unordered, or bulleted, list (when the order of operations is not essential). Ordered lists usually use numbers or letters to designate the sequence.

1. Take out two slices of fresh bread.
2. Spread one slice of bread with a thin layer of peanut butter.
3. Spread the other slice of bread with a layer of your favorite jam or jelly.
4. Place the two slices of bread together, coated sides facing each other.
5. Enjoy.

Bulleted lists highlight key ideas that do not require a specific order.

- Use bulleted lists to highlight key ideas that do not require a specific order.
- Use ordered lists to present ideas that must occur in a certain sequence.

Text boxes are useful in newsletters, brochures, or Web documents to set off headlines or other information that you wish to stand out. You can fill in the background of boxed text with shades of gray (for a black-and-white project) or colors, but be careful: make sure there is enough contrast between text and background to allow for easy reading.

For online research projects, you may also want to use the "list" feature to format your Works Cited or References list, as shown in Figure 20.8, since the

Works Cited

- Hamilton, Marcia A. "Why Suing College Students for Illegal Music Downloading Is Right." *CNN.com*/Law Center. 7 Aug. 2003. http://www.cnn.com/2003/LAW/08/07/findlaw.analysis.hamilton.music/inc (20 Aug. 2004).

- Kasaras, Kostas. "Music in the Age of Free Distribution: MP3 and Society." *First Monday* 7.1 (2002). http://firstmonday.org/issues/issue7_1/kasaras/index.html (20 Aug. 2004).

- Kontzer, Tony. "File Sharing's Close-Up." *Information Week* 27 Oct. 2003. http://www.informationweek.com/story/showArticle.jhtml?articleID=15600 233 (14 June 2004).

- "Napster Case." E-center for Business Ethics. http://www.e-businessethics.com/napster.htm (27 June 2004).

- Nguyen, Tim, Viet Nguyen, Jacob Scott, Igor Spivak, and Nicholas Stahl. "Ethics in a Peer-to-Peer World." Dept. of Nuclear Engineering. University of California, Berkeley. Spring 2003. http://www.nuc.berkeley.edu/courses/ classes/E-124/Ethics in a Peer-to-Peer World.pdf (1 July 2004).

- Read, Brock, and Jeffrey R. Young. "Music Denied." *Chronicle of Higher Education* 50.32 (2004): A30-32.

- Schultz, Jason. "File Sharing Must Be Made Legal." *Salon.com*. 12 Sep. 2003. http://archive.salon.com/tech/feature/2003/09/12/file_sharing_two (20 Aug. 2004).

- Traiman, Steve. "Boucher Wants Consumers' Fair-Use Rights Protected." *Billboard* 114.28 (2002): 67.

- Weinberger, David. "Copy Protection Is a Crime. *Wired* 11.06 (2003). http://www.wired.com/wired/archive/11.06/view.html?pg=1 (20 Aug. 2004).

FIGURE 20.8 A Works Cited list online, formatted using the "bulleted list" feature. Note that references to online sources are formatted as links and follow COS style.

"hanging indent" feature in your word processor, which formats the entries in a Works Cited or References list with the first line flush with the left-hand margin and subsequent lines indented, does not work well online.

Most Web page editors, like most word-processing applications, make formatting lists as easy as clicking a "List" button. Remember, however, that, as with figures, you need to introduce the information contained in lists within the body of your text, and be careful not to clutter your page.

20d Organize Web projects logically

For a Web site, you might try to imagine how a reader encountering it for the first time will search for information: Will users find what they are seeking with a minimum number of clicks? Do all the links work in both directions? Make sure there are no dead ends and that every page on your site provides a way to return to your home page or leads to another helpful location on the site. Make sure you include directions for returning to your site from any external links, if necessary.

Web pages offer a great deal of flexibility in design. But just as a traditional essay must follow a logical structure, a Web site needs coherent organization. Figure 20.9 depicts three organizational patterns for Web sites: hierarchical, sequential, and hub. Your project may follow any one of these patterns or a combination of them, depending on your rhetorical needs.

Like printed texts, Web pages also need transitional devices. Some of those transitions—such as titles, headings, and numerical sequences—are familiar because they are part of both printed and electronic texts. But hypertext also offers many special devices. For example, you can use page anchors (links to specific sections of a Web page) to scroll readers through lengthy online documents or establish links between pages. You can create arrows, image maps, or buttons to provide graphical transitions, and you can use pop-up browser windows or "rollovers" for digressions or explanations. Use these devices to be sure readers always know where they are in your material and how to get where they need to be.

You may also choose to include visual or multimedia elements to attract the reader's attention to important information (an email icon may alert the reader to information on contacting the author) and for navigation, but you will want to limit their file sizes, perhaps by including "thumbnail" (reduced-size) images or text descriptions on your pages with links to large multimedia files. Or you might treat interesting but unnecessary material, explanations, or definitions as separate linked files, similar to appendixes for technical reports.

20e Submit your project professionally

Bind a research paper modestly with a staple or a paper clip. Nothing more elaborate is needed, unless an instructor asks you to place the essay in a folder along with materials you used in developing it. For newsletters or brochures, make sure the information flows from one page to the next or from one panel to the next. If you have printed a newsletter on two sides of a single page, make sure that the print goes in the same direction on both sides! For brochures, you want to make sure the reader can follow the text from one panel (or "page") to the next and that space for a mailing address or contact information is in the appropriate place.

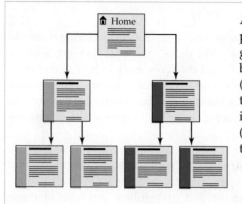

A **hierarchical** pattern organizes pages into increasingly specific groupings. Readers find material by starting with general categories (topics, areas, units) and working their way down to more specific information. Large organizations (such as colleges) often organize their Web sites this way.

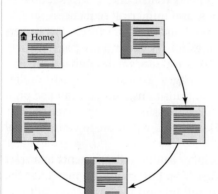

Sequential sites present readers with fewer options. If you are offering a proposal argument, your site might move readers step by step from problem to solution, with each stage of the argument building on material from the preceding screen. Readers are encouraged to click "Next Page" rather than select from a menu of options. Make sure to provide links back to the home page so readers won't reach a dead end.

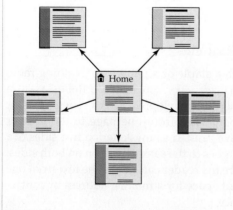

A **hub** structure encourages exploration. Here the home page links to related pages that neither require a specific order of reading nor fit into clear hierarchical groups. You might use a hub design to catalog items—say, all the native plants in a particular wetlands environment. Readers could browse each item, going back and forth from the home page. You might also provide direct links to related pages on the hub.

FIGURE 20.9 Three organizational patterns for a Web site.

When you submit an article for publication, be sure to follow all instructions for submission provided by the editors. Note in particular how many clean copies they require of your work, to whom those copies should be sent, and whether you should furnish a self-addressed, stamped envelope or separate, unattached postage for the return of your work.

When you publish your files on the Web, you will want to double-check them, preferably using different browsers and even different computers, to make sure they appear the way you want them to. Be certain that you upload any graphics files along with your HTML files (unlike print, graphics on the Web remain separate files), that you have set the necessary permissions to make your files readable, and that your links and file names all work. File names on the Web are case sensitive; you may want to use only lowercase letters for your file names to avoid problems. Avoid file names with spaces or special characters in them.

Electronic File Formats

When files are to be submitted electronically (in *WebCT* or *Blackboard*, via an email attachment, or saved on disk), you will want to be certain the file is in a format that is readable by your audience. Luckily, there are formats that are readable across platforms and applications. You can save your work as text-only, usually as ASCII-DOS Text or MS-DOS Text. But text-only files will strip your document of any special formatting features (italics, boldfaced fonts, colors, graphics). A better choice might be to save your work as Portable Document Format (PDF) or Rich Text Format (RTF) files. Check with your instructor for preferred file formats.

HTML files are readable regardless of the platform (DOS, Windows, Macintosh). However, embedded applications such as Java script or audio or video files may require certain browsers or plug-in applications. When this is the case, you can either include links to these applications or include a notice that readers need to acquire them before they can access your site.

Designing Web pages can be both frustrating and fun. It can take hours to find just the right graphic, to painstakingly proofread your work, and to eliminate all the bugs, but most students feel that the result is well worth the time and effort. Of course, Web pages aren't the only projects that require debugging; you'll pay the same careful attention to your print projects as you do to those published online. And you will want to take special care to give credit to all your sources in the proper format.

Many of the design principles for print and online projects apply to other types of projects as well. For example, an oral presentation often makes use of graphical aids, some of them electronically produced, and video essays make use of transitional devices. In Chapter 21 you will find more about how to apply design guidelines to oral and visual projects. Chapter 22 offers basic advice about authoring a Web page, along with annotated samples of a variety of print and nonprint projects.

WWW Web Sites Worth Knowing

20.2

- "Rhetorical Situation," http://www.bristol.mass.edu/department_pages/quest_writing_lab/writing/rhetoric.htm
- Writing Center at Colorado State University, " Writing Guides–Types of Documents," http://writing.colostate.edu/references/index.cfm?guides_active-documents

MANAGING YOUR PROJECT

1. Write an analysis of the rhetorical situation for your project. Who is your primary audience? What are their needs and expectations? What is your purpose in presenting your information to this audience? What is the occasion for presenting the information? What medium (paper or electronic) have you chosen, and why? Discuss your analysis with your peers, orally or by email, and compare your formatting decisions.

2. Carefully examine the structure of your project. Have friends test-drive a brochure you've designed. Does its arrangement of panels make sense? Are its headings logical? Will readers know where to go for additional information? For a Web site, ask an outsider to navigate the site. Does the structure direct readers logically to important information? Can readers navigate all levels of the site easily? Can they always return quickly to the home page? For an academic paper, check your headings and subheadings and your pagination.

CHAPTER 21

Preparing Oral and Visual Presentations

Your voice shakes; your fingers clench the podium so hard that your knuckles are white; you can't seem to find a comfortable position to stand, so you keep shifting your balance from one foot to the other. Sound familiar? If so, you're not alone! Most of us are nervous when called on to give a speech or oral presentation before a group of people. But with the right preparation and some practice, you can learn to make effective presentations.

Oral presentations require many of the same considerations as print-based projects. However, there are also important differences, since oral presentations are intended for *listeners* rather than *readers*. Nowadays, too, presentations are often supplemented by visual—usually electronic—media, and sometimes the entire presentation (including audio and perhaps video) is posted on the Web or otherwise remotely delivered.

This chapter will help you understand the principles of designing, drafting, and delivering effective oral and electronic presentations.

21a Designing oral and visual presentations

An effective oral presentation is usually carefully planned, often written on note cards. As with projects composed for print, you will need to consider your audience and purpose, the occasion for your presentation, and the media you will use. That is, in addition to presenting information orally, you may make extensive use of posters or electronic slides, you may need to prepare handouts, or you may even need to post your presentation to the Web for on-line delivery.

Electronic presentation software such as Microsoft's *PowerPoint* or Corel *Presentations* can also be used to create visuals for other media—for instance, to create transparencies to be shown with overhead projectors or to create slides or downloadable presentations for the Web. Or you may want to use presentation software to help you design posters or printed handouts (in black and white or in color) to give to your audience. All these considerations of medium are important to your design configurations.

Most oral presentations follow the same sequence as a formal written report: an introduction, a body, and a conclusion. You would do well to heed the sage advice of professionals—begin by telling your audience what you will tell them; tell them; then conclude by telling the audience what you have told them. Repetition, often berated in scholarly papers, is considered a key to effective oral presentations because it aids memory and reinforces important ideas.

You will want to begin with a strong introduction, one that will get your audience's attention. You may choose to appeal to the needs of your audience (for instance, they may need the information you provide in order to do something). Your introduction should introduce your topic, preview the information you will present, and identify your major points, as illustrated in Figure 21.1.

The body of your presentation should provide the necessary supporting details to make your point. But don't give the audience more—or less—than they need; too much information may overwhelm your audience, while too little will leave them unconvinced. You will also need to use transitions between slides, ideas, and supporting details to help your audience follow your train of thinking and to emphasize how ideas are related to each other and to your main points. In addition to repeating key ideas and terms to help your audience remember what you have already covered, parallel language can be especially helpful in oral presentations as an aid to memory. A well-known example of parallel language is found in the U.S. Declaration of Independence:

> We hold these truths to be self-evident, **that** all men are created equal, **that** they are endowed by their Creator with certain unalienable Rights, **that** among these are Life, Liberty, and the Pursuit of Happiness.

You will also want to make sure titles, headings, and subheadings, as well as any bulleted points in your slide show, are grammatically parallel.

Use plain language and avoid technical terms unless you are sure your audience will understand them or you can explain the terms adequately. Use active voice, and keep your sentences relatively short.

Visuals should be used to enhance your presentation, to clarify or emphasize important information, and to aid in understanding and retention. But be careful not to overuse them. A picture is *not* worth a thousand words: you must introduce and explain what you want the audience to see (just as with print documents). Keep visuals simple and uncluttered; address only one point or idea per visual. Presentation and word-processing software usually include a variety of clip art and audio and video selections that you may use in your presentation, or, with a little time and patience, you may choose to create your own. Make sure, however, that in addition to crediting any information (whether it is summarized, paraphrased, quoted, or included in a figure

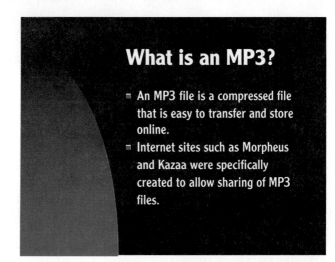

FIGURE 21.1 Preview your major points. Each point is then further developed in the slides that follow.

or table) you also give credit for any graphical or multimedia elements you borrow from other sources. (See Figure 21.2.)

When you're finishing up, don't just allow your presentation to trail off; provide a strong closing. Remind your audience of what you have said—your major points and arguments—and tell them what it means. Make clear to your audience what you want them to know or do with the information you have provided.

The questions in Checklist 21.1 on page 225 can also help you plan the design of your presentation.

Citing Graphics & Multimedia

Janice R. Walker

Backgrounds and graphics copyright Microsoft Corp. 2003

FIGURE 21.2
Cite the source of any graphics or multimedia files used in presentations.

21b Drafting oral and visual presentations

As with print projects, you will need to organize your presentation to suit the specific rhetorical situation. For example, your purpose may be to recommend a strategy, to report on the progress of a project, to provide a project overview—each of these purposes will entail choices of organization (see also Chapter 18). Many presentation software packages contain templates to help you organize your presentation for a variety of situations (see Figure 21.3 on page 226), but, of course, no software can foresee all the possibilities. You may find that some of the preformatted presentation types will fit your purpose, or you may be able to modify the templates slightly to make them fit. Or you may need to customize the layout, design, and organization to suit your own tastes and needs as well as those of your audience.

For many presentations, you will prepare posters, electronic slide shows, or handouts to accompany the information you present orally. But don't try to cram everything onto slides; remember that the slide presentation is not designed to present your entire speech. (There are, of course, exceptions to this, such as when your information will be presented online; see Section 21d.) You

CHECKLIST 21.1

Planning your presentation

○ What is your purpose? What do you want your audience to know or do with the information when you're done?

○ What does your audience already know? What do they need to know? Are they interested in your topic, or will you need to persuade them?

○ How big is the room? What time of day (or night) will it be?

○ What equipment is available? Will there be chalkboards, an overhead projector, computer and projection equipment, a microphone? Can you include other media, such as audio or video clips, in your presentation? Will you have access to the Internet?

○ How long do you have? How much time should you allow for introductions and questions?

○ Will visuals be useful to illustrate key concepts you need to make? Will you need to create your own visuals?

○ Should you prepare printed handouts to aid understanding and retention of useful or important information?

need a title and a few bulleted points on each slide—enough to keep the audience interested and on track. Crowd too much information on a slide, and you will distract viewers and may make the slide hard to read; offer too little information, and the slide will seem irrelevant or even distracting. Remember, it is up to you to provide the details orally.

In designing your slides, you can vary both font sizes and colors. Begin by considering the size of the room in which you will make your presentation and the projection equipment you will need. For electronic presentations you may want to consider using sans serif fonts (see Chapter 20): use a size large enough to be read easily (usually 20–36 points for body text, 40–44 for headings), and use high contrast (white or light backgrounds with dark text, or dark backgrounds with light text) for easy visibility. Use graphics or multimedia elements and colors with care—make sure they are important to your presentation and do not distract your audience's attention from what you have to say. Always test your slides to be certain they are readable by your audience and that they are in the correct order. Also proofread them carefully—your audience will have plenty of time to spot errors!

Review your entire presentation carefully. The questions in Checklist 21.2 can help.

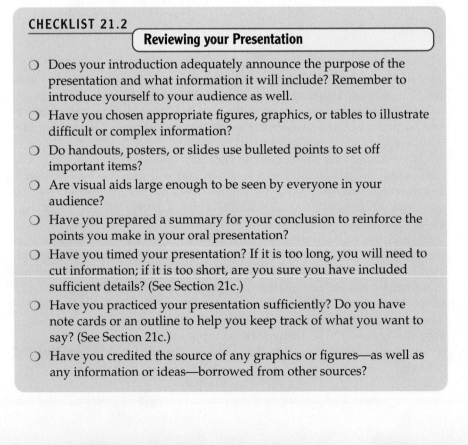

FIGURE 21.3 Templates for different types of presentations are included in Microsoft's *PowerPoint.*

CHECKLIST 21.2
Reviewing your Presentation

○ Does your introduction adequately announce the purpose of the presentation and what information it will include? Remember to introduce yourself to your audience as well.

○ Have you chosen appropriate figures, graphics, or tables to illustrate difficult or complex information?

○ Do handouts, posters, or slides use bulleted points to set off important items?

○ Are visual aids large enough to be seen by everyone in your audience?

○ Have you prepared a summary for your conclusion to reinforce the points you make in your oral presentation?

○ Have you timed your presentation? If it is too long, you will need to cut information; if it is too short, are you sure you have included sufficient details? (See Section 21c.)

○ Have you practiced your presentation sufficiently? Do you have note cards or an outline to help you keep track of what you want to say? (See Section 21c.)

○ Have you credited the source of any graphics or figures—as well as any information or ideas—borrowed from other sources?

21c Delivering oral and visual presentations

The most important advice we can give you is to relax. If you care about your subject—and you know what you're talking about—you may find that you can even forget you're making a "presentation" and instead simply *talk* to your audience. With practice, it does get easier!

You are much less likely to be nervous if you are well prepared. Use the following ideas to help you prepare so that, during your presentation, you can focus on getting your message across.

Plan what you're going to say. While you do not merely want to read a script to your audience, you will want to write out your information. Prepare notes or cards to help you remember facts or important points, and to make sure that you stay on track.

Plan how you will present your information. Will you stand at a lectern and deliver a speech? Will you use audiovisual equipment, electronic slide shows, handouts, or posters? Prepare your supplements with as much care as you do your speech.

Come early—check out the room and the equipment. Make sure everything works (and always have a backup plan in case it doesn't). Make sure you can be heard from every place in the room. Make sure your slides or other visual supplements are clear and visible. (Is the font large enough? Does the lighting in the room need to be adjusted? Is there anything—including the speaker's lectern—blocking the audience's view?)

Dress appropriately. How you dress will depend on the situation, of course. For many classroom presentations, instructors recommend that students dress in "business attire." At any rate, make sure that your clothing does not attract more attention than your presentation or detract from your credibility.

Introduce yourself and other members of your group—or have someone introduce you.

Greet your audience. Even a simple "Good morning!" or "Good afternoon!" can help your audience see you as a human being—and can help you see your audience as people rather than a fearsome horde.

Smile and gesture appropriately. Make appropriate eye contact, pay attention to your posture, and speak clearly and distinctly.

Involve your audience. Ask questions or plan some kind of interactivity. If the audience is involved in what you are saying, they're less likely to be judging you or, worse, falling asleep.

Pay attention to your audience—both their verbal and nonverbal cues. You may need to adjust your presentation based on this feedback. If they're shuffling in their seats or nodding off, maybe you need to

In a recent article in *Wired*, Edward Tufte likens the use of electronic presentation "slideware" to a drug with serious side effects that "induced stupidity, turned everyone into bores, wasted time, and degraded the quality and credibility of communication." Tufte doesn't blame the software, of course, but its misuse.

Just as it takes practice to create effective slide presentations, it takes practice to become comfortable speaking in front of an audience. There is no magic to mastering oral presentation skills, but there is help. In school, you may be able to take a class in public speaking or join the debate team to learn and practice your oral communication skills. Toastmasters International is a worldwide organization whose members practice leading meetings and giving both brief impromptu and prepared speeches, receiving constructive feedback as they learn.

speak louder or adjust your tone (for instance, avoid speaking in a monotone). Perhaps you need to plan breaks, add interactivity, or even adjust the thermostat!

Reserve time for questions—and for answers. Be polite and honest; if you don't know the answer, say so.

21d Considering special situations

Not all presentations involve one speaker standing in front of a group of people. You may need to present your information as part of a group; you may need to present a poster session; or you may need to prepare a presentation to publish on the Web.

Group presentations. Often, you may present information orally as part of a group. As with any group project, you may want to designate a team leader and assign roles or specific parts to each group member. Make sure that all members of the group play an active role in the presentation. The audience will notice if one or more "presenters" fails to participate.

Maintain consistency in your presentation. For instance, if you are each creating separate slide shows or handouts, or separate sections of the same slide show, consider whether using the same templates, backgrounds, and font choices will help to connect them. You will want to rehearse together as well. Introductions may be made at the beginning of the presentation, or you

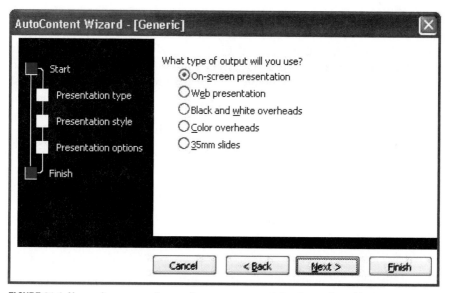

FIGURE 21.4 Your software may allow you to save your presentation in a variety of formats. (Microsoft *PowerPoint*)

may introduce each speaker as she or he comes to the podium. If one person is doing the speaking while another is working the slide presentation, practice when to move to the next slide, or devise a way of signaling.

Poster sessions. A poster session is usually a way of advertising your research rather than presenting it. Often, poster sessions take place in a large room, with several presenters vying for the attention of audience members, who may be milling about the room, moving from poster to poster. The key to an effective poster session is to design visual materials that will attract attention and, most important, communicate ideas clearly, succinctly, and quickly.

Unlike the case with oral presentations or written papers, you will have very little time—and space—to make an impact, so you must carefully consider how to focus your message. Think about the main point of your presentation and plan to draw readers' attention there first. Use tables, figures, or other visuals to condense information. And, above all, don't try to cram everything you have to say onto your poster; instead, use the poster as an opportunity to engage your audience, allowing you to fill in the details in further discussion.

Distance or online presentations. Electronic slide shows can easily be published on the Web: your presentation software may allow you to save it in different formats (see Figure 21.4). If so, you may decide to include links to other Web sites, audio and video files, or streaming text, so that the viewer can read the text along with the audio file and perhaps control the speed and volume of the presentation, skip through slides to access key points, or just sit back and enjoy the show.

In order to include necessary details without voice, you may need to add more slides or a copy of your accompanying speech. If you are using software such as *PowerPoint*, will users need to click on slides to advance them, or should you automate the presentation? If you decide to automate the slide show, be sure your timing is neither too fast nor too slow for your viewers! You may also want to consider using *Flash* movies or other media instead of *PowerPoint*.

In Chapter 22, we present samples of several different types of projects—from traditional essays to newsletters, brochures, and Web pages—along with checklists to make sure your project includes all the necessary parts.

WWW Web Sites Worth Knowing

21.2

- "The Art of Communicating Effectively," http://www.projectorsolution.com/effectivepresentations.asp?

- Toastmasters International, http://www.toastmasters.org

- Center at Colorado State University, Writing "Poster Sessions," http://writing.colostate.edu/references/speaking/poster/index.cfm

MANAGING YOUR PROJECT

1. Examine the templates available in your presentation software. Which presentation types might be well suited to your project? If you are preparing a persuasive presentation, for example, a template for marketing a product might work particularly well.

2. If possible, attend a lecture or presentation on campus or in your local community. Write a brief paper analyzing the lecture or presentation, including any handouts, slide presentations, or other media used. Evaluate its effectiveness in terms of its audience and purpose.

CHAPTER 22

Presenting Research in Many Genres

[Cue the drumroll. Hit the spotlights. Key the microphone.] *"Ladies and gentlemen!* You've completed your research and drafted your project! You've carefully considered your design options! You've analyzed your audience, your purpose, the occasion, and the media available! You've decided how you want to present your final project! And now, *it's showtime!"* [Cue thunderous applause.]

Sometimes the writing process can feel like a three-ring circus, but now that you've set up the tents and gotten the performers in place, you can enjoy the fun part: pulling it all together. While crafting your final product can be a time-consuming and sometimes frustrating process, it can also be the most satisfying part of your project. This chapter offers guidance to help you present your project professionally and completely.

22a Presenting your research in different genres

As you have learned, the results of your research project can be presented in many shapes, genres, and media, depending on your particular rhetorical situation. Both the genre and the medium you choose will entail choices about format and presentation and will ultimately shape the final product.

22.1

A traditional essay, prepared for submission to an instructor or a publisher, usually follows straightforward formatting (for instance, MLA or APA manuscript guidelines), with prescribed margins, line spacing, fonts, and other such decisions made for you. Newsletters and brochures may allow you more creativity, although you will certainly still need to work within limitations. (How many pages will you be allowed? How many colors can you use, if any? What equipment is available to you?) And, of course, for projects to be published on the Web, you will need to know how to publish your files on a server as well as how to think about design choices at a time when many of the "rules" for good Web page design are still being developed (and the technologies for creating, delivering, and accessing the Web are rapidly changing).

In the sections that follow, we present some brief samples of projects in a variety of genres, along with checklists to help ensure that you include all of the necessary parts for your project. You will also learn the basics of Web page design and authoring, using HTML code or a WYSIWYG (What You See Is What You Get, pronounced "wizzy-wig") editor.

22b Reports

Reports come in a variety of shapes and flavors, from brief, informal essays to more formal technical documents. They may be printed directly from your word processor in draft form (double spaced with standard margins and headers, for example), or they may be expensive, full-color glossy reports produced by professional printing companies.

Academic papers and essays. Most academic papers are relatively restrained in appearance, using diverse fonts, colors, and graphics only minimally. However, within limits, academic essays do include specific design criteria you must consider.

You will want to take advantage of the automatic formatting features of your word processor, such as italics, block indent, hanging indent, page numbering, headers, centering, and so on. Some word-processing packages include templates or style sheets that can help you set up your document following generic "research paper" guidelines; compare those style guidelines with the requirements of your project (see Chapter 1). Make sure you spell-check your document, use a good-quality printer and paper, and proofread your work carefully.

You can see an annotated sample research paper, "Swatting Flies with an Ax: File Sharing and the Recording Industry," formatted following MLA manuscript guidelines, in Chapter 24 (see pages 322–324). Also, Chapter 25 includes a sample paper formatted in APA style.

Checklist 22.1 presents important considerations for traditional research projects.

Articles for submission in hard copy to publishers. Many publishers follow the same guidelines for preparing manuscripts as outlined in MLA, APA, or another of the major style guides. However, some publishers have their own formatting requirements, which must be followed meticulously. Most prefer that design elements in manuscripts be kept to a minimum and that authors use few if any of the automatic formatting features available in their word processors. Instead, some require the use of special codes, or "tags" (similar to HTML; see Section 22d), to tell a printer exactly how to treat various elements. Follow the style manual or publisher's guidelines as required for your project, respecting any recommendations about length, margins, spacing, and placement of notes or references. Make sure your printouts are clean and legible and that you include separate camera-ready copies of all art-

CHECKLIST 22.1

Research Projects

○ For academic papers, have you placed your name, your instructor's name, the date, and the course name on the first or title page, if appropriate?

○ Is the title centered? Are only the major words and any proper nouns capitalized? (Do not use boldfaced type, underlining, italics, or different font sizes or types for titles.)

○ Did you number the pages? Are they in the right order?

○ Have you double-spaced your text?

○ Are tables and figures labeled correctly and introduced in the text?

○ Have you provided transitions and navigational aids such as subheadings, if appropriate?

○ Have you used quotation marks and parentheses correctly and in pairs? (The closing quotation mark and parenthesis are often forgotten.)

○ Have you indented all direct quotations of four typed lines or more (MLA) or of forty words or more (APA)?

○ Have you remembered that indented quotations are not placed between quotation marks?

○ Did you introduce all direct quotations with some identification of their author, source, or significance?

○ Have you handled titles correctly, italicizing or underlining the titles of books and putting the titles of articles between quotation marks?

○ Did you include a Works Cited or References page? Is it alphabetized correctly? Did you handle the formatting correctly?

○ Have you proofread your work carefully for errors?

work, as required. For electronic submissions, make sure your files are in the format specified in the guidelines and that you have included any graphics files.

Checklist 22.2 contains important considerations to keep in mind when submitting copy to a publisher.

Technical reports. Many companies have their own in-house style guidelines for technical reports. You will want to follow these guidelines scrupulously. When designing technical reports, you can usually include photographic images, line drawings, graphs, and tables. Some reports, such as corporate annual reports or technical manuals, may incorporate full-color reproductions, photographs, and other complex graphical elements. These reports may be costly and will have to be professionally printed. Thus most technical reports use color sparingly, if at all.

CHECKLIST 22.2

Submitting Articles to Publishers in Hard Copy

○ Have you followed the editor's instructions for placement of your name and affiliation?

○ Have you included all the parts required by the submission guidelines (abstract, author biography, etc.)?

○ Have you followed the editor's or required style guidelines *exactly*, including guidelines for formatting the document, for use of nonsexist language, and for citation of sources?

○ Did you include the required number of copies?

○ Did you include envelopes and/or sufficient postage as required by the editor's or publication's guidelines?

○ Have you included a cover letter with additional information?

Readers will find your report easy to follow when you use features such as headings or section numbers, lists, and tables to highlight significant information. You might also need to include a table of contents or an abstract that summarizes important information, especially for lengthy documents. See the annotated sample technical report on pages 235–240.

Review Checklist 22.3 to make sure your report includes all the necessary information.

CHECKLIST 22.3

Technical Reports

○ Have you followed the appropriate format for your report?

○ Have you included all the necessary parts, such as a title page, an abstract, a table of contents, appendixes, and/or a bibliography?

○ Do the page numbers on your table of contents or index page match those in your document?

○ Are headings and subheadings used appropriately? Are headings and subheadings at the same level formatted consistently, and are they parallel in grammatical structure?

○ Have you used figures, tables, and graphics appropriately? Have you stated the source of the information they contain?

○ Does your conclusion follow logically from the evidence you have provided? Does it agree with your stated purpose?

Sample Technical Report

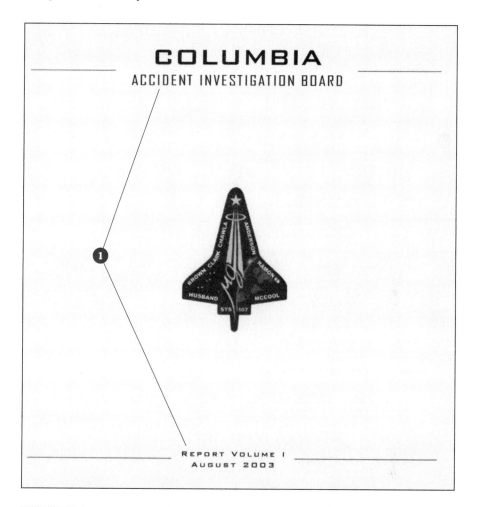

1. Title page for a technical report includes the title, the author or authoring agency, and the date. Other information may also be included, such as for whom the report was prepared.

Sample Technical Report (continued)

COLUMBIA
ACCIDENT INVESTIGATION BOARD

2. Since technical reports are often lengthy, they usually include a table of contents. Detailed contents pages usually include the top three levels (major headings and first- and second-level subheadings). A separate list of figures and/or tables may also be included.

Sample Technical Report (continued)

COLUMBIA
ACCIDENT INVESTIGATION BOARD

3 — EXECUTIVE SUMMARY

The Columbia Accident Investigation Board's independent investigation into the February 1, 2003, loss of the Space Shuttle *Columbia* and its seven-member crew lasted nearly seven months. A staff of more than 120, along with some 400 NASA engineers, supported the Board's 13 members. Investigators examined more than 30,000 documents, conducted more than 200 formal interviews, heard testimony from dozens of expert witnesses, and reviewed more than 3,000 inputs from the general public. In addition, more than 25,000 searchers combed vast stretches of the Western United States to retrieve the spacecraft's debris. In the process, *Columbia*'s tragedy was compounded when two debris searchers with the U.S. Forest Service perished in a helicopter accident.

The Board recognized early on that the accident was probably not an anomalous, random event, but rather likely rooted to some degree in NASA's history and the human space flight program's culture. Accordingly, the Board broadened its mandate at the outset to include an investigation of a wide range of historical and organizational issues, including political and budgetary considerations, compromises, and changing priorities over the life of the Space Shuttle Program. The Board's conviction regarding the importance of these factors strengthened as the investigation progressed, with the result that this report, in its findings, conclusions, and recommendations, places as much weight on these causal factors as on the more easily understood and corrected physical cause of the accident.

The physical cause of the loss of *Columbia* and its crew was a breach in the Thermal Protection System on the leading edge of the left wing, caused by a piece of insulating foam which separated from the left bipod ramp section of the External Tank at 81.7 seconds after launch, and struck the wing in the vicinity of the lower half of Reinforced Carbon-Carbon panel number 8. During re-entry this breach in the Thermal Protection System allowed superheated air to penetrate through the leading edge insulation and progressively melt the aluminum structure of the left wing, resulting in a weakening of the structure until increasing aerodynamic forces caused loss of control, failure of the wing, and breakup of the Orbiter. This breakup occurred in a flight regime in which, given the current design of the Orbiter, there was no possibility for the crew to survive.

The organizational causes of this accident are rooted in the Space Shuttle Program's history and culture, including the original compromises that were required to gain approval for the Shuttle, subsequent years of resource constraints, fluctuating priorities, schedule pressures, mischaracterization of the Shuttle as operational rather than developmental, and lack of an agreed national vision for human space flight. Cultural traits and organizational practices detrimental to safety were allowed to develop, including: reliance on past success as a substitute for sound engineering practices (such as testing to understand why systems were not performing in accordance with requirements); organizational barriers that prevented effective communication of critical safety information and

stifled professional differences of opinion; lack of integrated management across program elements; and the evolution of an informal chain of command and decision-making processes that operated outside the organization's rules.

This report discusses the attributes of an organization that could more safely and reliably operate the inherently risky Space Shuttle, but does not provide a detailed organizational prescription. Among those attributes are: a robust and independent program technical authority that has complete control over specifications and requirements, and waivers to them; an independent safety assurance organization with line authority over all levels of safety oversight; and an organizational culture that reflects the best characteristics of a learning organization.

This report concludes with recommendations, some of which are specifically identified and prefaced as "before return to flight." These recommendations are largely related to the physical cause of the accident, and include preventing the loss of foam, improved imaging of the Space Shuttle stack from liftoff through separation of the External Tank, and on-orbit inspection and repair of the Thermal Protection System. The remaining recommendations, for the most part, stem from the Board's findings on organizational cause factors. While they are not "before return to flight" recommendations, they can be viewed as "continuing to fly" recommendations, as they capture the Board's thinking on what changes are necessary to operate the Shuttle and future spacecraft safely in the mid- to long-term.

These recommendations reflect both the Board's strong support for return to flight at the earliest date consistent with the overriding objective of safety, and the Board's conviction that operation of the Space Shuttle, and all human spaceflight, is a developmental activity with high inherent risks.

A view from inside the Launch Control Center as Columbia rolls out to Launch Complex 39-A on December 9, 2002.

3. An executive summary presents the report's main findings and recommendations.

Sample Technical Report (continued)

CHAPTER 1

The Evolution of the Space Shuttle Program

More than two decades after its first flight, the Space Shuttle remains the only reusable spacecraft in the world capable of simultaneously putting multiple-person crews and heavy cargo into orbit, of deploying, servicing, and retrieving satellites, and of returning the products of on-orbit research to Earth. These capabilities are an important asset for the United States and its international partners in space. Current plans call for the Space Shuttle to play a central role in the U.S. human space flight program for years to come.

The Space Shuttle Program's remarkable successes, however, come with high costs and tremendous risks. The February 1 disintegration of *Columbia* during re-entry, 17 years after *Challenger* was destroyed on ascent, is the most recent reminder that sending people into orbit and returning them safely to Earth remains a difficult and perilous endeavor.

It is the view of the Columbia Accident Investigation Board that the *Columbia* accident is not a random event, but rather a product of the Space Shuttle Program's history and current management processes. Fully understanding how it happened requires an exploration of that history and management. This chapter charts how the Shuttle emerged from a series of political compromises that produced unreasonable expectations – even myths – about its performance, how the *Challenger* accident shattered those myths several years after NASA began acting upon them as fact, and how, in retrospect, the Shuttle's technically ambitious design resulted in an inherently vulnerable vehicle, the safe operation of which exceeded NASA's organizational capabilities as they existed at the time of the *Columbia* accident. The Board's investigation of what caused the *Columbia* accident thus begins in the fields of East Texas but reaches more than 30 years into the past, to a series of economically and politically driven decisions that cast the Shuttle program in a role that its nascent technology could not support. To understand the cause of the *Columbia* accident is to understand how a program promising reliability and cost efficiency resulted instead in a developmental vehicle that never achieved the fully operational status NASA and the nation accorded it.

1.1   GENESIS OF THE SPACE TRANSPORTATION SYSTEM

The origins of the Space Shuttle Program date to discussions on what should follow Project Apollo, the dramatic U.S. missions to the moon.[1] NASA centered its post-Apollo plans on developing increasingly larger outposts in Earth orbit that would be launched atop Apollo's immense Saturn V booster. The space agency hoped to construct a 12-person space station by 1975; subsequent stations would support 50, then 100 people. Other stations would be placed in orbit around the moon and then be constructed on the lunar surface. In parallel, NASA would develop the capability for the manned exploration of Mars. The concept of a vehicle – or Space Shuttle – to take crews and supplies to and from low-Earth orbit arose as part of this grand vision (see Figure 1.1-1). To keep the costs of these trips to a minimum, NASA intended to develop a fully reusable vehicle.[2]

Figure 1.1-1. Early concepts for the Space Shuttle envisioned a reusable two-stage vehicle with the reliability and versatility of a commercial airliner.

4. The body of the report usually begins with background information. Major headings (such as new chapters) begin on a new page; subheadings are usually designated with numbers and/or different fonts. Figures are numbered and labeled.

Sample Technical Report (continued)

COLUMBIA
ACCIDENT INVESTIGATION BOARD

and variable application, and the results of that imperfect process, as well as severe load, thermal, pressure, vibration, acoustic, and structural launch and ascent conditions.

5

Findings:

F3.2–1   NASA does not fully understand the mechanisms that cause foam loss on almost all flights from larger areas of foam coverage and from areas that are sculpted by hand.

F3.2–2   There are no qualified non-destructive evaluation techniques for the as-installed foam to determine the characteristics of the foam before flight.

F3.2–3   Foam loss from an External Tank is unrelated to the tank's age and to its total pre-launch exposure to the elements. Therefore, the foam loss on STS-107 is unrelated to either the age or exposure of External Tank 93 before launch.

F3.2–4   The Board found no indications of negligence in the application of the External Tank Thermal Protection System.

F3.2–5   The Board found instances of left bipod ramp shedding on launch that NASA was not aware of, bringing the total known left bipod ramp shedding events to 7 out of 72 missions for which imagery of the launch or External Tank separation is available.

F3.2–6   Subsurface defects were found during the dissection of three bipod foam ramps, suggesting that similar defects were likely present in the left bipod ramp of External Tank 93 used on STS-107.

F3.2–7   Foam loss occurred on more than 80 percent of the 79 missions for which imagery was available to confirm or rule out foam loss.

F3.2–8   Thirty percent of all missions lacked sufficient imagery to determine if foam had been lost.

F3.2–9   Analysis of numerous separate variables indicated that none could be identified as the sole initiating factor of bipod foam loss. The Board therefore concludes that a combination of several factors resulted in bipod foam loss.

Recommendation:

R3.2-1   Initiate an aggressive program to eliminate all External Tank Thermal Protection System debris-shedding at the source with particular emphasis on the region where the bipod struts attach to the External Tank.

3.3   WING LEADING EDGE STRUCTURAL SUBSYSTEM

The components of the Orbiter's wing leading edge provide the aerodynamic load bearing, structural, and thermal control capability for areas that exceed 2,300 degrees Fahrenheit. Key design requirements included flying 100 missions with minimal refurbishment, maintaining the aluminum wing structure at less than 350 degrees Fahrenheit, withstanding a kinetic energy impact of 0.006 foot-pounds, and the ability to withstand 1.4 times the load ever expected in operation.[5] The requirements specifically stated that the

REINFORCED CARBON-CARBON (RCC)

The basic RCC composite is a laminate of graphite-impregnated rayon fabric, further impregnated with phenolic resin and layered, one ply at a time, in a unique mold for each part, then cured, rough-trimmed, drilled, and inspected. The part is then packed in calcined coke and fired in a furnace to convert it to carbon and is made more dense by three cycles of furfuryl alcohol vacuum impregnation and firing.

To prevent oxidation, the outer layers of the carbon substrate are converted into a 0.02-to-0.04-inch-thick layer of silicon carbide in a chamber filled with argon at temperatures up to 3,000 degrees Fahrenheit. As the silicon carbide cools, "craze cracks" form because the thermal expansion rates of the silicon carbide and the carbon substrate differ. The part is then repeatedly vacuum-impregnated with tetraethyl orthosilicate to fill the pores in the substrate, and the craze cracks are filled with a sealant.

wing leading edge would not need to withstand impact from debris or ice, since these objects would not pose a threat during the launch phase.[6]

Reinforced Carbon-Carbon

The development of Reinforced Carbon-Carbon (RCC) as part of the Thermal Protection System was key to meeting the wing leading edge design requirements. Developed by Ling-Temco-Vought (now Lockheed Martin Missiles and Fire Control), RCC is used for the Orbiter nose cap, chin panel, forward External Tank attachment point, and wing leading edge panels and T-seals. RCC is a hard structural material, with reasonable strength across its operational temperature range (minus 250 degrees Fahrenheit to 3,000 degrees). Its low thermal expansion coefficient minimizes thermal shock and thermoelastic stress.

Each wing leading edge consists of 22 RCC panels (see Figure 3.3-1), numbered from 1 to 22 moving outward on each wing (the nomenclature is "5-left" or "5-right" to differentiate, for example, the two number 5 panels). Because the shape of the wing changes from inboard to outboard, each panel is unique.

Figure 3.3-1. There are 22 panels of Reinforced Carbon-Carbon on each wing, numbered as shown above.

5. Technical reports often make extensive use of formatting features such as lists, text boxes, shading, and figures to help facilitate communication of complex information.

Sample Technical Report (continued)

COLUMBIA
ACCIDENT INVESTIGATION BOARD

ENDNOTES FOR CHAPTER 10 — **6**

The citations that contain a reference to "CAIB document" with CAB or CTF followed by seven to eleven digits, such as CAB001-0010, refer to a document in the Columbia Accident Investigation Board database maintained by the Department of Justice and archived at the National Archives.

[1] "And stunningly, in as much as this was tragic and horrific through a loss of seven very important lives, it is amazing that there were no other collateral damage happened as a result of it. No one else was injured. All of the claims have been very, very minor in dealing with these issues." NASA Administrator Sean O'Keefe, testimony before the United States Senate Committee on Commerce, Science, and Transportation, May 14, 2003.

[2] An intensive search of over a million acres in Texas and Louisiana recovered 83,900 pieces of Columbia debris weighing a total of 84,900 pounds. (Over 700,000 acres were searched on foot, and 1.6 million acres were searched with aircraft.) The latitude and longitude was recorded for more than 75,000 of these pieces. The majority of the recovered items were no larger than 0.5 square feet. More than 40,000 items could not be positively identified but were classified as unknown tile, metal, composite, plastic, fabric, etc. Details about the debris reconstruction and recovery effort are provided in Appendix E.5, S. Altemis, J. Cowart, W. Woodworth, "STS-107 Columbia Reconstruction Report," NSTS-60501, June 30, 2003. CAIB document CTF076-20302182.

[3] The precise probability is uncertain due to many factors, such as the amount of debris that burned up during re-entry, and the fraction of the population that was outdoors when the Columbia accident occurred.

[4] "User's Guide for Object Reentry Survival Analysis Tool (ORSAT), Version 5.0, Volume I-Methodology, Input Description, and Results," JSC-28742, July 1999; W. Alior, "What Can We Learn From Recovered Debris," Aerospace Corp, briefing presented to CAIB, on March 13, 2003.

[5] "Reentry Survivability Analysis of Delta IV Launch Vehicle Upper Stage," JSC-29775, June 2002.

[6] Analysis of the recovered debris indicates that relatively few pieces posed a threat to people indoors. See Appendix D.16.

[7] Detailed information about individual fragments, including weight in most cases, was not available for the study. Therefore, some engineering discretion was needed to develop models of individual weights, dimensions, aerodynamic characteristics, and conditions of impact. This lack of information increases uncertainty in the accuracy of the final results. The study should be revisited after the fragment data has been fully characterized.

[8] K.M. Thompson, R.F. Rabouw, and R.M. Cooke, "The Risk of Groundling Fatalities from Unintentional Airplane Crashes," Risk Analysis, Vol. 21, No. 6, 2001.

[9] Ibid.

[10] The civil aviation study indicates that the risk to groundlings is significantly higher in the vicinity of an airport. The average annual risk of fatality within 0.2 miles of a busy (top 100) airport is about 1 in a million.

[11] Thompson, "The Risk of Groundling Fatalities," Code of Federal Regulations (CFR) 14 CFR Part 415, 415, and 417, "Licensing and Safety Requirements for Launch: Proposed Rule," Federal Register Vol. 67, No. 146, July 30, 2002, p. 49495.

[12] Code of Federal Regulations (CFR) 14 CFR Part 415 Launch License, Federal Register Vol. 64, No. 76, April 21, 1999; Range Commanders Council Standard 321-02, "Common Risk Criteria for National Test Ranges," published by the Secretariat of the RCC U.S. Army White Sands Missile Range, NM 88002-5110, June 2002; "Mitigation of Orbital Debris," Notice of Proposed Rulemaking by the Federal Communications Commission, FCC 02-80, Federal Register Vol. 67, No. 86, Friday, May 3, 2002.

[13] Air Force launch safety standards define a Hazardous Launch Area, a controlled surface area and airspace, where individual risk of serious injury from a launch vehicle malfunction during the early phase of flight exceeds one in a million. Only personnel essential to the launch operation are permitted in this area. "Eastern and Western Range Requirements 127-1," March 1995, pp. 1-12 and Fig. 1-6.

[14] Code of Federal Regulations (CFR) 14 CFR Part 431, Launch and Reentry of a Reusable Launch Vehicle, Section 35 paragraphs (a) and (b), Federal Register Vol. 65, No. 182, September 19, 2000, p. 56660.

[15] "Reentry Survivability Analysis of Delta IV Launch Vehicle Upper Stage," JSC-29775, June 2002.

[16] M. Tobin, "Range Safety Risk Assessments For Kennedy Space Center," October 2002. CAIB document CTF059-22802288; "Space Shuttle Program Requirements Document," NSTS-07700, Vol. I, change no. 76, Section 5-1. CAIB document CAB024-04120475.

[17] Here, ascent refers to (1) the Orbiter from liftoff to Main Engine Cut Off (MECO), (2) the Solid Rocket Boosters from liftoff to splashdown, and (3) the External Tank from liftoff to splashdown.

[18] Pete Cadden, "Shuttle Launch Area Debris Risk," October 2002. CAIB document CTF059-22682279.

[19] See Dennis R. Jenkins, Space Shuttle: The History of the National Space Transportation System — The First 100 Missions (Cape Canaveral, FL, Specialty Press, 2001), pp. 205-212 for a complete description of the Approach and Landing Tests and other testing conducted with Enterprise.

[20] Report of the Presidential Commission on the Space Shuttle Challenger Accident (Washington: Government Printing Office, 1986).

[21] The pre-declared time period or number of missions over which the system is expected to operate without major redesign or redefinition.

[22] "A crew escape system shall be provided on Earth to Orbit vehicles for safe crew extraction and recovery from in-flight failures across the flight envelope from pre-launch to landing. The escape system shall have a probability of successful crew return of 0.99."

[23] Report of the Aerospace Safety Advisory Panel Annual Report for 2002, (Washington: Government Printing Office, March 2002). CAIB document CTF014-25882645.

[24] Charlie Abner, "KSC Processing Review Team Final Summary," June 16, 2003. CAIB document CTF063-11801276.

[25] Julie Kramer, et al., "Minutes from CAIB / Engineering Meeting to Discuss CAIB Action / Request for Information B1-000193," April 24, 2003. CAIB document CTF042-00930095.

224   REPORT VOLUME I   AUGUST 2003

Source: NASA, Report of Columbia Accident Investigation Board, *Vol. 1, 26 Aug. 2003, http://anon.nasa-global.speedera.net/anon.nasa-global/CAIB/CAIB_lowres_full.pdf (4 Sep. 2004)*

6. Sources may be cited in footnotes, in endnotes, or in a separate bibliography or a References page at the end of the report, following a specified format. Detailed technical specifications or other useful information (such as author credentials) may be presented in appendixes.

22c Newsletters and brochures

Desktop publishing software such as Adobe *PageMaker* and Broderbund *Print Shop* enables you to create newsletters and brochures that rival those from professional printers, and many word-processing packages include templates to help you design effective publications, like the newsletter shown in Figure 22.1.

Newsletters are often printed on both sides of a single sheet of paper, although some newsletters include multiple pages. Brochures are usually printed on both sides of a single sheet of paper, in "panels" (similar to columns), so that they can be easily folded. Pay attention to the order of information in both. Use type sizes that are large enough to read (even though you may be tempted to use smaller fonts to squeeze in more information), and use colors, graphics, or other techniques for emphasis sparingly, and only when necessary (see Chapter 20 for more information on document design).

Often, newsletters and brochures fully justify the margins; that is, text continues to the very edge of the right-hand margin (as it does in this copy of *Bookmarks*). But be careful—unless you are using a proportional font, full justification may leave wide gaps between words on a line, requiring you to insert hyphens and word breaks manually. Type with "ragged" right-hand margins (called left justification because only the text on the left-hand margin is even) is easier to read with most font styles. Of course, when your newsletter or brochure is to be professionally typeset, you may have more choices.

Checklist 22.4 presents important considerations for creating newsletters.

CHECKLIST 22.4
Newsletters

○ Have you selected the paper size and method of binding and planned the number of pages you will use? Have you chosen a margin width that allows for binding or folding?

○ Have you decided whether you'll use images and how many colors you want to show? Did you keep in mind that colorful designs may be more costly to reproduce?

○ Will you use multicolumn pages, keeping in mind that while more columns usually mean more planning, when formatted carefully they make more efficient use of space?

○ Have you mapped out each page with two goals in mind: (1) showcasing the most important articles and (2) preventing your reader from having to jump from page to page to read a single article?

○ For your masthead, did you use a distinctive font that reflects the spirit of the organization represented by the newsletter? Have you adjusted headlines according to their importance, while maintaining a consistent font size and style throughout the body of the articles?

○ Have you kept paragraphs short and avoided long, unbroken stretches of print, especially when you're using narrow columns?

FRONT PAGE OF A NEWSLETTER

The **masthead** identifies a newsletter with a specific organization, often showing logos or catchphrases members recognize immediately. Mastheads also include publication date and issue number.

Lead articles appear on the front pages of newsletters—they reflect the most important recent events appearing in the issue.

Images are wrapped by text so that the space on each page is used efficiently, and related material is closely grouped.

Borders are *sometimes* used to frame text or decorate the margins.

PAGE 3 OF A NEWSLETTER

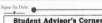

Running heads often include the same information appearing in the masthead and sometimes include page numbering.

Standard articles are introduced with enhanced headlines. This example uses a left-justified block style of paragraphing.

Regular features are columns that appear in each issue; they are often framed or otherwise distinguished from standard articles so they can be easily recognized.

Footers can include page numbering and information appearing in the masthead.

FIGURE 22.1 Sample newsletter

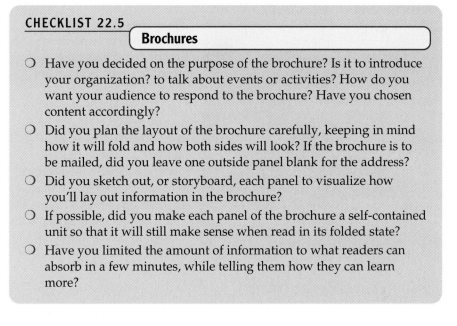

Brochures

○ Have you decided on the purpose of the brochure? Is it to introduce your organization? to talk about events or activities? How do you want your audience to respond to the brochure? Have you chosen content accordingly?

○ Did you plan the layout of the brochure carefully, keeping in mind how it will fold and how both sides will look? If the brochure is to be mailed, did you leave one outside panel blank for the address?

○ Did you sketch out, or storyboard, each panel to visualize how you'll lay out information in the brochure?

○ If possible, did you make each panel of the brochure a self-contained unit so that it will still make sense when read in its folded state?

○ Have you limited the amount of information to what readers can absorb in a few minutes, while telling them how they can learn more?

Brochures usually strive to stimulate interest or provide specific information about an organization, its activities, and its concerns. Figure 22.2 illustrates design principles that you will want to consider.

Checklist 22.5 will help ensure that your design suits your purpose.

22d Web sites

Creating a basic Web page is relatively easy and requires not much more skill than it takes to operate word-processing software. Many Web sites combine diverse design elements such as stylized text, graphics, animation, and even sound. We can't provide you with models and guidelines to suit every possible occasion, but what we can offer here is an outline of the basic processes involved in writing for the Web, which should be enough to get you started.

Plan your Web project carefully. Planning a Web project isn't much different from planning other types of documents (see Figure 22.3). You'll need to determine your audience, assess your resources, choose an effective layout, and make decisions about document style. Web projects, however, do have special demands.

First, you'll need to know that Web documents use Hypertext Markup Language (HTML) tags or codes to tell browsers how to display words and images and how to link documents. Think about what method you'll use to create your HTML documents, whether you'll use a single-page or a multi-

FRONT PANEL OF BROCHURE

Use **graphics** and **colors** to attract the eyes of readers. Keep in mind that most brochures must compete for attention.

The **logo** for the organization should appear on the front panel. This logo begins building a persona that the following panels will develop.

Show **addresses** and **contact** information so that readers get a clear idea of the organization's affiliations and institutional relationships.

INSIDE PANELS OF BROCHURE

Each **panel** includes a main heading with related passages of text. Panels have consistent layouts so readers can easily see the central points.

Headings are set apart from other text using inverted background and foreground colors. Provocative, eye-catching phrases draw readers in.

Contact information and the organizational **logo** reappear on the end panel, reminding readers that further details are available if they are interested.

Images have been carefully selected to portray themes and activities related to the organization. Here the images form a collage extending across all panels.

Paragraphs focus on the highlights of the organization, especially those that will seem most intriguing to the target audience.

FIGURE 22.2 Sample brochure

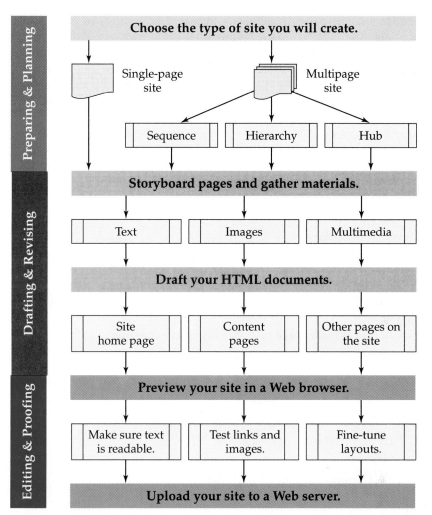

FIGURE 22.3 How to create a Web site.

page format, and how you'll lay out and link individual pages. If you plan to use more advanced features, such as Cascading Style Sheets or Java Script, for instance, make sure you know how to edit the scripts to make them work, and make sure your server will support these features.

You'll also need to adhere to the publication requirements of the Web. You'll eventually need to "upload" your documents to a Web server to make them accessible to the world. Here we focus on the design of Web pages. Check with your instructor or Internet provider for information on publishing your files.

Choose a single-page or multipage format. Decide early in your design process how you want to organize your Web page: will you create a single, scrolling page or multiple pages connected by links? When you have a limited amount of information to present—a personal home page or a brief report—consider choosing a single, scrolling page. If you have more than two or three screens of information or if your material breaks easily into sections, consider a set of pages connected by links.

A multiple-page site is harder to create than a single-page site. You have to decide how to arrange your information so readers can navigate the pages easily and intuitively. You'll need to create a home page as the entry into the site, but material deeper in the site may be connected to that home page in different ways, depending on your purpose and subject, to create a *hierarchy*, a *sequence*, or a *hub* (see Figure 20.9 on page 218.)

Create a storyboard. Storyboards are simply sketches of your page or pages, often drawn by hand with pencil and paper. For the sake of simplicity, new Web writers should focus on two types of pages: the *home page*, which clearly conveys the purpose of the site and how to navigate it; and *content pages*, which present, in a consistent and readable manner, the site's most important material.

As you prepare your page layouts, you'll have questions:

- How will you break up text onto separate pages?
- What text do you need to achieve your purpose on each page?
- Will you use images or multimedia?
- What materials can you gather from outside sources?
- What materials can you create yourself?
- How will you gather all these materials effectively to create your site?

Gather materials. Whatever materials you add to your site, you'll need to assemble them in electronic formats accessible to those browsing the Web. Although we don't have space here to explain how to digitize photographs, make animations, and record voices—all of which involve an understanding of specific software programs—we can give you guidelines for gathering material that has already been (or can easily be) converted to Web formats.

- **Create a working folder on your disk.** Place all your materials—HTML files, graphics files, and other media—for the project in this folder. When you're ready to publish your project, all you'll need to do is upload the folder to the Web server.
- **Write the text that will appear on your site.** Web sites need to be just as clear and grammatical as any other professional writing. Remember that what you post on a Web page is public. Proofread carefully, and edit to eliminate wordiness.

```
  htmltemplate.html - Notepad                        _ □ ×
File  Edit  Search  Help

 <HTML>

 <HEAD>

  <TITLE>HTML Template</TITLE>
  <META NAME="Author" CONTENT="your name">
  <META NAME="Date of Creation" CONTENT="day/month/year">

 </HEAD>

 <BODY>

   HTML Template

 </BODY>

 </HTML>
```

FIGURE 22.4 You can create an HTML template by typing the tags and words into your text editor exactly as shown above. Later, when you start making pages or customized templates, you'll put more personalized information into the areas highlighted above. The area between the <BODY> . . . </BODY> tags will contain the main content for each page. (*Microsoft ® Notepad is a trademark of Microsoft. Title bar screen shot reprinted by permission of Microsoft Corporation.*)

Draft your document using HTML. Depending on the page you're viewing, the HTML tags may seem daunting and difficult to learn. In fact, composing with HTML is relatively easy—if you start with the basics. While these basics won't allow you to make flashy, elaborate sites, they will allow you to publish material on the Web in a clear and organized fashion. Once you feel comfortable with the basics, you can then increase your HTML vocabulary, learning more striking Web design techniques as illustrated in Figure 22.7.

- Create an HTML template. All HTML documents have a basic structure, a required series of tags that tell browser programs necessary information about the organization of the page. Type the tags shown in Figure 22.4 into a new document using your HTML text editor. Save that document in your working folder as "htmltemplate.html"—you will make a copy of this document every time you start composing a new page, knowing that it will have the required structure.

- **Preview your HTML document in a browser.** By using a Web browser to open the pages you save in your working folder, you'll be able to see how they will appear once uploaded. To preview your HTML template, open your Web browser, choose "Open" from the "File" menu,

Basic HTML Tags

HTML TAGS	WHAT THEY DO
\<HTML> \</HTML>	Appear as the first and the last tags in an HTML document. These tags tell browser programs to translate codes on the page to a readable format.
\<HEAD> \</HEAD>	Follows the opening \<HTML> tag in a document. Tags between the \<HEAD> tags provide information about the document, but this material does not appear in the browser window.
\<TITLE> \</TITLE>	Identifies the title that will appear in the title bar on the browser when a page opens. The page title appears between the tags.
\<META . . . >	Provides extra information about the document, data often used by Web search engines to index the document once it has been uploaded to a Web server.
\<BODY> \</BODY>	Brackets the material in the body of the page, including the text, images, and any formatting that will appear in the browser window.
\<B> \</B>	Boldfaces text between the tags.
\<I> \</I>	Italicizes text between the tags.
\<P> \</P>	Formats text between the tags as a simple paragraph.
\<CENTER> \</CENTER>	Centers text between the tags.
\<H1> \</H1>	Forms a level-one heading—the largest HTML heading size. See Figure 20.3 on page 210.
\<A . . . > \</A>	Hyperlinks the text between the tags.
\<FONT . . . > \</FONT>	Sets the font for text between the tags.
\<UL> \<LI> \<LI> \<LI> . . . \</UL>	Creates a bulleted list. Place the \<LI> tag before each item in the list.
\ 	Inserts a line break. All text following the tag appears on the next line.
\<HR>	Inserts a horizontal line across the page.
\<IMG...>	Inserts an image onto the page.

FIGURE 22.5 Basic HTML tags.

and browse for the file you just saved in your working folder. You should then see something like what is shown in Figure 22.6. Other common HTML tags are shown in Figure 22.5.

Other ways of drafting HTML documents. If you aren't ready to learn the nuts and bolts of HTML, or if you need to produce an attractive Web document quickly, try a visual Web authoring program. The quality of the page you finally produce will depend on the software you have available—but most programs generate suitable layouts.

- **Choose your editing software.** Visual editors often cost money, but some computers come with them preinstalled. Netscape's free suite of Internet applications comes with both a Web browser (*Communicator*) and an editor (*Composer*). Other editors include Microsoft's *FrontPage*, Macromedia's *Dreamweaver*, and Apple's *HomePage*. Predictably, the more features offered, the more expensive the program.

- **Create a new HTML document.** In most programs all you'll need to do is select "New" from the "File" menu, just as you would in a word processor. Save the blank page in your project folder. Note that your editing software might provide predesigned templates. Choose a template for your new document if you find one that's appropriate. Make sure to adjust the template to suit your needs.

- **Set the document title.** Unlike HTML text editors, visual editors allow you to use the program's menus and dialog boxes to make modifications to your document. For this reason you'll need to explore your software for a few minutes, learning the available options. In particular, look for an option that allows you to change the title of your HTML document. This

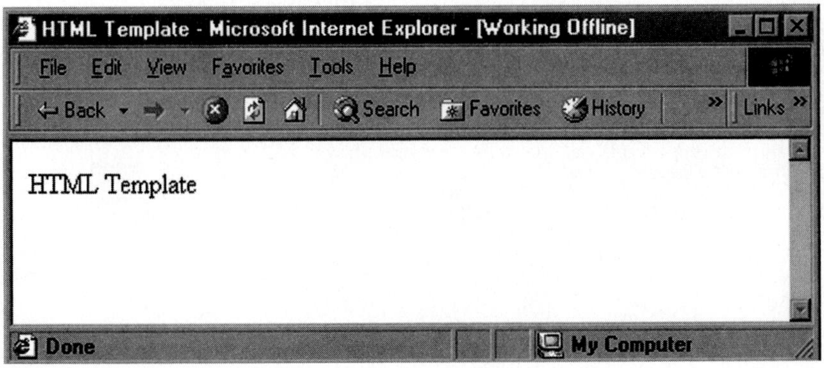

FIGURE 22.6 Preview your template and notice how little of what you typed appears on the final product. Browsers hide all HTML tags or convert them to special kinds of content such as images or empty lines. You'll need to review what different tags do in order to know how they can help you achieve the layout you want. (Title bar screen shot reprinted by permission of Microsoft Corporation.)

File   Edit   Search   Help

```
<HTML>

 <HEAD>
  <TITLE>Teaching Life's Lessons</TITLE>
  <META NAME="Author" CONTENT="Stella Galvan">
  <META NAME="Date of Creation" CONTENT="2000-12-15">
 </HEAD>

 <BODY BGCOLOR="TAN">

  <H1>Teaching Life's Lessons</H1>

  <IMG SRC="baum-bandit.jpg" ALIGN="RIGHT">

  <P>A great deal of criticism is leveled at modern media based upon their influence over
  children: too much violence, too much offensive language, too many adult situations.
  But is this a new trend? How did past ages teach children lessons about the world
  they live in, a world populated by adults and their problems? At right you'll see one
  method: through fairy tales, in this case Frank Baum's <I>Father Goose, His Book</I>
  (1899). Like Hans Christian Andersen, Baum accompanied illustrations with simple
  fables, making children his primary audience. But notice how the "bandit" is presented
  in a romanticized fashion, as "handsome." Isn't the romanticized criminal a primary
  target of critics of the late 20th century?

  <P>This section of the Modern Media Project takes up the question of how
  entertainment media--past and present--instruct children on harsh reality. On the
  group's <A HREF="conc.html">Conclusions</A> page, we'll consider more closely whether
  these lessons do more harm than good, and in what way they should be presented.

  <UL>
   <LI><A HREF="people.html">Bad people: Learn by watching or doing?</A>
   <LI><A HREF="places.html">Dangerous places: Ignorant bliss or sure knowledge?</A>
   <LI><A HREF="things.html">Harmful substances: Avoiding or experimenting?</A>
   <LI><A HREF="sources.html">Works Consulted and Image Credits</A>
  </UL>

  <CENTER>
  <HR>&copy 2001 Stella Galvan<BR>
  <A HREF="homepage.html"><B>Return to Modern Media Project Homepage</B></A>
  </CENTER>

 </BODY>

</HTML>
```

File   Edit   View   Favorites   Tools   Help

← Back • → • ⊗ ⟳ 🖶 | Search Favorites History | • • • | Links »

Teaching Life's Lessons

A great deal of criticism is leveled at modern media based upon their influence over children: too much violence, too much offensive language, too many adult situations. But is this a new trend? How did past ages teach children lessons about the world they live in, a world populated by adults and their problems? At right you'll see one method: through fairy tales, in this case Frank Baum's *Father Goose, His Book* (1899). Like Hans Christian Andersen, Baum accompanied illustrations with simple fables, making children his primary audience. But notice how the "bandit" is presented in a romanticized fashion, as "handsome." Isn't the romanticized criminal a primary target of critics of the late 20th century?

The Bandit is a handsome man,
In operas he sings;
He wears a wig and fierce moustache
And many other things.

corbis.com

This section of the Modern Media Project takes up the question of how entertainment media--past and present--instruct children on harsh reality. On the group's Conclusions page, we'll consider more closely whether these lessons do more harm than good, and in what way they should be presented.

- Bad people: Learn by watching or doing?
- Dangerous places: Ignorant bliss or sure knowledge?
- Harmful substances: Avoiding or experimenting?
- Works Consulted and Image Credits

© 2001 Stella Galvan
Return to Modern Media Project Homepage

My Computer

FIGURE 22.7 The top window shows the HTML codes used to generate the lower window for the page titled "Teaching Life's Lessons." (Microsoft ® Notepad is a trademark of Microsoft. Title bar screen shot reprinted by permission of Microsoft Corporation.)

menu item often appears under "Format" and "File" menus. Having found this option, your editor will display a dialog box that allows you to modify various properties of your document, including the name of the author (see Figure 22.8). The options will vary with the software you use.

- **Insert the text you have written into the new document.** Type your text into the visual editor as you would into any other program. Notice, however, that paragraphs are formatted differently for the Web, normally in single-spaced block style with no indention. You can change font and alignment by using options found in your program's formatting menus and toolbars.

- **Preview your page in a Web browser.** Most visual editors have a preview option among their menus and toolbars. This option will display your page in a Web browser program, allowing you to see how it will appear to readers on the Web. Ideally, your page won't change much from the editor to the browser program—that is, after all, the claim of WYSIWYG software. If the page does look significantly different, try upgrading either your editor or your browser; the versions you have may not include the latest standards. Most software makers provide free updates on the Web.

- **Insert an image into your page.** Most WYSIWYG editors have an "Insert" menu that allows you to add nontextual content to your page, such as pictures, tables, and horizontal rules. After moving your cursor to the location where you want the picture, select the menu option that allows you to place an image on your page. Select an image you have already saved in your Web project folder. After clicking "OK" in the dialog box, you should see the image on your page, as it will appear to browsers on the Web.

Page Properties	✕
Location:	file:///C|/MyWork/Media/lifelessons.html
Last Modified:	Unknown
Title:	Teaching Life's Lessons
Author:	Stella Galvan
Description:	A research project on the effect of media on children

Advanced users:
To edit other contents of the <head> region, use "HTML Source" in the View Menu or Edit Mode Toolbar.

[OK] [Cancel]

FIGURE 22.8 The "Page Properties" dialog box from *Netscape Composer* allows you to specify the title (as it will appear in the browser's title bar), the author, and a brief description, which search engines will use to index your page. After filling in the boxes, press the "OK" button.

- **Link your page to another.** Set the cursor where you want to add a link to another page. Type the text you would like to be linked, such as "Search at Google" or "Next Page." Select the text you just typed and choose the option to insert a link from your editor's menus. In the dialog box that appears, type the Internet address or page name. To link to a page in your working folder, simply enter the file name, as shown in Figure 22.9. To link to another Web site, include the full URL, including the protocol (for example, http://www.ablongman.com/bookmarks). Some editors allow you to edit other elements of the link, such as the target window. That is, if you wish a page to open in a second browser window, you can edit the "target" element in the anchor tag .

- **Change the page's background color.** One especially useful feature of visual editors is their ability to assign colors according to how they appear on the screen rather than through codes or names. To change the background color of your page, choose the appropriate menu option, probably "Change Background" or "Format Page." You will then see a dialog box displaying color options. To select your color, click on the box with the desired color and then select the "OK" button. When you return to the editor's main window, the background will have changed. A similar dialog box is often used to assist in picking colors for fonts, rules, and tables.

- **Add a footer.** Using the knowledge you have so far, try building a footer for your page. Insert a horizontal rule, a copyright symbol followed by the year and your name, and a link to your project's home page. Finally, use your editor's alignment tools to center the footer material.

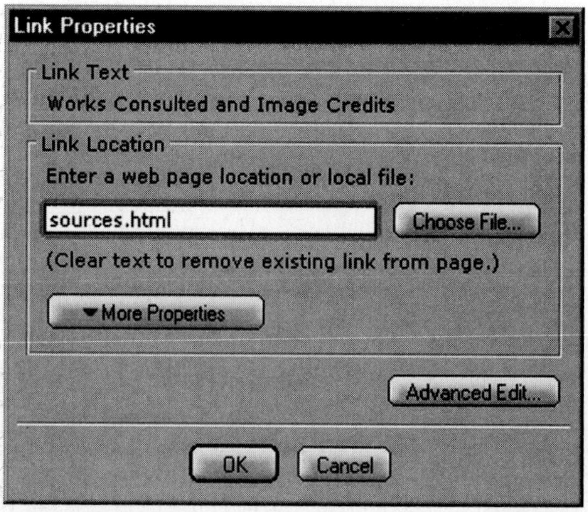

FIGURE 22.9 Creating hypertext links is easy with a Web page or WYSIWYG editor.

Your editor window should now look something like it would appear if it were viewed in a Web browser. What shows up in the browser may differ from the page you created in the program, but the inconsistencies don't usually outweigh the ease of laying out pages with a visual editor.

We suggest that you focus on the important parts of your page, namely, its ease of reading and navigation. It is often a good idea to leave some control over the layout of a page to your readers, who may have preferred settings for browsing the Web, such as large type, reduced colors, and text-only. If you prevent readers with special needs from using their preferences, they may decide not to read your page at all.

Draft by exporting from your word processor. This is the fastest and easiest method for creating Web documents. The latest word processors and spreadsheets allow you to open any existing document and convert it to HTML within seconds. The resulting pages may not have the layouts you expect, but they will be more or less Web compatible. If necessary, you may then be able to open the resulting page in a Web page or text editor and tweak it.

- **Open the text you've prepared in your word processor.** To make your text more readable onscreen, create block paragraphs. Feel free to use bullets and numbers for lists, and if your word processor allows, set background and font colors. Some word processors accommodate standard Web layouts, allowing you to identify different levels of headings to help organize your material.

- **Select the export option.** Some word processors allow you to "Save as" HTML; others permit you to "Export" the document to HTML. After selecting the appropriate option, you'll be prompted to name the file and storage location. Create a name that uses *.htm* or *.html* as an extension (for example, *index.html*) and store the document in your project folder. Note that your word processor may generate files besides the HTML document you explicitly name; this often occurs when you have images in your document. When you publish your document on the Web, you'll need to upload to the server all files and folders created by your word processor.

- **View the generated page in a browser.** To see the results created by your word processor, open the new HTML document in a Web browser. If the results aren't satisfactory, return to your word processor, experiment with simpler layouts, and try again. Alternatively, edit the HTML document directly using one of the other two methods discussed in this chapter.

Edit and proof your Web page. Although Web pages have many special features, the writing that appears on them requires the same care and attention that you would give to a print document. Besides editing for style and clarity, keep in mind some basic document design concerns. Will readers be able to move through the material in the manner you expect? Are the colors you have chosen readable onscreen? Have you cited your images correctly? Do your links work as they should?

In many ways, writing for the World Wide Web is similar to writing for print. You will still rely on text to convey a good deal of your message, and you are still writing to an audience—for a purpose and in response to an occasion. However, writing for electronic media involves additional constraints as well as additional opportunities, as you can see in the annotated sample Web site on pages 254–255.

Review Checklist 22.6 to make sure your Web site includes all the necessary information.

Before the final curtain call, you will want to review the chapters on documentation in Part VI to ensure that you have given proper credit, in the proper format—for any borrowings. Whatever format your project ultimately takes—a traditional paper report, a Web site, a newsletter or brochure, or some combination of genres—you will need to pay close attention to these details.

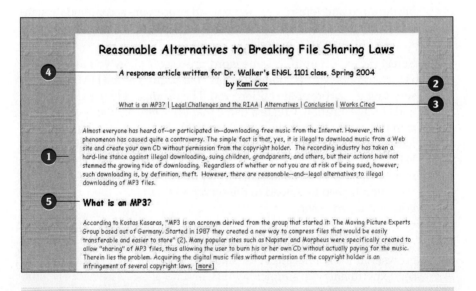

1. Background doesn't interfere with text or visuals.
2. Author's name is formatted as a link to student's email address.
3. Table of contents links to different sections of the page and to other pages.
4. Page includes information about the paper.
5. Subheadings help reader locate information.

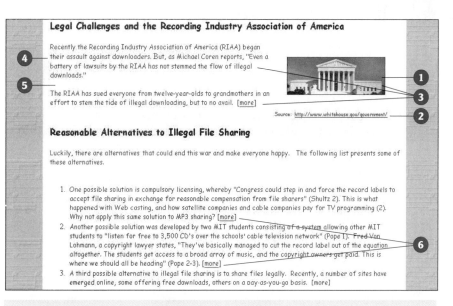

1. Graphic consistent with the topic adds interest.
2. Credit line links to source of graphics as requested by copyright owner.
3. Text and images are laid out on the page using tables without borders.
4. Paragraphs are smaller than for traditional print research papers.
5. Double spacing between paragraphs with no indention adds white space.
6. Links to additional information are included.

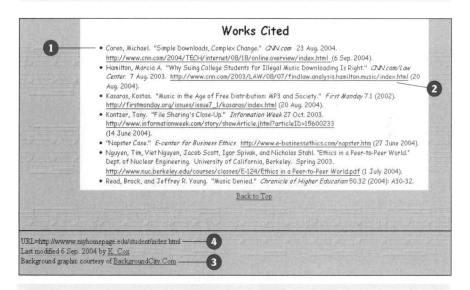

1. Works Cited entries are given in a bulleted list.
2. Links are provided for online sources in the Works Cited list.
3. Credit line for borrowed background image links to source.
4. Bibliographic information helps others evaluate and cite this page.

CHECKLIST 22.6

> ### Web Projects

○ Did you make sure all hypertext links are working? For external links, did you include a list describing each link in case the intended file moves or is changed?

○ Did you make sure your graphics print or load accurately and quickly?

○ Have you checked the appearance of your work carefully? For Web documents and files, did you try a variety of browsers? For documents to be read using electronic means, did you make sure files will transfer across platforms or applications?

○ Have you included bibliographical information—your name and a way to contact you (e.g., your email address) if appropriate, the title of your work or site, the date of creation or last modification, and the URL for the site if it is on the Web?

○ Did you give credit in the proper format to any sources you have borrowed from, including the source of any graphics?

WWW Web Sites Worth Knowing

22.2

- "About APA Style," http://www.apastyle.org/aboutstyle.html
- Modern Language Association (MLA) Home Page, http://www.mla.org
- Tips on Designing Brochures, http://www.peachpit.com/articles/article.asp?p=10297&reoir=1
- "Newsletter Design Tips," http://graphicdesign.about.com/library/weekly/aa121400a.htm?iam=spkask&terms=designing
- *IEEE Standards Style Manual* for Technical Publications, http://standards.ieee.org/guides/style/index.html
- Yale University Center for Advanced Instructional Media, *Web Style Guide*, http://info.med.yale.edu/caim/manual/contents.html
- Tutorials from the Web Developer's Virtual Library, http://www.wdvl.com/Authoring/Tutorials
- National Center for Supercomputing Applications, "A Beginner's Guide to HTML," http://archive.ncsa.uiuc.edu/General/Internet/WWW/HTMLPrimer.html
- Grids for Desktop Publishing, http://desktoppub.about.com/msub16grids.htm

MANAGING YOUR PROJECT

1. Using pencil and paper, sketch a layout for your Web site. If your site will include more than one page, include arrows designating links between pages. Prepare a one-page written explanation of your design choices and share it and your sketches with your peers. Ask for feedback and suggestions.

2. Create a template for your Web page, using either a visual editor or an HTML editor. Experiment with different layouts, using the table feature to place elements on your page. Save the different layouts to your disk and share them with your classmates. Ask classmates to review your designs and offer suggestions for improvement.

VI

DOCUMENTATION

DON'T MISS . . .

- **The overview of COS documentation in Section 23a.** When you expect to use many electronic sources in a project, Columbia Online Style (COS) may be your best choice of documentation system.
- **The sample MLA paper in Chapter 24.** If you are preparing a paper in language, literature, or the humanities, you may want to use MLA documentation.
- **The sample APA paper in Chapter 25.** If you are preparing a paper in the social sciences, you may want to use APA documentation.
- **The sample CMS paper in Chapter 26.** If you are preparing a paper in language, literature, or the humanities, you may want to use CMS documentation – especially if you prefer footnotes or endnotes to in-text parenthetical notes.
- **The explanation of CSE documentation in Section 27a.** If you are preparing a paper in the natural sciences, you may want to use CSE documentation.

EVERYDAY RESEARCH

ELIZABETH BRUNELL, Elementary School Teacher
Paul Revere School, Chicago

"There are two things in life about which I have always been passionate—teaching and volunteering. After college, I chose a career that incorporated both, working with underprivileged children in an inner city teaching program on Chicago's South side."

Because good teaching practices are constantly being modified and refined, Elizabeth constantly employs research in her career. "I like to use a variety of methods and activities to reach all of my students. When I first became a teacher, I spent hours making my lessons exciting and interesting; I soon found myself tired and out of good ideas." Elizabeth soon discovered the wealth of teaching resources available on the Internet, especially for those interested in varying their teaching techniques.

Observing other classrooms and teaching styles is also quite helpful in refining Elizabeth's own teaching skills. She is enrolled in a Master's program and is currently learning how to create interpretive questions and incorporate them into classroom discussions. "I have been engrossed in this concept and I've been reading other people's research and applying it in my class."

"My training in elementary and special education from college has helped me tremendously in my career. I reference my college notes and textbooks often. I also remain friendly with a college professor, who is both a mentor and a friend. She has been a tremendous help in my adjustment into a city school system, as she herself worked after college in an inner city elementary school. In addition, she is an avid researcher and has really helped me in narrowing down a topic for my Master's thesis that will ultimately benefit my classroom."

CHAPTER 23

COS Documentation

In preparing a college research project, you may use a wide variety of sources. However, conventional citation systems either don't mention the types of sources you are using, or the guidelines for documenting them are unwieldy.

The Columbia Guide to Online Style by Janice R. Walker and Todd Taylor (http://www.columbia.edu/cu/cup/cgos/idx_basic.html) presents a style (COS) designed expressly for electronically accessed material. Use *COS-humanities style* for projects following MLA or CMS guidelines and *COS-scientific style* for projects following APA or CSE guidelines. For other styles, COS guidelines can easily be adapted to conform to the specific format required.

23a How do you use COS documentation?

COS doesn't replace MLA, APA, CMS, or CSE styles; it supplements them so that writers can document electronic sources consistently and appropriately. In this chapter we provide separate COS form directories for humanities-style citations (Section 23b) and science-style citations (Section 23d).

Like the MLA and APA systems (see Chapters 24 and 25), Columbia Online Style documentation involves two basic steps.

Step 1: In the body of your paper, place a note in the appropriate form for every item you must document. The purpose of a parenthetical note is to guide your reader to the full citation in the list of Works Cited or References. The note also designates the exact location of information or quotations within the original source. When your source provides page or paragraph numbers, include them following the same format as for print sources (see also Chapters 24 and 25).

For electronic sources without page numbers or other consistent divisions (such as paragraph numbers), simply place the author's last name in parentheses after a passage that requires documentation.

Jim Lehrer may be America's most trusted newsperson, its new Walter

Cronkite (Shafer).

For Web pages that do not list an individual author or person responsible for maintaining the page, the sponsoring organization itself is considered the author. For example:

> The Educational Testing Service, or ETS, is a nonprofit organization that develops and administers educational assessment tests for schools throughout the world (ETS).

When no conventional author or other person or organization is listed, identify the source by its title or by the file name when no title is given (such as for a graphics file). When the title is very long, use a shortened version, but be sure to identify the piece in a way that will allow readers to locate the reference in your Works Cited or References list. The title of the following source is "Tobacco Wields Its Clout."

> USA Today was among those to editorialize against the tobacco industry's continuing influence on Congress ("Tobacco").

When citing an email message or chat room discussion you may have to include an author's alias or nickname.

> In a recent posting to the newsgroup alt.sport.paintball, jireem argued . . . .

To cite a source without page numbers multiple times, repeat the author's name (or the short title if there is no author) for each citation. But try to keep intrusions to a minimum—for example, by using a single note at the end of a paragraph when one source is cited throughout it. Eliminate the parenthetical note by naming the author or title of a source in the body of the paper.

> Shafer claims in a *Slate* column that PBS's Jim Lehrer is the new Walter Cronkite, America's most trusted newsperson.

> In "Tobacco Wields Its Clout," *USA Today* editorializes against the tobacco industry's continuing influence on Congress.

Some styles, such as Chicago, require that you use footnotes or endnotes instead of most parenthetical references.

The COS form for CMS notes can be adapted from the COS—Humanities Form Directory in Section 23b. You will need to study both the COS forms in that section and the CMS footnote forms in Sections 26a and 26c.

For scientific papers following APA or CSE styles for print sources, the in-text citation will include an author's last name followed by a date of publication in parentheses. For most types of publications, give only the year even when the source furnishes day and date.

> General Motors may soon find itself in the unenviable position of being unable to borrow money at favorable rates (Gross, 2004).

You can also name the author in the body of your text, following the name with year of publication in parentheses.

> Gross (2004) argues in a recent *Slate* article that General Motors may soon find itself unable to borrow money at favorable rates.

If the date of publication is not available use the day, month, and year you accessed the source.

Slipstream (21 May 2004) argues that the research design is flawed, but

ksmith (22 May 2004) rejects that claim.

As a general rule, make all parenthetical notes as brief and inconspicuous as possible. Remember that the point of a note is to identify a source of information, not to distract readers.

Step 2: On a separate page at the end of your paper, list every source you cited in a parenthetical note. This alphabetical list of sources is usually titled "Works Cited" in humanities projects and "References" in scientific projects. In Chicago style such a page is optional because the notes themselves include all essential bibliographical information. (See Chapter 26.)

COS items are assembled from a few basic components.

- **Author.** In **humanities** styles, list the full name of the author, last name first, followed by any additional authors' names in the usual order.

  Walker, Janice R., and Todd Taylor.

  In **scientific** styles, list the author's last name and initials, followed by any additional authors.

  Walker, J. R., & Taylor, T.

- **Title.** Depending on whether you are adapting COS to MLA or APA documentation style, titles of electronic works might be italicized, placed between quotation marks, or left with no special marking, following the format specified for print-based sources.

- **Editor, translator, or compiler.** Include the name of an editor, translator, or compiler, if not listed earlier. In **humanities** styles, give the appropriate abbreviation (*Ed., Trans.,* or *Comp.*) immediately followed by the full name. In **scientific** styles, the abbreviation is enclosed in parentheses and follows the name.

- **Print or previous publication information.** Include print or previous publication information just before the electronic publication information.

- **Date of publication and/or access.** When an online or electronic source is based on a printed source or appears in a dated format (such as the online version of a newspaper or magazine), give the original publication date of the material. For Web sites, check the home page for a copyright date or check the source code for dates of posting or updates.

  For most electronic sources, provide a date of access—the day, month, and year you examined the material—enclosed in parentheses and following the electronic address.

- **Electronic address.** Probably the most important information about a source you can provide is the electronic address (URL).

For very long URLs, allow your word processor to break the URL automatically. Ensure access to a source by pointing to the main URL for a given site instead and then listing the links or search terms followed to locate the particular site or document.

If you are publishing your project on the Web, do not try to force hanging indents. For traditional print projects, however, COS follows the hanging indent feature of other styles, with the first line of each bibliographic entry flush with the left-hand margin and subsequent lines indented one-half inch or five spaces.

Use Checklists 23.1 through 23.3 to understand the basic elements of citation for electronic sources.

Because there are so many variations in these general entries, you will want to check the COS form directories that follow in Sections 23b (humanities) and 23d (sciences) for the correct format of a particular entry.

CHECKLIST 23.1

Basic Format—COS-Humanities (MLA)

A typical Columbia Online Style Works Cited entry for an MLA-style paper in the humanities includes the following basic information.

○ Author, last name first, followed by a period and one space.

○ Title of the work, followed by a period and one space. Book titles are italicized; article titles appear between quotation marks.

○ Publication information (if any), followed by a period and one space. This will ordinarily include a date of publication if different from the date of access. List previous publication information (including print publication information), if known, followed by information on the electronic publication.

○ The electronic address and any path or directory information, followed by a space. No period follows the electronic address.

○ The date you accessed the information, in parentheses, followed by a period.

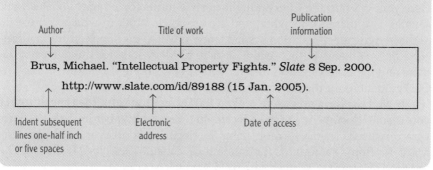

CHECKLIST 23.2

Basic Format—COS-Humanities (CMS)

A typical Columbia Online Style Works Cited entry for a CMS-style paper in the humanities includes the following basic information.

- ○ Author(s), last name first, followed by a period and one space.
- ○ Title of the work, followed by a period (or other final punctuation mark) and enclosed between quotation marks.
- ○ Publication information, followed by a period. This will ordinarily include a date of publication if different from the date of access. List previous publication information (including print publication information), if known, followed by information on the electronic publication.
- ○ The electronic address and any path or directory information, followed by a space. No period follows the electronic address.
- ○ The date you accessed the information, in parentheses, followed by a period.

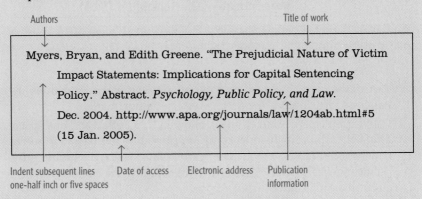

Authors   Title of work

Myers, Bryan, and Edith Greene. "The Prejudicial Nature of Victim
    Impact Statements: Implications for Capital Sentencing
    Policy." Abstract. *Psychology, Public Policy, and Law.*
    Dec. 2004. http://www.apa.org/journals/law/1204ab.html#5
    (15 Jan. 2005).

Indent subsequent lines   Date of access   Electronic address   Publication
one-half inch or five spaces   information

23b COS form directory—Humanities (MLA)

Here you will find the COS humanities-style forms for a variety of electronic sources. Use these forms when you are writing a paper in which you use an author–page number citation system (such as MLA) for nonelectronic sources. Note that the items in this section adhere to MLA style for the names of authors and the titles of works and for print publication information but follow COS guidelines for the electronic portions of the citation.

To find the form you need, look in the Format Index for the type of source you need to document and then locate that item by number in the COS Form Directory itself. To handle more complex electronic sources and to learn more about developing standards for online style, consult *The Columbia Guide to Online Style* by Janice R. Walker and Todd Taylor.

CHECKLIST 23.3

Basic Format—COS-Scientific (APA)

A typical Columbia Online Style "References" entry for an APA-style paper in the sciences includes the following basic information.

○ Author(s), last name first, followed by a period and one space.

○ Date of publication in parentheses, followed by a period and one space. Give the year first, followed by the month (do not abbreviate it), followed by the day (if applicable) for periodical publications; give only the year of publication for other works.

○ Title of the work, capitalizing only the first word and any proper nouns, followed by a period and one space.

○ Publication information (if any), followed by a period and one space. List previous publication information (including print publication information), if known, followed by information on the electronic publication if applicable.

○ The electronic address and any path or directory information, followed by a space. No period follows the electronic address.

○ The date you accessed the information, in parentheses, followed by a period.

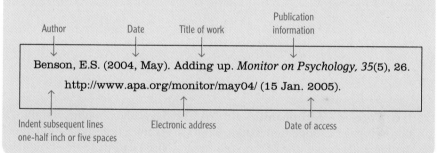

Author   Date   Title of work   Publication information

Benson, E.S. (2004, May). Adding up. *Monitor on Psychology, 35*(5), 26. http://www.apa.org/monitor/may04/ (15 Jan. 2005).

Indent subsequent lines one-half inch or five spaces   Electronic address   Date of access

---

11. Web site—online article—COS/MLA

12. Web site—article from a news service or online newspaper—COS/MLA

13. Web site—article from an archive—COS/MLA

14. Web site—with frames—COS/MLA

15. Web site—graphic, audio, or video file—COS/MLA

Online References and Databases

16. Online encyclopedia article—COS/MLA

17. Online dictionary or thesaurus entry—COS/MLA

18. Material from a CD-ROM—COS/MLA

19. Material from an online data-base—COS/MLA

Online Communication

20. Personal email—COS/MLA

21. Electronic mailing lists—COS/MLA

22. Newsgroup—COS/MLA

23. Blogs and Wikis—COS/MLA

24. Chats—COS/MLA

Miscellaneous Electronic Sources

25. MOOs, MUDs, and online games—COS/MLA

26. Software and video games—COS/MLA

27. *WebCT, Blackboard,* other course-ware—COS/MLA

28. Online course material—COS/MLA

29. Other electronic files—COS/MLA

1. **Web Page—COS/Humanities (MLA)** Cite the author's name, the title of the Web page in quotation marks, followed by any print publication information and/or the title of the Web site in italics, and the date of publication. Give the full URL followed by the date of access in parentheses.

Works Cited

Baron, Dennis. "From Pencils to Pixels: The Stages of Literacy Technology."

Passions, Pedagogies, and Twenty-First Century Technologies. Ed. Gail

Hawisher and Cynthia L. Selfe. Logan, UT: Utah State UP, 2000. 15–33.

http://netfiles.uiuc.edu/debaron/www/essays/pencils.htm (27 July 2004).

For a Web page with no known author, begin with the page title.

"Health Considered in Companies' Building Designs." *CNN.com.* 27 July 2004.

http://www.cnn.com/2004/HEALTH/diet.fitness/07/27/healthy

.architecture/index.html (27 July 2004).

For personal home pages, supply the description *Home page* after the author's name.

Brown, Kiwi. Home page. 31 Dec. 2001. http://www.geocities.com/shoe_polish/

   homepage.html (16 Jan. 2004).

2. **Web Site—COS/Humanities (MLA)** Many Web pages are part of a larger Web site. Italicize Web site titles.

Works Cited

"The Proved and the Unproved." Editorial. *The New York Times on the Web.* 13

   July 1997. http://www.nytimes.com/yr/mo/day/editorial/13sun1.html (13

   Aug. 2004).

For sites with no title, include a description of the site (e.g., *Home page*) or the name of the organization or corporate sponsor, as in the following example. Note that for government Web sites, you will identify the government (e.g., *United States*) in addition to the government agency (see model 7).

United States. National Aeronautics and Space Administration. Home page. Ed.

   Jim Wilson. 27 July 2004. http://www.nasa.gov/home (27 July 2004).

3. **Web Site, Revised or Modified—COS/Humanities (MLA)** You may specify a date that a page or a site was revised or updated when such a date is given.

Works Cited

Golombek, M., and Tim Parker. "PIGWAD: Layers in Motion." 21 Dec. 2000. Mod.

   21 Apr. 2003. *Science for a Changing World.* US Geological Survey.

   http://webgis.wr.usgs.gov/mer/revised_ellipse.htm (16 Sep. 2004).

4. **Web Site with a Group or Institutional Author—COS/Humanities (MLA)** Groups, organizations, and government agencies often author documents under the name of the group, organization, or agency instead of listing the names of individuals as authors.

Works Cited

Apple Computer, Inc. "Film Mogul in the Making." 2004.

   http://www.apple.com/education/profiles/brandl (16 Sep. 2004).

5. **Web Site, No Author or Title—COS/Humanities (MLA)** When no author or title can be assigned to a site, include the file name, followed by the date of publication or last modification, if known, the URL, and the date of access.

Works Cited

1993e-small.gif. http://encke.jpl.nasa.gov/images/1993e-small.gif (16 Sep. 2004).

6. **Web Site Maintained by an Individual—COS/Humanities (MLA)** A maintained site is one that usually contains links, routinely updated, to materials not created by the author(s) of the site. The site can be listed either by the person(s) maintaining it or by its name, depending on which emphasis suits your project.

Works Cited

Ley, Michael, maint. "DBLP Computer Science Bibliography." 2004. Universität

   Trier. http://dblp.uni-trier.de (16 Sep. 2004).

"DBLP Computer Science Bibliography." Maint. Michael Ley. 2004. Universität

   Trier. http://dblp.uni-trier.de (16 Sep. 2004).

7. **Web Site—Government—COS/Humanities (MLA)** Many government sites do not list individual authors. Treat these sites as you would a corporate or institutional author. Give the name of the government and the name of the agency or department, followed by the usual publication information.

Works Cited

United States. House of Representatives. "How Our Laws Are Made." Rev. by

   Charles W. Johnson. 30 June 2003. Last update 19 Nov. 2003. *THOMAS:*

   Legislative Information on the Internet.

   http://thomas.loc.gov/home/lawsmade.toc.html (3 Aug. 2004).

8. **Web Site—Corporate—COS/Humanities (MLA)** The corporation or institution should be listed as author of a corporate Web page or site.

Works Cited

Cedar Fair, L. P. "Spinning in Circles: Carousels." 2004.

   http://www.cedarpoint.com/public/news/carousel/index.cfm (4 Sep.

   2004).

Individual articles or pages within the site may or may not list authors (see model 11).

9. **Web Site—Book, Printed, Available Online—COS/Humanities (MLA)** Give the name of the author, the title of the work, and the publication information for the printed version if known (see also Chapter 24). Then provide the title of the electronic version, if different from the original title, and the electronic publication information.

Works Cited

Austen, Jane. *Pride and Prejudice.* 1813. *Pride and Prejudice Hypertext.* Ed. H.

    Churchyard. 1994. http://www.pemberley.com/janeinfo/pridprej.html (16

    Sep. 2004).

10. Web Site—Book, Published Electronically—COS/Humanities (MLA) Provide author, title, and date of publication followed by the URL and date of access.

Works Cited

Halsall, Paul, ed. *Internet Medieval Sourcebook.* Rev. 1999. Mod. 8 Jan. 2000.

    http://www.fordham.edu/halsall/sbook.html (18 Sep. 2004).

11. Web Site—Online Article—COS/Humanities (MLA) The title of the article in quotation marks is followed by the italicized title of the Web site or journal in which it appears. For journals, include the volume number of the periodical, followed by a period and the issue number (if available) and the date of publication.

Works Cited

DeFrancesco, Laura. "Beta Stem Cells: Searching for the Diabetic's Holy Grail."

    The Scientist 15.21 (29 Oct. 2001). http://www.the-scientist.com/

    yr2001/oct/research1_011029.html (16 Sep. 2004).

12. Web Site—Article from a News Service or Online Newspaper—COS/Humanities (MLA) When no author's name is given, list the name of the news source (such as *Reuters* or *Associated Press*), followed by the title of the article, the name of the news service or online newspaper, the date of the article if different from the date accessed, the electronic address, and the date of access. Include print publication information if available.

Works Cited

Associated Press. "Alaska Ruling Starts Debate on Gun Permits for Mentally Ill."

    The New York Times 11 Jan. 2002, late ed., sec. A: 18. *The New York Times*

    on the Web. http://www.nytimes.com/2002/01/11/national/

    11ALAS.html (16 Sep. 2004).

13. Web Site—Article from an Archive—COS/Humanities (MLA) Provide publication information as you would for a printed article (see Chapter 24), followed by the name of the archive site if applicable, the electronic address, and the date of access.

Works Cited

Shaw, Anna Howard. *The Story of a Pioneer.* New York: Harper, 1915. US Lib. of

Congress. *American Memory Collection.* http://

memory.loc.gov/cgi-bin/query/S?ammem/lhbumbib:

@field(TITLE+@od1(The+story+of+a+pioneer+)) (12 Sep. 2004).

For articles in archives with very long URLs or without direct access, give the address of the main page and include the publication information (if available), and link names and/or search terms used.

Shaw, Anna Howard. *The Story of a Pioneer.* New York: Harper, 1915. US Lib. of

Congress. *American Memory Collection.* http://memory.loc.gov (Links:

Search/story of a pioneer) (12 Sep. 2004).

14. **Web Site—with Frames—COS/Humanities (MLA)** A Web site that uses frames may present material from other sites as well as material from within its own site. To determine the URL for the material, you may be able to right-click inside the frame to view its properties. When you cannot determine the original URL of such material, list the document by author, title, and other publication information; then give the name of the site where the source appears within a frame; the electronic address of the site; and, in parentheses, the path, including the links followed to access the specific article or site (separating individual links by a forward slash). Conclude the entry with the date of access.

Works Cited

Lennie (#167). "AlaMOO Builder's Bible." *AlaMOO.* http://ranger.accd.edu:7000

(Links: Help Kiosk/Builder's Bible) (18 Sep. 2004).

If the file can be easily located from the frames page, using the publication information, then you may omit the links.

Kimelman, Reuven. "The Seduction of Eve and Feminist Readings of the Garden

of Eden." *Women in Judaism: A Multidisciplinary Journal* 1.2 (1998).

http://www.utoronto.ca/wjudaism/index.html (12 June 2004).

If the file is available in a nonframe version or if your browser provides site information for documents contained in frames, you may choose to cite the unique URL for the file being cited rather than that for the main site. Make sure, however, that the page is accessible from the URL given; some sites discourage this "deep linking" by using active server pages or other means to ensure that visitors will enter a site through its home page, so it is important that you double-check all URLs.

Kimelman, Reuven. "The Seduction of Eve and Feminist Readings of the Garden

of Eden." *Women in Judaism: A Multidisciplinary Journal* 1.2 (1998).

http://www.utoronto.ca/wjudaism/journal/vol1n2/eve.html (12 June

2002).

15. **Web Site—Graphic, Audio, or Video File—COS/Humanities (MLA)** Cite
a multimedia file in one of two ways: either by its own URL (which you can
usually find in the Netscape browser by selecting "View Page Info" or by
right-clicking to view the image alone; in *Internet Explorer*, right-click on the
image and view the properties), or cite the file by the Web page on which it
appears. Identify the creator, photographer, or artist (if known); then identify the title or file name, followed by the date of creation and/or publication (if known). Next, furnish the electronic address and date of access.

Works Cited

Van Gogh, Vincent. *Fourteen Sunflowers in a Vase*. 1888. http://www.artchive

.com/artchive/v/van_gogh/sunflowers.jpg (16 Sep. 2004).

To cite the file as it appears on a particular page, identify the artist, the title of the file, and the date of creation, if known. Then name the site on
which it appears, followed by any publication information and the electronic address for the page.

Works Cited

Van Gogh, Vincent. *Fourteen Sunflowers in a Vase*. 1888. *Web Gallery of Art*.

http://www.artchive.com/artchive/v/van_gogh/sunflowers.jpg.html (17 Sep.

2004).

Audio and video files are similar to graphic files: you may cite the direct
address or cite the file as a link from a Web site. Note that the file extension indicates the type of application necessary to access the file (*.mp3, .ra,
.mov*, etc.).

"Cherokee Traditional: Stomp Dance." http://realdl.ket.org/ramgen/realmedia/

humanities/music/cherokee.ra/dnet.ra?usehostname (17 Sep. 2004).

"Cherokee Traditional: Stomp Dance." *The Kentucky Network Distance Learning

Site*. 2002. http://www.dl.ket.org (Links: Humanities/Humanities through

the Arts/Music/Cherokee traditional: Stomp Dance) (17 Sep. 2004).

For audio and video files, you may include the name of the artist, composer, or director if known and depending on your focus.

Michael Ross Quartet. "Back at the Cathouse." *Year of the Dog*. Cooper-Alport

Productions, 2004. http://www.michaelrossquartet.com/

sounds04/05backatthecathouse.mp3 (30 Jan. 2005).

For files without titles, use the file name instead (see model 5).

16. **Online Encyclopedia Article—COS/Humanities (MLA)** Give the author of the article (if available); the title of the article or term, enclosed in quotation marks, and the name of the encyclopedia in italics. If the encyclopedia is based on a printed work, give place of publication, publisher, and date (see Chapter 24). For electronic publications, include online publication information.

Works Cited

Markie, Peter. "Rationalism vs. Empiricism." Last mod. 19 Aug. 2004. *Stanford*

   Encyclopedia of Philosophy. Ed. Edward N. Zalta. Stanford, CA: Stanford

   U, 2004. http://plato.stanford.edu/entries/rationalism-empiricism (20 Sep.

   2004).

Often online encyclopedias and reference works are available only through subscription. You may have free access through your library's portal or through an Internet service provider such as *America Online.* When this is the case, you need to give enough information to allow your readers to find the source regardless of the portal they use for access. Give the URL if it allows direct access for subscribers.

Fisher, William Weston. "Intellectual Property Law." *Encyclopaedia Britannica*

   Online. 2004. *Encyclopaedia Britannica.*

   http://search.eb.com/eb/article?tocId=231534 (20 Sep. 2004).

When you are unable to determine a URL for the article, give what information you have, including, where applicable, the name of the portal or service, and any keywords or search terms that differ from the title.

"Cathode Ray." *Encyclopaedia Britannica Online.* 2004. *Encyclopaedia*

   Britannica. Galileo. Georgia Southern U, Zach. S. Henderson Lib.,

   Statesboro, GA (30 Aug. 2004).

Stern, Robert M. "Eurodollar." *World Book Online Reference Center. America*

   Online (Keyword: World Book) (20 Sep. 2004).

17. **Online Dictionary or Thesaurus Entry—COS/Humanities (MLA)** List the entry by the word looked up, enclosed in quotation marks, followed by the name of the dictionary. If the dictionary is based on a printed work, give place of publication, publisher, and date (see Chapter 24). Give any publication information about the electronic version, including the service offering it (for example, *America Online*), the electronic address, links or keywords used to access the source, and the date accessed.

Works Cited

"Copyright." *Merriam-Webster Online Dictionary.* 2004. *Merriam-Webster*

   OnLine. http://www.m-w.com (17 Sep. 2004).

"Intellectual." *Thesaurus by Merriam Webster.* 2001. *America Online* (Links:

Research and Learn/thesaurus) (17 Sep. 2004).

18. **Material from a CD-ROM—COS/Humanities (MLA)** Provide an author (if available), the title of the entry or article (if applicable), and the name of the CD-ROM program or publication. Include any edition or version numbers, a series title if applicable, and available publication information. No date of access is necessary for CD-ROM publications (see also model 26).

Works Cited

Pearson Education. "What Is Plagiarism?" *Avoiding Plagiarism.* New York:

Longman, 2002.

19. **Material from an Online Database—COS/Humanities (MLA)** Provide as much information as possible to help your reader locate the source. Identify the author and the title of the entry or article, and give publication information for items that have appeared in print (see Chapter 24). Identify the database or information service in italics; give the name of the database publisher (if known), and furnish any retrieval data (if applicable), followed by the date of access. Unless the URL allows direct access to the source, do not include it.

Works Cited

Landau, Michael. "Digital Downloads, Access Codes, and US Copyright Law."

International Review of Law, Computers and Technology 16.2 (2002):

149-70. *Academic Search Premier.* EBSCO. DOI #10.1080/

1360086022000003973 (20 Sep. 2004).

Gallagher, David F. "Warner's Tryst with Bloggers Hits Sour Note." *The New*

York Times 16 Aug. 2004, late ed., sec. C: 1. *LexisNexis Academic Universe*

(17 Sep. 2004).

Often online databases are available only through subscription. When this is the case, you may include information on the portal or service you used to access the database.

Heinze, Denise. "Toni Morrison." *Dictionary of Literary Biography.* Vol. 143:

American Novelists Since World War II. 3rd series. Gale Group, 2001:

171–87. *Gale Literary Databases.* U of South Florida Lib., Tampa, FL

(21 Jan. 2004).

20. **Personal Email—COS/Humanities (MLA)** Identify the author of the email, and give the title of the message in quotation marks. Then identify the communication as *Personal email.* Include the date only if it differs

from the date you accessed (or read) the message; otherwise, you need only give the access date in parentheses.

Works Cited

Pemberton, Michael. "Bookmarks." Personal email (5 Mar. 2004).

21. **Electronic Mailing Lists—COS/Humanities (MLA)** Identify the author of the message to an electronic mailing list. If no author's name is given, use the author's alias or email name. (Do *not* include the author's entire email address.) Then give the subject line of the message (enclosed in quotation marks) as the title, followed by the date of the message (if different from the date of access); the name of the list in italics, if known; the address of the listserv; and the date of access.

Works Cited

Inman, James. "Re: Smart Thinking." *WCenter Listserv.*

   wcenter@edsel.tosm.ttu.edu (22 Sep. 2004).

djfoxwvgs. "Misleading Ads." 21 Sep. 2004. *WRIT 3230 Discussion List.*

   writ3230@yahoogroups.com (24 Sep. 2004).

For messages available through an online archive, see model 13.

22. **Newsgroup—COS/Humanities (MLA)** Give the author's name (or alias), the subject line of the message as the title (enclosed in quotation marks), the date of the message (if different from the date of access), the name and/or address of the newsgroup, and the name and address of the online archive (if applicable), followed by the date of access.

Works Cited

Allen, Tom. "What Medical Evidence Is Used to Evaluate Social Security Disability

   Cases?" 21 Aug. 2003. *misc.health.arthritis. Google Groups.*

   http://groups.google.com (23 Aug. 2003).

Wordblind. "Museum Redesign." 18 July 2003. news:alt.architecture.alternative

   (9 Aug. 2003).

23. **Blogs and Wikis—COS/Humanities (MLA)** Give the author's name or alias; the title of posting, if applicable; and the name of the blog or wiki site, followed by the date of posting. Include the electronic address and the date of access enclosed in parentheses.

Works Cited

Vaidhyanathan, Siva. "Universities, RIAA, and Academic Freedom."

   Sivacracy.net: Siva Vaidhyanathan' Weblog. 23 Apr. 2003.

http://www.nyu.edu/classes/siva/2003_04_23_blogarchive

.html#20187673 (30 Apr. 2003).

24. Chats—COS/Humanities To cite online conversations, give the name of the speaker; the title of the conversation (if applicable) enclosed in quotation marks, or a description of the conversation, the date of the conversation, and the name or location of the chat room.

Works Cited

Beckster. Personal communication. 3 Aug. 2003. *AOL Instant Messenger.*

Shoe_polish. Personal communication. 16 Aug. 2004. *Yahoo! Chat.*

  http://chat.yahoo.com (Links: Computers & Internet/Electronics).

Tch Tanya. Personal communication. 14 May 2003. *America Online* (Links:

  Research and Learn/Homework Help/English/Get Live Help).

If a transcript of the conversation is available, include information about the archive, including the title of the site (in italics), the URL, and the date of access. (See also Model 13.)

25. MOOs, MUDs, and Online Games—COS/Humanities (MLA) MOOs and MUDs and other synchronous communication sites or online games may contain information that needs to be cited: conversations, rooms and objects, command sequences, programming code, or even mailing lists. The form of the citation will depend on the type of information being cited and on what information is available. Include as much information as possible to allow future researchers to access the original source, if possible.

To cite an archived discussion, provide information about the conversation as well as information about the location of the archive. (See model 13.)

To cite an object, give the name of the object's owner (if available) followed by the name of the object, including the object number (if applicable) enclosed in quotation marks. Include any command sequences in parentheses after the URL or address.

Works Cited

Locke (#169). "Usability Lab (#836)." *TTU English MOO.*

  http://moo.engl.ttu.edu:7000/ (Command: @go #836) (22 Sep. 2004).

To cite programming code, give the name and object number of the author (if applicable); a description of the type of information (e.g., *Source code*); the name of the verb or program, in quotation marks; the name of the site (if applicable), in italics; the date of creation and/or last modification (if known); the protocol and address or URL; the command sequence; and the date accessed, in parentheses. If you are citing specific lines of the program, include the line number or numbers in the in-text citation.

Works Cited

Wizard. Source code. "Say." *DaMOO.* 13 May 1996. Last mod. 8 Mar. 2000.

  telnet://damoo.csun.edu:7777 (Command: @list #3:say) (22 Sep. 2004).

Cite MOO and MUD mail messages as you would other electronic mail, beginning with the name or alias of the author; the subject line of the posting; the date of the message; and the name and number of the list (if applicable) or the description (e.g., *Personal email*). Then list the name of the site; the protocol and address, or URL; and any commands necessary to access the message, followed by the date accessed, enclosed in parentheses.

Jai (#137). "Going Postal Goes PC?" 20 July 1997. *Social (#282). DaMOO.*

  telnet://damoo.csun.edu:7777 (Command: @read 1 on #282) (9 Sep. 2004).

Max (#11113). "Planet Maps." 31 July 2004. Personal email. *DaMOO.*

  telnet://lrc.csun.edu:7777 (24 Aug. 2004).

26. **Software and Video Games—COS/Humanities (MLA)** When citing software programs and video games, include the author, if known; the title of the game or software (in italics); the version or file number or other identifying information; the publisher of the software program; and the date of publication, if known. The date accessed is not necessary when citing software and video game programs.

Works Cited

ID Software. *Doom 3.* Santa Monica: Activision, 2004.

WordPerfect 12. Ottowa, ON: Corel, 2004.

To cite specific information in a software program or game, list the title of the screen or document referenced, enclosed in quotation marks; the title of the software, in italics; the version or other identifying information, if applicable; any commands or path information necessary to access the information, if applicable; and publication information (see also model 18).

U.S. Army. "212 Ways to Be a Soldier." *America's Army.* Army Game Project.

  2002. Washington: Department of Defense.

27. ***WebCT, Blackboard,* and Other Courseware—COS/Humanities (MLA)** Information may be published through various courseware packages such as *WebCT, Blackboard,* and a host of others. Some of this information may be part of the courseware package itself; some may be written by the instructor or by students in a given class. Other works may also be made available to students within the frame of a courseware package, such as scanned copies of print articles or links to external Web sites. Unfortunately, not all of this information may be adequately cited to begin with;

nonetheless, citing the course and instructor can allow future researchers to attempt to trace the original sources if necessary.

Works Cited

Collegeboard.com. "Financial Aid Myths: Don't Believe Everything You Hear."
2004. ENGL 1102: Composition II. Fall 2004. Jeff Todd, Instructor. *WebCT.*
Georgia Southern, Statesboro, GA (24 Sep. 2004).

Johnson, Terry. "Electronic Communication and Online Courses." Discussion
posting. 10 Sep. 2004. ENGL 1102: Composition II. Fall 2004. Jeff Todd,
Instructor. *WebCT.* Georgia Southern, Statesboro, GA (24 Sep. 2004).

28. **Online Course Materials—COS/Humanities (MLA)** Most citations of course materials should include the name of the instructor, the title and date of the course, and the name of the school. If the material is freely available on the Web, then include the URL and the date of access as well. Cite the home page for a course or online syllabus beginning with the name of the instructor, the name of the course, the description (e.g., *Home page*), and the date of the course. Include the name of the department offering the course (if known), the school or university, (including the city and state if the school is not well known), the URL, and the date of access.

Works Cited

Walker, Janice R. WRIT 3030: Writing for the WWW. Home page. Fall 2003. Dept.
of Writing and Linguistics. Georgia Southern U, Statesboro, GA.
http://www.georgiasouthern.edu/~jwalker/courses/fall03/writ3030/ (1 Sep.
2004).

Cite handouts and other documents beginning with the name of the author (if known) and the title of the document. Include the date of publication if known, followed by the title of the course, the date, the instructor's name, and the name of the school or university.

"Designing Print Documents: Brochures, Flyers, and Newsletters." PBAD 7120:
Written Communication for Public Managers. Fall 2002. Janice R. Walker,
Instructor. Georgia Southern U, Statesboro, GA. (25 Aug. 2003).

To cite email, discussion boards, or chat room conversations in courseware, include the name of the author or speaker, the subject line, and the posting date. Include any other information that may be helpful in accessing the information.

Walker, Janice. "IM-Speak." 24 Aug. 2003. Discussion Board. General Discussion.
WRIT3030: Writing the Digital World. Fall 2003. Janice Walker,

Instructor. Georgia Southern, Statesboro, GA. http://www.blackboard.com

(25 Aug. 2003).

Sanders, Ruth. Personal interview. *WebCT* Chat. PBAD 7120: Written

Communication for Public Managers. Fall 2002. Janice R. Walker,

Instructor. Georgia Southern, Statesboro, GA. (24 Oct. 2002).

29. **Other Electronic Files—COS/Humanities (MLA)** How you access electronic information will usually determine the format in which it is cited. For example, an electronic presentation may be accessed on the Web, from a diskette or CD-ROM, or through a courseware package. Many types of files can be made accessible on the Web, including electronic presentations, Portable Document Format (PDF) files, electronic spreadsheet files, plain text files, or files created using a word processor. Generally, the file extension (the letters after the "dot" in the file name) provides the information necessary for most browsers to open the file. Include the URL for files available on the Internet or on an intranet; include the drive designation and directories, along with the file name, for items available through a shared network, as well as any links necessary to access the cited file.

List the name of the author (if known), the title of the file, and the date of creation or publication. Include any other information that will help locate the original source.

Works Cited

Association of Internet Researchers (AOIR). "Ethical Decision Making and Internet

Research: Recommendations from the AOIR Ethics Working Committee." 27

Nov. 2002. http://www.aoir.org/reports/ethics.pdf (24 Aug. 2003).

Lehman, Carol M., and DuFrene, Debbie D. "Chapter 7: Delivering Bad-News

Messages." *Business Communication.* 14th ed. Cincinnati: South-Western

College Publishing, 2005. http://www.swlearning.com/bcomm/lehman/

lehman_14e/lehman.html (Links: PowerPoint/7) (23 Aug. 2004).

Nichols, L. R. "Return on Investment: Second Quarter." 2002. p:\public\roi2q.xls

(24 Aug. 2003).

23c Sample COS pages—Humanities (MLA)

Excerpts from a research paper that uses MLA format for printed sources and COS-humanities style for electronically accessed sources appear on pages 279–281. Note that titles of complete works are italicized rather than underlined. If you compare the examples here with the sample MLA-style paper in Chapter 24, you will notice that the COS entries resemble MLA entries in arrangement, capitalization, and punctuation; the main difference is in how COS references electronic sources.

CHECKLIST 23.4

Body of the Essay—COS-Humanities Style

Like MLA style, COS-humanities style uses parenthetical or in-text citations to designate material from other sources. The parenthetical note generally includes the author's last name and a page number, if applicable.

○ A book is cited following MLA format, giving the author's last name and the exact page number of the reference.

○ A Web site is listed by the author's last name (here the author is a government agency). Since page numbers are not designated in the Web site, this information is omitted from the citation. Even when the source is named in the text, a parenthetical note is included for direct quotations. Note that long quotations are indented, with the parenthetical note placed outside the closing punctuation.

○ When there are two or more references with the same author, the title (or a shortened version of the title) is included in the parenthetical citation.

○ Journal and magazine articles, accessed using an online database, are also listed by the author's last name. Page numbers are omitted unless specifically included in the electronic text.

○ A posting to an online newsgroup is cited by the author's last name.

○ A newspaper article of only one page, following MLA format, may omit the page number from the parenthetical citation.

Brown 2

Although water covers most of the earth's surface, most of this water is not usable for industrial or human consumption (Carson 44). Nonetheless, many of us take water for granted:

> We watch the rain fall or stand on the bank of a river and assume that our water needs will be taken care of[,] that water is a "free good" readily available to all. But a closer look reveals that it's not that simple. (U.S. Environmental Protection Agency, "Cleaner Water")

Water is so inexpensive, argues the US Environmental Protection Agency (EPA), that we often ignore little leaks, even though these small leaks can add up to "big waste" (US Environmental Protection Agency, "Ground Water Primer").

Along with water conservation measures, increasing the amount of available freshwater supplies is an urgent concern. One method often suggested to address this problem is desalination, the process of removing salt from ocean water to produce fresh, drinkable water. There are several desalination methods, including reverse osmosis, electrodialysis, flash evaporation, and freezing (Lewin). Reverse osmosis entails pumping salt water at high pressure through special membranes that, while allowing fresh water to pass through, repel the salts (Uehling 83). Tom Pankrantz notes that "Desalination technology has been available since the turn of the century. However, economic considerations have limited its widespread use."

Brown 8

Works Cited

Carson, Rachel. *Silent Spring.* Boston: Houghton, 1962.

Heller, Jean. "Water Woes May Find Salty Solution." *St. Petersburg Times* 2 Apr. 1995, state ed., Tampa Bay and State: 1B.

Kensmark, John. "Re: Desalination." 15 Sep. 1998. news:rec.arts.sf. science (16 Sep. 2004).

Lewin, Seymour Z. "Water." *Microsoft Encarta.* Santa Rosa, CA: Microsoft, 1993.

Pankrantz, Tom. "Dissecting Desalination." *Water and Environment International* 9.64 (2000): 8–9. *Academic Search Premier.* EBSCO. AN #3058652 (2 Sep. 2004).

Uehling, Mark D., and J. Brenning. "Salt Water on Tap." *Popular Science* 238.4 (Apr. 1991): 82–85.

US Environmental Protection Agency (EPA). *Cleaner Water Through Conservation.* April 1995. http://www.epa.gov/water/ you/intro.html (17 Sep. 2004).

---. "Ground Water Primer." 8 May 1998. http://www.epa.gov/seahome/ groundwater/src/ground.htm (18 Sep. 2004).

CHECKLIST 23.5

> **Works Cited Page—COS-Humanities Style**

The Works Cited list (see pages 280–281) contains full bibliographic information on all sources used in composing the paper. Electronic sources are cited using COS-humanities format; other sources are cited using MLA style. Titles are italicized rather than underlined for both types of sources. Begin the list of works cited on a separate page immediately following the body of the essay; number the pages sequentially throughout the paper (including the Works Cited page).

○ Center the title "Works Cited" at the top of the page.

○ Include full bibliographic information for all sources mentioned in the paper.

○ Arrange the items in the list alphabetically by the last name of the author, or, when no author is given, by the first major word of the title.

○ For two or more entries with the same author, use three hyphens (---) followed by a period in place of the name(s) of the author(s).

○ Use the hanging indent feature of your word processor to format entries, with the first line of each entry flush with the left-hand margin and subsequent lines indented five spaces or one-half inch.

○ Double-space the entire list. Do not add extra spacing between entries.

○ Use MLA style to cite nonelectronic sources; for electronic sources, follow COS-humanities style.

23d COS form directory—Sciences (APA)

Here you will find the COS science-style forms for a variety of electronic sources. Use these forms when you are writing a paper in which you use an author-date citation system (such as APA) for nonelectronic sources. Note that the items in this section adhere to APA style for the names of authors and the titles of works but follow COS guidelines for the electronic portion of the citation.

To find the form you need, look in the Format Index for the type of source you need to document and then locate that item by number in the COS Form Directory that follows. To handle more complex electronic sources and to learn more about developing standards for online style, consult *The Columbia Guide to Online Style* by Janice R. Walker and Todd Taylor.

COS Format Index—Sciences (APA)

World Wide Web Citations

30. Web page—COS/APA
31. Web site—COS/APA
32. Web site, revised or modified—COS/APA
33. Web site with a group or institutional author—COS/APA
34. Web site, no author or title—COS/APA
35. Web site maintained by an individual—COS/APA
36. Web site—government—COS/APA
37. Web site—corporate—COS/APA
38. Web site—book, printed, available online—COS/APA
39. Web site—book, published electronically—COS/APA
40. Web site—online article—COS/APA
41. Web site—article from a news service or online newspaper—COS/APA
42. Web site—article from an archive—COS/APA
43. Web site—with frames—COS/APA
44. Web site—graphic, audio, or video file—COS/APA

Online References and Databases

45. Online encyclopedia article—COS/APA
46. Online dictionary or thesaurus entry—COS/APA
47. Material from a CD-ROM—COS/APA
48. Material from an online database—COS/APA

Online Communication

49. Personal email—COS/APA
50. Electronic mailing list—COS/APA
51. Newsgroup—COS/APA
52. Blogs and wikis—COS/APA
53. Chats—COS/APA

Miscellaneous Electronic Sources

54. MOOs, MUDs, and online games—COS/APA
55. Software and video games—COS/APA
56. WebCT, Blackboard, and other courseware—COS/APA
57. Online course material—COS/APA
58. Other electronic files—COS/APA

30. **Web Page—COS/Sciences (APA)** List the author's last name and first initial, the date of publication, and the title of the Web page, capitalizing the first word and any proper nouns. Do not enclose the title in quotation marks or italicize it. Include any print publication information (see also Chapter 25), followed by electronic publication information and the date of access. When no author is listed, begin with the title of the page, followed by the date of publication in parentheses.

References

Baron, D. (2000). From pencils to pixels: The stages of literacy technology. In G.

Hawisher & C. L. Selfe (Eds.), *Passions, pedagogies, and twenty-first*

century technologies (pp. 15-33). Logan, UT: Utah State UP.

http://netfiles.uiuc.edu/debaron/www/essays/pencils.htm (27 July 2004).

31. **Web Site—COS/Sciences (APA)** The title of an entire Web site is italicized with only the first word and any proper noun capitalized. This information follows the title of the Web page or article (or the author's name when the entire site is being referenced) and the publication date.

References

Harris, R. (2001). Human-factor phenomena in problem solving. *Virtual salt.*

http://www.virtualsalt.com/crebok3a.htm (17 Jan. 2002).

32. **Web Site, Revised or Modified—COS/Sciences (APA)** You may specify the date that a page or site was revised or updated if such a date is given. In this case, the date of modification follows the article title.

References

Golombek, M., & Parker, T. (2000, December 21). PIGWAD: Layers in motion (Mod.

21 April 2003). *Science for a Changing World.* U.S. Geological Survey.

http://webgis.wr.usgs.gov/mer/revised_ellipse.htm (24 Aug. 2003).

When no publication date is given, you may include the date of revision or last modification in place of the publication date.

United States Congress. (Last updated 2004, May 26). About THOMAS. *THOMAS:*

Legislative information on the Internet.

http://thomas.loc.gov/home/abt_thom.html (25 Sep. 2004).

33. **Web Site with a Group or Institutional Author—COS/Sciences (APA)** Instead of listing the names of individual authors, sometimes a group or institution will co-author or take responsibility for authorship. List the name of the group or institution in place of an author's name.

References

Apple Computer, Inc. (2004). Film mogul in the making.

  http://www.apple.com/education/profiles/brandl (16 Sep. 2004).

34. **Web Site, No Author or Title—COS/Sciences (APA)** When no author or institution can be assigned to a site with no title, begin the entry with the file name, followed by the date of publication in parentheses, if known.

References

1993e-small.gif. (1993). http://encke.jpl.nasa.gov/images/1993e-small.gif (16 Sep.

  2004).

35. **Web Site Maintained by an Individual—COS/Sciences (APA)** A maintained site is one that collects resources or links, such as an online bibliography. The site can be listed either by the person(s) maintaining it or by its title, depending on which emphasis suits your project.

References

Ley, M. (Maint.). (2004). DBLP computer science bibliography. Universität Trier.

  http://dblp.uni-trier.de (16 Jan. 2004).

DBLP computer science bibliography. (2004). M. Ley (Maint.). Universität Trier.

  http://dblp.uni-trier.de (16 Sep. 2004).

36. **Web Site—Government—COS/Sciences (APA)** Government agencies are treated like group or institutional authors.

References

U.S. House of Representatives. (2003, June 30). How our laws are made (Updated

  19 November 2003). *THOMAS: Legislative information on the Internet.*

  http://thomas.loc.gov/home/lawsmade.toc.html (3 Aug. 2004).

37. **Web Site—Corporate—COS/Sciences (APA)** The corporation or institution should be listed as the author.

References

Cedar Fair, L.P. (2004). Spinning in circles: Carousels.

  http://www.cedarpoint.com/public/news/carousel/index.cfm (4 Sep. 2004).

Individual articles or pages within the site may or may not list authors (see also model 40).

38. **Web Site—Book, Printed, Available Online—COS/Sciences (APA)** Give the name of the author, the year of publication, the title of the work, and

the publication information for the printed version if known. Then provide the title of the electronic version, if different from the original title, and the electronic publication information.

References

Austen, J. (1813). *Pride and prejudice. Pride and prejudice hypertext.* H.

Churchyard (Ed.). 1994. http://www.pemberley.com/janeinfo/

prideprej.html (16 May 2004).

39. Web Site—Book, Published Electronically—COS/Sciences (APA) Provide an author, date of publication, and title. In this example, the publication of the book is sponsored by an organization listed after the title.

References

Baker, C. (1999). *Your genes, your choice: Exploring the issues raised by genetic*

research. American Association for the Advancement of Science.

http://www.nextwave.org/ehr/books/index.html (16 July 2004).

40. Web Site—Online Article—COS/Sciences (APA) In this entry the complete date of publication is included in the parenthetical note after the author's name. Notice also that in APA style, the volume number of the periodical is italicized and all major words in magazine, journal, and newspaper titles are capitalized. Provide an issue number (if available) in parentheses after the volume number. The issue number is not italicized. (See also Chapter 25.)

References

DeFrancesco, L. (2001, October 29). Beta stem cells: Searching for the diabetic's

holy grail. *The Scientist, 15*(21). http://www.the-scientist.com/

yr2001/oct/research1_011029.html (16 Sep. 2004).

41. Web Site—Article from a News Service or Online Newspaper—COS/Sciences (APA) When no author's name is given, list the name of the news source (such as *Reuters* or *Associated Press*), followed by the date of the article if different from the date accessed, the title of the article, the name of the online news service or newspaper, the electronic address, and the date accessed.

References

Associated Press. (2002, January 11). Alaska ruling starts debate on gun permits

for mentally ill. *The New York Times on the Web.* http://www.nytimes

.com/2002/01/11/national/11ALAS.html (16 Sep. 2004).

42. **Web Site—Article from an Archive—COS/Sciences (APA)** Provide author, date of publication, title, and publication information (if applicable), followed by the name of the archive site (if available), the electronic address, and date of access.

References

Shaw, A. H. (1915). *The story of a pioneer.* New York: Harper and Brothers. U.S.

    Library of Congress. *American memory collection.*

    http://memory.loc.gov/cgi-bin/query/S?ammem/lhbumbib:

    @field(TITLE+@od1(The+story+of+a+pioneer+)) (12 Sep. 2004).

For articles in archives with very long URLs or without direct access, give the address of the main page and include the links followed or search terms used.

Shaw, A. H. (1915). *The story of a pioneer.* New York: Harper and Brothers. U.S.

    Library of Congress. *American memory collection.* http://memory.loc.gov

    (Links: Search/story of a pioneer) (12 Jan. 2002).

43. **Web Site—with Frames—COS/Sciences (APA)** Documents published in frames do not always indicate a unique URL for each page. To cite a file from the main page, include the links followed to access the specific page or file being cited.

References

Lennie (#167). AlaMOO builder's bible. *ALAMOO.* http://ranger.accd.edu:7000

    (Links: Help Kiosk/Builder's Bible) (24 Aug. 2004).

If the file can be located within the frame from the publication information, then you may omit the links.

Kimelman, R. (1998). The seduction of Eve and feminist readings of the Garden

    of Eden. *Women in Judaism: A Multidisciplinary Journal, 1*(2).

    http://www.utoronto.ca/wjudaism/index.html (12 June 2004).

If the file being cited is available in a nonframes version or if your browser allows you to discern site information for documents presented in frames, you may choose to cite the unique URL for the file being cited rather than that for the main site.

Kimelman, R. (1998). The seduction of Eve and feminist readings of the Garden of

    Eden. *Women in Judaism: A Multidisciplinary Journal, 1*(2).

    http://www.utoronto.ca/wjudaism/journal/vol1n2/eve.html (12 June 2004).

44. **Web Site—Graphic, Audio, or Video File—COS/Sciences (APA)** Cite a multimedia file in one of two ways: either by its own URL (which you can

usually find in the Netscape browser by selecting "View Page Info") or by the Web page on which the file appears. For a graphic alone, identify the author, photographer, or artist (if known); then give the date of creation or publication (if known); and give the title of the work, followed by a description of the source in square brackets. For files with no title information available, you may use the file name (*sunflowers.jpg*) instead.

References

Van Gogh, V. (1888). *Fourteen sunflowers in a vase* [Painting]. http://

www.artchive.com/artchive/v/van_gogh/sunflowers.jpg (16 Sep. 2004).

To cite the file as it appears on a particular page, identify the artist, date of creation, and title of the file or the file name when no title is given; then name the page or site on which it appears, followed by any publication information and the electronic address for the page.

References

Van Gogh, V. (1888). *Fourteen sunflowers in a vase* [Painting]. *Web gallery of

art.* http://www.artchive.com/artchive/v/van_gogh/sunflowers.jpg.html (17

Sep. 2004).

Audio and video files are similar to graphic files; you may cite the direct address or cite the file as a link from a Web site. Note that the file extension indicates the application necessary to access the file (*.mp3, .ra, .mov*, etc.). The year of publication in the second example [below] refers to the date of publication of the Web site, not to the audio file being cited.

Cherokee traditional: Stomp dance [Audio file]. http://realdl.ket.org/ramgen/

realmedia/humanities/music/cherokee.ra/dnet.ra?usehostname (17 Sep.

2004).

Cherokee traditional: Stomp dance [Audio file]. *The Kentucky network distance

learning site.* (2002). http://www.dl.ket.org (Links: Humanities/

Humanities through the Arts/Music/Cherokee traditional: Stomp Dance)

(17 Sep. 2004).

For files without author names or titles, see model 34.

45. Online Encyclopedia Article—COS/Sciences (APA) Give the author of the article (if available), the date of the article, its title, and the name of the encyclopedia. If the encyclopedia is based on a printed work, identify the place of publication and the publisher. Give publication information for the electronic version, including the electronic address, any directories or pathways, and the date accessed.

References

Markie, P. (2004). Thought experiments (Mod. 19 August 2004). In E. N. Zalta

    (Ed.), *Stanford encyclopedia of philosophy*. Stanford, CA: Stanford

    University. http://plato.stanford.edu/entries/rationalism-empiricism (20

    July 2004).

Often online encyclopedias and reference works are available only through subscription. You may have free access through your library's portal or through an Internet or information service provider such as *America Online*. When this is the case, you need to give enough information to allow your readers to find the source regardless of the portal they use for access. Give the URL if it allows direct access.

Fisher, W. W. (2004). Intellectual property law. In *Encyclopaedia Britannica*

    online. Encyclopaedia Britannica.

    http://search.eb.com/eb/article?tocId=231534 (20 Sep. 2004).

When you are unable to determine a URL for the article, give what information you have, including (where applicable) the name of the portal or service and any keywords or search terms that differ from the title.

Cathode ray. (2001, December 30). In *Encyclopaedia Britannica online*.

    Encyclopaedia Britannica. Galileo. Henderson Library, Georgia Southern

    University, Statesboro, GA (30 Aug. 2004).

Stern, R. M. (2004). Eurodollar. In *World book online reference center. America*

    Online (Keyword: World Book) (20 Sep. 2004).

46. **Online Dictionary or Thesaurus Entry—COS/Sciences (APA)** List the entry by the word looked up, followed by the date of publication and the name of the dictionary or thesaurus. If the dictionary is based on a printed work, give the place of publication and the publisher (see Chapter 25). Give any publication information about the electronic version, including the service offering it (for example, *America Online*), if applicable; the electronic address; links or keywords necessary to access the source; and the date accessed.

References

Copyright. (2004). In *Merriam-Webster collegiate dictionary. Merriam-Webster*

    online. http://www.m-w.com (17 Sep. 2004).

Intellectual. (2001). In *Thesaurus by Merriam-Webster. America Online* (Links:

    Research and Learn/thesaurus) (17 Sep. 2004).

47. **Material from a CD-ROM—COS/Sciences (APA)** Give the name of the author or, as in this example, the corporate author, the date of publication,

and the title of the entry, followed by the title of the software. Include any edition or version numbers and/or series title (if applicable), along with available publication information. No date of access is necessary for CD-ROM publications. (See also model 55.)

References

Pearson Education. (2002). What is plagiarism? *Avoiding plagiarism*. New York:

 Longman.

48. **Material from an Online Database—COS/Sciences (APA)** Identify the author, the date of publication, and the title of the entry or article, and give publication information for items that have appeared in print (see Chapter 25). Next, identify the name of the database or information service in italics, and give the name of the database publisher (if known). Furnish retrieval data (for example, Digital Object Identifier, or DOI, numbers; file numbers; or other identifying information) followed by the date of access. Remember that your goal is to provide as much information as possible to help your reader locate the source; however, unless the URL allows direct access to the source, do not include it.

References

Landau, M. (2002). Digital downloads, access codes, and US copyright law.

 International Review of Law, Computers and Technology, 16(2), 149-170.

 Academic Search Premier. EBSCO [DOI #10.1080/

 1360086022000003973] (20 Sep. 2004).

Gallagher, D. F. (2004, August 16). Warner's tryst with bloggers hits sour note.

 The New York Times. Late ed., sec. c, p. 1. *LexisNexis Academic Universe*

 (17 Sep. 2004).

Often online databases are available only through subscription. You may have free access through your library's portal or through an Internet or information service provider such as *America Online*. When this is the case, you may want to include information on the portal or service you used to access the database.

Heinze, D. (2001). Toni Morrison. In *Dictionary of Literary Biography*. Vol. 143:

 American novelists since World War II (3rd series). Gale Group: p.

 171–187. *Gale Literary Databases*. Henderson Library, Georgia Southern

 University, Statesboro, GA (21 Jan. 2002).

49. **Personal Email—COS/Sciences (APA)** In APA style, you do not include personal email messages in the References list. Instead, cite them in the body of your text.

50. **Electronic Mailing List—COS/Sciences (APA)** Identify the author of the message to an electronic mailing list. If no author's name is given, use the author's alias or email name (do not include the author's entire email address, however). Then give the date followed by the subject line of the message; the name of the list, if applicable, in italics; the address of the listserv; and the date of access. For messages available through an online archive, see model 42.

References

Inman, J. (2004, September 22). Re: Smart thinking. *WCenter listserv.*

    wcenter@edsel.tosm.ttu.edu (24 Sep. 2004).

51. **Newsgroup—COS/Sciences (APA)** Give the author's name (or alias), the date of the posting, the subject line of the message as the title, the name and address of the newsgroup, and the date of access.

References

Allen, T. (2003, August 21). What medical evidence is used to evaluate social

    security disability cases? *misc.health.arthritis. Google Groups.*

    http://groups.google.com (23 Aug. 2003).

52. **Blogs and Wikis—COS/Sciences (APA)** Give the author's name or alias, followed by the posting date and title or subject line (if applicable). Include the title of the blog or wiki site (in italics), the electronic address, and the date of access enclosed in parentheses.

References

Kiwi. (2003, April 23). Re: How do you cite a blog post in your bibliography?

    Kairosnews: A weblog for discussing rhetoric, technology and pedagogy.

    http://kairosnews.org/node/view/1830#comment (30 Apr. 2003).

53. **Chats—COS/Sciences (APA)** APA does not include personal conversations in the list of References. You will, however, want to provide information about the conversation in the body of your text.

54. **MOOs, MUDs, and Online Games —COS/Sciences (APA)** Give the author or owner of the material you are citing (if available); the date of creation or publication (if available); the title of the material; the site name; the protocol and address, including any steps or commands necessary to access the information; and the date of access.

References

Locke (#169). Usability lab (#836). *TTU English MOO.*

    http://moo.engl.ttu.edu:7000 (Command: @go #836) (22 Sep. 2004).

To cite programming code, include a description of the type of information (e.g., "Source code").

Wizard. (1996, May 13). Say [Source code] (Mod. 8 March 2000). *DaMOO.*

    telnet://damoo.csun.edu:7777 (Command: @list #3:say) (22 Sep. 2004).

Cite messages to MOO or MUD mailing lists as you would for messages to other electronic mailing lists (see model 50), including any necessary commands to access the messages.

Jai (#137). (1997, July 20). Going postal goes PC? *#Social (#282). DaMOO.*

    telnet://damoo.csun.edu:7777 (Command: @read 1 on #282) (19 Sep. 2004).

55. **Software and Video Games—COS/Sciences (APA)** List software by its individual or corporate author. When no author is given or the corporate author is the same as the publisher, list the software by its title. APA style does not italicize the title of software in a References list. Note also the placement of the version number in parentheses and the description of the source in brackets, both following the title.

References

Norton Systemworks (Version 2002.05) [Computer software]. (2002). Cupertino,

    CA: Symantec.

ID Software. (2004). Doom 3 [video game]. Santa Monica, CA: Activision.

To cite specific information in a software program or game, give the title of the screen or document referenced, including any paths or commands necessary to access it if not readily discernible from the publication information given (see also model 47).

U.S. Army. (2002). 212 ways to be a soldier. America's army [video game]. Army

    Game Project 2002. Washington, DC: Department of Defense.

56. *WebCT, Blackboard,* **and Other Courseware—COS/Sciences (APA)** Formats for citing information published through various courseware packages depend on the type of information being cited. Some of this information may be part of the courseware package itself; it may be written by the instructor or by students in the class; or it may have been linked or scanned in from other sources. Unfortunately, not all of this information may include the necessary publication information; however, citing the course and instructor can allow future researchers to trace the original source, if necessary.

References

Collegeboard.com. (2004). Financial aid myths: Don't believe everything you hear.

    In J. Todd (Instructor), ENGL 1102: Composition II (Fall 2004). *WebCT.*

  Georgia Southern University, Statesboro, GA (24 Sep. 2004).

Johnson, T. (2004, September 10). Electronic communication and online courses
[discussion posting]. In J. Todd (Instructor), ENGL 1102: Composition II
(Fall 2004). *WebCT*. Georgia Southern University, Statesboro, GA (24 Sep.
2004).

57. Online Course Material—COS/Sciences (APA) To cite online course materials, include the instructor's name, the date of the course, and the course title, followed by the name and location of the school, if applicable. If the material is freely available on the Web, include the URL and date of access.

References

Walker, J. R. (2003, Fall). Home page. WRIT 3030: Writing for the WWW.
Department of Writing and Linguistics. Georgia Southern University,
Statesboro, GA. http://www.georgiasouthern.edu/~jwalker/courses/
fall03/writ3030/(1 Sep. 2003).

Cite handouts and other documents beginning with the author's name (if known) and the title of the document. Include the date of publication (if known) immediately after the author's name or after the title when no author is listed.

Designing print documents: Brochures, flyers, and newsletters. In J. R. Walker
(Instructor), PBAD 7120: Written Communication for Public Managers (Fall
2002). *WebCT*. Georgia Southern University, Statesboro, GA.

Email, discussion boards, or chat room conversations in courseware are not included in the list of references in scientific styles; instead, cite them in the text as for other types of personal communications (see models 49–53).

58. Other Electronic Files—COS/Sciences (APA) The format for citing other types of electronic files depends largely on how they are accessed. For example, a PowerPoint presentation may be accessed on the Web, from a diskette or CD-ROM, or through a courseware package such as *WebCT* or *Blackboard*. Many types of files can be made accessible electronically, often in multiple formats (electronic presentations, PDF files, spreadsheet files, plain text, etc.). Generally, the file extension (the letters after the "dot" in the file name) provides sufficient information to allow browsers or computer operating systems to recognize the type of file and open it (providing that the user has the necessary software installed). Include the URL for files available on the Web or the drive designation and directories for items available through a shared network drive, along with any links necessary to access the cited file.

References

Association of Internet Researchers (AOIR). (2002, November 27). Ethical
decision making and Internet research: Recommendations from the AOIR

ethics working committee. http://www.aoir.org/reports/ethics.pdf (24 Aug. 2003).

Lehman, C. M., & DuFrene, D. D. (2005). Chapter 7: Delivering bad-news messages. *Business communication* (14th ed.). Cincinnati: South-Western College Publishing. http://www.swlearning.com/bcomm/lehman/lehman_14e/lehman.html (Links: PowerPoint/7) (23 Aug. 2004).

Nichols, L.R. (2004). Return on investment: Second quarter. p:\public\roi2q.xls (24 Aug. 2004).

23e Sample COS pages—Sciences (APA)

Excerpts from a research paper that uses APA format for printed sources and COS-sciences style for electronically accessed sources appear on pages 293–294. You will notice that the COS entries resemble APA entries in arrangement, capitalization, and punctuation. However, COS electronic entries are more compact than comparable APA entries.

Sanders 2

The Human Genome Project began more than two decades ago in 1988 when the Congress of the United States allocated approximately $3 billion to support a 15-year multiuniversity endeavor to complete the mapping of the human genome (Caskey, 1994). The human genome is the set of 23 chromosomes and 60,000 to 80,000 genes that provide the blueprint for our bodies (U.S. Department of Energy, 2004). . . .

Throughout the project, scientists also hope to identify some of the key ethical issues in gene research, to address the societal implications of the research, to bring genetic issues to public attention, and to formulate policy options designed to benefit both individuals and society (U.S. Department of Energy, 2004). In an email discussion with D. Swinbanks, a writer for the magazine *Nature*, . . .

Swinbanks (1992) observes, however, that since many scientists believe that . . .

Sanders 10

References

Caskey, T. C. (1994). Human genes: The map takes shape. *Patient Care, 28,* 28–32.

Swinbanks, D. (1992). When silence isn't golden. *Nature, 368,* 368–370.

U.S. Department of Energy Office of Science. (Last modified 2004, September 15). *Human Genome Project information.* http://www.ornl.gov/sci/techresources/Human_Genome/ home.shtml (24 Sep. 2004).

CHECKLIST 23.6

Body of the Essay—COS-Sciences Style

Like APA style, COS-sciences style uses parenthetical or in-text citations to designate material from other sources. A parenthetical citation generally includes the author's last name and the year of publication. APA requires that page numbers be included for citing a specific part of a text and for direct quotations. In COS-sciences style, however, page numbers may be omitted for electronically accessed sources that do not specifically designate pagination.

○ An article in a print journal is cited in the paper by the author's last name and the year of publication, separated by a comma. Since this reference is to the work as a whole, no page number is given.

○ A Web site authored by an organization (in this case, a government agency) is listed by the name of the organization, followed by the year of publication.

○ Personal conversations, including email, are referenced in the body of the text only.

○ For both print and electronic sources, when the author's name is given in the essay, the parenthetical reference directly follows it and includes only the year of publication.

CHECKLIST 23.7

References Page—COS-Sciences Style

○ List sources used in the paper alphabetically by the author's last name or, when no author is given, by the first major word of the title. Use italics rather than underlining for titles throughout.

○ Begin the list of references on a separate page immediately following the body of the essay; number the pages sequentially throughout (including the References page).

○ Center the title "References" at the top of the page.

○ Include full bibliographical information for all sources mentioned in the paper.

○ Use the hanging indent capability of your word processor to format entries, with the first line of each entry flush with the left-hand margin and subsequent lines indented five spaces or one-half inch.

○ Double-space the entire list. Do not add extra spacing between entries.

○ Use APA style to cite nonelectronic sources; for electronic sources, follow COS-sciences style.

CHAPTER 24

MLA Documentation

In many professional fields in the humanities (including both English and rhetoric and composition) writers are expected to follow the conventions of documentation and format recommended by the Modern Language Association (MLA). The basic procedures for MLA documentation are spelled out in this chapter. If you encounter documentation problems not discussed here, you may want to refer to the *MLA Handbook for Writers of Research Papers*, sixth edition (2003), by Joseph Gibaldi. Style updates are available at the MLA Web site at **http://www.mla.org**.

Citing Electronic Sources in the Humanities

When citing electronic sources, you may want to use the documentation style recommended by the *Columbia Guide to Online Style*, developed explicitly for electronic environments. Columbia Online Style (COS) for humanities papers is described in Chapter 23. MLA items that have a Columbia equivalent are marked in the MLA Form Directory in this chapter with a distinctive icon: COS p. 000 . COS-humanities style is designed to work with MLA format for citing print sources and to replace MLA recommendations for citing electronic sources. Consult your instructor about using COS in your research project.

24a How do you use MLA documentation?

MLA documentation involves two basic steps:

Step 1: In the body of your paper, place a note in parentheses to identify the source of each passage or idea you must document. Such a note ordinarily consists of an author's last name and a page number. Here is a sentence that includes a direct quotation from *Ralph Bunche: An American Life,* by Brian Urquhart.

Ralph Bunche never wavered in his belief that the races in America had to

learn to live together: "In all of his experience of racial discrimination

Bunche never allowed himself to become bitter or to feel racial hatred"

(Urquhart 435).

The author's name and the page number of the source are separated by a single typed space. Page numbers are *not* preceded by *p.* or *pp.* or by a comma.

Do not repeat the first digit of the page number when it is over one hundred.

(Bly 253–54)

You can shorten a note by naming the author of the source in the body of the essay; then the note consists only of a page number. This is a common and readable form, one you should use regularly, since it also accomplishes the important goal of helping your reader discern the authority behind your use of the information.

Brian Urquhart, a biographer of Ralph Bunche, asserts that "in all of his

experience of racial discrimination Bunche never allowed himself to become

bitter or to feel racial hatred" (435).

Note that the period is placed outside the parenthetical note; a single blank space separates the closing quotation marks from the opening parenthesis.

As a general rule, make all parenthetical notes as brief and inconspicuous as possible. The point of a note is to identify a source of information, not to distract or impress readers. A parenthetical note should begin with the same name as the entry in your list of Works Cited as shown in Figure 24.1; when appropriate, indicate the exact location of information in the source by providing a page number, if available.

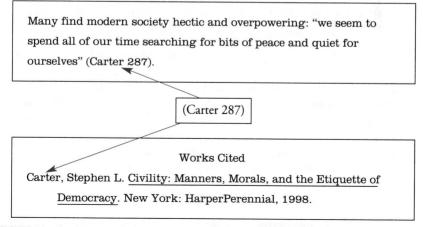

FIGURE 24.1 In-text notes are keyed to specific entries in the list of Works Cited.

The parenthetical note is usually placed after a passage needing documentation, typically at the end of a sentence, before the final punctuation mark. When a quotation is long enough (more than four typed lines) to require indention, the parenthetical note falls after the final punctuation mark. Compare the following examples.

SHORT QUOTATION (NOT INDENTED)

Ralph Bunche never wavered in his belief that the races in America had to learn to live together: "In all of his experience of racial discrimination Bunche never allowed himself to become bitter or to feel racial hatred" (Urquhart 435). He continued to work . . .

LONG QUOTATION (INDENTED TEN SPACES)

Winner of the Nobel Peace Prize in 1950, Ralph Bunche, who died in 1971, left an enduring legacy:

> His memory lives on, especially in the long struggle for
> human dignity and against racial discrimination and bigotry,
> and in the growing effectiveness of the United Nations in
> resolving conflicts and keeping the peace. (Urquhart 458)

Generally you will want to rely on primary sources in your research projects (see Chapter 5). When you need to cite a quotation included in another source and you are using only the quoted material, note that you obtained it secondhand by including *qtd. in* in the parenthetical note.

One handbook includes a quotation from Roger Parker's Looking Good in Print that makes even more sense as we begin considering rhetorical concepts for hypertextual writing: "Graphic design should provide a road map that steers your readers from point to point" (qtd. in Hairston et al. 268).

The Hairston book, not Roger Parker's book, would be listed on your Works Cited page. In this way you protect yourself (if there are errors in the quotation, they are Hairston's, not yours), and you show that you are honest (you cited the source where you actually found the information). If at all possible, and to eliminate any chance of error or academic dishonesty, you should check the original for yourself.

Another situation you may encounter is a quotation within a quotation. In this case, alternate your use of double and single quotation marks: the entire quotation will be surrounded by double quotation marks, the interior quotation enclosed within single quotation marks.

Mikhail Bakhtin "segregates language into three aspects--thematic content, style, and compositional structure, in which all three are 'inseparably linked to the whole of utterance'" (Walker 36).

Make sure you close both sets of quotation marks.

Use the following guidelines when preparing in-text notes:

1. **When two or more sources are cited within a single sentence,** the parenthetical notes appear right after the statements they support.

> While the budget cuts might go deeper than originally reported (Kinsley 42), there is no reason to believe that "throwing more taxpayers' dollars into a bottomless pit" (Doggett 62) will do much to reform "one of the least productive job training programs ever devised by the federal government" (Will 28).

   Notice that a parenthetical note is always placed outside quotation marks but before any punctuation, including the period that ends the sentence.

2. **When you cite more than one work by a single author in a paper,** a parenthetical note listing only the author's last name could refer to more than one book or article on the Works Cited page. To avoid confusion, place a comma after the author's name and use a shortened title to identify the particular work being cited. For example, a Works Cited page might list four works by Richard D. Altick.

Works Cited

Altick, Richard D. <u>The Art of Literary Research</u>. New York: Norton,
   1963.

- - -. <u>The Shows of London</u>. Cambridge: Belknap-Harvard, 1978.

- - -. <u>Victorian People and Ideas</u>. New York: Norton, 1973.

- - -. <u>Victorian Studies in Scarlet</u>. New York: Norton, 1977.

   When you refer to a work by Richard Altick, you need to identify it by including a shortened title in the parenthetical note.

   (Altick, <u>Shows</u> 345)

   (Altick, <u>Victorian People</u> 190-202)

   (Altick, <u>Victorian Studies</u> 59)

3. **When you need to document a work without an author**—an unsigned article in a magazine or newspaper, for example—give the title, shortened if necessary, and the page number. Remember that the goal is to help your reader locate the citation in your list of Works Cited.

   ("In the Thicket" 18)

   ("Students Rally" A6)

Works Cited

"In the Thicket of Things." <u>Texas Monthly</u> Apr. 1994: 18.

"Students Rally for Academic Freedom." <u>Chronicle of Higher Education</u>
28 Sept. 1994: A6.

4. **When you need to cite more than a single work in one note,** separate the citations with a semicolon.

(Polukord 13–16; Ryan and Weber 126)

5. **When a parenthetical note would be awkward,** refer to the source in the body of the essay itself.

In "Hamlet's Encounter with the Pirates," Wentersdorf argues . . . .

Under "Northwest Passage" in <u>Collier's Encyclopedia</u> . . . .

The <u>Arkansas State Highway Map</u> indicates . . . .

Software such as Microsoft's <u>FoxPro</u> . . . .

Occasions when parenthetical notes might be awkward include the following:

- When you wish to refer to an entire article, not just to a passage or several pages
- When the author is a group or institution—for example, the editors of *Time* or the Smithsonian Institution
- When the citation is to a personal interview or an unpublished speech or letter
- When the item doesn't have page numbers: a map, a cartoon, a work of art, a videotape, a play in performance
- When the item is a reference work arranged alphabetically
- When the item is a government document with a name too long for a convenient in-text note
- When the item is computer software or an electronic source without conventional page numbers (see Section 23a on using parenthetical notes with electronic sources)

You may still need a parenthetical note to indicate the page number or location of an exact quotation or reference.

Step 2: On a separate page at the end of your project, list every source included in the parenthetical notes. The alphabetical list of sources is titled "Works Cited" and begins on the page immediately following the body of your essay. (See the sample essay beginning on page 322.)

The Works Cited page itself follows the body of the essay. It lists bibliographical information on all the materials you used in composing an essay. (You do not include sources you examined but did not cite in your paper.) For a sample Works Cited list, see Figure 24.2.

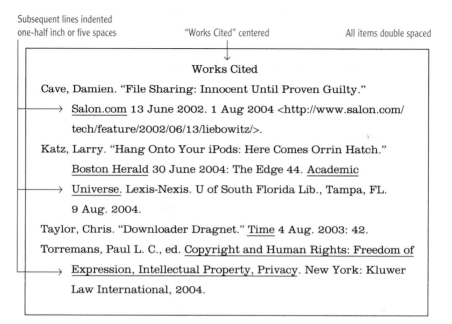

Subsequent lines indented
one-half inch or five spaces   "Works Cited" centered   All items double spaced

Works Cited

Cave, Damien. "File Sharing: Innocent Until Proven Guilty."

   Salon.com 13 June 2002. 1 Aug 2004 <http://www.salon.com/
   tech/feature/2002/06/13/liebowitz/>.

Katz, Larry. "Hang Onto Your iPods: Here Comes Orrin Hatch."

   Boston Herald 30 June 2004: The Edge 44. Academic

   Universe. Lexis-Nexis. U of South Florida Lib., Tampa, FL.

   9 Aug. 2004.

Taylor, Chris. "Downloader Dragnet." Time 4 Aug. 2003: 42.

Torremans, Paul L. C., ed. Copyright and Human Rights: Freedom of

   Expression, Intellectual Property, Privacy. New York: Kluwer

   Law International, 2004.

FIGURE 24.2 Sample Works Cited list in MLA format

When an author has more than one work on the Works Cited list, those works are listed alphabetically under the author's name (see page 299).

Works published since 1900 include the publisher's name. Publishers' names should be shortened whenever possible. Drop the words *Company, Inc., Ltd., Bros.,* and *Books.* Abbreviate *University* as *U* and *University Press* as *UP.* When possible, shorten a publisher's name to one word. Here are some suggested abbreviations.

Barnes and Noble Books	Barnes
Doubleday and Co., Inc.	Doubleday
Harvard University Press	Harvard UP
University of Chicago Press	U of Chicago P
The Viking Press	Viking

Because there are so many variations to these general entries, you will want to check the MLA Form Directory that follows for the correct format of any unusual entry.

24b MLA Form Directory

Here you will find the MLA Works Cited and parenthetical note forms for fifty kinds of sources. First find the type of source you need to cite in the Format Index; then locate that item by number in the list that follows. The "COS"

CHECKLIST 24.1

Basic Format—Books

A typical MLA Works Cited entry for a book includes the following basic information.

○ Author, last name first, followed by a period and one space.

○ Title of the work, underlined or italicized, followed by a period and one space.

○ City of publication (including two-letter state designation for cities that are not well known), followed by a colon.

○ Name of publisher (see list of abbreviations), followed by a comma and one space.

○ Date of publication, followed by a period.

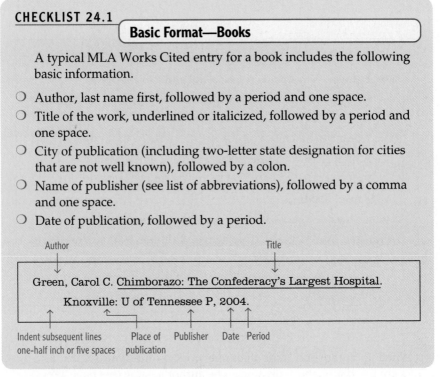

Author

Title

Green, Carol C. Chimborazo: The Confederacy's Largest Hospital.
    Knoxville: U of Tennessee P, 2004.

Indent subsequent lines one-half inch or five spaces   Place of publication   Publisher   Date   Period

icon next to an entry indicates that a Columbia Online Style (COS) form is available for that source (see Chapter 23 on COS).

CHECKLIST 24.2

> **Basic Format—Scholarly Journals**

A typical MLA Works Cited entry for an article in a scholarly journal (where the pagination is continuous throughout a year) includes the following basic information.

○ Author, last name first, followed by a period and one space.

○ Title of the article, followed by a period (or other final punctuation mark) and enclosed between quotation marks.

○ Name of the periodical, italicized or underlined, followed by one space.

○ Volume number, followed by one space.

○ Date of publication in parentheses, followed by a colon.

○ Page or location, followed by a period. Page numbers should be inclusive, from the first page of the article to the last, including notes and bibliography.

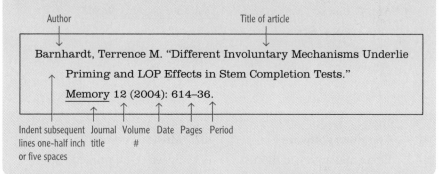

Author   Title of article

Barnhardt, Terrence M. "Different Involuntary Mechanisms Underlie Priming and LOP Effects in Stem Completion Tests."
Memory 12 (2004): 614–36.

Indent subsequent   Journal   Volume   Date   Pages   Period
lines one-half inch   title   #
or five spaces

77. Book published before 1900

78. Book issued by a division of a publisher—a special imprint

79. Dissertation or thesis—published (including publication by UMI)

80. Dissertation or thesis—unpublished

81. Article in a scholarly journal

[COS] 82. Journal article, accessed through an online database

[COS] 83. Journal, electronic

84. Article in a popular magazine

[COS] 85. Article in an online magazine

86. Article in a newspaper

[COS] 87. Online newspaper

[COS] 88. Reviews

89. Cartoon, newspaper or magazine

[COS] 90. Encyclopedia and reference articles

91. Bulletin or pamphlet

92. Biblical citation

[COS] 93. Government publication

[COS] 94. Web page or site

CHECKLIST 24.3

Basic Format—Magazines and Newspapers

A typical MLA Works Cited entry for an article in a popular magazine or newspaper includes the following basic information.

○ Author, last name first, followed by a period and one space.

○ Title of the article, followed by a period or other end punctuation and enclosed between quotation marks.

○ Name of the periodical or newspaper, underlined or italicized, followed by one space.

○ Date of publication, followed by a colon and one space. Abbreviate all months except May, June, and July.

○ Page and/or location (section number for newspapers), followed by a period. Pages should be inclusive.

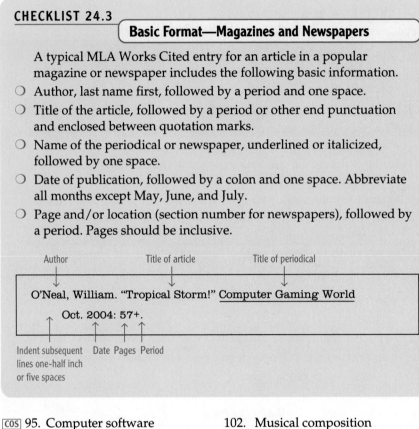

Author   Title of article   Title of periodical

O'Neal, William. "Tropical Storm!" Computer Gaming World

Oct. 2004: 57+.

Indent subsequent   Date Pages Period
lines one-half inch
or five spaces

[COS] 95. Computer software	102. Musical composition
[COS] 95. Email and archived discussions	103. Speech—no printed text
	104. Speech—printed text
[COS] 97. Publication or database on CD-ROM/diskette	105. Letter—published
	106. Letter—unpublished
[COS] 98. Film and sound recordings	107. Artwork
99. Microfilm or microfiche	108. Drama or play
100. Television and radio programs	
101. Personal interview	

59. **Book, One Author—MLA** Give the author, last name first, followed by the title of the book in italics or underlined, city of publication, name of publisher, and year of publication.

Works Cited

Lutz, Dick. Patagonia: At the Bottom of the World. Salem, OR: Dimi, 2002.

Parenthetical note: (Lutz 24)

CHECKLIST 24.4

Basic Format—Electronic Sources

A typical MLA Works Cited entry for an electronic source may include the following information, though few will require all the elements. (See also COS-humanities style in Chapter 23.)

○ Author, last name first, followed by a period and one space.

○ Title of the document, followed by a period and one space. Book and Web site titles are underlined or italicized; individual Web page or article titles appear between quotation marks.

○ Print publication information (if any), followed by a period and one space.

○ Title of the electronic site, underlined or italicized, followed by a period and one space.

○ Editor (if any) of the electronic site, database, or text, with role indicated (for example, *Ed.*), followed by a period and a space.

○ Version or volume number (if any) of the source, usually followed by a period.

○ Date of electronic publication or most recent update, followed by a period.

○ Identity of institution or group (if any) sponsoring the electronic site, followed by a period and a space.

○ Date you accessed the information, followed by a space.

○ Electronic address between angle brackets (< >), followed by a period.

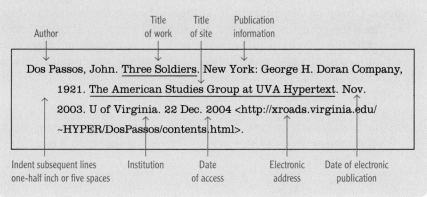

60. **Book, Two or Three Authors or Editors—MLA** The names of second and third authors are given in normal order, first names first.

Works Cited

Ivins, Molly, and Lou Dubose. <u>Bushwhacked: Life in George W. Bush's America</u>.

New York: Random House, 2003.

Parenthetical note: (Ivins and Dubose 115)

61. **Book, Four or More Authors or Editors—MLA** You have two options. You may name all the authors in both the Works Cited entry and any parenthetical note.

Works Cited

Gillespie, Paula, Alice Gillam, Lady Falls Brown, and Byron Stay, eds. <u>Writing</u>

<u>Center Research: Extending the Conversation</u>. Mahwah, NJ: Erlbaum,

2002.

Parenthetical note: (Gillespie, Gillam, Brown, and Stay 43)

Alternatively, you may name only the first author listed on the title page, followed by the Latin abbreviation *et al.,* which means "and others."

Gillespie, Paula, et al. <u>Writing Center Research: Extending the Conversation</u>.

Mahwah, NJ: Erlbaum, 2002.

Parenthetical note: (Gillespie et al. 43)

62. **Book, Group or Organizational Author—MLA** In the Works Cited entry, treat the group as the author. But to avoid a confusing parenthetical note, identify the group author in the body of your paper and place only relevant page numbers in parentheses. For example, you might use a sentence such as "The Reader's Digest <u>Fix-It-Yourself Manual</u> explains the importance of a UL label (123)."

Works Cited

Society for Human Resource Management. <u>Strategic Management</u>. Alexandria,

VA: SHRM, 2002.

63. **Book, Author Unknown—MLA** List the book by its title, alphabetized by the first major word (excluding *The, A,* or *An*).

Works Cited

<u>Illustrated Atlas of the World</u>. Chicago: Rand, 1985.

Parenthetical note: (<u>Illustrated Atlas</u> 88)

64. **Book, Revised by a Second Author—MLA** Sometimes you may need to cite a book by its original author, even when it has been revised. In such a case, place the editor's name after the title of the book.

Works Cited

Corbett, Edward P.J. Classical Rhetoric for the Modern Student. Ed. Robert J.

Connors. 4th ed. Oxford: Oxford UP, 1999.

Parenthetical note: (Corbett 43)

65. **Book, Edited—Focus on the Editor—MLA** When you cite an edited work by the editor's name, identify the original author after the title of the work.

Works Cited

Walker, Keith, ed, John Dryden: The Major Works. By John Dryden. Oxford:

Oxford UP, 2003.

Parenthetical note: (Walker iv)

Treat multiple editors just as you would multiple authors, but place the abbreviation for editors (*eds.*) after their names.

Works Cited

Behrens, Laurence, and Leonard J. Rosen, eds. Writing and Reading Across the

Curriculum. 8th ed. New York: Longman, 2003.

Parenthetical note: (Behrens and Rosen v)

66. **Book, Edited—Focus on the Original Author—MLA** Because the sample Works Cited entry shown here is an edition of Shakespeare, the parenthetical note furnishes the act, scene, and line numbers for a particular play—not the author and page numbers one might expect with another kind of book.

Works Cited

Shakespeare, William. The Tragedy of Coriolanus. Ed. Reuben Brower. New

York: Signet, 1966.

Parenthetical note: (Cor. 3.3.119–35)

67. **Work of More Than One Volume—MLA** When you use only one volume of a multivolume set, identify both the volume you used and the total number of volumes in the set.

Works Cited

Brenner, Frederic. Diaspora: Homelands in Exile. Vol. 1. New York:

HarperCollins, 2003. 2 vols.

Parenthetical note: (Brenner 12–13)

If you use more than one volume of a set, list only the total number of volumes in that set. Then, in your parenthetical notes, identify the specific volumes as you cite them.

Brenner, Frederic. Diaspora: Homelands in Exile. 2 vols. New York:

>   HarperCollins, 2003.

Parenthetical note: (Brenner 1: 12–13); (Brenner 2: 95)

68. **Book, Revised or Subsequent Edition—MLA** The edition number follows the title of the book.

Works Cited

Gauntlett, David, and Ross Horsley, eds. Web Studies. 2nd ed. New York: Oxford

>   UP, 2004.

Parenthetical note: (Gauntlett and Horsley 231–36)

COS
p. 269 69. **Book, Electronic—MLA** Since most online books do not have page numbers, avoid parenthetical citations by identifying the site in the text of your project. Give both an original date of publication and the date of publication of the electronic source as well as the date you accessed the information.

Works Cited

Dickens, Charles. A Christmas Carol. London, 1843. The Electronic Text Center.

>   Ed. David Seaman. Dec. 1997. U of Virginia Lib. 4 Feb. 2004

>   <http://etext.lib.virginia.edu/cgibin/browse-mixed?id=

>   DicChri&tag=public&images=images/modeng&data=/lv1/Archive/

>   eng-parsed>.

70. **Book, a Collection or Anthology—MLA** List the entry by the name(s) of the editor(s), followed by the abbreviation *ed.* or *eds.* To cite a selection within an anthology, see model 72.

Works Cited

Pemberton, Michael A., and Joyce Kinkead, eds. The Center Will Hold: Critical

>   Perspectives on Writing Center Scholarship. Logan, UT: Utah State UP,

>   2003.

Parenthetical note: (Pemberton and Kinkead 4–8)

71. **Introductions, Prefaces, Forewords, etc.—MLA** The note below refers to information in Tony Tanner's introduction, not to the text of Jane

Austen's novel. Do not underline, italicize, or enclose in quotation marks the words *Introduction, Preface,* or *Foreword.* See model 72 for how to cite chapters or articles in an anthology or collection.

Works Cited

Tanner, Tony. Introduction. Mansfield Park. By Jane Austen. Harmondsworth,

　　Eng.: Penguin, 1966. 7–36.

Parenthetical note: (Tanner 9–10)

72. **Article or Selection from a Reader or Anthology—MLA** List the item on the Works Cited page by the author of the piece you are citing, not the editor(s) of the collection. Then provide the title of the particular selection, the title of the overall collection, the editor(s) of the collection, and publication information. Conclude with the page numbers of the selection.

Works Cited

Lerner, Neal. "Writing Center Assessment: Searching for the 'Proof' of Our

　　Effectiveness." The Center Will Hold: Critical Perspectives on Writing

　　Center Scholarship. Ed. Michael A. Pemberton and Joyce Kinkead. Logan:

　　Utah State UP, 2003. 58-73.

Parenthetical note: (Lerner 62)

When you cite two or more selections from a reader or an anthology, list that collection fully on the Works Cited page. (see model 70.) Then, elsewhere in the Works Cited list, identify the authors and titles of all articles you cite from that reader or anthology, followed by the name(s) of the editor(s) and the page numbers of those selections.

Carino, Peter. "Power and Authority in Peer Tutoring." Pemberton and Kinkead

　　96–113.

Kail, Harvey. "Separation, Initiation and Return: Tutor Training Manuals and

　　Writing Center Lore." Pemberton and Kinkead 74–95.

When necessary, provide the original publication information first and then give the facts about the collection.

Hartman, Geoffrey. "Milton's Counterplot." ELH 25 (1958): 1–12. Rpt. in Milton:

　　A Collection of Critical Essays. Ed. Louis L. Martz. Twentieth Century

　　Views. Englewood Cliffs: Spectrum-Prentice, 1966: 100–08.

Parenthetical note: (Hartman 101)

73. **Book, Translation—Focus on the Original Author—MLA** Include the name of the translator, preceded by the abbreviation *Trans.*, after the title of the book.

Works Cited

Freire, Paulo. Learning to Question: A Pedagogy of Liberation. Trans. Tony

Coates. New York: Continuum, 1989.

Parenthetical note: (Freire 137–38)

74. **Book, Translation—Focus on the Translator—MLA** In this example the author is unknown. If known, the author's name would follow the title of the book, preceded by the word *By.*

Works Cited

Heaney, Seamus, trans. Beowulf. New York: Norton, 2001.

Parenthetical note: (Heaney 53–54)

75. **Book in a Foreign Language—MLA** Copy the title of the foreign language work *exactly* as it appears on the title page, paying special attention both to accent marks and to capitalization.

Works Cited

Bataille, Georges. Romans et Récits. Paris: Editions Gallimard, 2004.

Parenthetical note: (Bataille 23)

76. **Book, Part of a Series—MLA** Give the series name just before the publishing information. Do not underline or italicize a series name or enclose it in quotation marks.

Works Cited

Fleckenstein, Kristie S. Embodied Literacies: Imageword and a Poetics of

Teaching. Studies in Writing and Rhetoric. Carbondale: Southern Illinois

UP, 2003.

Parenthetical note: (Fleckenstein 183)

77. **Book Published Before 1900—MLA** You may omit the name of the publisher in citations of works published prior to 1900.

Works Cited

Bowdler, Thomas, ed. The Family Shakespeare. 10 vols. London, 1818.

Parenthetical note: (Bowdler 2: 47)

78. **Book Issued by a Division of a Publisher—a Special Imprint—MLA** Attach the special imprint (Vintage in this case) to the publisher's name with a hyphen.

Works Cited

James, P. D. The Murder Room. New York: Vintage-Random, 2004.

Parenthetical note: (James 192–93)

79. **Dissertation or Thesis—Published (Including Publication by UMI)— MLA** The abbreviation *Diss.* indicates that the source is a dissertation. Include the name of the university and the year of graduation. If the dissertation you are citing is published by University Microfilms International (UMI), provide the publication information and order number as the last item in the Works Cited entry.

Works Cited

Moldenhauer, Zendi. Adolescent Depression: A Primary Care Pilot Intervention

    Study. Diss. U of Rochester School of Nursing, 2004. Ann Arbor: UMI,

    2004. AAT 3120695.

Parenthetical note: (Moldenhauer 143)

80. **Dissertation or Thesis—Unpublished—MLA** The title of an unpublished dissertation appears between quotation marks.

Works Cited

Talmadge, William Tracy. "Exploring the Hope Construct in Psychotherapy."

    Diss. U of Georgia, 2002.

Parenthetical note: (Talmadge 79)

81. **Article in a Scholarly Journal—MLA** Issues of scholarly journals are usually identified by volume number or season (rather than day, week, or month of publication). Such journals are usually paginated year by year, with a year's work treated as one volume.

Works Cited

Barnhardt, Terrence M. "Different Involuntary Mechanisms Underlie Priming

    and LOP Effects in Stem Completion Tests." Memory 12 (2004): 614–36.

Parenthetical note: (Barnhardt 620)

When a scholarly journal is paginated issue by issue, place a period and the issue number after the volume number.

Blitz, Mark. "Responsibility and Biotechnology." <u>ReVision</u> 25.4 (2003): 38–46.

Parenthetical note: (Blitz 42)

COS
p. 273 82. **Journal Article, Accessed Through an Online Database—MLA** In addition to print publication information, supply the name of the database or subscription service, including the publisher, and the date of access. You may also include the name and location of the library.

Works Cited

Landau, Michael. "Digital Downloads, Access Codes, and US Copyright Law."

<u>International Review of Law, Computers and Technology</u> 16.2 (2002):

149–70. <u>Academic Search Premier</u>. EBSCO. U of South Florida Lib.,

Tampa, FL. 20 Jan. 2004.

Include the word *abstract* if your database does not provide the article in full text or full image. You may also include the direct URL to the database if you know it.

Ealey, Robert F., John G. Michel, and Saray Devaraj. "The MP3 Open Standard

and the Music Industry's Response to Internet Piracy." <u>Communications</u>

<u>of the ACM</u> 46.11 (2003): 90–96. Abstract. <u>Academic Search Premier</u>.

EBSCO. Georgia Southern U, Zach S. Henderson Lib., Statesboro, GA.

20 Jan. 2004 <http://www.ebsco.com/home>.

COS
p. 269 83. **Journal, Electronic—MLA** Since most online articles do not have page numbers, avoid parenthetical citations by identifying the site in the text of your paper.

Works Cited

Austen, Veronica, "Writing Spaces: Performances of the Word." <u>Kairos: A Journal</u>

<u>of Rhetoric, Technology, and Pedagogy</u> 8.1 (2003). 22 Dec. 2004.

<http://english.ttu.edu//kairos/8.1/index.html>.

84. **Article in a Popular Magazine—MLA** Magazines are paginated issue by issue and identified by the monthly or weekly date of publication (instead of by volume number). If an article does not appear on consecutive pages in the magazine, give the first page on which it appears, followed by a plus sign: *64+*. Use the three-letter abbreviation for months of more than four letters.

O'Neal, William. "Tropical Storm!" <u>Computer Gaming World</u> Oct. 2004: 57+.

Parenthetical note: (O'Neal 62)

For weekly magazines, give the entire date of publication in day-month-year format as stated on the issue.

Ghosh, Aparisim. "The Great Sunni Hope." <u>Time</u> 13 Dec. 2004: 33.

Parenthetical note: (Ghosh 33)

COS p. 269 85. Article in an Online Magazine—MLA Since most online articles do not have page numbers, avoid parenthetical citations by identifying the site in the text of your project.

Works Cited

Levin, Josh. "Locker Room Affairs: The Sordid History of the Biggest Taboo in

Sports." <u>Slate</u> 22 Dec. 2004. 18 Jan. 2005.

<http://slate.msn.com/id/2111295/>.

86. Article in a Newspaper—MLA For page numbers, use the form in the newspaper you are citing; many newspapers are paginated according to sections.

Works Cited

Broder, John M. "Groups Debate Slower Strategy On Gay Rights." <u>The New York</u>

<u>Times</u> 9 Dec. 2004: A1.

Parenthetical note: (Broder A1)

A plus sign following the page number (for example, 7+) indicates that an article continues beyond the designated page but not on consecutive pages.

Weir, Tom. "Drug-Free Sports Might Be Thing of the Past." <u>USA Today</u> 8 Dec.

2004: 1A+.

Parenthetical note: (Weir 1)

To cite an editorial with no known author, begin with the title of the editorial, if applicable, followed by the description *Editorial.*

"Europe, Turkey, and Darwin." Editorial. <u>Christian Science Monitor</u> 15 Dec.

2004: 8.

Parenthetical note: ("Europe" 8)

To cite a letter to the editor, give the author's name, followed by the description *Letter.* In this example the particular edition of the newspaper is noted after the date of publication.

Doremire, Joe. Letter. <u>Los Angeles Times</u> 21 Dec. 2004, home ed.,

sec. B:12.

Parenthetical note: (Doremire 12)

COS
p. 269 87. **Online Newspaper—MLA** Here the date of the editorial and the date of access to it are the same.

> Works Cited
>
> "Grim Realities in Iraq." Editorial. The New York Times on the Web 22 Dec.
>
> > 2004. 22 Dec. 2004 <http://www.nytimes.com/2004/
> >
> > 12/22/opinion/22wed1.html>.

Pay special attention to daily publications online; materials may be archived each day, so the URL for today's headline will change tomorrow. In such cases, you may need to provide the URL for the site's search page. Note, too, that for some online publications, the URL you provide may require a subscription or fee to access. (See also Chapter 23.)

COS
p. 269 88. **Reviews—MLA** Not all reviews have titles, so the Works Cited form can vary slightly. Notice that a book or film title (*Uncle Tom's Cabin*) within another book or film title (Uncle Tom's Cabin *and American Culture*) is not underlined or italicized.

> Works Cited
>
> Baym, Nina. Rev. of Uncle Tom's Cabin and American Culture, by Thomas F.
>
> > Gossett. Journal of American History 72 (1985): 691–92.
>
> Keen, Maurice. "The Knight of Knights." Rev. of William Marshall: The Flower
>
> > of Chivalry, by Georges Duby. New York Review of Books 16 Jan. 1986:
> >
> > 39–40.
>
> **Parenthetical note:** (Baym 691–92); (Keen 39)

89. **Cartoon, Newspaper or Magazine—MLA** To avoid a confusing parenthetical note, describe a cartoon in the text of your essay. For example, you might use a reference such as "In 'Squib' by Miles Mathis. . . ."

> Works Cited
>
> Amend, Bill. "Fox Trot." Cartoon. Savannah Morning News 20 Dec. 2004: 3D.

COS
p. 272 90. **Encyclopedia and Reference Articles—MLA** With familiar reference works, especially those revised regularly, identify the edition you are using by its date. You may omit the names of editors and most publishing information. No page number is given in the parenthetical note when a work is arranged alphabetically.

> Works Cited
>
> Benedict, Roger William. "Northwest Passage." Encyclopaedia Britannica:
>
> > Macropaedia. 1974 ed.
>
> **Parenthetical note:** (Benedict)

A citation for an online encyclopedia article would include a date of access and an electronic address.

Fisher, William Weston. "Intellectual Property Law." Encyclopaedia Brittanica

Online. 2004. Encyclopaedia Britannica. 20 Sep. 2004.

<http://search.eb.com/eb/article?tocId=231534>.

With less familiar reference tools, a full entry is required.

Kovesi, Julius. "Hungarian Philosophy." The Encyclopedia of Philosophy. Ed.

Paul Edwards. 8 vols. New York: Macmillan, 1967.

Parenthetical note: (Kovesi)

91. **Bulletin or Pamphlet—MLA** Treat bulletins and pamphlets as if they were books.

Works Cited

United States. Environmental Protection Agency. Protect Your Family from Lead

in Your Home. Washington: GPO, 2003

92. **Biblical Citation—MLA** Note that titles of sacred works, such as the Talmud or the Bible, are not underlined. Titles of editions, however, are underlined. The parenthetical note references the book, chapter, and verse.

Works Cited

The New Jerusalem Bible. Henry Wansbrough, gen. ed. Garden City: Doubleday,

1990.

Parenthetical note: (John 18.37–38)

93. **Government Publication—MLA** Give the name of the government (national, state, or local) and the agency issuing the report, the title of the document, and publishing information. If it is a congressional document other than the *Congressional Record,* identify the Congress and, when important, the session (for example, *99th Cong., 1st sess.*) after the title of the document. Avoid a lengthy parenthetical note by naming the document in the body of your essay and placing only the relevant page numbers between parentheses: "This information is from the 2003–04 Official Congressional Directory (182–84)."

Works Cited

United States. Cong. Joint Committee on Printing. 2003–04 Official

Congressional Directory. 108th Cong., 1st sess. Washington: GPO, 2004.

To cite the *Congressional Record,* give only the date and page number.

Cong. Rec. 8 Feb. 2004: 3942–43.

COS
pp. 266–67 94. **Web Page or Site—MLA** The variety of Web pages is staggering, so you will have to adapt your documentation to particular sources. In general, provide author, title of the work, print publication information (if any), electronic publication information, and access information. Note that MLA encloses URLs with angle brackets (< >). Since most Web sites do not have page numbers, avoid parenthetical citations by identifying the site in the text of your project. (See also Chapter 23.)

Works Cited

Baron, Dennis. "From Pencils to Pixels: The Stages of Literacy Technology."

    Passions, Pedagogies, and Twenty-First Century Technologies. Ed. Gail

    Hawisher and Cynthia L. Selfe. Logan: Utah State UP, 2000. 15–33. 27

    July 2004 <http://netfiles.uiuc.edu/debaron/www/essays/pencils.htm>.

For a Web page with no known author, begin with the page title.

"Health Considered in Companies' Building Designs." CNN.com. 27 July 2004.

    27 July 2004 <http://www.cnn.com/2004/HEALTH/diet.fitness/07/27/

    healthy.architecture/index.html>.

A citation of an entire Web site (consisting of multiple Web pages) might be somewhat different.

United States. National Aeronautics and Space Administration. Ed. Jim Wilson.

    27 July 2004. 27 July 2004 <http://www.nasa.gov/home/>.

For a personal home page, you may want to supply the description *Home page* after the author's name.

Brown, Kiwi. Home page. 31 Dec. 2004. 16 Jan. 2005

    <http://www.geocities.com/shoe_polish/homepage.html>.

COS
p. 276 95. **Computer Software—MLA** Give the author, if known; the version number, if any (for example, *Microsoft Word*. Vers. 7.0); the manufacturer; the date; and (optionally) the system needed to run the software. Name the software in your text rather than use a parenthetical note: "With software such as AnyDVD. . . ."

Works Cited

AnyDVD. Vers. 4.3.0.1. St. John's, Antigua: 2004.

Include the URL for downloaded software.

enCore. Vers. 4.0.1. 25 July 2004 <ftp://ftp.utdallas.edu/pub/ah/moo/

    enCore-latest.tar.gz>.

COS
p. 273
96. Email and Archived Discussions—MLA When citing material from a list-serv, identify the author of the document or posting; put the subject line of the posting between quotation marks, followed by the words *Online posting* and the date on which the email was originally posted. Include the name of the discussion list, followed by the date you accessed the item, and the electronic address of the list in angle brackets. Because there will be no page number to cite, avoid a parenthetical citation by naming the author in the text of your project: "Cook argues in favor of . . . ."

Works Cited

Carbone, Nick. "RE: Searching PDF Files." Online posting. 29 Oct. 2004.

> WCenter Listserv. 12 Dec 2004 <wcenter@lyrics.acs.ttu.edu>.

Heady, Christy. "Buy or Lease? Depends on How Long You'll Keep the Car."

> Online posting. 7 July 1997. 14 July 2004

> <news:clari.biz.industry.automotive>.

For online discussions provide the speaker and/or site, the title of the session or event or its description, the date of the session, the forum for the communication (if specified), the date of access, and the electronic address.

Inept Guest. "Discussion of Disciplinary Politics in Rhet/comp." 12 Mar. 2004.

> LinguaMOO. 12 Mar. 2004 <telnet://lingua.utdallas.edu:8888>.

COS
p. 273
97. Publication or Database on CD-ROM/Diskette—MLA To cite a publication or database on CD-ROM, diskette, or other external storage medium, provide basic information about the source itself: author, title, and publication information. Identify the name of the database (italicized or underlined), the publication medium (*CD-ROM, Diskette, Magnetic tape*), and the name of the vendor if applicable. (The vendor is the company publishing or distributing the database.) If the publication is available in more than one medium, you may list them all or cite only the medium you actually used. Conclude with the date of electronic publication. (For material from online databases, see also model 82.)

Works Cited

Bevington, David. "Castles in the Air: The Morality Plays." The Theatre of

> Medieval Europe: New Research in Early Drama. Ed. Simon Eckehard.

> Cambridge, Eng.: Cambridge UP, 1993. MLA Bibliography. CD-ROM.

> SilverPlatter. Feb. 1995.

Parenthetical note: (Bevington 98)

For a CD-ROM database that is often updated (*ProQuest,* for example), you must provide publication dates for the item you are examining and for the data disk itself.

Alva, Sylvia Alatore. "Differential Patterns of Achievement Among Asian-

American Adolescents." Journal of Youth and Adolescence 22 (1993):

407–23. Proquest General Periodicals. CD-ROM. UMI-Proquest. June

1994.

Parenthetical note: (Alva 407-10)

Cite a book, encyclopedia, play, or other item published on CD-ROM or diskette just as if it were a printed source, adding the medium of publication (*CD-ROM, Diskette*). When page numbers aren't available, name the author in the text of your project to avoid using a parenthetical citation: "Bolter argues. . . ."

Bolter, Jay David. Writing Space: A Hypertext. Diskette. Hillsdale: Erlbaum,

1990.

COS
p. 271 98. **Film and Sound Recordings—MLA** Cite a video entry by title in most cases. Include relevant information about the producer, designer, performers, and so on. Identify the distributor, and provide a date. Avoid parenthetical citations to items on videocassette or DVD by naming the work in the body of your essay: "In Oliveri's video Dream Cars of the 50s & 60s. . . ."

Works Cited

Dream Cars of the 50s & 60s. Comp. Sandy Oliveri. Videocassette. Goodtimes

Home Video, 1986.

Movies are usually listed by title unless your emphasis is on the director, producer, or screenwriter. Provide information about actors, producers, cinematographers, set designers, and so on to suit your purpose. Identify the distributor, and give a date of production. Avoid parenthetical citations to films by naming the works in the body of your paper: "In Emmerich's film The Day After Tomorrow. . . ."

The Day After Tomorrow. Dir. Roland Emmerich. Perf. Dennis Quaid. 20th

Century Fox, 2004.

List commercial recordings by composer, performer, or song title, depending on your emphasis. Song titles are enclosed in quotation marks; album and CD or DVD titles are italicized or underlined.

Pavarotti, Luciano. Pavarotti's Greatest Hits. London, 1980.

To cite a sound recording or clip you obtained online, include the URL and any path information, along with the date of access.

Michael Ross Quartet. "Back at the Cathouse." <u>Year of the Dog</u>. Cooper-Alport

Productions, 2004. 20 Jan. 2005

<http://www.michaelrossquartet.com/sounds04/05backatthecathouse.mp3>.

99. **Microfilm or Microfiche—MLA** Treat material on microfilm as if you had seen its original hard-copy version. Then add information about the source, including the title of the microform (if applicable) and any volume, fiche, or grid numbers or other publication information if applicable.

Works Cited

Rhodes, Michael. "Bio-Terrorism Expert Warns of Crises to Come." <u>Valley News</u>

19 Sep. 2001: A1–2. <u>Newsbank: Social Problems</u> 12 (2001):fiche 5, grids

8–11.

100. **Television and Radio Programs—MLA** List the program by episode or name of series or program. Enclose episode or segment names in quotation marks; italicize or underline program or series names. Avoid parenthetical citations to television shows by naming the programs in the body of your paper.

Works Cited

"No Surrender, No Retreat." Dir. Mike Vejar. Writ. Michael Straczynski. Perf.

Bruce Boxleitner, Claudia Christian, and Mira Furlan. <u>Babylon 5</u>. KEYE,

Austin. 28 July 1997.

101. **Personal Interview—MLA** Refer to the interview in the body of your essay rather than in a parenthetical note: "In an interview, Peter Gomes explained. . . ." Identify the type of interview (*Personal, Telephone,* or *E-mail interview*) and give the interview date in the Works Cited entry.

Works Cited

Gomes, Rev. Peter. Personal interview. 23 Apr. 2005.

102. **Musical Composition—MLA** List the work on the Works Cited page by the name of the composer. Note that song titles are enclosed in quotation marks; the titles of operas, ballets, and symphonies are italicized or underlined. When you have sheet music or a score, you can furnish complete publication information.

Works Cited

Joplin, Scott. "The Strenuous Life: A Ragtime Two Step." St. Louis: Stark Sheet

Music, 1902.

When you don't have a score or sheet music to refer to, provide a simpler entry. In either case, naming the music in the essay text is preferable to using a parenthetical citation.

Porter, Cole. "Too Darn Hot." 1949.

To cite recordings, see model 98.

103. Speech—No Printed Text—MLA Include the location and date of the speech. Naming the speech in the text of your project is preferable to using a parenthetical citation.

Works Cited

Yancey, Kathleen Blake. "Made Not Only in Words: Composition in a

New Key." Conf. on Coll. Composition and Communication.

Henry B. Gonzalez Convention Center, San Antonio. 25 Mar.

2004.

When there is no title, include a description (*Lecture, Keynote speech, Address, Reading*).

Walker, Janice R. Lecture. WRIT 5550: Technologies of Writing. Georgia

Southern U, Statesboro, GA. 29 Jan. 2004.

104. Speech—Printed Text—MLA Give the location and date of the speech, followed by the publication information, including page numbers.

Works Cited

Farmer, Jr., John J. "The Rule of Law in an Age of Terror." Rutgers U Law

School, Newark. 10 Nov. 2004. Rpt. Vital Speeches of the Day 71.4 (2004):

98–106

Parenthetical note: (Farmer 99)

105. Letter—Published—MLA A published letter is cited in the same manner as an article in a collection.

Works Cited

Eliot, George. "To Thomas Clifford Allbutt." 1 Nov. 1873. In Selections from

George Eliot's Letters. Ed. Gordon S. Haight. New Haven: Yale UP,

1985: 427.

Parenthetical note: (Eliot 427)

106. **Letter—Unpublished—MLA** Identifying the letter communication in the text of your project is preferable to using a parenthetical citation.

Works Cited

Newton, Albert. Letter to Agnes Weinstein. 23 May 1917. Albert Newton Papers.
     Woodhill Lib., Cleveland.

107. **Artwork—MLA** Titles of works of art are generally underlined or italicized. Include information on the location of the collection, if applicable. Naming the artwork in the text of your essay is preferable to using a parenthetical citation.

Works Cited

Fuseli, Henry. Ariel. Folger Shakespeare Lib., Washington.

108. **Drama or Play—MLA** Citing the printed text of a play, whether individual or collected, differs from citing a performance. For printed texts, provide the usual Works Cited information, taking special care when citing a collection in which various editors handle different plays. In parenthetical notes give the act, scene, and line numbers if the work is so divided; give page numbers if it is not.

Works Cited

Shakespeare, William. The Tragedy of Hamlet, Prince of Denmark. Ed. Frank
     Kermode. The Riverside Shakespeare. Ed. G. Blakemore Evans and J. J. M.
     Tobin. 2nd ed. Boston: Houghton, 1997. 1183–1245.
Stoppard, Tom. Rosencrantz and Guildenstern Are Dead. New York: Grove, 1967.
Parenthetical note: (Ham. 5.2.219–24); (Stoppard 11–15)

For performances of plays, give the title of the work, the author, and then any specific information that seems relevant—director, performers, producers, set designer, theater company, and so on. You may also begin the entry with the name of a person (director, performer, etc.) if you are focusing on the work of that person. Conclude the entry with a theater, its location, and a date. Refer to the production directly in the body of your essay to avoid using a parenthetical citation.

Timon of Athens. By William Shakespeare. Dir. Michael Benthall. Perf. Ralph
     Richardson, Paul Curran, and Margaret Whiting. Old Vic, London. 5 Sept.
     1956.

24c Sample MLA paper

John Brown

Professor J. Kline

ENGL 101

16 December 2003

Swatting Flies with an Ax: File Sharing

and the Recording Industry

In the last few years, downloading and file sharing of CD-quality music files has become both a popular practice and a source of legal and social controversy. To music fans, obtaining music from the Internet or sharing it on the Internet has become a new way of enjoying music, no more reprehensible than recording music from the radio. To the recording industry, it is theft, and they have responded with harsh legal action against file sharers. In the following discussion, it will be suggested that the industry has a legitimate case, but that its heavy-handed response has served only to alienate its own customers without providing a creative response to new technologies for providing music to listeners.

Copying music at home is not new. For decades, people used tape recorders to record music from the radio, or from friends' albums, and thus obtain their own copies. For an equally long period, the recording industry has fought this practice, seeking, for example, to ban sales of blank audiocassette tapes in the 1970s (Cave). That conflict was strictly a boardroom battle, however, pitting the recording industry against one of its own suppliers, the tape manufacturing industry. It had no direct impact on home recorders. The recording industry lost in any case, the first of a long series of setbacks in its struggle against home copying of music, a history perhaps reflected in the industry's hard-line posture today.

Moreover, home tape recording was never as widespread as file sharing is today. The primary reason, in a nutshell, is that the quality of home recordings was relatively low, not a substitute for commercially produced records, tapes, or CDs. Also, repeated

CHECKLIST 24.5

Title Page—MLA

MLA does not require a separate cover sheet or title page. If your instructor expects one, center the title of your paper and your name in the upper third of the paper. Center the course title, your instructor's name, and the date of submission on the lower third of the sheet, double-spacing between the elements.

The first page of a paper without a separate title page will look like the [facing page]. Be sure to check all the items in this list.

○ Place your name, your instructor's name, the course title, and the date in the upper left-hand corner, beginning one inch from the top of the page. These items are double spaced.

○ Identify your instructor by an appropriate title. When uncertain about academic rank, use *Mr.* or *Ms.*

○ Center the title. Capitalize the first word and all major words and proper nouns.

   Swatting Flies with an Ax: File Sharing and the Recording Industry

○ Do not underline or boldface the title of your paper. Do not use all caps, place the title between quotation marks, or end it with a period. Titles may, however, end with question marks or include words or phrases that are italicized, underlined, or between quotation marks.

   Violence in Shakespeare's Macbeth

   Dylan's "Like a Rolling Stone" Revisited

○ Begin the body of the essay immediately below the title. Double-space the entire essay, including quotations.

○ Use one-inch margins at the sides and bottom of this page.

○ Number the first page in the upper right-hand corner, one-half inch from the top, one inch from the right margin. Precede the page number with your last name.

recordings would lead to a steady decrease in quality, due to the nature of so-called analog reproduction (Muroff). It is possible to make extremely high quality analog copies, but this requires expensive equipment not owned by ordinary music fans.

These constraints were dramatically reduced, almost eliminated, by the technology of digital recording and by the spread of high-speed Internet access. A digital recording can be digitally copied with no loss in quality (Leubitz 421); even multiple generations of duplication will produce no degradation. (Taping a digital recording is an "analog" process and results in degradation.) A digital recording can also be stored as a computer file and transferred over the Internet like any other file. Music fans could digitally copy CDs onto their computers and send perfect copies to friends, in the form of files. Soon, fans began providing music available for downloading by anyone. Commercial services such as Napster appeared, providing software to facilitate this process, making it fast, easy, and convenient.

The total volume of music downloading is enormous. If the average CD is assumed to have ten songs, the number of songs downloaded was estimated by 2002 as equal to about five times US sales of CDs, or about 1.5 times world sales (Cave). Nearly all of this downloading is illegal; downloading over legal services is equivalent to only about 2 percent of CD sales (Cave). Whether file sharing and downloading have severely undermined CD sales is, however, much less certain. The same study that produced the estimates cited above found that CD sales had fallen by a modest 5 percent, a dip that could be attributed to the state of the economy (Cave). A more recent study has found sales of the most popular CDs are actually increased by downloading, with about one additional CD being sold for each one hundred downloads. Less popular CDs, however, suffered if songs on them had larger numbers of downloads (Potier).

CHECKLIST 24.6

Body of the Essay—MLA

The body of an MLA research paper continues uninterrupted until the separate Notes page (if any) and the Works Cited page.

○ Use margins of one inch all around. Left-justify your margins. Do not hyphenate words at the end of lines.

○ Use the "header" feature of your word processor to automatically include your last name and the page number in the upper right-hand corner of each page, one inch from the right edge of the page and one-half inch from the top.

○ Indent the first line of each paragraph one-half inch, or five spaces.

○ Indent long quotations one inch, or ten spaces. In MLA documentation, long quotations are any that exceed four typed lines in the body of your essay. Double-space these indented quotations. Note that parenthetical citations are placed *outside* the closing punctuation for indented quotations and *inside* closing punctuation for in-text quotations.

○ All information and quotations from outside sources are noted in the text and keyed to entries in the list of Works Cited. Include exact page numbers for direct quotations. (See Chapter 23 for information on documenting electronic sources without pagination.)

Brown 3

The reasons for these phenomena—particularly the resilience of CD sales in the face of an enormous volume of music file sharing—are uncertain and have been a considerable surprise to experts who have studied file sharing (Cave). One factor may be convenience. Since music files are generally available online in the form of individual songs or tracks, a music downloader still faces a significant amount of work in downloading all the tracks of an album, then burning them onto a blank CD in the desired order. Many downloaders, perhaps most, may decide that if they like an album enough to download all of it, the convenience of buying the CD is worth the cost (Cave).

We may speculate that a related pattern of behavior explains why file sharing would help regular CDs while hurting less popular ones. Suppose that some substantial fraction of downloading is done by music fans who are "sampling" music. Perhaps they heard a cut on the radio, or a friend recommended the artist. If file sharing were not available, some of these fans would take a chance on buying a CD, but others would not. It would not be surprising if more popular artists benefited from such sampling, due to downloaders choosing to buy the whole CD, while less popular artists suffered, potential buyers passing on a CD they would have ended up rarely playing. The above is speculation, but it seems clear that the relationship between file sharing and buying CDs is not a simple matter of the one replacing the other.

In any case, file sharing has become a widespread practice. To the recording industry, it is an alarming one, in spite of the lack of clear evidence that it has hurt CD sales to date. While historical data on home taping are not available, almost certainly far more people are making digital copies than previously made analog ones. Moreover, due to the poor quality of analog copies, those who made them might still buy the higher-quality record or commercial tape. A copied digital file is as good as the original CD from which it was

Brown 4

reproduced, so a fan who has made one may have no motivation to go out and pay for the CD. To recording industry executives, the spread of file sharing is at least painful, and it looms as a potential catastrophe. The market for music CDs might nearly evaporate, with only a handful of original CDs being sold, while everyone else gets free copies off the Internet.

If this were to happen, the recording industry in anything like its present form would collapse. With CD sales insignificant, the industry would go out of business. Artists would still earn money from live concerts and radio airplay licensing, but a large fraction of their income would also evaporate. File sharers would find that they had strangled their own source of supply—digitally recorded CDs— and the practice of file sharing itself would collapse from lack of new files to share. Everyone involved would end up a loser. In this respect, the Recording Industry Association of America (RIAA) has a legitimate case that illegal file sharing has a destructive potential. The industry can also legitimately argue that not only recording firms but artists are hurt by file sharing. To whatever extent CD sales are currently being hurt by file sharing, recording artists are losing deserved royalties for their creative efforts.

In response to the spread of file sharing, the RIAA has invoked intellectual property laws in the specific form of copyright protection. "Intellectual property" is a modern term for an old concept, namely, that people who create music, words, or some other intellectual product of value should have a right to their work. They should be able to sell it and profit from the sale (US Patents and Trademarks Office 19-20). Without intellectual property rights, most creative artists could not make a living. Musicians can perform at concerts, which people will pay to attend, but writers depend entirely on selling copies of their works. Even musicians depend heavily on sales of their recorded music.

The unusual feature of intellectual property is that it is not physical. People don't buy recorded CDs for the physical CD itself, but for the music recorded on it, and that same music can be put in a computer file and transmitted on the Internet. Moreover, stealing intellectual property is not like most kinds of theft. If I steal your CD player, you're left without it. If I copy your CDs, you still have them. This reflexive reaction of file sharers and downloaders is undoubtedly at the root of their lack of moral qualms about the practice. Nevertheless, the RIAA has issued hundreds of subpoenas to Internet service providers (ISPs) and others, demanding the names of file sharers (Taylor 42). In response, software designers are working on software that will provide file sharers with anonymity even from their ISPs. The battle over file sharing has thus developed into a cat-and-mouse game between the recording industry and file sharers (Taylor 42).

Just as casual home recording is not new, the recording industry has long struggled against commercial pirates. By the 1990s it was seeking crackdowns on commercial pirates overseas, firms that made and sold bootleg copies of CDs (Cave). This industry demand was not controversial. Piracy of this sort was done for money, not for the sake of the music, and the musicians got no royalties for bootleg copies. Retail buyers of commercial pirate CDs had no way to know they were buying counterfeits, and they were, in a sense, also victims (though unlikely to feel victimized so long as the recording was high quality).

So long as making high-quality copies of music or other intellectual property was an expensive and difficult process, a sharp line existed between commercial piracy and casual home copying. Digital recording blurred the technical distinction. It did not, however, blur the perceptual distinction. Casual copying of music by fans, though also technically illegal, is a very different issue (Katz). In attacking it the same way, the recording industry is swatting

Brown 6

flies with an ax. The perceptual distinction is fundamentally a matter of motives.

Most people probably would agree that someone should not make money from intellectual property without paying the owner, usually the creator, such as a musician receiving royalties from sales. File sharers, however, are doing it not for the money but for love of music. In fact, most are paying at least a small amount to maintain Internet servers to make their music files available. People who download files are saving money by not buying the CD, but they are not <u>making</u> money. They too are in it for the music. This is at the root of the attitude described by <u>PC Magazine</u> editor Michael Miller, who found in talking to students that "most of the students didn't buy my argument; they just don't see what they're doing wrong."

More ambiguous is the situation of commercial services that provide file-sharing access software. They are arguably in it for the money, not the music. However, their service is not limited to piracy; it can also provide legal copies of noncopyrighted music files. The RIAA succeeded in shutting down Naptser in its original form, on the basis that it was specifically facilitating illegal copying by providing a sort of clearinghouse of available files (Enos). Other technologies soon appeared that decentralized the file-searching process. The RIAA then turned to direct legal action against individual file sharers.

From the point of view of the RIAA, there is no difference between a bootleg CD made and sold by a firm in China and a music file made available for file sharing online by a music fan. It is still theft of intellectual property, and theft is theft, no matter the motive. Members of the public, however, particularly music fans, see a profound distinction between commercial copying for profit and making or providing copies for personal enjoyment. One downloader of file-shared music describes herself as "having the same moral

problem with sharing digital music that I have with public libraries—
i.e., none" (Cullen 45).

Moreover, the companies that make up the RIAA are large
corporations, which themselves are in it for the money. They are also
faceless entities to music fans, who may have loyalty to musicians
but feel no connection to labels. Attempts by labels to launch their
own for-pay downloading services failed for this reason; fans look for
performers or groups, not labels (Cullen 44). Efforts by the RIAA to
shame music fans into refraining from file sharing have swayed few
fans, while the RIAA's heavy-handed legal actions, such as offering
"amnesties" to file sharers that, in fact, leave them exposed to legal
action (Yu), have alienated many more.

In fact, a strong case can be made that the RIAA's tactics
amount to shooting itself in the foot. The more it cracks down, the
more it is despised by music fans. For many, transferring files may
become a means not only of getting music for less but of thumbing
their noses at the heavy-handed corporations. While file sharing may
be both illegal and open to legitimate moral criticism for robbing
artists of royalties as well as recording firms of revenue, legal action
against an activity that few regard as a crime is rarely successful in
the long run. As noted above, new technologies, providing anonymity
to file sharers, may render effective legal action nearly impossible.
The end result might be just the catastrophe that the RIAA fears—a
spread of illegal file sharing, collapse of CD sales, and perhaps
collapse of digital music recording itself.

What alternatives are available? The industry has looked into
technological solutions to the problem of file sharing, such as Digital
Rights Management (DRM) codes that will prevent copying of
copyrighted material. Codings of this sort tend to be inconvenient
even for legal users because of incompatible systems. A downloaded
song, for example, may be playable on your iPod, but not on your

Brown 8

car's CD player (Levy). Legal downloading for payment cannot become a popular alternative so long as it suffers from such compatibility limitations.

Software firms depend on sales of manuals and technical support to limit their losses from copying of software programs. No manual or tech support is needed to play a music CD. However, some music CD makers are starting to include booklets and similar supplemental material with CDs. This approach has been recommended by industry consultants and appears to be attractive to music customers (Howe). Another possible approach is one used in European countries, which charge a fee on each sale of blank CDs or other recording media (Yu). Revenue from these fees supplies a fund from which artists are compensated for lost royalties from sales of recordings. Low-priced, intercompatible forms of legal downloading of music are also starting to catch on.

Illegal file sharing and downloading remain a real problem, undermining not only the recording industry but, ultimately, the very artists whose music the fans wish to listen to. It is time for the industry to step back, take a breath, and explore more creative and consumer-friendly approaches to solving the problem of piracy while making music available online.

Brown 9

Works Cited

Cave, Damien. "File Sharing: Innocent Until Proven Guilty."
  Salon.com 13 June 2002. 1 Aug. 2004
  <http://www.salon.com/tech/feature/ 2002/06/13/liebowitz/>.

Cullen, Lisa Takeuchi. "How To Go Legit." Time 22 Sep. 2003: 44–45.

Enos, Lori. "RIAA Slams Napster Defense." E-Commerce Times 17
  July 2000. 4 Aug. 2004
  <http://www.ecommercetimes.com/story/ 3792.html>.

Howe, Jeff. "File-Sharing Is, Like, Totally Uncool." Wired 12.5 (2004).
  7 Oct. 2004
  <http://www.wired.com/wired/archive/12.05/mpaa.html>.

Katz, Larry. "Hang Onto Your iPods: Here Comes Orrin Hatch."
  Boston Herald 30 June 2004: The Edge 44. Academic Universe.
  Lexis-Nexis. U of South Florida Lib., Tampa, FL. 9 Aug. 2004.

Levy, Steven. "iTunes and Lawsuits: The Labels Still Don't Get It."
  Newsweek 3 May 2004. 7 Oct. 2004 <http://msnbc.msn.com/id/
  4891711/>.

Leubitz, Brian. "Digital Millenium? Technological Protections for
  Copyright on the Internet." Texas Intellectual Property Law
  Journal 11.2 (2003): 417–446.

Miller, Michael J. "More Squabbles over Digital Music." PC Magazine
  20 May 2003. 7 Oct. 2004 <http://www.pcmag.com/article2/
  0,1759,1091444,00.asp>.

Muroff, Andrew S. "Some Rights Reserved: Music Copyright in the
  Digital Era." Detroit College of Law at Michigan State
  University Law Review 4 (1997). 4 Oct. 2004
  <http://www.law.msu.edu/lawrev/
  97-4/muroff.htm>.

Potier, Beth. "File Sharing May Boost CD Sales." Harvard University
  Gazette 15 Apr. 2004. 17 Aug. 2004
  <http://www.news.harvard.edu/gazette/2004/04.15/
  09-filesharing.html>.

CHECKLIST 24.7

> ### The Works Cited Page—MLA

The Works Cited list contains full bibliographical information on all the books, articles, and other resources used in composing the paper.

○ Center the title "Works Cited" at the top of the page.

○ Include in the Works Cited list all the sources actually mentioned in the paper. Do not include materials you examined but did not cite in the body of the paper itself.

○ Arrange the items in the Works Cited list alphabetically by the last name of the author or the first major word of corporate or organizational authors. If no author is given for a work, list it according to the first word of its title, ignoring articles (*The, A, An*).

○ Be sure the first line of each entry touches the left-hand margin. Subsequent lines are indented one-half inch or five spaces, using the hanging indent capability of your word processor.

○ Double-space the entire list. Do not insert extra space between entries unless that is the form your instructor prefers.

○ Punctuate items in the list carefully. Don't forget the period at the end of each entry.

○ Follow this form if you have two or more entries by the same author:

Ro, Ronin. Bad Boy: The Influence of Sean "Puffy" Combs on the Music
    Industry. New York: Pocket Books, 2001.

---. Have Gun Will Travel: The Spectacular Rise and Violent Fall of Death
    Row Records. New York: Doubleday, 1998.

Brown 10

Taylor, Chris. "Downloader Dragnet." Time 4 Aug. 2003: 42.

US Patents and Trademarks Office. Working Group on Intellectual
    Property Rights. "Intellectual Property and the National
    Information Infrastructure." Mod. 15 Nov. 1995. 4 Oct. 2004
    <http://www.uspto.gov/web/offices/com/doc/ipnii/>.

Yu, Peter K. "Music Industry Hits Wrong Note Against Piracy."
    Detroit News 14 Sep. 2003. 7 Oct. 2004
    <http://www.detnews.com/2003/ editorial/0309/14/a13-
    269781.htm>.

CHAPTER 25

APA Documentation

In many social science and related courses (anthropology, education, home economics, linguistics, political science, psychology, sociology) writers are expected to follow the conventions of documentation recommended by the American Psychological Association (APA). The basic procedures for APA documentation are spelled out in this chapter. A full explanation of APA procedures is provided by the *Publication Manual of the American Psychological Association,* fifth edition (2001), available in most college libraries. Style updates are also available at the APA Web site at **http://apastyle.org**.

Citing Electronic Sources in the Social Sciences

APA documentation includes forms for some electronic sources, which we present in this chapter. However, you may want to use the COS-sciences documentation style recommended by the *Columbia Guide to Online Style* instead. Developed explicitly for electronic forms, COS-sciences style is designed to *work with* APA forms for citing conventional print sources and *replace* APA style for the citation of electronic sources. APA forms that have a Columbia equivalent are marked in the APA Form Directory in this chapter with a distinctive icon: COS p. 000 .

25a How do you use APA documentation?

APA documentation involves two basic steps.

Step 1: In the body of your paper, place a note to identify the source of each passage or idea you must document. In its most common form, the APA note consists of the last name of the source's author, followed in parentheses by the year the material was published.

> According to Murphy (2003) , current assessment practices can sometimes
> have a negative effect on both teaching and learning.

Another basic form of the APA note, used when the author's name is not mentioned in the sentence, places both the author's last name and a date between parentheses. Notice that a comma follows the author's name.

> Current assessment practices can sometimes have a negative effect on both
>
> teaching and learning (Murphy, 2003).

A page number may be given for indirect citations and *must* be given for direct quotations. A comma follows the date when page numbers are given, and page numbers are preceded by *p.* or *pp.*

> Omitting teachers from the design of assessment tests can "have the
>
> unintended consequence of marginalizing teachers and making them less
>
> enabled to respond to student needs" (Murphy, 2003, p. 42).

For electronic sources, page numbers are omitted (most electronic sources do not have pagination) since the "search" or "find" feature of most applications will allow readers to locate specific words or phrases within the file. (See also Chapter 23.)

When appropriate, the documentation may be distributed throughout a passage.

> Murphy (2003) observes that current assessment practices "can be effective
>
> when the work is routine, mechanistic, and highly predictable" (p. 42).

Parenthetical notes should be as brief and inconspicuous as possible. Because the purpose of a note is to identify a source of information, it should begin with the same name as the entry in your References list, as shown in Figure 25.1.

> According to Murphy (2003), current assessment practices can
>
> sometimes have a negative effect on both teaching and learning.

Murphy (2003)

References

Murphy, S. (2003). That was then, this is now: The impact of changing

assessment policies on teachers and the teaching of writing in

California. *Journal of Writing Assessment, 1*(1), 23–45.

FIGURE 25.1 In-text notes are keyed to specific entries in the References list.

1. **When two or more sources are used in a single sentence,** the notes are inserted as needed after the statements they support.

   > While Porter (2003) suggests that the ecology of the aquifer might be hardier than suspected, "given the size of the drainage area and the nature of the subsurface rock" (p. 62), there is no reason to believe that the county needs another shopping mall in an area described as "one of the last outposts of undisturbed nature in the state" (Martinez, 2004, p. 28).

   Notice that a parenthetical note is placed outside quotation marks but before the period ending the sentence.

2. **When a single source provides a series of references, you need not repeat the name of the author until other sources interrupt the series.** After the first reference, page numbers are sufficient until another citation intervenes. Even then you need repeat only the author's last name, not a date, when the additional reference occurs within the same paragraph.

   > The council vetoed zoning approval for a mall in an area described by Martinez (2004) as the last outpost of undisturbed nature in the state. The area provides a "unique environment for several endangered species of birds and plant life" (p. 31). The birds, especially the endangered vireo, require breeding spaces free from encroaching development (Harrison & Cafiero, 1979). Rare plant life is similarly endangered (Martinez).

3. **When you cite more than one work written by an author in a single year,** assign a small letter after the date to distinguish between the author's works.

   > (Rosner, 2004a)
   >
   > (Rosner, 2004b)
   >
   > The charge is raised by Rosner (2004a), quickly answered by Anderson (2004), and then raised again by Rosner (2004b).

4. **When you need to cite more than a single work in one note,** separate the citations with a semicolon and list them in alphabetical order.

   > (Searle, 2002; Yamibe, 2002)

5. **When you are referring to a Web site** (though not to a particular Web document), you can give the electronic address in the text of your paper. The site need not be added to the References list according to

APA style. (See Chapter 23 for COS-sciences style on citing electronically accessed sources.)

> More information about psychology as a profession is available
> on the American Psychological Association's Web site at
> http://www.apa.org .

In-text notes to specific electronic sources in the body of an APA paper should include the author's last name, a comma, the year of publication followed by a comma, and the page number (or, if given in the source, the paragraph number designated by the symbol ¶ or the abbreviation *para.*).

> Ensuring Web site accessibility includes "not only making the
> language clear and simple, but also providing understandable
> mechanisms for navigating within and between pages"
> (W3C, 1999, ¶ 2.2) .

For most electronic sources, however, you will not have page or paragraph designations. When this is the case, give the heading or subheading (if applicable) and the number of the paragraph following it. Make certain you count the paragraphs accurately! See Chapter 23 for more information on citing electronic sources.

> The first scientific journal was published in 1665 by the Royal
> Society of London (Walker, 1998, The Evolution of Scientific
> Publishing section, para. 1) .

Step 2: On a separate page at the end of your paper, list every source cited in an in-text note. This alphabetical list of sources is titled "References." Tebeaux's article would appear in the References list of a *college paper* in APA "final copy" style in this form.

> Tebeaux, E. (1991). Ramus, visual rhetoric, and the emergence of page
> design in medical writing of the English Renaissance. *Written
> Communication, 8*, 411–445.

We use hanging indents for APA References entries, and use italics to designate titles of major works (books, journals, newspapers, magazines, etc.). For projects to be submitted to publishers, see the recommendations in the fifth edition of the APA *Publication Manual*.

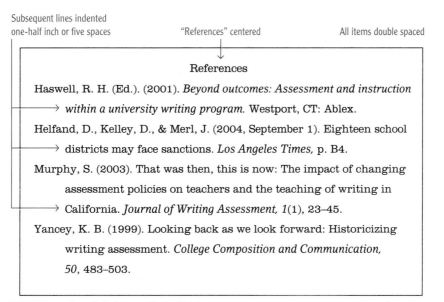

Subsequent lines indented one-half inch or five spaces   "References" centered   All items double spaced

References

Haswell, R. H. (Ed.). (2001). *Beyond outcomes: Assessment and instruction within a university writing program.* Westport, CT: Ablex.

Helfand, D., Kelley, D., & Merl, J. (2004, September 1). Eighteen school districts may face sanctions. *Los Angeles Times,* p. B4.

Murphy, S. (2003). That was then, this is now: The impact of changing assessment policies on teachers and the teaching of writing in California. *Journal of Writing Assessment, 1*(1), 23–45.

Yancey, K. B. (1999). Looking back as we look forward: Historicizing writing assessment. *College Composition and Communication, 50,* 483–503.

FIGURE 25.2 Sample References list in APA format.

CHECKLIST 25.1

Basic Format—Books

A typical APA References entry for a book includes the following basic information.

○ Author(s), last name first, followed by a period and one space. Initials are used instead of first and middle names unless two authors mentioned in the paper have identical last names and initials.

○ Date of publication in parentheses, followed by a period and one space.

○ Title of the work, italicized, followed by a period (unless some other information separates the name of the title from the period) and one space. Only the first word of the title, the first word of a subtitle, and proper nouns are capitalized.

○ City of publication, followed by a colon and one space.

○ Publisher, followed by a period.

(Continued)

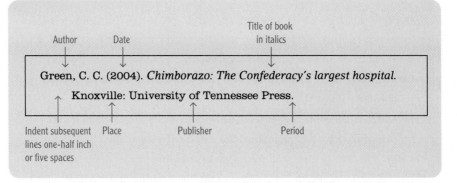

Author   Date   Title of book in italics

Green, C. C. (2004). *Chimborazo: The Confederacy's largest hospital.*
    Knoxville: University of Tennessee Press.

Indent subsequent   Place   Publisher   Period
lines one-half inch
or five spaces

CHECKLIST 25.2

Basic Format—Scholarly Journals and Scholarly Magazines

A typical APA References entry for an article in a scholarly journal or magazine includes the following basic information.

○ Author(s), last name first, followed by a period and one space.

○ Date of publication in parentheses, followed by a period and one space.

○ Title of the article, followed by a period and one space. Only the first word of the title, the first word of a subtitle, and proper nouns are capitalized. The title does not appear between quotation marks.

○ Name of the periodical, italicized, followed by a comma and one space. Notice that all major words are capitalized in periodical names.

○ Volume number, italicized, followed by a comma and one space.

○ Page numbers, followed by a period.

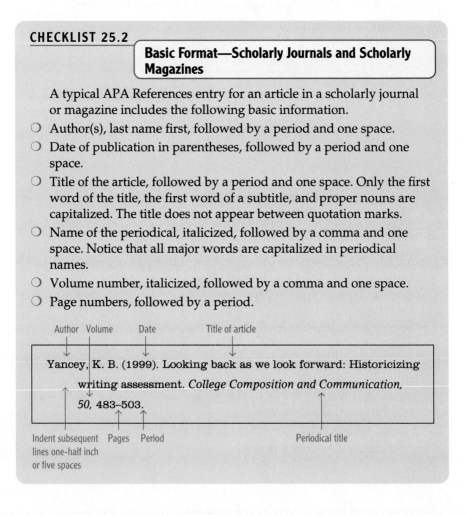

Author Volume   Date   Title of article

Yancey, K. B. (1999). Looking back as we look forward: Historicizing
    writing assessment. *College Composition and Communication,*
    50, 483–503.

Indent subsequent   Pages   Period   Periodical title
lines one-half inch
or five spaces

CHECKLIST 25.3

Basic Format—Magazines and Newspapers

A typical APA References entry for an article in a popular magazine or newspaper includes the following basic information.

○ Author(s), last name first, followed by a period.

○ Date of publication in parentheses, followed by a period and one space. Give the year first, followed by the month (do not abbreviate it) and the day, if necessary.

○ Title of the work, followed by a period and one space. Only the first word and proper nouns are capitalized. The title does not appear between quotation marks.

○ Name of the periodical, italicized, followed by a comma. All major words are capitalized.

○ Page or location, followed by a period.

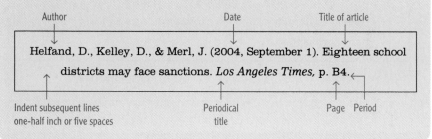

Author   Date   Title of article

Helfand, D., Kelley, D., & Merl, J. (2004, September 1). Eighteen school districts may face sanctions. *Los Angeles Times*, p. B4.

Indent subsequent lines one-half inch or five spaces   Periodical title   Page Period

CHECKLIST 25.4

Basic Format—Electronic Sources

APA offers only a few models for citing electronic sources, and those models may be unwieldy. For papers and projects that follow APA models for citing print sources, consider following COS-science models instead (see Chapter 23). A typical APA References entry for an online or Web document includes the following basic information.

○ Author(s), last name first, followed by a period and one space.

○ Date of publication in parentheses, followed by a period and one space. Give the year first, followed by the month (do not abbreviate it) and the day, if necessary.

○ Title of the work, followed by a period and one space unless other information intervenes.

(Continued)

○ Title of the journal in italics, followed by a comma; a single blank space; and, if applicable, the volume number, also in italics and the issue number, not italicized, enclosed by parentheses then another comma, a single space, and the page numbers, followed by a period.

○ For Internet articles that are based on a print source, include the description *Electronic version*, enclosed in square brackets, after the title of the journal.

○ For Internet-only articles or for articles that you believe are different from the printed version, include the word *Retrieved*, followed by the date you accessed the information, a comma, the word *from*, and the Internet address. Do not use a period or other punctuation at the end of the URL.

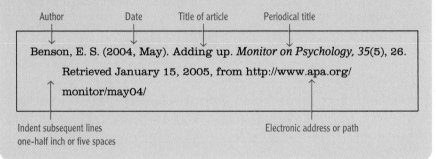

Benson, E. S. (2004, May). Adding up. *Monitor on Psychology, 35*(5), 26.

    Retrieved January 15, 2005, from http://www.apa.org/

    monitor/may04/

There are many variations to these generic entries, so you should consult the *Publication Manual of the American Psychological Association* (2001) when you do a major APA-style project. For the latest updates on electronic documentation, check the APA Web site at http://www.apa.org/students. You may also want to review COS-sciences style in Chapter 23.

The References list appears on its own page following the body of the essay (and any endnote page). It lists bibliographical information for all the materials you used in composing your paper. See Checklist 25.9 on page 371 on setting up a References list.

25b APA Form Directory

Here you will find the APA References and parenthetical note forms for a variety of sources. First find the type of source you need to cite in the Format Index, and then locate the item by number in the list that follows. The COS icon next to an entry indicates that a Columbia Online Style (COS) form is available for that source (see Chapter 23 on COS).

109. Book, One Author or Editor—APA Give the author's last name and initials, followed by a period; the year of publication in parentheses, followed by a period; and the title of the book in italics, capitalizing only the first word, proper nouns, and the first word in subtitles (designated by a colon). Then give the city of publication (include the two-letter state designation only when the city is not well-known), followed by a colon and the name of the publisher.

References

Haswell, R. H. (Ed.). (2001). *Beyond outcomes: Assessment and instruction within a university writing program.* Westport, CT: Ablex.

Parenthetical notes:

Haswell (2001) found. . . .

(Haswell, 2001)

(Haswell, 2001, p. 49)

110. **Book, Two or Three Authors or Editors—APA** An ampersand (&) appears between the authors' names in the References list and in parenthetical notes. The word *and* is used when the authors are identified in the text.

References

Ivins, M., & Dubose, L. (2003). *Bushwhacked: Life in George W. Bush's America.*
New York: Random House.

Parenthetical notes:

Ivins and Dubose (2003) found. . . .

(Ivins & Dubose, 2003)

(Ivins & Dubose, 2003, pp. 210–213)

111. **Book, Four or More Authors or Editors—APA** For books with three to six authors, supply all authors' names in both the References list and in the first parenthetical note; subsequent notes will give only the first author's name and the abbreviation *et al.*

References

Gillespie, P., Gillam, A., Brown, L. F., & Stay, B. (Eds.). (2002). *Writing center
research: Extending the conversation.* Mahwah, NJ: Erlbaum.

Parenthetical notes:

First note: Gillespie, Gillam, Brown, and Stay (2002) found . . .

Subsequent notes: Gillespie et al. (2002) found. . . .

First note: (Gillespie, Gillam, Brown, & Stay, 2002)

Subsequent notes: (Gillespie et al., 2002)

When a work has seven or more authors, give the first six authors' names, followed by *et al.*, in the References list; for all parenthetical references, including the first, give only the first author's name, followed by *et al.* (including the period).

112. **Book, Group or Organizational Author—APA** Provide the full name of the group or organization in the text, in parenthetical notes, and in the References list.

References

Council of Biology Editors. (1994). *Scientific style and format: The CBE manual
for authors, editors, and publishers* (6th ed.). Cambridge: Cambridge
University Press.

Parenthetical notes:

The Council of Biology Editors (1994) recommends. . . .

(Council of Biology Editors, 1994, pp. 210–213)

You may include an abbreviation in the text (in parentheses) or in the notes (in square brackets) the first time you cite the source; subsequent references may then use the abbreviation only.

First note: The Council of Science Editors (CSE) (1994) recommends . . .

Subsequent notes: CSE (1994) suggests. . . .

First note: (Council of Science Editors [CSE], 1994)

Subsequent notes: (CSE, 1994)

113. **Book, Author Unknown—APA** The entry begins with the title of the book, followed by the year of publication, in parentheses, and a period. Notice that the book title is also italicized in the parenthetical note.

References

Illustrated atlas of the world. (1985). Chicago: Rand McNally.

Parenthetical notes:

In *Illustrated Atlas* (1985). . . .

(*Illustrated Atlas*, 1985, pp. 88–89)

When the author of a work is actually given as "Anonymous," cite the work that way in the References list and a parenthetical note.

(Anonymous, 1995)

114. **Book, Edited, Focus on the Editor—APA** APA uses an ampersand (&) to join the names of two editors or authors.

References

Behrens, L., & Rosen, L. J. (Eds.). (2003). *Writing and reading across the*
    curriculum (8th ed.). New York: Longman.

Parenthetical notes:

Behrens and Rosen (2003) observe. . . .

(Behrens & Rosen, 2003)

115. **Book, Edited, Focus on the Original Author—APA** Begin the entry with the author's last name and initials. Include the name of the editor(s) in parentheses after the title. List the entry in any parenthetical notes by the author's name.

References

Vygotsky, L. S. (1986). *Thought and language* (Rev. ed.) (A. Kozulin, Ed.).
    Boston: MIT Press.

Parenthetical notes:

Vygotsky (1986). . . .

(Vygotsky, 1986, pp. 88–89)

116. **Work of More Than One Volume—APA** List the total number of volumes in parentheses following the title in the References list to refer to the work as a whole; if you reference only one volume of a multivolume work, then specify the volume number and/or title. In the parenthetical note, include only the volume actually referenced unless you are referring to the work as a whole.

References

Brenner, F. (2003). *Diaspora: Homelands in Exile* (Vols. 1–2). New York:

HarperCollins.

Parenthetical notes:

Brenner (2003). . . .

(Brenner, 2003, Vol. 1, pp. 12–13)

117. **Book, Revised or Subsequent Edition—APA** Provide revision information, enclosed in parentheses, following the book title.

References

Edelmann, A. T. (1997). *Latin American government and politics* (Rev. ed.).

Homewood, IL: Dorsey.

Parenthetical notes:

Edelmann (1997) found. . . .

(Edelmann, 1997)

(Edelmann, 1997, p. 62)

COS
p. 285 118. **Book, Electronic—APA** Provide the electronic address of the home or entry page of a book published on the Internet. Note that no punctuation follows the URL in APA format. In the parenthetical note, include the chapter or section title or identifier in place of page numbers.

References

Rheingold, H. (1998). *The virtual community: Homesteading on the electronic*

frontier. Retrieved December 28, 2004, from

http://www.rheingold.com/vc/book

Parenthetical notes:

Rheingold (1998) claims. . . .

(Rheingold, 1998)

(Rheingold, 1998, chap. 3)

119. **Book, a Collection or Anthology—APA** Begin the entry with the editor(s') name(s), the description *Ed.* or *Eds.* enclosed in parentheses, and a period.

References

Pemberton, M. A., & Kinkead, J. (Eds.). (2003). *The center will hold: Critical perspectives on writing center scholarship.* Logan, UT: Utah State University Press.

Parenthetical notes:

Pemberton and Kinkead (2003) found. . . .

(Pemberton & Kinkead, 2003)

120. **Introductions, Prefaces, Forewords, etc.** Begin with the author's name, followed by the year of publication and, the title or description (for example, *Introduction*), capitalizing only the first word of the title and subtitle, if any, and any proper nouns.

References

Winchester, S. (1998). Preface. In *The professor and the madman: A tale of murder, insanity, and the making of the* Oxford English Dictionary (pp. xi–xiii). New York: HarperPerennial.

Parenthetical notes:

Winchester (1998) dramatizes. . . .

(Winchester, 1998)

If the author of the material you are citing is different from the author or editor of the book, include the name of the book's author(s) or editor(s) preceding the book title.

Hawisher, G. E. (2003). Foreword. In G. E. Kirsch, F. S. Maor, L. Massey, L. Nickoson-Massey, & M. P. Sheridan-Rabideau (Eds.), *Feminism and composition: A critical sourcebook* (pp. xv–xx). Boston: Bedford/ St. Martin's.

Parenthetical notes:

Hawisher (2003) introduces. . . .

(Hawisher, 2003)

121. **Work Within a Collection, Anthology, or Reader—APA** List the item on the References page by the author of the piece you are citing, not the editor(s) of the collection. Then provide the date of the particular selection, its title, the editor(s) of the collection, the title of the collection, the pages on which the selection appears, and publication information.

References

Lerner, N. (2003). Writing center assessment: Searching for the "proof" of our effectiveness. In M.A. Pemberton & J. Kinkead (Eds.), *The center will hold:*

Critical perspectives on writing center scholarship (pp. 58–73). Logan, UT: Utah State University Press.

Parenthetical notes:

Lerner (2003) found. . . .

(Lerner, 2003)

122. **Article in a Scholarly Journal—APA** Scholarly journals are usually identified by volume number or season (rather than day, week, or month of publication) and are paginated year by year, with a full year's work gathered and treated as one volume. Cite articles from these scholarly journals by providing author, date, title of article, and journal, volume, and page numbers.

References

Yancey, K. B. (1999). Looking back as we look forward: Historicizing writing assessment. *College Composition and Communication, 50,* 483–503.

Parenthetical notes:

Yancey (1999) observes. . . .

(Yancey, 1999, p. 411)

COS p. 285   123. **Article in an Electronic Journal—APA** Cite an article published in an electronic journal as you would a print journal, but include the URL and date of access. Note that no punctuation follows the URL. Instead of page numbers, the in-text note includes section titles and/or paragraph numbers.

References

Haynes, C. (2003). Rhetoric/slash/composition. *Enculturation, 5* (1). Retrieved July 10, 2004, from http://enculturation.gmu.edu/5_1/haynes.html

Parenthetical notes

Haynes (2003) concludes. . . .

(Haynes, 2003, Slash as Scapegoat section, para. 1)

COS p. 289   124. **Journal Article, Full-Text, Accessed Through Online Database—APA** Cite as you would the print article, including page numbers if available. Include the name of the electronic database and the date of retrieval. You may include the item or accession number, if desired, in parentheses following the retrieval statement.

References

Clark, M. M. (2004). Hemingway's early illness narratives and the lyric dimensions of "Now I Lay Me." *Narrative, 12* (2), 167–177. Retrieved May 24, 2004, from EBSCOhost database.

Parenthetical notes

Clark (2004) shows. . . .

(Clark, 2004, p. 175)

125. **Article in a Popular Magazine—APA** To cite a magazine published monthly, give the author's name, the date as given on the publication, the title of the article, the name of the magazine and volume number if applicable (in italics), and the page numbers.

References

O'Neal, W. (2004, October). Tropical storm! *Computer Gaming World,*

57–62.

Parenthetical notes:

O'Neal (2004) notes. . . .

(O'Neal, 2004)

To cite a weekly or biweekly periodical or magazine, give the author's name, the date (including month and day), the title of the article, the name of the magazine and volume number if applicable (in italics), and the page numbers.

Ghose, A. (2004, December 13). The great Sunni hope. *Time, 164,* 33.

Parenthetical notes:

Ghosh (2004) observes. . . .

(Ghosh, 2004)

(Ghosh, 2004, p. 33)

COS **p. 285** 126. **Article in an Online Magazine—APA** Cite the article as you would for an article in a print magazine, but include the date of access and the URL. Note that no punctuation follows the URL.

References

Sandel, M. J. (2004, April). The case against perfection. *The Atlantic Online.*

Retrieved July 10, 2004, from http://www.theatlantic.com/issues/2004/

04/sandel.htm

Parenthetical notes:

Sandel (2004) argues. . . .

(Sandel, 2004, para. 6)

127. **Article in a Newspaper—APA** If the article does not appear on consecutive pages in the newspaper, give all the page numbers, separated by a

comma. Note that abbreviations for *page* (*p.*) and *pages* (*pp.*) are used with newspaper entries.

References

Helfand, D., Kelley, D., & Merl, J. (2004, September 1). Eighteen school districts

      may face sanctions. *Los Angeles Times*, p. B4.

Parenthetical notes:

Helfand, Kelley, and Merl (2004) report. . . .

(Helfand, Kelley, & Merl, 2004, p. B4)

If the author is not named, then the entry begins with the title of the article, followed by the date of publication.

No child left behind: Schools on the underperformers list—and why. (2004,

      August 27). *Star Tribune* [Minneapolis, MN], p. 14A.

Parenthetical notes:

In the article "No Child Left Behind" (2004). . . .

("No Child," 2004)

COS
p. 285

128. Online Newspaper—APA Cite articles in online newspapers as you would print articles, but include the URL and date of access. Note there is no punctuation following the URL.

References

Holland, J. J. (2004, May 24). Kidnapped children alerts work but flawed.

      Boston.com. Retrieved July 10, 2004, from http://www.boston.com/news/

      nation/articles/2004/05/24/kidnapped_children_alerts_work_but_flawed

Parenthetical notes:

Holland (2004) notes. . . .

(Holland, 2004, para. 10)

COS
p. 285

129. Reviews—APA Brackets surround the description of an article that has no title. When a review has a title, the title precedes the bracketed description, which would still appear.

References

Farquhar, J. (1987). [Review of the book *Medical power and social knowledge*].

      American Journal of Psychology, 94, 256.

Parenthetical notes:

Farquhar (1987) observes. . . .

(Farquhar, 1987)

COS p. 287
130. Encyclopedia and Reference Articles—APA Cite an encyclopedia or reference article as you would an article in a print collection. For entries with no author, begin with the title or search term followed by the year of publication.

References

Rosenthal, M. (1996). Thomas Gainsborough. In J. Turner (Ed.), *The Dictionary of Art* (Vol. XI, pp. 906–913). London: MacMillan.

Parenthetical notes:

Rosenthal (1996) depicts. . . .

(Rosenthal, 1996)

To cite an entry in an online encyclopedia or reference work, include the URL and date of access.

Intellectual-property Law. (2004). In *Encyclopaedia Britannica Online*. Retrieved July 13, 2004, from http://search.eb.com/eb/article?eu=369684

131. Biblical Citation—APA APA does not require reference entries for citations of classical works or biblical references if these works are well-known. However, these works still need to be cited in a parenthetical note.

Parenthetical note: (John 13:29)

COS p. 284
132. Government Publication—APA If no individual author is listed, list the entry by the government agency or department responsible for the document. Include document or publication numbers if available.

References

U.S. General Accounting Office. (1999). National archives: Preserving electronic records in an era of rapidly changing technology (GAO/GDD-99-94). Washington, DC: U.S. Government Printing Office.

Parenthetical notes:

In a U.S. General Accounting Office (1999) report, . . .

(U.S. General Accounting Office, 1999)

COS p. 283
133. Web Page or Site—APA Give the author's name, the date of publication or last modification or *n.d.* (for not dated), and the title of the page, followed by the word *Retrieved,* the date of retrieval, and the Internet address. No period follows the URL.

References

Templeton, B. (n.d.). Ten big myths about copyright explained. Retrieved July 13, 2004, from http://www.templetons.com/brad/copymyths.html

Parenthetical notes:

Templeton (n.d.) introduces. . . .

(Templeton, n.d.)

When the author is not known, begin with the title of the page, followed by the date of publication or *n.d.* in parentheses if the page is not dated. If the Web page is part of a larger Web site, include the name of the host organization or other relevant information.

Law about copyright: An overview. (n.d.). Retrieved July 13, 2004, from

Cornell University Legal Information Institute Web site:

http://www.law.cornell.edu/topics/copyright.html

Parenthetical notes:

"Law About Copyright: An Overview" (n.d.) provides. . . .

(Law About Copyright, n.d.)

134. **Computer Software—APA** Do not underline or italicize the titles of software. List authors only when they own a proprietary right to the product. APA does not require most common software packages (such as Microsoft *Word*) to be included in the References list.

References

AnyDVD (Version 4.3.0.1) [Computer software]. (2004). St. John's Antigua.

Parenthetical note: In AnyDVD (2004). . . .

COS
pp. 289–90 135. **Email and Archived Discussions—APA** Electronic communications not stored or archived have limited use for researchers. APA style treats such information (and email) as personal communication. Because personal communications are not available to other researchers, no mention is made of them in the References list. Personal communications should, however, be acknowledged in the body of the paper in parenthetical notes. References to personal communications should include the initials as well as the last name of the speaker.

Parenthetical note:

According to J. G. Rice (personal communication, October 14, 2004). . . .

(J. G. Rice, personal communication, October 14, 2004)

Messages posted to newsgroup or electronic discussion lists and archives of virtual conference proceedings should be included in the list of references.

References

Rhodes, K. (2001, August 22). Re: Need for student consent. Message posted to

    Writing Program Administration List, archived at http://lists.asu.edu/ cgi-

    bin/wa?A2=ind0108&L=wpa-l&D=1&O=D&F=&S=&P=29383

Parenthetical note: Rhodes (2001). . . .

COS
pp. 286–87

136. **Film and Sound Recordings—APA** This is also the basic form for films, audiotapes, slides, charts, and other nonprint sources. The specific medium is described between brackets, as shown here for a motion picture. In most cases APA movie references are listed by the screenwriter, though that varies, as the example shows. Include the country of origin as well as the name of the studio.

References

Zeffirelli, F. (Director). (1968). *Romeo and Juliet* [Motion picture]. United States:

    Paramount Pictures.

Parenthetical notes:

Zeffirelli (1968) features. . . .

(Zeffirelli, 1968)

Music is ordinarily listed by the composer, followed by the date of copyright and the title of the song. You may include the name of the recording artist if different from the composer and the name of the album or CD on which the song is recorded, identifying the medium, followed by the location and label. Include the recording date in parentheses if different from the coypright date.

Dylan, B. (1989). What was it you wanted? [Recorded by Willie Nelson]. On

    Across the borderline [CD]. New York: Columbia.

Parenthetical note: In the song "What Was It You Wanted?" (Dylan, 1989,

    track 10). . . .

25c   Sample APA Paper

In the social sciences, articles published in professional journals often follow a form designed to connect new findings to previous research. Your instructor will usually indicate whether you should follow this structure for your paper or report.

The following APA-style research report by Chad Briggs and faculty adviser Fred Ribich originally appeared in volume 1 of *Psych-E*, an online journal of psychology for undergraduates. We have modified the essay to show how it would look as a paper a student might turn in for a college course. Because of space limitations, we've also shortened the article slightly. But we have not altered its basic style, which reflects the conventions of the social sciences, particularly a heavier use of passive voice than might appear in an MLA or Chicago-style article.

For easy reference, we've numbered the paragraphs (these numbers would *not* appear in an actual APA paper).

CHECKLIST 25.5

The Components of a Social Science Report

○ **An abstract**—a concise summary of the research article.

○ **A review of literature**—a survey of published research that has a bearing on the hypothesis advanced in the research report. The review establishes the context for the research essay.

○ **A hypothesis**—an introduction to the paper that identifies the assumption to be tested and provides a rationale for studying it.

○ **An explanation of methods**—a detailed description of the procedures used in the research. Since the validity of the research depends on how the data were gathered, this is a critical section for readers assessing the report.

○ **Results**—a section reporting the data, often given through figures, charts, graphs, and so on. The reliability of the data is explained here, but little comment is made on its implications.

○ **Discussion/conclusions**—a section in which the research results are interpreted and analyzed.

○ **References**—an alphabetical list of research materials and articles cited in the report.

○ **Appendixes**—a section of materials germane to the report but too lengthy to include in the body of the paper.

The Relationship Between Test Anxiety, Sleep Habits, and
Self-Perceived Academic Competency

Chad S. Briggs[1] and Fred Ribich

1. Email: briggs@siu.edu

Wartburg College

CHECKLIST 25.6

Title Page for a Paper—APA

APA style requires a separate title page; use the facing page as a model and review the following checklist.

○ Type your report on white bond paper. Preferred typefaces (when you have a choice) include Times Roman, American Typewriter, and Courier.

○ Arrange and center the title of your paper, your name, and the name of your school.

○ Use the correct form of the title, capitalizing all important words and all words of four letters or more. Articles, conjunctions, and prepositions are not capitalized unless they are four letters or more. Do not underline the title or use all capitals.

○ Give your first name, middle initial, and last name.

○ Number the title page and all subsequent pages in the upper right-hand corner. Place a short title for the paper on the same line as the page number as shown; the short title consists of the first two or three key words of the title.

Abstract

One hundred fifty-eight college students completed questionnaires and tests that measure test anxiety, sleep habits, and self-perceived academic competency. It was hypothesized that test anxiety and irregular sleep patterns will lower college students' self-perceived academic competency. The results showed that high test anxiety and poor sleep habits negatively affected students' self-perceived academic competency. It was also found that high self-perceived academic competency was positively correlated with GPA (a measure of performance). This study shows the need for further research that deals with the relationship between self-perceived academic competency and academic performance. This will enable professionals to look in more detail at another variable that affects academic performance.

CHECKLIST 25.7

Abstract for a Paper—APA

○ Abstracts are common in papers using APA style.

○ Place the abstract on a separate page, after the title page.

○ Center the word *Abstract* at the top of the page.

○ Place the short title of the essay and the page number (2) in the upper right-hand corner.

○ Double-space the abstract.

○ Do not indent the first line of the abstract. Type it in block form.

○ Strict APA form limits abstracts to 960 characters or fewer.

The Relationship Between Test Anxiety, Sleep Habits, and

Self-Perceived Academic Competency

Introduction

¶1   Self-perceived academic competency has been shown to be a

significant contributor to the academic success of college students.

Bandura (1986) defines self-perceived competency as "people's

judgments of their capabilities to organize and execute courses of

action required to attain designated types of performances" (p. 10). It

has been found by Lee and Babko (1994) that when in a difficult

situation such as a college-type test, a person with a strong sense of

self-perceived academic competency will devote more attention and

effort to the task at hand, therefore trying harder and persisting

longer, than will those who have lower levels of self-perceived

competency.

¶2   Self-perceived academic competency can be affected by a

plethora of variables. In this study, the variables of test anxiety and

sleep habits will be examined in relationship to college students' self-

perceived academic competency.

¶3   Lewis (1970) defines anxiety as "an unpleasant emotion

experienced as dread, scare, alarm, fright, trepidation, horror or

panic" (p. 63). Test anxiety, then, is the debilitating experience of

anxiety, as described by Lewis, during the preparation for a test or

during the test itself. Although anxiety is often detrimental, it may

be beneficial if it is not extreme. Simpson, Parker, and Harrison

(1995) convey this through two well-known principles of anxiety: "A

minimal amount of anxiety" (an optimal amount is more accurate)

"can mobilize human beings to respond rapidly and efficiently," while

"excessive amounts of anxiety may foster poor response and

sometimes inhibit response" (p. 700). Knox, Schacht, and Turner

CHECKLIST 25.8

The Body of a Research Paper—APA

The body of the APA paper runs uninterrupted until the separate References page. The first page of an APA paper will look like the facing page, except for the paragraph numbers, included here for reference only.

○ Repeat the title of your paper, exactly as it appears on the title page, on the first page of the research essay.

○ Be sure the title is centered and properly capitalized.

○ Begin the body of the essay two lines (a double space) below the title.

○ Double-space the body of the essay.

○ Use at least one-inch margins at the sides, top, and bottom of this and all subsequent pages.

○ Indent the first line of each paragraph five to seven spaces.

○ Indent long quotations (more than forty words) in a block five to seven spaces from the left margin. In student papers, APA permits long quotations to be single spaced.

○ Include the short title of the essay and the page number (3) in the upper right-hand corner. Number all subsequent pages the same way.

○ Do not hyphenate words at the right-hand margin. Do not justify the right-hand margin.

○ Label figures and tables correctly. Be sure to mention them in the body of your text: (*see Figure 1*).

○ Provide copyright/permission data for figures or tables borrowed from other sources.

(1993) state that test anxiety can include performance anxiety and content (e.g., math) anxiety. Both of these make it hard for students to concentrate and perform adequately on tests. Knox et al. (1993) also recognize the consequences of poorly managed test anxiety. "Failure to manage test anxiety can result in failing courses, dropping out of school, a negative self-concept and a low earning potential" (p. 295).

¶4   Research on test anxiety has identified three models that explain the origin of test anxiety: (1) The problem lies not in taking the test, but in preparing for the test. Kleijn, Van der Ploeg, and Topman (1994) have identified this as the learning-deficit model. According to this model, the student with high test anxiety tends to have or use inadequate learning or study skills while in the preparation stage of exam taking. (2) The second model is termed the interference model (Kleijn et al., 1994). The problem for people in this model is that during tests, individuals with test anxiety focus on task-irrelevant stimuli that negatively affect their performance (Sarason, 1975). The attention diverted from the task at hand can be categorized into two types, according to Sarason. The first type of distraction can be classified as physical and includes an increase in awareness of heightened autonomic activity (e.g., sweaty palms, muscle tension). The second type of distraction includes inappropriate cognitions, such as saying to oneself, "Others are finishing before me, so I must not know the material," or "I'm stupid, I won't pass." The presence of either of these two task-irrelevant cognitions will affect the quality of a student's performance. (3) The third model of test anxiety includes people who think they have prepared adequately for a test, but in reality, did not. These people question their abilities after the test, which creates anxiousness during the next test.

¶5   Sleep patterns are believed to be more irregular among college students, and irregular sleep patterns are believed to affect both self-perceived academic competency and academic performance. Sleep, therefore, seems to be an important factor in a college student's success and self-perceived ability. An optimal sleep pattern, as defined here, is one in which an individual goes to bed and wakes up at about the same time every day while allowing an adequate amount of time in each of the five stages of the sleep cycle. The function of the body that keeps our sleep patterns in this constant waking and sleeping cycle is called the circadian rhythm. During the night a person enters into and out of five different stages of sleep, the most important being REM (rapid eye movement) sleep. When the circadian rhythm of a person's sleep is thrown off, less time is spent in REM sleep (Lahey, 1995). People deprived of REM sleep are likely to experience irritability, inefficiency, and fatigue (Hobson, 1989; Webb & Bonnet, 1979). Furthermore, they are more likely to experience irritability and fatigue when switched from the day shift to the night shift rather than from the night shift to the day shift (Wilkinson, Allison, Feeney, & Kaminska, 1989). This phenomenon known as "jet lag" is consistent with our natural tendency to lengthen our circadian rhythms. For example, one experiment demonstrated that participants' circadian rhythms continued even when they were isolated in constantly lighted chambers. However, their rhythms quickly changed to a twenty-five-hour cycle (Aschoff, 1981; Horne, 1988). This phenomenon suggests that college students are particularly prone to sleep deprivation because college students are notorious for "cramming" information into their memories the night before a test. To do this, they stay up longer and wake up earlier than they usually would. The impact of sleep deprivation on academic performance is negative; consequently, it is hypothesized that students with poor sleep habits will have a lower level of self-perceived academic competency since each test is taken in a state marked by inefficient, irritable, or fatigued thinking.

¶6   While there have been numerous studies on self-perceived competency and academic performance, on test anxiety and performance, and on sleep and performance, little direct information exists on the relationship among these variables taken together. It is believed that in our findings it will be shown that test anxiety and irregular sleep patterns will lower college students' self-perceived academic competency.

Methods

Participants

¶7   One hundred fifty-eight college students participated in the study. There were 89 first- and second-year students and 64 third- and fourth-year students. Among the participants, there were 67 males and 89 females. Demographic data obtained from the participants included gender, age, year in school, major, and their estimated current grade point average (GPA).

Instruments

¶8   The Test Attitude Inventory (TAI), created by Spielberger (1980), was used to measure test anxiety. The TAI subscales measure self-reported worry and emotionality. The TAI contains twenty items that are situation-specific to academically related test situations and environments. A five-point Likert scale (5 represented "usually" and 1 represented "never") was used to obtain the participants' responses.

¶9   To measure sleep habits, the Sleep Questionnaire constructed by Domino, Blair, and Bridges (1984) was used. The questionnaire contains fifty-four questions pertaining to various sleep and related behaviors. The same five-point Likert scale that was used for the TAI was used by this instrument as well. In addition, three closed-ended questions help reveal the approximate time of sleep onset, the approximate time of awakening, and whether or not the participants take naps during the day.

¶10   The College Academic Self-Efficacy Scale (CASES), created by Owen and Froman (1988), was administered to determine the degree of confidence participants believe they have in various academic settings (e.g., note taking during class or using the library). A five-point Likert Scale was also used here, where 5 represented "a lot of confidence," and 1 represented "little confidence." This scale consists of thirty-three questions covering a wide variety of academic settings and situations that are pertinent to the students' overall academic self-competency rating. Owen and Froman (1988) found the alpha internal consistency of the CASES, in two different trials, to be .9 and .92.

Procedure

¶11   Packets were prepared which contained a demographic data sheet, consent form, test anxiety inventory, CASES, and the sleep habits questionnaire, in that order. Next, professors in the selected classes were given information on the purpose of the study, shown the survey instruments, and told approximately how long it would take for students to complete the entire packet (20–30 minutes). We were invited to six different class meetings. The students were informed verbally that the purpose of the study was to examine the relationships between test anxiety, sleep habits, and self-perceived academic competency. The students were also informed that

Test Anxiety   8

participation in the experiment was completely voluntary and that their responses would be kept anonymous. The students who agreed to participate in the study signed a consent form. These students then filled out the demographic data and the four surveys. The participants were then thanked for their willingness to participate in the study.

Results

¶12   The mean score for test anxiety was 52.67 (out of a possible 100), with a high score of 95 and a low score of 24. In order to see if differences existed between people with high test anxiety and low test anxiety, the participants' test anxiety scores were divided into three levels (low, moderate, and high) and compared to the CASES using an ANOVA. Those people in the low test anxiety group scored 124.50 (a higher score indicates greater self-perceived academic competency) on the CASES. Those people in the moderate test anxiety group scored 113.75 on the CASES. Those people in the high test anxiety group scored 106.21 on the CASES. The p-value was found to be .001. This finding is represented in Figure 1.

It was also found that there were significant differences between test anxiety groups and GPA (a measure of performance).

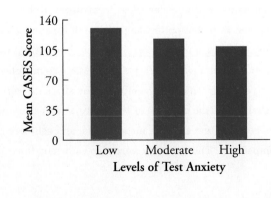

FIGURE 1. Test Anxiety CASES Scores

Test Anxiety   9

The low test anxiety group reported having a 3.29 GPA, the group that reported moderate anxiety had a 3.13 GPA, and the group with high test anxiety reported having a 3.02 GPA. The *p*-value was found to be .05.

¶13   Similarly, the sleep scores were also divided into three groups (bad sleep, moderate sleep, and good sleep) for the purpose of comparing mean differences. The mean sleep score was 130.28 (out of 200), with a high score of 163 and a low score of 90. The lower sleep scores represent better sleep habits. The people in the bad sleep group scored 110.42 on the CASES, the moderate sleepers scored 114.98 on ¶14   the CASES, and the people in the good sleep group scored 119.33. This is represented in Figure 2.

¶15   Furthermore, grade point averages were significantly different depending on which sleep group the student was associated with. Students in the bad sleep group reported having a 3.02 GPA, while students in the moderate sleep group reported having a 3.11 GPA. Also, those students who fell into the good sleep group reported having a 3.31 GPA. The *p*-value was found to be .03.

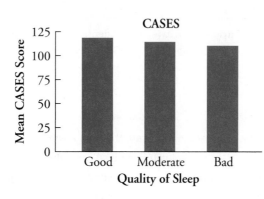

FIGURE 2. Sleep Quality and CASES Scores

¶16   Correlations were also figured for the following variables
(shown in Table 1): quality of sleep habits, test anxiety, self-perceived
academic competency, and GPA. It was found that the quality of sleep
habits and test anxiety were negatively correlated at the –.26 level
(p-value of .001). The quality of sleep habits was also found to be
positively correlated with self-perceived academic competency at the
.19 level (p-value of .016). Additionally, it was found that the quality
of sleep habits was positively correlated with GPA at the .18 level
(p-value of .024). Test anxiety and self-perceived academic
competency were negatively correlated at the –.41 level (p-value of
.001). GPA and test anxiety were negatively correlated at the –.21
level (p-value of .01). Lastly, self-perceived academic competency and
GPA were positively correlated at the .47 level (p-value of .001). This
can be seen in Table 1.

Table 1

*Correlations Calculated to Find the Relationships Between Main
Variables in the Study*

	GPA	TA	CASES	Sleep
GPA	1.0			
TA	–.21**	1.0		
CASES	.47***	–.41***	1.0	
Sleep	.18*	–.26***	.19*	1.0

Note. The main variables include the students' GPA, test anxiety (TA),
self-perceived academic competency (CASES), and sleep habits (Sleep).
*$p < 0.05$
**$p < 0.01$
***$p < 0.001$

Discussion

¶17   The findings presented indicate that bad sleep habits and high
test anxiety negatively affect self-perceived academic competency, as
was hypothesized. Additionally, it was found that low self-perceived
academic competency negatively affected students' GPA.

¶18   Quality of sleep habits was found to be a factor in self-perceived academic competence. If college students do experience REM sleep deprivation more than the average population, then the findings of this study need to be passed on to college students. The findings in this study suggest that college students with poor sleep habits may perceive themselves as having lower academic competency. The study also showed that self-perceived academic competency was positively correlated to academic performance. Thus, according to Hobson (1989), Webb & Bonnet (1979), and this study, those college students who do have poor sleep habits will negatively affect their academic performance.

¶19   It was also found that test anxiety and grade point average are negatively correlated, and that quality of sleep and grade point average are positively correlated. This finding, and the fact that quality of sleep and test anxiety are negatively related, suggest interrelationships among the variables test anxiety, sleep habits, self-perceived academic competency, and academic performance. This result highlights the fact that professors need to instruct their students on how to manage test anxiety. Students also need to be aware of the effects that poor sleep and low self-perceived academic competency have on academic performance. Thus, the phrase "I think I can, I think I can . . ." may be beneficial only if students reduce their test anxiety and develop better sleep habits. More research needs to be done to find other variables that affect self-perceived academic competence.

Test Anxiety   12

References

Aschoff, J. (1981). *Handbook of behavioral neurobiology* (Vol. 4).
    Biological rhythms. New York: Plenum.

Bandura, A. (1986). *Social foundations of thought and action: A social
    cognitive theory.* Englewood Cliffs, NJ: Prentice Hall.

Domino, G., Blair, G., & Bridges, A. (1984). Subjective assessment of
    sleep by sleep questionnaire. *Perceptual and Motor Skills, 59,*
    163–170.

Hobson, J. A. (1989). *Sleep.* New York: Scientific American Library.

Horne, J. (1988). *Why we sleep: The functions of sleep in humans and
    other mammals.* New York: Oxford University Press.

Kleijn, W. C., Van der Ploeg, H. M., & Topman, R. M. (1994). Cognition,
    study habits, test anxiety, and academic performance.
    Psychological Reports, 75, 1219–1226.

Knox, D., Schacht, C., & Turner, J. (1993). Virtual reality: A proposal
    for treating test anxiety in college students. *College Student
    Journal, 27,* 294–296.

Lahey, B. B. (1995). In M. Lange, S. Connors, A. Fuerste, K. M. Huinker-
    Timp, & L. Fuller (Eds.), *Psychology: An Introduction.* Dubuque,
    IA: Brown & Benchmark.

Lee, C., & Babko, P. (1994). Self-efficacy beliefs: Comparison of five
    measures. *Journal of Applied Psychology, 79,* 364–369.

Lewis, A. (1970). The ambiguous word "anxiety." *International Journal
    of Psychiatry, 9,* 62–79.

Owen, S. V., & Froman, R. D. (1988). *Development of an academic self-
    efficacy scale.* Paper presented at the annual meeting of the
    National Council on Measurement in Education, New Orleans, LA.

Sarason, I. G. (1975). Test anxiety and the self-disclosing coping model.
    Journal of Consulting and Clinical Psychology, 43, 148–152.

CHECKLIST 25.9

> ### References Pages—APA

Sources contributing directly to the paper are listed alphabetically on a separate page immediately after the body of the essay.

○ Center the title (*References*) at the top of the page.

○ All sources mentioned in the text of the paper must appear in the References list, except personal communications; similarly, every source listed in the References must be mentioned in the paper.

○ Arrange the items in the References list alphabetically by the last name of the author. Give only initials for first names. If no author is given for a work, list and alphabetize it by the first word in the title, excluding articles (*A, An, The*).

○ The first line of each entry is flush with the left-hand margin. Subsequent lines in an entry are indented five spaces or one-half inch.

○ The list is ordinarily double spaced. In student papers, APA style does permit single spacing of individual entries; double spacing is preserved between the single-spaced items.

○ Punctuate items in the list carefully. Do not forget the period at the end of each entry, except those entries that terminate with an electronic address.

○ In the References list, capitalize only the first word and any proper names in the title of a book or article. Within a title, capitalize the first word after a colon.

○ When you have two or more entries by the same author, list them by year of publication, from earliest to latest. If an author publishes two works in the same year, list them alphabetically by title and place a lowercase letter immediately after the year: (*1998a*).

Test Anxiety   13

Simpson, M. L., Parker, P. W., & Harrison, A. W. (1995). Differential performance on Taylor's Manifest Anxiety Scale in black private college freshmen, a partial report. *Perceptual and Motor Skills, 80,* 699–702.

Spielberger, C. D. (1980). *Preliminary professional manual for the Test Attitude Inventory.* Palo Alto, CA: Consulting Psychologists Press.

Webb, W. B., & Bonnet, M. H. (1979). Sleep and dreams. In M. E. Meyer (Ed.), *Foundations of contemporary psychology.* New York: Oxford University Press.

Wilkinson, R., Allison, S., Feeney, M., & Kaminska, Z. (1989). Alertness of night nurses: Two shift systems compared. *Ergonomics, 32,* 281–292.

CHAPTER 26

CMS Documentation

Writers who prefer full footnotes or endnotes rather than in-text notes often use the documentation style recommended in *The Chicago Manual of Style.* Basic procedures for the CMS documentary-note system are spelled out in the following sections. If you encounter documentation problems not discussed below or prefer CMS's author-date style, refer to the full manual or to Kate L. Turabian's *A Manual for Writers of Term Papers, Theses, and Dissertations,* sixth edition (1996), or check *The Chicago Manual of Style* FAQ at http://www.press.uchicago.edu/Misc/Chicago/cmosfaq.html.

A Note on Citing Electronic Sources

CMS documentation offers specific forms for several electronic sources in Chapter 17 of The *Chicago Manual of Style* (15th ed., 2003). However, when citing such items, you may want to use the documentation style recommended by the *Columbia Guide to Online Style* instead, described in Chapter 23. It was developed explicitly for research in electronic documents and is designed to work *with* CMS-style formats for citing print-based sources. CMS items that have a Columbia equivalent are marked in the CMS Form Directory in this chapter with a distinctive icon: COS p. 000 . Consult your instructor about using Columbia style for electronic sources.

Because notes in CMS humanities style include full publishing information, bibliographies are optional in CMS-style papers. However, both note and bibliography forms are described in the following section.

26a CMS notes

CMS documentation involves two basic steps.

Step 1: In the text of your paper, place a raised number after a sentence or clause you need to document. These note numbers follow any punctuation mark except a dash, and they run consecutively throughout a paper. A direct quotation from Brian Urquhart's *Ralph Bunche: An American Life* is followed here by a raised note number.

> Ralph Bunche never wavered in his belief that the races in America had to
> learn to live together: "In all of his experience of racial discrimination
> Bunche never allowed himself to become bitter or to feel racial hatred."[1]

The number is keyed to the first note (see below). To create this raised, or superscript, number, select "Superscript" from your word-processing font options or select the "endnote" or "footnote" feature in your word processor.

Step 2: Link every note number to a footnote or endnote. The basic CMS note consists of a note number, the author's name (in normal order), the title of the work, full publication information within parentheses, and the appropriate page numbers or the URL and date of access for electronic sources (see also Chapter 23). The first line of the note is indented like a paragraph.

> 1. Brian Urquhart, *Ralph Bunche: An American Life* (New York:
> Norton, 1993), 435.

To document particular types of sources, including books, articles, magazines, and electronic sources, see the CMS Form Directory on page 379.

CMS style allows you to choose whether to place your notes at the bottom of each page (footnotes) or in a single list titled "Notes" at the end of your paper (endnotes). Endnotes are more common now than footnotes and easier to manage. Individual footnotes are single spaced, with double spaces between them.

Use the following guidelines when preparing notes.

1. **When two or more sources are cited within a single sentence,** the note numbers appear right after the statements they support.

   > While some in the humanities fear that electronic technologies may
   > make the "notion of wisdom" obsolete,[2] others suggest that technology
   > must be the subject of serious study even in elementary and secondary
   > school.[3]

   The notes for this sentence would appear in this form:

   > 2. Sven Birkerts, *The Gutenberg Elegies: The Fate of Reading in
   > an Electronic Age* (Boston: Faber & Faber, 1994), 139.

   > 3. Neil Postman, "The Word Weavers/The World Makers," in *The
   > End of Education: Redefining the Value of School* (New York: Alfred A.
   > Knopf, 1995), 172–93.

   Observe that note 2 documents a particular quotation while note 3 refers to a full chapter in a book.

2. **When you cite a work several times in a paper,** the first note gives full information about author(s), title, and publication.

> 1. Helen Wilkinson, "It's Just a Matter of Time," *Utne Reader,*
> May/June 1995, 66–67.

Then, in shorter papers, subsequent citations require only the last name of the author(s) and page number(s).

> 2. Wilkinson, 66.

In longer papers the entry may also include a shortened title to make references from page to page clearer.

> 3. Wilkinson, "Matter of Time," 66.

When you cite the same work again immediately after a full note, you may use the Latin abbreviation *Ibid.* (meaning "in the same place") followed by the page number(s) of the citation.

> 4. Newt Gingrich, "America and the Third Wave Information Age,"
> in *To Renew America* (New York, HarperCollins, 1995), 51.

> 5. Ibid., 55.

To avoid using *Ibid.* when documenting the same source in succession, give a page reference—for example (*55*)—within the text itself. When successive citations are to the same page, *Ibid.* alone can be used.

> 4. Newt Gingrich, "America and the Third Wave Information Age,"
> in *To Renew America* (New York: HarperCollins, 1995), 51.

> 5. Ibid.

Here's how a sequence of notes using several sources and subsequent short references might look. Notice that note 4 refers to the Gingrich chapter and notes 6 and 7 refer to the Wilkinson article.

Notes

> 1. Helen Wilkinson, "It's Just a Matter of Time," *Utne Reader,*
> May/June 1995, 66–67.
> 2. Paul Osterman, "Getting Started," *Wilson Quarterly,* Autumn
> 1994, 46–55.
> 3. Newt Gingrich, "America and the Third Wave Information Age,"
> in *To Renew America* (New York: HarperCollins, 1995), 51.
> 4. Ibid., 54.

5. Wilkinson, 66.

6. Ibid.

7. Ibid., 67.

8. Osterman, 48–49.

9. Gingrich, 60.

26b CMS bibliographies

Because CMS notes are quite comprehensive, a Works Cited or Bibliography list may be optional, depending on the assignment; check with your instructor or editor about including such a list. The Works Cited list includes only works actually mentioned in your paper; a Bibliography list also includes works consulted in preparing the project but not cited. Individual entries in a Works Cited or Bibliography are listed alphabetically and single spaced, with a double space between each entry (see the sample CMS paper on pages 388–393).

When an author has more than one work in the bibliography, those works are listed alphabetically under the author's name in this form.

Fischer, David Hackett. *The Great Wave: Price Revolutions and the*

Rhythm of History. New York: Oxford University Press, 1996.

---. *Liberty and Freedom.* New York: Oxford University Press, 2005.

---. *Washington's Crossing.* New York: Oxford University Press, 2004.

Checklists 26.1 through 26.4 provide general information about citing sources of information in CMS style.

CHECKLIST 26.1

Basic Format—Books

A typical CMS Works Cited/Bibliography entry for a book includes the following basic information.

○ Author(s), last name first, followed by a period and one space.
○ Title of the work, italicized, followed by a period and one space.
○ Place of publication, followed by a colon and one space.
○ Publisher, followed by a comma and one space.
○ Date of publication, followed by a period.

Author   Title

Green, Carol C. *Chimborazo: The Confederacy's Largest Hospital.*
   Knoxville: University of Tennessee Press, 2004.

Indent subsequent lines one-half inch or five spaces   Place of publication   Publisher   Date   Period

CHECKLIST 26.2

Basic Format—Magazines

A typical CMS Works Cited/Bibliography entry for an article in a popular magazine includes the following basic information.

○ Author(s), last name first, followed by a period and one space.
○ Title of the article, followed by a period and enclosed between quotation marks.
○ Name of the periodical, italicized, followed by a comma and one space.
○ Date of publication, followed by a comma and one space. Do not abbreviate months.
○ Page and/or location, followed by a period. Pages should be inclusive.

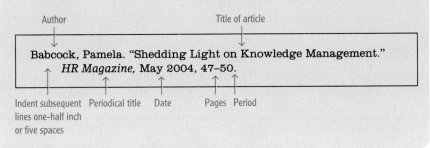

Author   Title of article

Babcock, Pamela. "Shedding Light on Knowledge Management."
  HR Magazine, May 2004, 47–50.

Indent subsequent Periodical title Date Pages Period
lines one-half inch
or five spaces

CHECKLIST 26.3

Basic Format—Scholarly Journals

A typical CMS Works Cited/Bibliography entry for an article in a scholarly journal (where the pagination is continuous throughout a year) includes the following basic information.

○ Author(s), last name first, followed by a period and one space.
○ Title of the article, followed by a period (or other final punctuation mark) and enclosed between quotation marks.
○ Name of the periodical, italicized, followed by one space.
○ Volume number, followed by one space.
○ Date of publication in parentheses, followed by a colon and one space.
○ Page or location, followed by a period. Page numbers should be inclusive, from the first page of the article to the last, including notes and bibliography. *(Continued)*

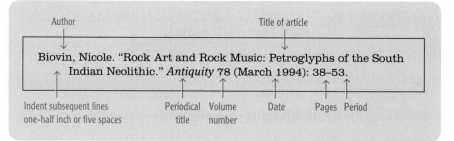

CHECKLIST 26.4

Basic Format—Electronic Sources

A typical CMS Works Cited/Bibliography entry for an electronic source is arranged and punctuated like a printed source, with some additions.

○ Author and title, arranged and punctuated as for a printed source.

○ Publication information (if available), including city, publisher, and date for books or volume number/date for periodicals, followed by a period and one space.

○ The URL (that is, the address that begins *http*) for Internet sources, or a description of the medium (for example, *CD-ROM*).

○ The date of access for material that may change frequently.

Because there are so many variations to these general entries, you will want to check the CMS Form Directory that follows for the correct format of any unusual entry. Note that you may need to consult more than one model for a particular type of source.

26c CMS Form Directory

Here you will find the CMS note and bibliography forms for more than twenty types of sources. For each type, you will find sample note forms, complete with page references, followed by the corresponding bibliography entries. The COS icon next to an entry indicates that a Columbia Online Style (COS) form is available for that source (see Chapter 23 on COS).

137. **Book, One Author or Editor—CMS** Give the author's name, the title of the book in italics, and the publication information. Notice that footnotes and endnotes do not invert the author's name and that they use commas to separate information and parentheses to enclose the publication information. Notes include page references for quotations or the exact location of information. The bibliography format uses periods to separate elements and does not enclose the publication information in parentheses, and the author's name is inverted and alphabetized by last name. Page numbers are omitted unless a specific article or chapter is being referenced.

1. Jeffrey S. Young, *Forbes Greatest Technology Stories: Inspiring Tales of the Entrepreneurs and Inventors Who Revolutionized Modern Business* (New York: John Wiley & Sons, 1998), 238.

Young, Jeffrey S. *Forbes Greatest Technology Stories: Inspiring Tales of the Entrepreneurs and Inventors Who Revolutionized Modern Business.* New York: John Wiley & Sons, 1998.

138. Book, Two or Three Authors or Editors—CMS For footnotes and endnotes, list the names of the authors in normal order; for bibliography citations, invert only the first author's name.

2. Ron White and Michael White, *MP3 Underground: The Inside Guide to MP3 Music, Napster, RealJukebox, MusicMatch, and Hidden Internet Songs* (Indianapolis, IN: Que, 2001), 124.

White, Ron, and Michael White. *MP3 Underground: The Inside Guide to MP3 Music, Napster, RealJukebox, MusicMatch, and Hidden Internet Songs.* Indianapolis, IN: Que, 2001.

139. Book, Four or More Authors or Editors—CMS Use *et al.* or *and others* after the first author's name in a note, but list all authors in the bibliography when that is convenient.

3. Philip Curtin and others, eds., *African History* (Boston: Little, Brown, 1978), 77.

Curtin, Philip, Steve Feierman, Leonard Thompson, and Jan Vansina, eds. *African History.* Boston: Little, Brown, 1978.

140. Book, Group or Organizational Author—CMS List the organization or group name as the author, even if it is repeated in the title or publication information.

4. Council of Biology Editors, *Scientific Style and Format: The CBE Manual for Authors, Editors, and Publishers,* 6th ed. (Cambridge: Cambridge University Press, 1994).

Council of Biology Editors. *Scientific Style and Format: The CBE Manual for Authors, Editors, and Publishers.* 6th ed. Cambridge: Cambridge University Press, 1994.

141. Book, Author Unknown—CMS List the book by its title, alphabetized by the first major word (excluding *The, A,* or *An*).

    5. *The Baseball Encyclopedia: The Complete and Definitive Record of Major League Baseball*, 9th ed. (New York: Macmillan, 1993).

The Baseball Encyclopedia: The Complete and Definitive Record of Major League Baseball, 9th ed. New York: Macmillan, 1993.

142. Book, Edited—Focus on the Editor—CMS When you cite an edited work by the editor's name, identify the original author after the title of the work.

    6. Scott Elledge, ed., *Paradise Lost*, by John Milton (New York: Norton, 1975).

Elledge, Scott, ed. *Paradise Lost*, by John Milton. New York: Norton, 1975.

143. Book, Edited—Focus on the Original Author—CMS In footnotes or endnotes, use the abbreviation *ed.* for *edited by.* In the bibliography entry, either use the abbreviation or spell it out.

    7. William Shakespeare, *The Complete Works of Shakespeare*, 4th ed., ed. David Bevington (New York: Longman, 1997).

Shakespeare, William. *The Complete Works of Shakespeare*. 4th ed. Edited by David Bevington. New York: Longman, 1997.

144. Work of More Than One Volume—CMS Indicate the total number of volumes after the title of the work when you are citing the work as a whole.

    8. Frederic Brenner, *Diaspora: Homelands in Exile*, 2 vols. (New York: HarperCollins, 2003).

Brenner, Frederic. *Diaspora: Homelands in Exile*. 2 vols. New York: HarperCollins, 2003.

When citing only a particular volume, include the specific volume number.

    9. Frederic Brenner, *Diaspora: Homelands in Exile* (New York: HarperCollins, 2003), 1:12–13.

Brenner, Frederic. *Diaspora: Homelands in Exile*. Vol. 1. New York: HarperCollins, 2003.

145. **Work in a Series—CMS** Do not underline or italicize a series name. You may omit series titles if the work can be located without it, and you may omit the name(s) of series editor(s).

> 10. Grayson Kirk and Nils H. Wessell, eds., *The Soviet Threat: Myths and Realities,* Proceedings of the Academy of Political Science 33 (New York: Academy of Political Science, 1978), 62.

> Kirk, Grayson, and Nils H. Wessell, eds. *The Soviet Threat: Myths and Realities.* Proceedings of the Academy of Political Science 33. New York: Academy of Political Science, 1978.

146. **Work in Second or Subsequent Edition—CMS** Include the edition number and the abbreviation *ed.* following the title. Do not italicize.

> 11. University of Chicago Press, *The Chicago Manual of Style,* 15th ed. (Chicago: University of Chicago Press, 2003), 676.

> University of Chicago Press. *The Chicago Manual of Style,* 15th ed. Chicago: University of Chicago Press, 2003.

COS p. 269 147. **Book, Electronic—CMS** For books published on the World Wide Web, include the URL and the access date.

> 12. Howard Rheingold, *The Virtual Community: Homesteading on the Electronic Frontier* (1998), http://www.rheingold.com/vc/book (accessed May 20, 2004).

> Rheingold, Howard. *The Virtual Community: Homesteading on the Electronic Frontier.* 1998. http://www.rheingold.com/vc/book (accessed May 20, 2004).

For electronic books in other formats (on CD-ROM or downloaded in specific e-book formats, for example), include a designation of the format.

> 13. Vernor Vinge, *A Fire Upon the Deep* (New York: St. Martin's Press, 2002), Microsoft Reader e-book.

> Vinge, Vernor. *A Fire Upon the Deep.* New York: St. Martin's Press, 2002. Microsoft Reader e-book.

148. **Introductions, Prefaces, Forewords, etc.—CMS** When referring to a section such as an introduction written by the author or editor of the book, include the generic title (e.g., *introduction*) preceding the book title.

14. James Inman, preface to *Computers and Writing: The Cyborg Era* (Mahwah, NJ: Lawrence Erlbaum, 2004), ix.

Inman, James. Preface to *Computers and Writing: The Cyborg Era*. Mahwah, NJ: Lawrence Erlbaum, 2004.

If the reference is to a section written by someone other than the author or editor of the book, then include the name(s) of the book's author(s) or editor(s) after the book title.

149. Article or Selection from a Reader or an Anthology—CMS Give the author and title of the article being cited, followed by *in* (capitalized for bibliography entries), the book title, the name(s) of editor(s), and publication information. Include the page numbers for the article or selection. Include page numbers for the article or selection in the bibliographic entry. In the note, include the page number of an exact reference or quotation, or, for references to the entire article, include beginning and ending page numbers.

15. Patricia Fitzsimmons-Hunter and Charles Moran, "Writing Teachers, Schools, Access, and Change," in *Literacy Theory in the Age of the Internet*, ed. Todd Taylor and Irene Ward, 158–170 (New York: Columbia University Press, 1998).

Fitzsimmons-Hunter, Patricia, and Charles Moran. "Writing Teachers, Schools, Access, and Change." In *Literacy Theory in the Age of the Internet*, edited by Todd Taylor and Irene Ward, 158–70. New York: Columbia University Press, 1998.

150. Article in a Scholarly Journal—CMS Scholarly journals are usually identified by volume and issue numbers. Such journals are usually paginated year by year, with a year's work treated as one volume.

16. Bill McCarron and Paul Knoke, "Images of War and Peace: Parallelism and Antithesis in the Beginning and Ending of *Cold Mountain*," *Mississippi Quarterly* 52, no. 2 (1999): 278.

McCarron, Bill, and Paul Knoke. "Images of War and Peace: Parallelism and Antithesis in the Beginning and Ending of *Cold Mountain*." *Mississippi Quarterly* 52, no. 2 (1999): 273–85.

COS
p. 269

151. Electronic Journal—CMS Include the URL and the date the material was last accessed online. Omit page numbers for online articles that do not include them.

17. Adrian Miles and others, "I Link Therefore I Am: Symposium on Digital Literacy 2002," *Kairos: Rhetoric, Technology, Pedagogy* 8, no. 1 (2003), http://english.ttu.edu/kairos/8.1/binder2.html?coverweb/vot/index.html (accessed May 24, 2004).

Miles, Adrian, Darren Tofts, Mark Amerika, Jenny Weight, Pia Ednie-Brown, and Jeremy Yuille. "I Link Therefore I Am: Symposium on Digital Literacy 2002." *Kairos: Rhetoric, Technology, Pedagogy* 8, no. 1 (2003). http://english.ttu.edu/kairos/8.1/binder2.html?coverweb/vot/index.html (accessed May 24, 2004).

152. Journal Article, Full-text, Accessed Through an Online Database—CMS Include the name of the database; the database publisher (*ProQuest, EB-SCOhost*, etc.); the URL; and the Digital Object Identifier (DOI), an accession number, or a descriptive phrase. Omit page references for quotations in the note unless the electronic version provides such page numbers.

18. Miriam Marty Clark, "Hemingway's Early Illness Narratives and the Lyric Dimensions of 'Now I Lay Me,'" *Narrative* 12, no. 2 (2004), 169, *Academic Search Premier* (EBSCOhost), http://search.epnet.com/direct.asp?an=12474315&db=aph (accession number 12474315; accessed May 24, 2004).

Clark, Miriam Marty. "Hemingway's Early Illness Narratives and the Lyric Dimensions of 'Now I Lay Me.'" *Narrative* 12, no. 2 (2004): 167–77. *Academic Search Premier* (EBSCOhost). http://search.epnet.com/direct.asp?an=12474315&db=aph (accession number 12474315; accessed May 24, 2004).

153. Article in a Popular Magazine—CMS Magazines are paginated issue by issue and identified by monthly or weekly dates of publication (instead of by volume number). When an article does not appear on consecutive pages, omit page numbers in the bibliography entry.

19. Eleanor Cooney, "Death in Slow Motion: A Descent into Alzheimer's," *Harper's*, October 2001, 43.

Cooney, Eleanor. "Death in Slow Motion: A Descent into Alzheimer's." *Harper's*, October 2001, 43–58.

154. Article in an Online Magazine—CMS COS p. 269 Include the date of publication as shown on the masthead of the online magazine, the URL, and the date of last access.

20. Michael J. Sandel, "The Case against Perfection," *eWeek: The Atlantic Online,* April 2004, http://www.theatlantic.com/issues/2004/04/sandel.htm (accessed July 10, 2004).

Sandel, Michael J. "The Case Against Perfection." April 2004.
http://www.theatlantic.com/issues/2004/04/sandel.htm (accessed July 10, 2004).

155. **Article in a Newspaper—CMS** Individual news stories are usually not listed in a bibliography, but they must be identified in notes or parenthetical references. Identify the section and edition of the newspaper (*national edition, home edition,* etc.) except when citing editorials or features that appear in all editions. Since an individual story may move in location from edition to edition, page numbers are not ordinarily provided.

21. Celestine Bohlen, "A Stunned Venice Surveys the Ruins of a Beloved Hall," *The New York Times,* January 31, 1995, national edition, sec. B.

COS p. 269 156. **Online Newspaper—CMS** Cite online newspapers the same as for print ones, except include the URL and the date last accessed.

22. Jesse J. Holland, "Kidnapped Children Alerts Work but Flawed," *Boston.com,* May 24, 2004, http://www.boston.com/news/nation/articles/2004/05/24/kidnapped_children_alerts_work_but_flawed/ (accessed July 10, 2004).

157. **Reviews—CMS** List the author of the review, if named; the title of the review, if applicable; the words *review of* followed by the name of the work being reviewed, if not included in the review title; and the author, composer, director, or other party responsible for the work being reviewed.

23. David G. Holmes, review of *African American Literacies,* by Elaine Richardson, *College Composition and Communication* 55, no. 3 (2004), 575.

Holmes, David G. Review of *African American Literacies,* by Elaine Richardson. *College Composition and Communication* 55, no. 3 (2004): 575–77.

158. **Encyclopedia and Reference Articles—CMS** When a reference work is a familiar one (encyclopedias, dictionaries, thesauruses), omit the names of authors and editors and most publishing information. No page number is given when a work is arranged alphabetically; instead the item referenced is named, following the abbreviation *s.v.* (*sub verbo,* meaning "under the word"). Familiar reference works are not listed in the bibliography.

24. *The Oxford Companion to English Literature,* 4th ed., s.v. "Locke, John."

159. **Biblical Citation—CMS** Biblical citations appear in notes but not in the bibliography. If it is important, you may name the version of the Bible cited.

> 25. John 18:37–38 (Jerusalem Bible).

160. **Government Publications—CMS** Name the government division or legislative body or committee responsible for the document, the title of the document, and any individual author(s) or editor(s), if listed. Include any report or document number, followed by the publisher (if applicable), the date of publication, and the page number(s), if relevant.

> 26. U.S. House of Representatives Committee on Armed Services,
>
> *National Defense Authorization Act for Fiscal Year 2004*, 108th Cong., 1st sess.,
>
> 2003, H.R. 1588, 309.

> U.S. House of Representatives. Committee on Armed Services. *National Defense*
>
> > *Authorization Act for Fiscal Year* 2004. 108th Cong., 1st sess., 2003.
>
> > H.R. 1588.

COS pp. 266–67

161. **Web Page or Site—CMS** Include as much information about the page or site as is available, including the name(s) of the author(s), editor(s), or compiler(s); the title of the page and/or site; the date of publication or last modification; the URL; and the date of access.

> 27. Emil Kren and Daniel Marx, *Web Gallery of Art*, modified January
>
> 17, 2004, http://gallery.euroweb.hu/welcome.html (accessed May 25, 2004).

> Kren, Emil, and Daniel Marx. *Web Gallery of Art*. Modified January 17,
>
> > 2004. http://gallery.euroweb.hu/welcome.html (accessed May 25,
>
> > 2004).

COS p. 276

162. **Computer Software—CMS** CMS recommends that references to computer software be included in the text rather than in endnotes or footnotes, with full citation information, if necessary, included in the bibliography. CMS does not italicize the titles of software packages. The version number should be included, but no date of publication is necessary.

> Netscape Navigator Ver. 7.1. Netscape Communication Corp., Mountain
>
> > View, CA.

COS p. 273

163. **Email—CMS** Include the name of the author; the words *e-mail to* and the name of the mailing list or, for personal email, the words *e-mail to author;* and the date of the email. If the message is archived, include the URL. Email is generally not included in the bibliography.

26. Pat Belanoff, e-mail to Writing Program Administration mailing list, April 24, 2004, http://lists.asu.edu/cgi-bin/wa?A2=ind0404&L= wpa-l&D=1&O=D&F=&S=&P=41666.

27. Todd Taylor, e-mail to the author, May 24, 2004.

26d Sample CMS paper

The following sample CMS paper, Diomedes as Hero of *The Iliad* provides an example of the sort of literary analysis that might be done for a classics or an English course. The paper has been lightly edited for style and revised to incorporate CMS-style endnotes and a Works Cited page.

The sample paper demonstrates how to use both endnotes and a Works Cited page. However, the Works Cited page is optional in CMS style because the endnotes themselves include full bibliographical information. Following the sample paper, we provide a single page reformatted to demonstrate the use of CMS-style footnotes. If you choose to use footnotes, do not also include endnotes. You may, however, present a Works Cited or Bibliography page. (A Works Cited page lists only those works mentioned in the paper itself; a Bibliography page includes all works cited in the paper as well as sources you consulted but did not mention in the paper.)

The sample paper shows titles italicized. You may either italicize or underline titles in CMS style, but be consistent: do not mix italicized and underlined titles within the same paper. In numbering the pages of CMS papers, count the title page as page 1, but do not number it. Note that footnotes are single spaced. Indented quotations are also single spaced. For more on typing student papers in CMS style, see Kate L. Turabian, *A Manual for Writers of Term Papers, Theses, and Dissertations,* sixth edition.

DIOMEDES AS HERO OF *THE ILIAD*

BY

JEREMY A. CORLEY

E 309K--TOPICS IN WRITING

DIVISION OF RHETORIC AND COMPOSITION

THE UNIVERSITY OF TEXAS AT AUSTIN

28 FEBRUARY 2004

Diomedes as Hero of *The Iliad*

Achilles is the central character of *The Iliad*, but is his prominence alone enough to make him the story's hero? There are many examples that would say otherwise. One of the most interesting aspects of the epic is its use of a lesser character, rather than the technical protagonist, as the tale's benchmark for heroism. This lesser character is Diomedes, and his leadership skills and maturity prove to be far superior to those of Achilles. Book V of *The Iliad* is devoted almost entirely to Diomedes' feats, and there are many scenes in which he is presented as a leader and hero throughout the rest of the text. While Diomedes is singled out for his gallantry, Achilles is, by contrast, noted for his immaturity and selfishness. Homer depicts Diomedes in a much more positive light than Achilles, despite the latter's obvious natural superiority as a soldier. It seems evident that Homer is emphasizing the total use of one's abilities, rather than just the presence of those abilities, as the basis of heroism. Diomedes, therefore, is the actual hero of *The Iliad*.

Achilles is immediately placed at the focal point of the story, and his pride and immaturity surface almost instantaneously. In Book I, Agamemnon embarrasses Achilles publicly with an outward display of his power as the Achaians' commander: "Since Apollo robs me of Chryseis . . . I will take your beautiful Briseis . . . to show you how much stronger I am than you are."[1] Achilles can hardly be faulted for taking offense at this incident, as it "threatened to invalidate . . . the whole meaning of his life."[2] Achilles' refusal to fight afterward must be looked at from more than one perspective. This is the first example of Achilles acting according to his pride, as proven by his regard for himself as "the best man of all."[3] While it is understandable for a soldier such as Achilles, who "towers above all the other characters of *The Iliad*," to be hesitant to fight for and under the man who embarrassed him, Agamemnon, it is also folly for a soldier to stop fighting because of anything as relatively unimportant as an insult, even a public one.[4] A soldier's duty is to defend his homeland and fight in its wars, and Achilles misses this greater duty because of his own

Diomedes as Hero 3

selfishness. This refusal to fight is compounded by his request to his mother, Thetis, to "see if he [Zeus] will help the Trojans and drive the Achaians back to their ships with slaughter!"[5] This is wholly selfish. Achilles is willing to put the fate of the entire Greek army in peril to feed his own wounded ego. Achilles is acting nothing like the leader that his divine gifts give him the power to be. Homer clearly leaves his central character open for some significant character development.

In contrast to Achilles' infantile behavior, which is consistent throughout most of the story, Diomedes is cast in a different light. Athena gives Diomedes "courage and boldness, to make him come to the front and cover himself with glory."[6] While not Achilles' equal as a soldier, "Diomedes was extremely fierce" and proved to be a terrific leader for the Achaians.[7] Diomedes kills off many Trojan warriors in Book V, acting as many hoped Achilles would, and even fighting through an injury suffered from the bow of Pandaros.[8] Rather than back down, Diomedes prayed to Athena for aid and joined the battle even more fiercely than before, slaying even more Trojan soldiers.[9] It is clear at this point that Diomedes is "obviously a paradigm of heroic behavior in Achilles' absence."[10] Diomedes represents a well-behaved, properly subservient soldier in the Achaian army who uses his courage and his honor to accomplish feats that are beyond his natural abilities. Diomedes exhibits self-control above all else, which is the element most wanting in Achilles' character.[11] His courage is further proven when he speaks against Agamemnon at the beginning of Book IX when the Achaian commander is advocating a Greek retreat: "Two of us will go on fighting, Sthenelos and I, until we make our goal!"[12] This is the moment when Diomedes is confirmed as one of the Greeks' greatest leaders, as even in a time when the army was "possessed by Panic,"[13] we see that "all cheered bold Diomedes in admiration."[14] The scene underscores Diomedes' rise to greatness in the Achaian army.

Achilles and Diomedes finally come into direct conflict with one another in Book IX, after Agamemnon has decided to make a peace offering to Achilles in hopes of the latter's return to battle. Agamemnon makes an offer to Achilles that is outrageously

generous in exchange for Achilles' return to battle. Achilles' response
is far from heroic and borders on cowardly: "If I go home to my
native land, there will be no great fame for me, but I shall live long
and not die an early death."[15] These words show utter selfishness on
the part of the man who is supposedly the greatest warrior in Greek
history, and Achilles is certainly not, at this point, living up to his
reputation or his potential. Observing that Achilles "shall appear in
battle once more whenever he feels inclined or when God makes him
go," Diomedes speaks against Achilles for the first time, effectively
casting himself as something of an adversary to Achilles in the hopes
of bringing him back into the battle, an action that serves the overall
good of the Achaians.[16] Once more, Diomedes is doing what is best
for his people and his army while Achilles thinks only of himself.
Peter Toohey observes that "Homer likes to juxtapose," and here he
uses that device to highlight the stark contrast between the
protagonist of the story and the true hero of the story.[17]

Homer centers *The Iliad* around Achilles, whose actions are
notably selfish and immature. Homer then uses Diomedes, at first a
lesser character, as a dramatic foil. Diomedes comes across as an
example of the ideal young Greek soldier. Achilles' capacities as a
warrior are far superior to those of any man alive, yet Diomedes
betters him in both words and actions throughout most of the story.
Achilles is finally brought to realize his supreme military prowess,
but it is the death of his friend Patroclos that spurs his fighting
spirit, still another example of Achilles' penchant for acting on
emotion rather than judgment. Achilles is finally reconciled to
Diomedes' example when he meets Priam at the end of the story and
responds honorably: "I mean myself to set your Hector free,"
agreeing to return the corpse of Priam's son for a proper burial.[18]
Achilles at last achieves a measure of respect that his abilities could
have earned him long before. It is in that time, however, when
Achilles was still selfish and immature that Diomedes shone as the
example of leadership and valor. Diomedes is, at least in a measure of
consistency, the true hero of *The Iliad*.

Diomedes as Hero 5

NOTES

1. Homer, *The Iliad,* trans. Robert Fitzgerald (New York: Anchor Press, 1974), 14.

2. R. M. Frazer, *A Reading of "The Iliad"* (Lanham, MD: University Press of America, 1993), 12.

3. Homer, 15.

4. Frazer, 11.

5. Homer, 18.

6. Ibid., 58.

7. Scott Richardson, *The Homeric Narrator* (Nashville: Vanderbilt University Press, 1990), 159.

8. Homer, 59.

9. Ibid., 60–61.

10. W. Thomas MacCary, *Childlike Achilles: Ontogeny and Philogeny in "The Iliad"* (New York: Columbia University Press, 1982), 95.

11. G. S. Kirk, *"The Iliad": A Commentary,* vol. 2 (New York: Cambridge University Press, 1990), 34.

12. Homer, 103.

13. Ibid., 102.

14. Ibid., 103.

15. Ibid., 110.

16. Ibid., 115.

17. Peter Toohey, "Epic and Rhetoric: Speech-making and Persuasion in Homer and Apollonius," *Arachnion: A Journal of Ancient Literature and History on the Web* 1 (1995), http://www.cisi.unito.it/arachne/num1/toohey.html (accessed February 21, 1996).

18. Homer, 293.

WORKS CITED

Frazer, R. M. *A Reading of "The Iliad."* Lanham, MD: University Press of America, 1993.

Homer. *The Iliad.* Translated by Robert Fitzgerald. New York: Anchor Press, 1974.

Kirk, G. S. *"The Iliad": A Commentary.* Vol. 2. New York: Cambridge University Press, 1990.

MacCary, W. Thomas. *Childlike Achilles: Ontogeny and Philogeny in "The Iliad."* New York: Columbia University Press, 1982.

Richardson, Scott. *The Homeric Narrator.* Nashville: Vanderbilt University Press, 1990.

Toohey, Peter. "Epic and Rhetoric: Speech-making and Persuasion in Homer and Apollonius." *Arachnion: A Journal of Ancient Literature and History on the Web* 1 (1995). http://www.cisi.unito.it/ arachne/num1/toohey.html (accessed February 21, 1996).

Sample CMS page with footnotes. In CMS style you have the option of placing all your notes on pages following the body of a paper, as shown on page 392, or you may locate them at the bottom of each page as they occur in the text.

In Book I, Agamemnon embarrasses Achilles publicly with an outward display of his power as the Achaians' commander: "Since Apollo robs me of Chryseis . . . I will take your beautiful Briseis . . . to show you how much stronger I am than you are."[1] Achilles can hardly be faulted for taking offense at this incident, as it "threatened to invalidate . . . the whole meaning of his life."[2] Achilles' refusal to fight afterward must be looked at from more than one perspective. This is the first example of Achilles acting according to his pride, as proven by his regard for himself as "the best man of all."[3] While it is understandable for a soldier such as Achilles, who "towers above all the other characters of *The Iliad*," to be hesitant to fight for and under the man who embarrassed him, Agamemnon, it is also folly for a soldier to stop fighting because of anything as relatively unimportant as an insult, even a public one.[4] A soldier's duty is to defend his homeland and fight in its wars, and Achilles misses this greater duty for his own selfishness. This refusal to fight is compounded by his request to his mother, Thetis, to "see if he [Zeus] will help the Trojans and drive the Achaians back to their ships with slaughter!"[5] This is wholly selfish. Achilles is willing to put the fate of the entire Greek army in peril to feed his own wounded ego. Achilles is acting nothing like the leader that his divine gifts give him the power to be. Homer clearly leaves his central character open

1. Homer, *The Iliad*, trans. Robert Fitzgerald (New York: Anchor Press, 1974), 14.

2. R. M. Frazer, *A Reading of "The Iliad"* (Lanham, MD: University Press of America, 1993), 12.

3. Homer, 15.

4. Frazer, 11.

5. Homer, 18.

CHAPTER 27

CSE Documentation

Disciplines that study the physical world—physics, chemistry, biology—are called the natural sciences; disciplines that examine (and produce) technologies are described as the applied sciences. Writing in these fields is specialized, and no survey of all forms of documentation can be provided here. For more information about writing in the following fields, we suggest that you consult one of these style manuals. Check with your library for availability.

- **Chemistry:** *The ACS Style Guide: A Manual for Authors and Editors,* second edition (1997)—American Chemical Society

- **Geology:** *Suggestions to Authors of the Reports of the United States Geological Survey,* eighth edition (1997)—U.S. Geological Survey, http://www.nwrc.usgs.gov/lib/lib_sta.htm

- **Medicine:** *American Medical Association Manual of Style: A Guide for Authors and Editors,* ninth edition (1997)

- **Physics:** *AIP Style Manual,* fourth edition (1998)—American Institute of Physics, http://www.aip.org/pubservs/style/4thed/toc.html

A highly influential manual for scientific writing is *Scientific Style and Format: The CBE Manual for Authors, Editors, and Publishers,* sixth edition (1994). The Council of Science Editors, or CSE (formerly known as the Council of Biology Editors) is currently at work on a new edition; in the meantime, updates, corrections, and additional suggestions for citing electronic sources are available on the CSE Web site at http://www.cbe.org.

CSE style offers the choice of two principal methods of documenting sources used in research: a name-year system that resembles APA style (see Chapter 25) and a citation-sequence system that lists sources in the order of their use in a paper. In this chapter we briefly describe the second system.

Citing Electronic Sources in the Natural and Applied Sciences

CSE follows the National Library of Medicine Recommended Formats for Bibliographic Citation for Internet sources. However, when citing such items, you may want to use the documentation style recommended by the *Columbia Guide to Online Style* for scientific papers, described in Chapter 23. Consult your instructor about using COS for electronic and computerized sources.

27a Provide in-text citations

Where a citation is needed in the text of a paper, insert either a raised number (the preferred form) or a number in parentheses. Citations should appear immediately after the word or phrase to which they are related, and they are numbered in the order in which you use them.

> Oncologists[1] are aware of trends in cancer mortality.[2]

> Oncologists (1) are aware of trends in cancer mortality (2).

Source 1 thus becomes the first item to be listed on the References page, source 2 the second item, and so on.

> 1. Urowski B. Enhanced outcomes in a managed care model. Admin Rad J 1996;15:19-23.
>
> 2. Kongstvedt PR. The managed care handbook. Boston: Jones & Bartlett; 2001. 1408 p.

You can refer to more than one source in a single note, with the numbers separated by a dash if they are in sequence and by commas if out of sequence.

IN SEQUENCE

> Cancer treatment[2-3] has changed over the decades. But Damberg[4] shows that the politics of cancer research remains constant.

OUT OF SEQUENCE

> Cancer treatment[2,5] has changed over the decades. But Damberg[4] shows that the politics of cancer research remains constant.

If you cite a source again later in the paper, refer to it by its original number.

> Great strides have occurred in epidemiological methods[5] despite the political problems in maintaining research support and funding described by Damberg.[4]

27b List sources used

On a separate page at the end of your project, list the sources you used in the order they occurred. These sources are numbered: source 1 in the project will be the first source listed on the References page, source 2 the second item, and so on. Notice, then, that this References list is *not* alphabetical. The first few entries on a CSE list might look like this.

Subsequent lines begin under first words of first line   "References" centered   All items double spaced

References

1. Urowski B. Enhanced outcomes in a managed care model. Admin
   Rad J 1996; 15:19–23.

2. Kongstvedt PR. The managed care handbook. Boston: Jones &
   Bartlett; 2001. 1408 p.

3. Loeb LA, Essigmann JM, Kazazi F, Zhang J, Rose KD, Mullins JI.
   Lethal mutagenesis of HIV with mutagenic nucleoside analogs.
   Proc Natl Acad Sci USA 1999; 96:1492–1497.

4. Damberg CL. Evaluating the feasibility of developing national
   outcomes databases to assist patients with making treatment
   decisions. Santa Monica: Rand, 2003. 131 p.

5. US Natl Inst of Health [homepage on the Internet]. Bethesda (MD):
   Natl Cancer Inst (US); [cited 2004 Dec 30]. Available from http://
   www.cancer.gov/

FIGURE 27.1 Sample References list in CSE format

CHECKLIST 27.1

Basic Format—Books

A typical CSE citation-sequence style References entry for a book includes the following basic information.

○ Number assigned to the source.

○ Name of author(s), last name first, followed by a period. Initials are used in place of full first and middle names. Commas ordinarily separate the names of multiple authors.

(Continued)

○ Title of work, followed by a period. Only the first word and any proper nouns in a title are capitalized. The title is not underlined or italicized.

○ Place of publication, followed by a colon.

○ Publisher, followed by a semicolon. Titles of presses can be abbreviated.

○ Year of publication, followed by a period.

○ Total number of pages, followed by *p* and a period.

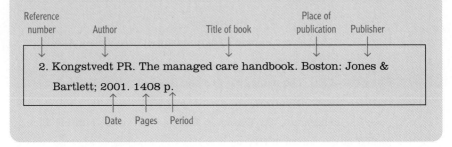

Reference number | Author | Title of book | Place of publication | Publisher

2. Kongstvedt PR. The managed care handbook. Boston: Jones & Bartlett; 2001. 1408 p.

Date   Pages   Period

CHECKLIST 27.2

Basic Format—Scholarly Journals

A typical CSE citation-sequence–style References entry for an article in a scholarly journal (where the pagination is continuous through a year) includes the following basic information.

○ Number assigned to the source.

○ Name of author(s), last name first, followed by a period. Initials are used in place of full first and middle names. Commas ordinarily separate the names of multiple authors.

○ Title of article, followed by a period. Only the first word and any proper nouns in a title are capitalized. The title does not appear between quotation marks.

○ Name of the journal. All major words are capitalized, and the journal title is not underlined or italicized. A space (but no punctuation) separates the journal title from the publication date. Journal titles of more than one word can be abbreviated following the recommendations in *American National Standard Z39.5-1985: Abbreviations of Titles of Publications*.

- ○ Year (and month for journals not continuously paginated; date for weekly journals), followed immediately by a semicolon.
- ○ Volume number, followed by a colon, and the page numbers of the article. No spaces separate these items. A period follows the page numbers.

Reference
number   Title of article   Author(s)

1. Loeb LA, Essigmann JM, Kazazi F, Zhang J, Rose KD, Mullins JI.

   Lethal mutagenesis of HIV with mutagenic nucleoside analogs.

   Proc Natl Acad Sci USA 1999; 96:1492–1497.

   Name of periodical   Year Volume Pages Period

CHECKLIST 27.3

Basic Format—Magazines

A typical CSE citation-sequence–style References entry for an article in a popular magazine includes the following basic information.

- ○ Number assigned to the source.
- ○ Name of author(s), last name first, followed by a period. Initials are substituted for first names unless two authors mentioned in the paper have identical last names and first initials.
- ○ Title of article, followed by a period. Only the first word and any proper nouns in a title are capitalized. The title does not appear between quotation marks. (Where quotation marks are needed, CSE recommends British style. See the *CBE Manual*, pages 180–81.)
- ○ Name of magazine, abbreviated. All major words are capitalized, but the journal title is not underlined or italicized. A space (but no punctuation) separates the magazine title from the year and month.
- ○ Year, month (abbreviated, using three-letter abbreviation for months with more than four letters), and day (for a weekly magazine). The year is separated from the month by a space. A colon follows immediately after the date, followed by page number(s). The entry ends with a period.

(Continued)

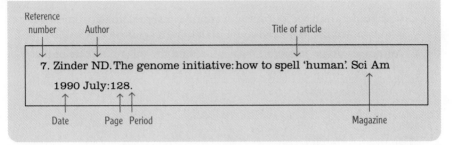

CHECKLIST 27.4

Basic Format—Electronic Sources

A typical CSE citation-sequence–style References entry for an electronic item includes the basic information provided for a print document (author, title, publication information, page numbers) with the following additions.

○ Electronic medium, identified between brackets [*Internet*]; for books and monographs, this information comes after the title; for periodicals, it follows the name of the journal.

○ Date cited, following the year of publication but before the volume and issue numbers.

○ Availability statement, following the publication information or page numbers. No punctuation follows the Internet address.

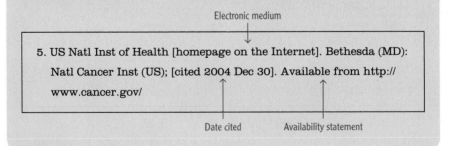

There are so many variations to these basic entries that you will want to consult the *CBE Manual* when you do a major CSE-style paper.

Use the following considerations as a guide when formatting a paper in CSE style.

CHECKLIST 27.5

> **CSE Style**

○ CSE style normally requires a separate title page. The title of the essay can be centered about a third of the way down the page, followed by the word *by* on a separate line and the writer's name, also on a separate line. Other information such as instructor's name, course title, and date can be included on the bottom third of the page.

○ CSE style normally requires an abstract of about 250 words on a separate page immediately following the title page. The title "Abstract" is centered on the page.

○ Double-space the body of a CSE paper. Avoid hyphenating words at the end of lines.

○ Number pages consecutively in the upper right-hand corner, counting the title page as page 1, using the automatic page numbering feature of your word processor, if available.

○ Take special care with figures and tables. They should be numbered in separate sequences. The *CBE Manual* includes an entire chapter on handling illustrative material.

○ The References page follows the text of the CSE essay on a new page. Remember that the items on this page are *not* listed alphabetically. References pages can also be titled "Literature Cited" or "References Cited."

○ All works listed on the References page should be cited at least once in the body of your paper.

○ Entries on the References page are single spaced, with a space between entries.

Credits

Austen, Jane. Excerpt from *Pride and Prejudice*, 1813.

Blake, William. "The Tyger," 1794.

Briggs, Chad S. and Fred Ribich. "The Relationship Between Test Anxiety, Sleep Habits, and Self-Perceived Academic Competency," *Psych-E*, Vol. I (Dec. 1, 1998). Reprinted by permission of Chad S. Briggs.

Brown, John. Sample MLA paper, "Swatting Flies with an Ax." Reprinted by permission of John Brown.

Clarke, Arthur C. Quote from *Profiles of the Future*. New York: Warner Books, 1985.

Design International's Newsletter. From *DI: Communicator*, 2000. Reprinted by permission of Design International.

Diagram of OrbView-2 Satellite from SeaStar Image catalog, http://Seawifs.gsfc.nasa.gov/SEAWIFS/SEASTAR/Seastar_images_diagram.html. OrbView-2/SeaStar Satellite is reprinted by permission of Orbital Sciences Corporation.

"File Sharing Is Not Threat to Music Sales." Reprinted from *Broadcast Engineering*, April 12, 2004. Reprinted with the permission of Primedia Business Magazines & Media. Copyright © 2004. All rights reserved.

Google screen shot search results for "Mp3 downloading" from www.google.com. Google screen shot. Reproduced with permission of Google, Inc.

Anthony Grafton, quotes from "The Death of the Footnote (Report on Exaggeration)," *The Wilson Quarterly* (Winter 1997).

"Homepage" from *MotherJones.com*, July 7, 2004, http://www.motherjones.com. *MotherJones* Homepage screen shot. Reprinted with permission from *MotherJones* Magazine.

"HTML Template-Microsoft Internet Explorer" Title Bar Screen Shot. Title Bar screen shot reprinted by permission of Microsoft Corporation.

Lincoln, Abraham. Excerpt from First Inaugural Address, March 4, 1861.

Microsoft PowerPoint screen shot Templates "Select the Type of Presentation You're Going to Give." From Microsoft's PowerPoint® presentation graphics program. © 2003 Microsoft Corporation. Screen shot reprinted by permission from Microsoft Corporation.

Microsoft PowerPoint screen shot "What Type of Output Will You Use?" From Microsoft's PowerPoint® presentation graphics program. © 2003 Microsoft Corporation. Screen shot reprinted by permission from Microsoft Corporation.

NASA. From "Report of Columbia Accident Investigation Board," Volume 1, August 2003. The Columbia Accident Investigation Board; distributed by the National Aeronautics and Space Administration and the Government Printing Office, Washington, DC, (2003).

Netscape Composer "Page Properties" screen shot. Netscape is a registered trademark of Netscape Communications Corporation. Used with permission.

"Number of Automated Banking Machines Per 1,000,000 Inhabitants" extracted from Table 5 of CPSS Publications No. 54, April 2003, Bank for International Settlements. Reprinted by permission of Secretariat of the Committee on Payment and Settlement Systems (CPSS), Bank for International Settlements, Basel, Switzerland, from Table 5 "Cards with a Cash Function and ATMs" in *Statistics on Payments and*

Stern, Barbara Lang. Quote from "Tears Can Be Crucial to Your Emotional Health," *Vogue*, June 1979.

Title bar screen shots "lessons.html-Notepad" (HTML Codes) and "Teaching Life's Lessons–Microsoft Internet Explorer." Microsoft ® Notepad is a trademark of Microsoft. Title Bar screen shots reprinted by permission of Microsoft Corporation.

University of Texas online library search menu (UTnetCat). UTnetCat Online Library Catalog at the University of Texas at Austin. Provided courtesy of The General Libraries, The University of Texas at Austin.

Williams, Terry Tempest. Quote from *Refuge: An Unnatural History of Family and Place.* New York: Pantheon Books, 1991.

Yahoo! Chat room. http://chat.yahoo.com/ Reproduced with permission of Yahoo! Inc. © 2004 by Yahoo! Inc. YAHOO! and the YAHOO! logo are trademarks of Yahoo! Inc.

Yankelovich, Daniel. Quote from "The Work Ethic Is Underemployed," *Psychology Today*, May 1982.

Yu, Peter K. "Music Industry Hits Wrong Note Against Piracy," *The Detroit News*, September 14, 2003. Approved by Mark Silverman, Publisher and Editor. Reprinted with permission from *The Detroit News.*

Photo Credits

Page 3: Photo courtesy of Thiago "Elvis" DaCumba. Page 45: Photo courtesy of Anne Nathan. Page 99: Photo courtesy of Tim Cockey. Page 152: Photo courtesy of Frederick L. Whitmer. Page 203: Photo courtesy of Dr. Irwin Hollander. Page 259: Photo courtesy of Elizabeth Brunell.

Index

Glossary of Computer Terms

address The route or path followed to access a specific file or person. An email address usually consists of a log-in name and a domain name. A Web address usually includes a domain name, a directory or directories, and a file name.

asynchronous In Internet communication, electronic mail and other communication wherein messages are not dependent on timing.

BBS Bulletin Board Service. An online service, generally hosted by an individual user, that allows others to post messages and share files.

blog Short for "Web log." Typically, a personal journal posted on a public Web site for others to read. Blog entries can be modified only by the original poster.

bookmarks Called "Favorites" in some browsers, bookmarks are a way of marking a specific file, an online address, or a location within a file for later retrieval.

Boolean operators Search terms based on logic that allow you to limit and define search criteria. The most commonly used Boolean operators are AND, OR, and NOT.

browser Software that allows users to access files on the World Wide Web and move through hypertext links. Some browsers such as *Lynx* offer text-only access, while browsers such as Netscape *Navigator* and Microsoft *Internet Explorer* use graphical interfaces and point-and-click technology.

chat room A virtual room; an address where multiple users may communicate with each other in real time, usually by inputting text on a keyboard.

cookie A small piece of computer code stored on personal computers by some Web sites. Cookies allow sites to recognize return visitors and often include information such as a user's name and the last time the site was visited.

directory A structure for organizing files on a computer or host, similar to a file folder containing individual files.

domain name The unique name assigned to an individual host address, such as www.whitehouse.gov.

download The act of moving a file from a host or server directory to a local storage medium such as a diskette or hard drive.

FAQ Frequently Asked Questions. A file providing information about a newsgroup, a listserv, or another online service, including details of membership, discussion topics, and rules or netiquette guidelines.

FTP File Transfer Protocol. A means of transferring files between machines.

GUI Graphical User Interface. An interface (such as the Windows and Macintosh desktops) that uses icons, pictures, and pointers to control programs.

HTTP HyperText Transfer Protocol. The process by which hypertext files are transferred between remote computers on the Internet using browser software.

hypertext Text, graphics, or files that are linked together, as designated by the hypertext author, using a special system of tags called HyperText Markup Language (HTML).

Internet An international network of computers originally designed by the U.S. Department of Defense to ensure communication abilities in the event of a catastrophe. The Internet today connects millions of individual users, universities, governments, businesses, and other organizations using telephone lines, fiber-optic cabling, and other technologies to link machines to each other.